D1337060

Affectionately yours
Charles Hodge,

PRINCETON SERMONS

Outlines of Discourses
Doctrinal and Practical

CHARLES HODGE

THE BANNER OF TRUTH TRUST

THE BANNER OF TRUTH TRUST
3 Murrayfield Road, Edinburgh EH12 6EL
PO Box 621, Carlisle, Pennsylvania 17013, USA

*

First published 1879
First Banner of Truth Trust edition 1958
Reprinted 1960
Reprinted 1979

ISBN 0 85151 285 2

Printed in Great Britain by
Billing & Sons Limited,
Guildford, London and Worcester

FOREWORD

In the annals of the Reformed Churches throughout the world for the last hundred years no name is better known than that of Charles Hodge, the distinguished professor for more than half a century at Princeton Theological Seminary in New Jersey. He is best known, no doubt, for his massive work in three volumes, *Systematic Theology*. Perhaps equally well known is his commentary on the Epistle to the Romans. In both works the genius of Hodge as a theologian and expositor of Scripture is plainly evident, and if one perused only these he would be able to understand the reason for the eminence accorded to this Princeton divine. Not only the erudition which Hodge possessed and which he brought to bear upon his work appears in these volumes, but also the simplicity and depth of his personal devotion as one committed to the Saviour of men and to the infallible truth and sufficiency of Holy Scripture as God's Word are likewise apparent.

But our acquaintance with the work and labours of Dr. Hodge would be too limited for an adequate assessment of the influence he exerted if we were to take into account only the aforementioned fruits of his pen. For nearly fifty years in the pages of what was first called the *Biblical Repertory*, begun in 1825, later on called *The Biblical Repertory and Theological Review* and, finally, *The Biblical Repertory and Princeton Review*, there regularly appeared articles and reviews which probably more than anything else demonstrated the fertility and versatility of Hodge's mind. He was always abreast of the latest in the movements of thought, especially as these movements affected the Christian faith. And, besides, this literary output shows how intense was his interest in the practical concerns of the church of Christ. It is not surprising, therefore, that one of the volumes from his pen bears the title, *The Church and its Polity*.

Another facet of his interest and character appears in what may, from one viewpoint, be called his masterpiece, a work not so well known in many circles but one that, above all else, meets the need of the lay reader. It is *The Way of Life*, written for and published by the American Sunday School Union in 1841. It is a simple statement of the way of salvation and life. Here are manifest the tenderness and fervency of a saint of God devoted to the cure and care of souls. A quotation from the first paragraph of his preface should suffice to whet the appetite as well as indicate the theme. "It is one of the clearest principles of divine revelation, that holiness is the fruit of truth ; and it is one of the plainest inferences from that principle, that the exhibition of the truth is the best means of promoting holiness."

The same interests and characteristics so apparent in *The Way of Life* come to expression in the volume, *Princeton Sermons*, now being republished. These are but outlines of addresses given on Sabbath afternoons to the students at Princeton Seminary. But they offer Hodge's mature thought on a great many subjects and they breathe the warmth of devotional fervour. Here is a fund of succinct definition on the great themes of theology as they are related to the most practical concerns of the Christian and of the pastor. The brevity arising from the fact that they are but outlines, though in some respects a handicap, in other respects is a virtue—thought is stimulated to reflection and heart-searching, and when these outlines are studiously and meditatively used for the same kind of exercise as that for which they were originally prepared, they will prove for the reader to be the means of cultivating that intelligent piety of which the Seminary at Princeton was the nursery. One can but earnestly hope that the Sabbath afternoons of many will be restored to and enriched by the same kind of concentrated and devoted reflection on the great themes of our holy faith which these addresses exemplify. Meditation is not detached dreaming. To be fruitful it requires intense application to the riches of truth deposited for us in God's Word. And the reward will be visions of the mountains of God. Rest of soul will then have reached the summit of its exercise, for we shall behold the majesty of the Lord.

These analyses of discourses will have to be read with the discrimination which is required in the use of the work of all fallible men. Sometimes the reader will have to diverge from the interpretations of the learned and devout professor. At times more exegetical distinction could be desired than Dr. Hodge, great though he was as an expositor, had been able to muster. In exegetical penetration he was excelled by some of his contemporaries and successors at Princeton. But this necessity of using the critical faculty will only enhance the profit to be derived from these studies, and the greater will be the challenge to careful thought. The masterful survey provided by this volume is calculated to rehabilitate in the thinking and practice of the present day those very patterns which are largely lost and which are our clamant need. May it be that by God's grace this may be the fruit.

JOHN MURRAY

Philadelphia,
Pennsylvania.
October 29, 1957.

PREFACE.

From the time of its foundation it has been the habit of the professors of Princeton Theological Seminary to meet the students every Sabbath afternoon, for prayer and conference on themes relating to the life of God in the soul, and to the practical duties having their root therein. The members of all the successive classes will bear testimony to the unique character and singular preciousness of these Sabbath afternoon Conferences in that sacred old Oratory, whose walls are still eloquent to them with imperishable associations. Here the venerable professors appeared rather as friends and pastors than as instructors. The dry and cold attributes of scientific theology, moving in the sphere of the intellect gave place to the warmth of personal religious experience, and to the spiritual light of divinely illuminated intuition. Here in the most effective manner did these teachers of teachers set the crown upon their work, and herein they exerted by far, their most widely extended and permanent influence. Here they sought rather to build up Christian men, than to form accomplished scholars, and to infuse into their pupils the highest motives, and to instruct them in the wisest methods for their future work of saving souls and of edifying the Church of Christ.

The text or topic for consideration was announced at the preceding meeting. The professors presided in turn, and were called upon to speak in the inverse order of seniority, the professor presiding for the day coming last. For many years, the discussion was opened by remarks volunteered by the students, but in later times, the entire hour has been occupied by the professors.

The historical character of this remarkable service is of course derived from the peerless endowments, intellectual and spiritual, of the first three professors in the institution. Men so different, yet together constituting such a singular completeness of excellence by the combination of their complementary graces.

Dr. Miller, the model Christian gentleman and typical divine, whose original, generous and genial nature had been transfigured by the long indwelling of the Holy Ghost, and whose outward manner had evidently been conformed by long self-training to the highest models, would have been the first to attract the eye and to impress the ear of the stranger. His long and active life had furnished him with rich stores of experience of men as well as a vast volume of learning derived from books. All this he poured forth with a deliberate and stately copiousness, in a manner serene and dignified, yet full of impressive force and tender unction. His adoring sense of the majesty of God, and of the seriousness of human life, of the reality and solemnity of divine things, and of the obligations attending the Christian profession, and above all attending the office of the Christian ministry gave form and color to all he said. His instructions were always wise and practical, and were characteristically illustrated from an inexhaustible fund of apt and often witty, but always dignified anecdote, drawn from all literature, sacred and profane, and from his own extensive intercourse with men as a pastor and as a citizen.

Dr. Archibald Alexander, incomparably the greatest, as he was the first of that illustrious family, though neither more learned, nor more holy than his older colleague, was far more original. He was modeled upon nothing, but every thing in him and about him to the last detail of thought or glance, or inflexion, or gesture was immediately determined by spontaneous forces working straight outward from within. It was this entire absence of self-consciousness, this absolute simplicity of thought, emotion and' expression, and its spontaneous directness to its point, which, added to his other natural and gracious endowments, gave this great teacher his singular pre-eminence. His intellect was intuitive rather than logical. Although he exhibited flashes of acute analysis, as sharp and rapid as a Damascus blade, yet he did not characteristically excel in broad views of truths in their relations, nor in lengthened processes of consecutive thought. He was eminently quick in his observation, and penetrating in his insight, accurately noting facts and reading character in rapid glances. He held in his retentive mind the spoils of a vast and widely selected reading. All the treasures of divine wisdom and grace, which the Holy Ghost communicates to life-long students of the word, when to high intellect is added all the simplicity and docility of a little child, irradiated his soul, and made it luminous to others. All the secrets of the human heart and its various experiences under the discipline of the natural conscience and of the word and Spirit of God were known to him, and he possessed the finest skill in interpreting and in treating with acute precision, the states and frames of all who sought his counsel or listened to his instructions.*

This utter simplicity, this all-penetrating insight, accompanied with a wonderful spontaneousness of thought, imagination and speech were personal attributes, inseparable from his presence and manner, and incapable of being transmitted to the printed page. During his later years, when urged to put the results of his studies and reflections in the permanent form of writing, he often said, " No, if I have any talent, it is to talk sitting in my chair." And however much he may have been mistaken in failing to recognize the value of his writings to the Church, there is no doubt that his gifts as a talker on the themes of Christian experience were without parallel among his contemporaries. He more than any man of his generation, appeared to those who heard him to be endued with the knowledge, and clothed with the authority of a prophet sent immediately from God. He was to us as the highest peak of the mountains, on whose pure head the heavens, beyond the common horizon, pour the wealth of their iridescent radiance.

In his early and middle life he had been an orator endowed with

---

* "For Dr. Alexander I have the most profound reverence and respect, and particularly for this thing, which impressed me more than any thing else, his wonderful knowledge of the human heart, and of the Christian heart, in all its morbid and its healthful exercises, so that you may call him the Shakspeare of the Christian heart. I have never seen a man, nor do I ever expect to see the man, who has impressed me more in this particular." Dr. Theodore D. Woolsey, ex-President of Yale College, at Dr. Hodge's' Semi-Centennial Commemoration April 24th, 1872.

singular powers of dramatic representation. In his old age he was always calm and quiet, but such was his intense sense of the reality of the subjects on which he discoursed, that often, as he spoke of angels, of heaven, of the beatific vision of saints, of Christ, and of his second coming and judgment, his hearers felt that their eyes also were opened to discern the presence of things invisible and eternal.

Every Wednesday evening Dr. Alexander presided at the public prayers in the Oratory. The instant the students were in their seats he came in rapidly, his cloak hanging, often diagonally, from his bent shoulders, his head inclined as in revery, yet flashing sudden glances on either side with his piercing eyes, which seemed to penetrate all the secrets of those upon whom they fell. He sat down with his back to the windows and his right side to the students; sitting low, almost hidden by the desk. Drawing the large Bible down before him he seemed to lose at once all sense of human audience, and to pass alone into the presence of God. As he read, and mused, and ejaculated the utterances of all the holy exercises of his soul upon the Divine Word, a solemn hush fell upon us, and we felt, not as those who listen to a teacher, but as those who are admitted to approach with the shoes from off their feet, to gaze in and listen through an opened window to the mysterious workings of a sanctified soul under the immediate revelations of the Holy Ghost.

Dr. Hodge was by a whole generation younger than these venerable fathers. Hence during the first years of his professorship his part in these Sabbath afternoon Conferences, although regularly discharged, was less prominent than theirs. During the long period, however, from about 1848 to his death in 1878, he was recognized by all as the central sun which gave light and heat to the entire service.

As all acquainted with his life-work know, Dr. Hodge's distinguishing attributes were, great tenderness and strength of emotion, and the power of exciting it in others—an habitual adoring love for Christ, and absolute submission of mind and will to His word—a chivalrous disposition to maintain against all odds, and with unvarying self-consistency through all the years of a long life, the truth as he saw it—crystalline clearness of thought and expression—and an unsurpassed logical power of analysis, and of grasping and exhibiting all truths in their relations. Dr. Alexander once said to a friend that the mental constitution of Dr. Hodge was more than that of any man he knew—like that of John Calvin, without his severity. As he sat in the Conference he spoke freely, without paper, in language and with illustration spontaneously suggested at the moment. To the hearer the entire exercise appeared extemporaneous. The *matter* presented was a clear analysis of the scriptural passage, or theme, doctrinal or practical, chosen for the occasion. An exhaustive statement and clear illustration of the question. An exhibition of the evidence of the doctrine, and of the grounds and reasons and of the methods, conditions and limits of the experience or duty. A development of each doctrine on the side of experience and duty, and a demonstration of the practical character of all doctrine, and of the doctrinal basis of all genuine religious experience and practice.

As to the *manner* the entire discourse was in the highest degree earnest, fervent and tender to tears; full of conviction and full of love. While the temporary impression made upon most hearers was less remarkable than that produced by Dr. Alexander, in his happiest moods, all the students, and especially those who were diligent in taking notes, felt that they took away with them from Dr. Hodge a far larger mass of coherent thought for permanent use, than from any of the rest. The reason for this is abundantly evident when the drawers of his study are opened, and the large accumulation of careful preparations for this exercise are examined. He prepared and wrote out a careful analysis or skeleton of every Conference discourse. Although designed to meet no eye but his own, these analyses are fully written out, and, are verbally complete in all their articulations. And although his audience was completely changed every three years, it appears that he never used the same preparation twice, but prepared, even after he had passed his 80th year a new paper for each Conference, often constructing analyses of the same theme several times.

This was his method of mental preparation. He habitually thought with his pen in his hand. He prepared an analysis of his subject before he wrote his sermons. He did the same before writing his theological lectures, or the several divisions of his Systematic Theology. He also made a written analysis of every important book he read, especially if it presented views of truth antagonistic to his own.

A volume of these papers is now published, not only because they will afford a reminiscence of past sacred scenes, grateful to his surviving pupils, but chiefly because it is believed that in their present form they will be widely useful.   Although the brain and heart, which through the beaming countenance and tremulous voice, infused these skeletons with life, are absent, they yet remain in themselves very remarkable examples of that analysis, that logical grouping and perspicuous exhibition of truth which is an essential faculty of the effective preacher.   They present in this analytic form an amount and quality of homiletical example and suggestion probably not surpassed in the same number of pages in the English language.   As an effective exhibition of the great principle that all genuine religious experience is only the realization in experience of Christian doctrine, and that all true doctrine does immediately go out into the practical issues of the inward and outward life, this volume is eminently fitted to vindicate and supplement the three volumes of Systematic Theology, which were the last work of the author's life.

The classification of these papers is entirely the work of the editor. The reader will find instances of repetition, some of which, under the circumstances are neither avoidable nor objectionable; some of which may be attributed to the incompetence of the editor, but none of which, if the several dates and original purpose of these papers be considered, can be regarded as the fault of the beloved and venerated author. As there is no Index of Subjects, the Table of Contents is made unusually, and it is hoped, sufficiently full and explicit.

A. A. HODGE.

Princeton, March 30, 1879.

CHARLES HODGE

1797–1878

In the pleasant little town of Princeton, situated on the fertile slopes of New Jersey, a theological seminary was founded in 1812. From here were to go forth a long line of distinguished ministers and missionaries who made the name of their seminary revered throughout the English-speaking world. For over a hundred years, while great and sad changes were taking place within the Protestant churches, "Princeton theology" was to remain a synonym for orthodoxy, and, long after other colleges had gone down before the inroads of error, Princeton was to stand firm in its reverent and faithful allegiance to the Word of God.

At the inaugural service, held in the old Presbyterian church, a youthful figure could be seen, leaning against the rail of the gallery, listening with rapt attention to the address of Dr. Archibald Alexander, one of the senior professors of the new seminary. It was an event which fourteen year old Charles Hodge was never to forget. That same year he had left his home in Philadelphia and entered Princeton College, one of the old American seats of learning—associated with the names of such men as Jonathan Edwards. As it provided a general education, the College remained distinct from the Seminary which was specifically theological, but it quickly became the custom for students entering the ministry to pass from one to the other. Thus, after graduating from the College in 1815, Hodge enrolled his name, on 9th November, 1816, as one of the twenty-six students attending the Seminary.

From his childhood Hodge had never wavered in his sense of a call to the ministry, though the profession did not run in his family

His grandfather, an emigrant from Northern Ireland in 1730, had been a successful merchant, and his father—who died only six months after his birth—had been a medical practitioner. It was to his mother, Hodge used later to say, that, under God, he owed everything. Before her marriage in 1790, she had been known as "the beautiful Mary Blanchard of Boston"; her family were of Huguenot extraction, and she inherited their strong character and earnest piety. Left a widow at an early age, Mrs. Hodge by her example brought her youngest son, Charles, under the power of godliness from his infancy and by self-denying economy she was able to give him a first-class education. Hodge later wrote concerning the influence of his home: "I think that in my childhood I came nearer to conforming to the apostle's injunction, 'Pray without ceasing', than in any other period of my life. As far back as I can remember, I had the habit of thanking God for everything I received, and asking him for everything I wanted. If I lost a book, or any of my playthings, I prayed that I might find it. I prayed walking along the streets, in school and out of school, whether playing or studying. I did not do this in obedience to any prescribed rule. It seemed natural. I thought of God as an everywhere-present Being, full of kindness and love, who would not be offended if children talked to Him. I knew he cared for sparrows. I was as cheerful and happy as the birds, and acted as they did."

At Princeton Seminary Hodge showed himself an earnest and successful student, diligent at his books, ardently devoted to his professors (then two in number), and warmly attached to his friends. He graduated on 28th September, 1819, and a month later the presbytery of Philadelphia licensed him to preach the Gospel. Missionary zeal was already a marked characteristic in his life; "I would give the world," he recorded, "were my desire of honouring Christ and of saving souls so strong that I should be indifferent to what related merely to myself." When, therefore, he received a proposal about this time to become an assistant-teacher of Biblical literature and exegesis in his former seminary, we find him writing: "Did the duties of the contemplated office require me to give up the prospect of preaching altogether, I think I should not hesitate in declining it; for I believe that preaching the Gospel is a privilege superior to any other entrusted to men." The office did not call for the relinquishment of any directly spiritual duties, and Hodge, well

aware of the intimate connection between the prosperity of the
Church and the propagation of sound theology, accepted the appointment in 1820. After two years his two senior professors, Dr. Alexander
and Dr. Samuel Miller, were so satisfied with his abilities that they
successfully recommended to the Assembly his appointment to a
regular professorial chair. A month later he married Sarah Bache, a
young lady of unusual beauty both of person and character who
attributed her conversion to his instrumentality. A new house was
built for them near the Seminary and it became the scene of Hodge's
life and labours for more than half a century to come. Here his eight
children, except the eldest, were born, and here his loved partner
was reft from him by death in 1849. His two sons, A. A. Hodge, and
Caspar Wistar Hodge, and his grandson, Caspar Wistar Hodge Junr.,
were themselves later to become professors in the Seminary and his
eminent successors.

From this early period in Hodge's life till the day of his death his
activities were almost entirely of the same character. Year after
year his life was one uniform devotion to the training of men to
preach the glorious gospel of the grace of God. Some 3,000 students
passed through his classes, and for over fifty years he continued to
mould the current opinions of his Church and country. Hodge was
a man of wide outlook; at an early period in his life he spent two
years at German Universities listening to men of very different views
from his own, yet he never faltered in his conviction that historic
Calvinism provides the only sound basis for true exposition and
evangelical preaching. By deep study he arrived at the settled
conclusion that the doctrinal standards of the Reformers and Puritans
were the truth, and in 1872 at his jubilee, when multitudes were
elsewhere confounding novelty with truth, he boldly declared—
"I am not afraid to say, that a new idea never originated in this
seminary." Strife was not congenial to his nature, but he could not,
and did not, shun controversy on these doctrinal principles. In an
age of increasing uncertainty, compromise and confusion, he saw
clearly, in the words of his son, that "The last issue must be between
Atheism and its countless forms and Calvinism. The other systems
will be crushed as the half-rotten ice between two great bergs."
Dr. Shedd spoke the truth when he said, "Dr. Hodge has done more
for Calvinism than any other man in America." It was a fact which
his opponents unconsciously recognised when they referred to him

as the greatest hindrance to theological "progress" that the century had seen!

Hodge's life is itself the best answer to those who have wrongly deemed narrowness and coldness to be the necessary accompaniments of the Reformed Faith. He was no abstract systematizer, but ever concerned with the living application of the great truths of Scripture to men's spiritual experience. He did not forget the warning of an old Puritan divine, "Beware of a strong head and a cold heart." The mention of the love of Christ would sometimes, even in the class-room, affect him to tears, and in no spirit of exaggeration a life-long friend testified—"Not Rutherford himself was more absorbed with the love of Christ." Professor B. B. Warfield, who later succeeded to Hodge's theological chair, gives the following description of his manner of teaching: "After his always strikingly appropriate prayer had been offered, and we were settled back into our seats, he would open his well-thumbed Greek Testament—on which it was plain that there was not a single marginal note—look at the passage for a second, and then, throwing his head back and closing his eyes, begin his exposition. He scarcely again glanced at the Testament during the hour: the text was evidently before his mind, verbally, and the matter of his exposition thoroughly at his command. In an unbroken stream it flowed from subject to subject, simple, clear, cogent, unfailingly reverent. Now and then he would pause a moment, to insert an illustrative anecdote—now and then lean forward suddenly with tearful, wide-open eyes to press home a quick-risen inference of the love of God to lost sinners."

In his home Hodge was ever found to be a humble, lovable Christian. "Clear light did not interfere with warm love in good old Dr. Hodge," declared one visitor. "I remember his parlour-study as one of the cheeriest glimpses I had of an American interior." His study was in fact the family thoroughfare through which the children, boys and girls, went in and out for work and play. Often, if too busy to rise and open his door, he would leave it off the latch "so that the least child might toddle in at will unhindered." A. A. Hodge, recalling his father's influence in the home, wrote: "He prayed for us all at family prayers, and singly, and with such soul-felt tenderness taught us to pray at his knees, that, however bad we were, our hearts all melted to his touch. During later years he always caused his family to repeat after him at morning worship

the Apostles' Creed, and a formula of his own composition, professing
personal consecration to the Father, and to the Son, and to the
Holy Ghost. But that which makes those days sacred in the retro-
spect of his children is the person and character of the father himself,
as discovered in the privacy of his home, all radiant as that was with
love, with unwavering faith, and with unclouded hope."

Charles Hodge finally bade farewell to his beloved Princeton and
entered his eternal rest on the 19th of June, 1878. The last consecutive
utterance of his expiring moments was, "To be absent from the body
is to be present with the Lord; to be present with the Lord is to
see Him; to see Him is to be like Him." A great life's work was done,
but behind him in his books he left a legacy to enrich the Church of
God till the end of time. He was a great writer and his pen seems
never to have been idle. For over forty years he had been the editor
of, and chief contributor to, the "Biblical Repertory and Princeton
Review", and through its pages he had exerted a very weighty
influence. In 1835 he issued his great commentary on Romans
which was followed later by his fine expositions on I and II Corinthians
and Ephesians. "The more we use Hodge, the more we value him.
This applies to all his commentaries," wrote Spurgeon. At length,
after his sixty-ninth birthday, his masterpiece and "magnum opus"
on "Systematic Theology" was written and published. These
volumes have in recent years all been made available again in America,
but one book which is worthy of being compared with his finest
works and in some respects excels them, has long been unobtainable,
new or second-hand, on both sides of the Atlantic. That is the book
which is now in the reader's hands. Here are the rich outlines of
sermons—full of doctrine and devotion—delivered by Hodge over
many years to his students on Sunday afternoons. "There it was,"
said one who attended these meetings, "as nowhere else perhaps,
that the 'old Doctor' made his power felt, as, with glistening eye and
quivering lip, he bent forward to press home some practical truth
that had a powerful hold on his own inner experience. He seemed to
yearn over his young disciples as Paul did over Timothy; and every
week he spoke as earnestly and tenderly as though it might be
his last."

These outlines, as A. A. Hodge truthfully asserts, "present in
analytic form an amount and quality of homilectical example and
suggestion probably not surpassed in the same number of pages in

the English language." Such sermons have a peculiar advantage in the present day. Our busy times call loudly for conciseness and simplicity. It is not a reading age, and we have to face the fact that attention to study is no longer common either among Christians or their ministers. Yet there is a growing awareness that we have been too long concerned with activity at the expense of doctrine, there is some awakening to the realization that our fathers were much more deeply acquainted with God's Word than we are, and there is a call for books that set out clearly the truths upon which the Church was fed and nourished in the days of her spiritual prosperity. All these needs are eminently met in this volume. To the prayerful and meditative reader these outlines will provide an inexhaustible supply of spiritual light and strength. May the unction that marked their first delivery attend this re-publication and lead to the blessing of God's people everywhere!

LONDON, 1958

TABLE OF CONTENTS.

III.

IV.

V.

CONVERSION—ENTRANCE UPON THE CHRISTIAN LIFE 116–141

VI.

CHRISTIAN EXPERIENCES, CHARACTERISTICS AND PRIVILEGES.............142-236

VII.

VIII.

THE MEANS OF GRACE—THE SCRIPTURES, MINISTRY, SACRAMENTS, &C.

IX.

DEATH, AND THE CONSUMMATION OF REDEMPTION.

X.

I.

GOD AND HIS ATTRIBUTES.

I. Omnipresence of God.

[*April 15th*, 1855.]

I. *Its Nature.* In regard to God himself and to all his attributes, there is a simple, scriptural, popular mode of conception which answers all the purposes of piety. There is, however, another mode not inconsistent with or contradictory of the former, demanded by the understanding to avoid confusion and inconsistency. Thus, in reference to the omnipresence of God, the simple, popular idea that God is equally present every where is enough. The understanding, however, requires a more particular statement to avoid our conceiving of God as extended. The nature of time and space involved in this conception is among the most difficult of philosophical questions. Happily, some of the most simple truths are the most mysterious. We know that our spirits are here and not elsewhere, and yet the relation of our souls to space is inscrutable. So we know that God is every where, but his relation to space is past finding out.

He is every where present as to his essence, for he does not admit of division. He is every where present as to his knowledge, for nothing escapes his notice. He is every where present as to his power, as he worketh all things after the counsel of his own will. This attribute, therefore, includes the idea—

1. That the universe exists in God. For of all creatures it is said that in him they live and move and have their being.

2. That all the intelligence indicated in nature is the omnipresent intelligence of God. Rational creatures he has endowed with an intelligence of their own.

3. That all the efficiency manifested in nature is the "potestas ordinata" of God.

II. *Hence the universe is a manifestation of God.* The stars, the earth, all vegetable and animal life, our bodies, insects the most minute, all reveal a present God. We see God in every thing.

III. *Hence all events,* the falling of a sparrow, the fall of king-doms, the course of history, the events of our own life, are all mani-festations of his presence.

IV. *Hence we are ever in God's presence.* All our thoughts and feelings are exercised in his sight, all our acts are performed under his eye.

V. *Hence an infinite Helper and portion is ever near to us;* a loving merciful, long-suffering, omnipotent Father is ever with us, to sustain, to guide, to aid and comfort. The infinite fountain of all blessedness is always at hand, from which we may derive inexhaustible supplies of life.

VI. *Hence all sin and sinners are enveloped, as it were, with a consuming fire.* They can no more escape than we can escape out of the atmosphere which now surrounds us.

The contemplation of this doctrine, therefore, serves—

1. To exalt our conceptions of God by making all things the manifestation of his glory and power.

2. To promote our peace and security, because we know God is every where and controls all events.

3. To promote fear—knowing that our thoughts and acts are open to his view.

4. To promote joy and confidence, because our almighty helper is ever at hand, and he whose presence constitutes the blessedness of heaven is near to us.

5. To teach sinners the certainty and fearfulness of their doom.

As all religion consists in communion with God, and as all communion supposes his presence, this doctrine lies at the foundation of all religion.

II. In him we live and move and have our being: Acts xvii. 28.

[*October 7th,* 1860.]

Wrong views of the nature of God and of our relation to him lie at the foundation of all false theories of religion. Wrong views of the nature of God are—

I. *That he is a limited being,* dwelling in temples, receiving gifts from man. Such was the popular notion of the ancient Greeks to whom Paul spoke.

II. *That he is an infinite being,* the creator of all things, but a God removed from us, not watching over us and ordering the events of his providence, and not a moral governor.

III. *That he is an infinite being,* and in fact the only being, all that is being merely phenomena of God; so that there is no individual separate existence, no self-activity, no sin, no holiness, no responsibility, no hereafter.

IV. *The true doctrine here taught by the Apostle is—*

1. That God is a personal being distinct from the world; its creator and preserver.

2. That he is not far from any one of us, but is everywhere present beholding, directing and controlling all things; a being on whom we are dependent, and to whom we are responsible.

3. That our dependence upon him is absolute for being, for life, for activity, but at the same time it is consistent with separate personal existence, with liberty, with accountability.

These are the fixed points in Paul's Theism. How are these points to be understood? Or, in other words, how is our relation to God to be apprehended by us? There are two ways of determining these points.

First, by the reason, or the understanding.

Second, by the intuitions of our moral and religious nature as enlightened by the Scriptures.

First. The intellectual method, or the way of speculation. The problem to be solved is, how the omnipresent, universal, omnipotent agency of the first cause—God—stands related to the phenomenal world.

The most natural solution of this problem is the Pantheistic. 1. Because it is the simplest and most intelligible. 2. Because as an historical fact, it has been the solution most generally received. Brahm of the East was the universal substance of which all things are the manifestation. This principle underlay the nature worship of the Egyptians. It was the Esoteric faith of the higher Greek philosophers. It passed over into the Alexandrian school and the doctrine of the New Platonists. It reappears among the schoolmen, and has become the popular faith of the philosophers of modern times.

But this doctrine does such violence to the moral and religious nature of man, that it never can be the real faith of any class of men any more than Idealism can.

The rebound from this extreme is Deism, *i. e.,* a God, indeed extra-mundane, but indifferent and unconcerned as to any efficiency of his in the events and changes of the world.

Second. What the Scriptures teach is congenial to our whole nature, intellectual and moral.

1. That all existence is from God and in God.

2. That all life is from him, and in him.

3. That all activity is from and in him, so far as that unsustained by him no second cause could act.

From all this it follows:

1. That we are always most near to God. This presence includes a presence of knowledge, of power, of approbation or disapprobation.

2. That we are thus dependent for natural, for intellectual, and for spiritual life.

3. That this concursus of the divine and human is according to fixed laws ; laws, which concern our natural, intellectual and spiritual life ; laws, however, under the control of a personal God, who can suspend, counteract or ignore them, at will.   If we recognize these laws, and act according to them, we experience their normal working, we become more and more the recipients of the life of God.   If we ignore them, or transgress them, the opposite result is unavoidable.

4. That as the whole being and blessedness of the soul, thus depends on keeping the true relation between God and ourselves, we should be ever on our guard never to violate his laws ; in all things to act in accordance with his will, feeling our dependence, our obligation, rendering him trust, gratitude and love.

5. Under all circumstances we are ever in contact with the infinite source of knowledge, being, blessedness, holiness and life.

6. The wicked are always in contact with him as a consuming fire.

III. The Sovereignty of God.

[*April* 3*d*, 1859.]

I. *Sovereignty—What it is.*

It is the right of absolute dominion. The right to act in reference to ourself and others according to the dictate of our own will. It is thus among men. An absolute sovereign is an autocrat; a ruler whose will is law, which no one has a right to dispute or to disobey. This does not imply that any ruler has a right to do wrong; to violate the eternal principles of justice and mercy. But it implies that the ruler is responsible for the wisdom and justice of his acts to no one on earth.

So when we speak of the sovereignty of God, we mean his right to work all things after the counsel of his own will ; to do what he wills with his own ; that he has in reference to the whole universe the most absolute dominion and right to deal with his creatures just as seems good in his sight; to allow them to sin or to prevent their sinning ; and when they have sinned, to allow them to perish or to provide salvation ; and, if salvation be provided, to reveal it to one nation and not to another; to apply it to one person and not to another. Of course he has an equal right to determine their destiny on earth, whether it shall be civilized or savage, rich or poor, learned or ignorant, healthy or infirm, happy or miserable.

The sovereignty of God supposes that the whole plan of creation, providence and redemption, was adopted on the ground of God's good pleasure; that the carrying out of that plan in all its infinitude of details is determined by his absolute will. So that if it be asked why Adam fell; why salvation was provided for man and not angels; why that salvation was revealed at first to Jews and not to the Gentiles; why now it is made known to us and not to the Chinese; why you and not others are made partakers of this redemption; why one man is a noble and another a peasant; one sick and another well; one happy and another miserable; we have nothing to say but: "Even so, Father, for so it seemed good in thy sight."

This sovereignty of God is not what the schoolmen meant by absolute power; which supposes that God could make sin, holiness, and holiness, sin. For although there is no being above God to whom he is responsible, and no eternal principle to which he is subject, yet it is involved, in the idea of God as a rational and holy being that his acts are subject to his reason. Infinite reason cannot be unreasonable, nor can infinite holiness be unholy.

II. *The ground of this sovereignty.*

The only legitimate ground of authority is superiority on the one hand and dependence on the other. So it is in the relation of parents and children; so, in theory, is it in human society. The sovereign is assumed to have more power and resources, and the people for this reason to be dependent. Or, according to another theory, the magistrate represents the state which is superior to any of its members. So the ground of God's sovereignty is, on the one hand his infinite superiority to his creatures, not only as their creator and proprietor, but in all his attributes. He is entitled, in virtue of this infinite superiority of wisdom, power and goodness, to do his pleasure among the armies of heaven and the inhabitants of earth. On the other hand it rests on the absolute dependence of his creatures on his power, and of sinners on his grace. They have no claim upon him.

III. *Proof of this sovereignty.*

Three sources of proof apart from the *à priori* reasonableness of the claim.

1. The express and innumerable declarations of the Scriptures on the subject.

2. The actual administration of the providence of God, and the actual dispensations of his grace.

3. The consciousness and experience of all believers.

IV. *The practical importance of this great doctrine is plain.*

1. Because it determines our relation to God which determines our religion. If a man misconceives his relation to God, of course his re-

ligion will be perverted. If he regards himself as a mere machine, a manifestation of God's agency, then all responsibility, sense of guilt, and all religion disappear. If he considers himself independent of God, deciding his own character and destiny, then again he is in a false position. But if he conceives of God as infinitely good, his rightful sovereign, and himself as dependent and as unworthy, then all is right.

2. It is only on this ground that we can have any security for our personal well being or salvation.

3. This is the ground of our confidence as to the issue of all things. It is well that infinite wisdom, power and goodness, and not fate or chance control the world.

V. *How this doctrine lies in the Scriptures, and how it should be preached.*

It is to all other doctrines of Scripture what the granite formation is to the other strata of the earth. It underlies and sustains them, but it crops out only here and there. So this doctrine should underlie all our preaching, and should be definitely presented and asserted only now and then.

IV. The Lord Reigneth. Ps. 93:1.

[*April 23d*, 1865.]

The Lord, that is, Jehovah, the self-existent, the immutable, the infinite.

1. This is not an idea, nor a force, nor a principle of being, but a personal God.

2. As such He is infinite in wisdom, in power, in goodness.

3. He is the only God—the triune God of whom this dominion is predicated.

4. But the manifested Jehovah, the person of the Trinity in whom the Godhead is revealed, and through whom the dominion spoken of is exercised—is the Logos, and that Logos has assumed our nature, and, therefore, the Lord to whom the kingship is ascribed is the Theanthropos. "Alleluia; for the Lord God omnipotent reigneth."

Reigneth. This implies,

1. Absolute power over all things. As there is nothing to limit his dominion, his power extends over the whole universe and all it contains; over all orders and classes of beings, rational and irrational, sensible and insensible, great and small.

2. That his power is not only over all things, so that he can if he please destroy or preserve them, but that he actually exercises this controlling influence. The universe is not left to itself, to chance, to fate,

or to the powers of darkness. The Lord is the controlling force. His will, his wisdom, his power determines all events.

3. This dominion is absolutely sovereign. He has no counsellors. He has none to hinder or to thwart his designs. His dominion is absolute and irresistible.

4. It is of course, being the dominion of God, the dominion of infinite wisdom and of infinite love, directing all things to the attainment of the highest conceivable ends.

This doctrine is the ground,

1. Of confidence and joy. The whole universe has reason to rejoice that the Lord reigneth.

2. Of submission and of resignation under the most adverse circumstances. This the people of God have ever done, and we ought now to do.

3. If the Lord reigns it is unspeakably wicked not to acknowledge his authority.

4. Those who set themselves in opposition to him must perish.

5. The high office and favor bestowed on those who are commissioned to teach men that the Lord reigns, and to bring them to acknowledge their allegiance to him.

Go with this graven on your hands.—The Lord, Our Lord, the Lord Jesus Christ reigneth.

V. Dependence on God.

[*September 7th*, 1862.]

I. *The fact that we are dependent is assumed in all religions.* It is one of those truths which is practically admitted, even when theoretically denied. It is admitted by Deists, Israelites, Pantheists, as well as by Rationalists and Pelagians, diverse as their theories are.

II. *As to the nature of this dependence, there are two extremes.* First, some refer it only to the existence and subsistence of second causes, and not to their operation or their effects. Second, others exclude second causes and merge all things into God.

The Scriptures teach that there is a two-fold dependence of man upon God; first, as creature, and second, as believer; as to his natural and as to his spiritual life. These are very different. The one has reference to our relation to the providential efficiency of God, the other to his spiritual influence.

III. *As to our dependence on God as creatures,* or as to the relation between God and the world, the Scriptures teach; 1st. That the world owes its existence to God. 2d. Its continuance in being is also owing to him. 3d. It nevertheless has a real existence, and that second causes have a real efficiency of their own. 4th. In the exercise of that efficiency there is (1) a general superintendence and control, so that where there is design there is mind present and active; and (2) an ordering of second causes for specific ends; so that whether there shall be rain or drought, abundance or want, success or defeat depends upon the will of God, and not on the mere operation of second causes.

IV. *As to our dependence upon God spiritually, the Scriptures teach* 1st. that the origin of spiritual life and its continuance is not due to any natural law. It is not brought about in the way of nature. There was a great difference between the dependence of a healthy man for the exercise of sight and the dependence of a blind man upon Christ for the restoration of vision. So we are dependent upon God for the origin of spiritual life as something supernatural. 2d. The Scriptures teach that we are dependent for the continuance and exercise of this spiritual life; 3d. that we are dependent for the success of our efforts to benefit others. Here our dependence is absolute. 4th. But the supplies of divine influence are made in the use of appropriate means. Those means cannot be neglected. If faithfully used, they are always more or less blessed.

Inferences. 1. We should constantly recognize this doctrine, and not feel and act as though we were independent of God and could do without him. 2. We should earnestly seek his presence and aid. 3. Avoid grieving his Spirit.

VI. Thy Word is Truth.

[*September* 16*th*, 1866.]

By truth is meant that which sustains, which answers expectation; which never disappoints; which is and is ever found to be consistent with reality. Falsehood and error, on the other hand, is that which is empty, vain; which does not sustain; which disappoints; which does not correspond with the real.

The truth concerning the eternal world, its phenomena and its laws, is that which represents what really is, and what may be relied upon, and which when assumed as real never disappoints. So the truth concerning the internal world of mind is what corresponds to the phenomena and laws of that world, and which we can always safely assume and rely upon.

So the truth concerning God is that representation of his nature, attributes, mode of being and acting which corresponds with what he really is and does. And the truth concerning our moral and spiritual state, our relation to God, our delivery, the mode and condition of salvation, is what in all these matters is found worthy of confidence, which never disappoints.

Now, the proposition, " Thy word is truth," is a very wide one. By the word of God is meant, or may be meant,

1. Any revelation of God. A word is a revelation. It is an outward manifestation of thought. Anything, therefore, by which God reveals himself, his purposes, or any fact, is his word. In this sense the whole creation is an outspoken word of God. It reveals him. And all that it makes known of him, of his ways, his character, will or purposes is truth. It accords exactly with what God is, and what it legitimately teaches concerning him may, therefore, be relied upon with implicit confidence.

The external world is not a phantasm, an empty show. It is not delusive, but is what it reveals itself to be, and never disappoints those who rely upon its teachings.

The foundation of this reality, the reason why the world, as the word of God, is thus real and reliable, is because it is his word. It must be studied as his word.

2. By the word of God is often meant in the Scriptures, any particular declaration, whether a promise, a threatening, or revelation of what is, or is to be.

3. It means the revelation concerning God and divine things contained in the Scriptures. In that sense the proposition " Thy word is truth " is equivalent to, the Scriptures are true ; all they teach concerning God, man, his character and state, his relation to God, concerning the person and work of Christ, the plan of salvation, the future life, and the future state of the Church, is true. Everything conforms to what is real. Everything may be confidently relied upon. Nothing will ever disappoint legitimate expectation. Those who assume the Scriptures to be true and act upon them will attain the end they promise. Those who assume that what they teach is false and act accordingly, will find their mistake.

Now, 1. It is an unspeakable blessing to know what is truth, and where it may be found. This is the great pursuit. Men seek it here and there, but it is found only in God and his word, in all the senses mentioned.

2. It is also an unspeakable blessing not only to know where truth may be found, but to have it made accessible to us. If we seek it ourselves in reason, in consciousness, in the wisdom and teaching of men, the history of the race, we shall be disappointed. All who seek truth elsewhere than in the word of God (and especially the Scriptures) will and must be in doubt, darkness and error.

Hence we have an immovable and everlasting foundation.

VII. God is Light.

[*December* 11*th*, 1859.]

The knowledge of God is essential to all religion. 1. Because religion consists in the relation of the soul to God. 2. Because that relation, being that of a person to a person, is of necessity a rational relation. That is, it supposes knowledge of the person to whom the relation is sustained. Our inward state is determined by our cognitions; not by mere speculative apprehension, but by the apprehension of the true nature of the objects of knowledge in their relation to ourselves. Therefore, if we have wrong views of God, and of his relation to us, we necessarily have wrong feelings ; that is, we cannot have true religion. Thus, if we conceive of God, 1. As a principle or power, or as the unconscious life of the world, whose life is the life of the world, then we cannot stand to him in the relation of creatures or of children. He cannot be our father, protector, governor or portion. 2. Or if we conceive of God as a being who created the world and exercises no providential care over it, and holds its inhabitants to no responsibility, then we cannot stand in the true relation to him. 3. If we regard God as all benevolence without justice, then again all is wrong as to our internal state.

The knowledge of God being thus essential, the Scriptures employ all methods of communicating it. His names, his attributes, his works, his word, his Son, are all modes of revealing God. God is described sometimes in a word, sometimes by an enumeration of his attributes or acts. We are not to consider any one name, or any one work, or any one description as exhausting the idea as made known to us. When it is said God is a refuge, he is that and more. When it is said he is love, he is that and more. There are two things intended by that declaration. One is that there is nothing in him inconsistent with love ; the other is that love exists in him in an infinite degree.

When, therefore, it is said God is Light, we are not to understand that there is nothing in God but what light represents, but only that there is nothing in him inconsistent with the idea expressed by light, (in him there is no darkness at all ;) and that all that the word expresses belongs to him in an infinite degree.

Two things are intended, when it is said God is Light. 1. What he is in his own nature. 2. What he is to us.

I. *God in his own nature is Light.* We know nothing of material things but their phenomena. We know nothing of light but its effects and its laws. What it is in itself we do not know. Therefore its essential nature is not the point of comparison between God and light.

He is called light simply because his nature agrees with what we know of light. 1. Light is transparent and revealing. It is therefore the fit emblem of knowledge, just as darkness is the emblem of ignorance. God, is light, therefore, because his infinite intelligence embraces all truth, there is no obscurity or doubt in any of his apprehensions. In him is no darkness in the sense of ignorance. And as light manifests immediately, as it reveals instantly, so it properly represents the intuitive nature of God's knowledge. He sees all things, knows by seeing, not by searching or reasoning.

2. Light is pure. It cannot be defiled. So it is the fit emblem of holiness. God is absolute holiness. There is nothing in him of an opposite character. He stands opposed to evil as light does to darkness by an opposition of nature, necessary, immutable, eternal. Darkness cannot exist in the light. The one excludes or is the negative of the other. God and sin are opposed and cannot exist in fellowship. What fellowship hath light with darkness? We therefore, as sinners, cannot have fellowship with God. No possession, no external relations, nothing done for us which leaves us unchanged can bring us into communion with God. Without holiness no man can see God.

3. Light is calm. It is not disturbed by any storms. It is therefore the emblem of the harmony and blessedness of the divine nature. There is nothing in him inconsistent with perfect harmony. His blessedness is infinite, immutable, eternal. God is light in all these aspects, in his unclouded intelligence, absolutely holy and infinite in his undisturbed blessedness.

II. *In his relation to us God is light.*

1. Light is the great medium of revelation. Darkness hides, light reveals. So God to us is the only, the infinite and inexhaustible fountain of all knowledge; objective, in what he has revealed, and subjective in his illumination of our understanding. In his light we see light. He only can banish darkness from our minds and bring us to the knowledge of the truth.

2. Light in the natural world is the source or necessary condition of life. So God is to us the source of all spiritual life. We can only live, grow, and flourish in his presence and under the light of his countenance. His favor is our life. All holiness springs from reconciliation to him and fellowship with him.

3. Light is the source of all beauty, so God is the source of all blessedness. Absence from him is that outer darkness in which the wicked are plunged. What light is to the natural world, therefore, that in a far greater degree God is to us.

VIII. God is Love. 1 John 4: 8 and 14.

[January 20th, 1855.]

I. *Meaning of the proposition.*

1. Love includes, *a.* desire of communion, *b.* complacency, and *c.* benevolence.

2. When it is affirmed that God is love, it is not meant that he is nothing else, nor that all his moral perfections may be resolved into one, much less into one form of one.

3. But it means negatively that there is nothing in God incompatible with love; no malice or malignity, no coldness or indifference. This is infinitely much, if the omnipotence and knowledge of God are not controlled for evil.

4. Positively, it means that love in God, as desire, complacency and benevolence, is essential, eternal and infinite. *a.* It is universal, extending to all his creatures. *b.* It is intelligent. *c.* It is holy. *d.* It is unfathomable. *e.* It is sovereign and discriminating. One creature is an angel, another a man, and another a brute, another an insect. Of rational creatures, some are preserved holy, some left to sin. Of the latter some are redeemed and others are not. *f.* It is affluent, rejoicing in enriching and adorning his creatures. *g.* It is immutable in all its forms, whether of simple benevolence or of electing saving love. *h.* It is manifold, manifesting itself in one form towards merely sentient creatures, in another towards rational beings, in another towards the unholy, and in another towards the redeemed, his peculiar ones, his יְחִידִים (if that word can have a plural.)

II. *Proof that God is love.*

1. Negatively, there is no evidence of malignity in him. 2. Creation and providence constantly manifest it. 3. Redemption is the great overwhelming demonstration of it. 4. It is declared in a thousand forms in the Scriptures, that God is merciful, long-suffering, tender, compassionate; that his love is stronger than a father's, or a mother's, or a husband's.

III. *Importance of this truth.*

1. It is the foundation of repentance, faith and obedience. 2. It is important to the promotion of holiness. Our life consists in the knowledge of God, and God is love. This must be known, believed and appreciated before it can produce in us the proper impressions. 3. We are God's children if we love; for God is love. 4. It is the ground of all confidence as to the issue of the universe, as to the course of providence, and as to our own affairs. 5. If God is love, then it is only by loving that we have fellowship with him, and that he dwells in us. The proposition thus becomes to us a test of character.

IX. Love of God to Us.

[*December* 23*d*, 1855.]

I. *Nature of love in God.*

Everything in the nature of God is incomprehensible. He is, on the one hand, like us, because we are like him. But, on the other hand he is infinite, eternal, without succession, and therefore not in time. We can not understand the Almighty unto perfection.

1. If God be conceived of as mere law or power, it is impossible that we can predicate love of him.

2. If God be conceived of as intelligent and personal, and yet as acting only by law, establishing general principles in his moral government, analogous to the laws of nature, he may be benevolent, but cannot love. If he simply ordains that virtue shall produce happiness, or that certain external things shall minister enjoyment, this is benevolence but not love. It has no regard to individuals. He includes in it nothing more than a desire to promote happiness. It has no more respect to one class of beings than to another. It has no more regard to one person than to another. We know that love in us is something more than a desire that creatures or that man should be happy.

3. It is only on the assumption that God is not only a person, but as such can have and has intercourse with persons, that we can attribute love to him. Love has regard, *a.* To individuals. *b.* It is complacency and delight in them. *c.* It is desire of possession and fellowship. *d.* It is desire to render good and happy, and a desire to be loved.

a. Being to individuals it is not indiscriminate. It is not equal. We see in Christ, benevolence to all, love to his people. He loved John more than any other of his disciples. *b.* It is a complacent delight in them. *c.* It is expressed in intercourse. God communes with his creatures. His love is shed abroad in our hearts. *d.* It is manifested in making its objects perfectly blessed.

It is objected to such views that they are inconsistent with the nature of God. We can learn, however, what God is only by his word and by what he does. Men think, because God is infinite, that nothing minute is worthy of his notice. But the Bible teaches that because he is infinite, nothing is so minute as to require any effort of attention. Everywhere, deep in the sea and in the stars, God's intelligence is at work. As he intelligently operates everywhere, in the least as in the greatest, so he can consciously love everywhere.

II. *The love of God is infinite, eternal, immutable, sovereign.*

III. *It is the source of all holiness.* We can love him because he loved us. It produces gratitude, delight, zeal, filial reverence, obedience.

It elevates the soul above the creature. It purifies all the affections. This is its legitimate effect. Where God is understood, and where his love is really enjoyed, these effects follow. When it is assumed that he loves where he does not, and love is regarded as mere respect of persons, then it produces, as it did in the Jews, spiritual pride, bigotry, malignity, contempt and arrogance. So it is among the Romanists, who hate all out of their church. If it is the source of holiness, the assurance of it should be cherished.

2. It is the source of happiness.

Love is the great source of blessedness. All the happiness of life depends upon it. Its power depends much on the character and dignity of those who exercise it. Love in the infinite God is an infinite source of blessedness. It fills and satisfies the whole soul.

3. It sustains and strengthens us under all trials and for all duties.

4. It exalts the full perfection of our nature.

God's benevolence is manifested in his works of creation and providence. God's love is shown to his people as a whole, by the gift of his Son, and by all the provisions of his grace. God's love to each individual is manifested by the work of his Spirit in him.

X. The Tender Mercies of God. Ps. 146: 9.

[March 11th, 1860.]

There are two ways of conceiving of God, the philosophical and the religious, as he stands related to the reason and as he stands related to the heart. According to the one method we regard God as the first ground and cause of all things, as infinite, immutable, eternal, incapable of any relation to space or duration, without succession and without passion or change.

According to the other, we regard him as a person to whom we bear the relation of creatures and children, of responsibility and dependence, to whom we must look for all good, and with whom we can have intercourse, who has towards us the feelings of a father and to whom we can make known our joys and sorrows.

Both these are right, so far as limited and determined by the Scriptures. The one limits the other. If we press the philosophical method so far as to lose the object of the religious affections, we end in Atheism. If we let our affections have full scope we lose the infinite and absolutely perfect, as did the mystic enthusiasts. In the Bible both elements are harmonized; though the latter is the predominant, as it should be with us.

In the interpretation of all such passages as this in which human affections are attributed to God, two things are to be avoided. 1. That we do not ascribe to him anything inconsistent with his nature as the eternal and immutable Jehovah, any perturbation or excitement. 2. That we do not merge everything into figure, as though nothing real was intended ; as though the God we worship was a God without consciousness, without knowledge, without regard for his creatures. There is in him something which really answers to the words we use, and which is the proper object of the affections which we exercise.

I. *What is meant by the tender mercy of the Lord.* The word רַחֲמִים is always used of natural affection of parents for children, at least the verb is always so used, and the noun expresses the paternal feeling, especially the maternal feeling. It is always rendered *tender mercies*, because there is no feeling in our nature more tender than that of a mother for her child.

The objects of the mercy of God, therefore, are not his works, not the universe, not irrational creatures, but his rational creatures. It expresses the relation which God sustains to them. Or it teaches that there is something in him analogous to parental love.

II. *The characteristics of this mercy.*

1. It is universal. All rational creatures and especially all men are its objects. It is merciful to the just and to the unjust. It takes no regard of character or conduct. This is illustrated in the arrangements of creation, in the dispensations of his providence, in the provisions of his grace, which are adapted to all and sufficient for all.

2. It is instinctive and natural as opposed to what is founded on congeniality, or conduct, or reciprocation of benefits. So it is with the love of parents.

3. It is indestructible. A parent never ceases to love his child, and cannot do it. Let the child be ever so ungrateful and wicked, and return to his father's house, he is received with rejoicing as the prodigal. So with God, his mercy is everlasting.

4. It is untiring, long-suffering, tender.

5. It is perfectly consistent with holiness, and therefore with God's hatred of sin, with his justice, and therefore with his determination to punish sinners.

III. *The evidences of God's mercy are to be found in creation, in providence, in redemption, in his dealings towards us personally.*

IV. *The importance of faith in this divine perfection.* That is, it is important we should believe that there is in God this universal instinctive, and therefore indiscriminate love, which is indestructible. It gives us, 1. A ground of trust under all circumstances. If our fathers or mothers were only omnipresent and almighty and infinitely wise, we would be secure of blessedness. Why cannot we feel since God has this רַחֲמִים or tender mercy for us ? 2. It gives encouragement to the vilest sinner to return. It gives no encouragement to sin, and no ground to hope for impunity for the impenitent.

XI. God so Loved the World. John 3: 16.

[*February 22d*, 1863.]

The object of God's love. The greatness of that love. The design of God in its manifestation.

I. *The object of God's love.*

Man, in distinction from all other orders of beings. This determines nothing more. It does not teach that benevolence merely was the motive of the act here spoken of. Nor does it assert that philanthropy, or indiscriminate or equal love for all mankind was the form of the love here spoken of. This may be true. The passage is consistent also with the assumption that it was the distinguishing or peculiar love to his people. Which is the real or true view of the matter depends on the analogy of Scripture. When it is said that Christ is the Saviour of the world, the Saviour of men, that is consistent with the doctrine that he does not save all men, or that he saves only his people. In either case he is the Saviour of men.

Man being considered as the object of God's love, there are considerations which enhance the character of that love. 1. The insignificance of man, absolutely and relatively. What is man in the immensity of God's works, and what is he in comparison with the higher order of intelligences? 2. His guilt. He is not himself the proper object of love or recipient of favors. He deserves nothing but the wrath and curse of God. 3. He is unattractive. In the highest degree repulsive and unlovely.

That God therefore should love man is wonderful and mysterious. It is unaccountable. It is something for which no reason can be given. It is, therefore, something hard to be believed. Hard, not for the impenitent and insensible, but for the enlightened and convinced sinner. It needs, therefore, not only the repeated assurances and assertions of the Scriptures, but also the clearest manifestation, and even this is not enough. It requires the special revelation and witnessing of the Holy Spirit that we are the objects of the love of God.

II. *The greatness of the love of God*—of God as manifested in the gift of Christ. We must take the doctrines of the Bible as they are presented, and hold them in the form in which they are presented. We must not, on the plea that God is an infinite Being, and that the truth is presented in human forms, *i. e.*, in forms adapted to our mode of conception, explain them away, or expand them into more general philosophical formulas. Whether we can comprehend them or not, we must receive, believe and live upon them as revealed. It is declared in the Scriptures: 1. That there is only one God. 2. That there are three distinct persons in the Godhead, and that the Son, or second person, is the object of the infinite love of the Father. 3. That something is true of the Son that is not true of the Father or the Spirit. It was the Son, and neither of the other persons of the trinity, who became incarnate and suffered and died for our sins. 4. That this involved a great sacrifice on the part of the Father; not a painful one, but involved something which love to the Son would, if allowed exclusive control, have prevented. The person given up to humiliation, suffering and death was the Son of God: not in the sense in which angels and men are called the sons of God, but his only begotten Son, the partaker of his nature, the same in substance and equal in power and glory with the Father.

The importance of the object to be obtained or the strength of the feeling which prompts to its attainment, is to be measured by the means adapted to that end. To give up an angel, or a world, or a myriad of worlds, would indicate that the feeling was strong and the object of vast importance. But to give up his Son places these things beyond our comprehension. It shows the love to be absolutely infinite —such as admits of no limit or measure.

III. *The design of God in giving his Son was that men should not perish but have everlasting life.* The perdition to which they were exposed included eternal misery and eternal sinfulness. The salvation includes deliverance from that perdition, and eternal holiness and eternal blessedness.

2. It is here, as well as elsewhere taught, that it was the design of God to render the salvation of all men possible, by the gift of his Son. There was nothing in the nature, or the value, or the design of his work to render it available for any one class of men only. *Whosoever* believeth, etc. This is not inconsistent with other representations that it entered into God's design to render the salvation of his people certain by the death of his Son.

3. The passage teaches that faith is the only condition of salvation; not descent from Abraham, nor circumcision, not church connection, not outward rite, not goodness, but simple faith, which indeed secures all goodness, etc.

4. It teaches that faith includes trust. We believe upon Christ, *i. e.*, we trust in him as our Saviour. This includes or supposes the apprehension of his glory as the Son of God; the renunciation of all other grounds of reliance; the knowledge of what he has done and has promised to do for our salvation, and the actual committing ourselves into his hands believing that he will save us.

This is a passage to which we must constantly recur for our own instruction, confirmation and consolation, and for the instruction and guidance of those committed to our care.

XII. "Who will have all men to be saved and to come unto the knowledge of the truth." 1 Tim. 2 : 4.

[*March 1st*, 1868.]

There are two principles which must control the interpretation of the Scriptures. That is, when a passage admits of two interpretations, the choice between them is to be determined, first, by the analogy of Scripture. If one interpretation contradicts what the Bible elsewhere teaches and another accords with it, then we are bound to accept the latter. Or, secondly, the interpretation must be decided by established facts. That is, if one interpretation agrees with such facts and another contradicts them, then the former must be true.

This passage admits of two interpretations so far as the signification of the words are concerned. *First*, that God *wills*, in the sense of purposing or intending, the salvation of all men. This cannot be true, first, because it contradicts the Scriptures. The Scriptures teach 1st, that the purposes of God are immutable, and that they cannot fail of their accomplishment. 2d. That all men are not to be saved. It is clearly taught that multitudes of the human race have perished, are now perishing, and will hereafter perish. That God intends and purposes what he knows is not to happen, is a contradiction. It contradicts the very idea of God, and is an impossibility. Secondly, this interpretation contradicts admitted facts as well as the explicit statements of the Bible.

1. It is a fact that God does not give saving grace to all men. 2. It is a fact that he does not and never has brought all men to the knowledge of the truth. Multitudes of men are destitute of that knowledge, and ever have been. By truth it is clear the apostle means saving truth, the truth as revealed in the gospel, and not merely the truth as revealed by things that are made. This interpretation therefore cannot be correct.

The *second* interpretation is that God desires the salvation of all men. This means 1st, just what is said when the Scriptures declare that God is good; that he is merciful and gracious, and ready to forgive; that he is good to all, and his tender mercies over all his works. He is kind to the unthankful and to the evil. This goodness or benevolence of God is not only declared but revealed in his works, in his providence, and in the work of redemption. 2d. It means what is said in Ezek. xxxiii. 11. "As I live, saith the Lord God, I have no pleasure in the death of the wicked," and in Ezek. xviii. 23, "Have I any pleasure at all that the wicked should die, saith the Lord God, and not that he should return from his ways and live?" Also Lam. iii. 33, "For he doth not afflict willingly nor grieve the children of men." It means what Christ taught in the parable of the prodigal son, and of the lost sheep and the lost piece of money; and is taught by his lament over Jerusalem.

All these passages teach that God delights in the happiness of his creatures, and that when he permits them to perish, or inflicts evil upon them, it is from some inexorable necessity; that is, because it would be unwise and wrong to do otherwise. His relation is that of a benevolent sovereign in punishing crime, or of a tender judge in passing sentence on offenders, or, what is the familiar representation of Scripture, that of a father who deals with his children with tenderness, yet with wisdom and according to the dictates of right.

This is the meaning of the passage. That it is the correct one is plain,

1. Because it is agreeable to the meaning of the word θέλειν. In innumerable cases it means to love, delight in, to regard with satisfaction as a thing desirable. "Sacrifice and offerings thou wouldst not," "neither hadst pleasure therein." "Ye cannot do the things that ye would." "For what I would, that do I not, but what I hate, that I do." "We would see a sign from thee." "Be it unto thee even as thou wilt." "If he delight in him" is εἰ θέλει αὐτόν. 2. This passage thus interpreted teaches just what the Scriptures elsewhere teach of the goodness of God. 3. It does not contradict the Scriptures as the other does, or make God mutable or impotent. 4. It is accordant with all known facts. It agrees with the fact, that God is benevolent, as shown in his works, and yet that he permits many to perish.

This truth is of great importance, 1. Because all religion is founded on the knowledge of God and on the proper apprehensions of his character. We should err fatally if we conceived of God as malevolent.

2. The conviction that God is love, that he is a kind Father, is necessary to encourage sinners to repent. The prodigal hesitated because he doubted his father's love. It was his hope that encouraged him to return.

3. This truth is necessary to our confidence in God. It is the source of gratitude and love.

4. It is to be held fast to under all circumstances. We are to believe though so much sin and misery are allowed to prevail. We are not to resort to false solutions of this difficulty, to assume that God cannot prevent sin, or that he wills it as a means to happiness. He allows it because it seems good in his sight to do so, and this is the highest and the last solution of the problem of evil.

XIII. The Promises of God.

[*December 2d*, 1860.]

The promises of God bear an important part in the work of redemption, both as to justification and as to sanctification. They are the objects of faith and hope.

I. *They are objects of faith.*

The promise to fallen Adam; to Abraham, to David; to the people of God in all ages. The promise of the Messiah, of justification and salvation through him, was and is now held up as the proper object of faith.

This faith includes self-renunciation, assent, and trust. And as such, it has ever been the condition of justification.

II. *They are the objects of hope*, because the blessings to which they relate, not only of the present but also of the future, are the blessings which we specially need, and include all we need, in order to our deliverance from the guilt of sin, from hell, and to secure the full perfection, happiness, and exaltation of our nature, here and hereafter, for time and for eternity.

As the objects of hope and faith, they,

III. *Sanctify.* By them we are made partakers of the divine nature, as Peter says in his 2d Epistle 1: 4, unless the word be taken for the things promised, as when it is said, we inherit the promise, or we receive the promise, or wait for the promise. In either sense the declaration is true. By the divine promises we are made partakers of the divine nature, *i. e.*, of holiness, because, 1. Were it not for those promises, we should have neither faith nor hope, and divine life would be impossible. 2. Because it is by the power of the promises as revealed by the power of the Spirit, that the soul is purified, the heart weaned from things of earth and set on things above.

Or, if the word *promises* there means the blessings promised, then the meaning is that by the redemption of Christ, his work outside of ourselves to satisfy divine justice, and the work of his Spirit in the heart, and by the whole administration of his kingdom of grace, we are exalted to the participation of the divine nature, φύσις, not in the sense of essence, but of character, or disposition; so that we concur with God in judgment and feeling.

IV. *They are the source of consolation and strength*, 1. in times of affliction. 2. In times of conflict. 3. In times of temptation. They fill the soul with confidence and joy, and excite the purpose to persevere even unto the end, assured that we shall become more than conquerors.

These promises relate not merely to individuals, but to the church and to the government of the world.

V. *The attributes of the divine promises are,*

1. That they are exceeding great and precious. The blessings promised are exceeding great, and are such as give them value to us.

2. They are sure, *a.* Because spoken by God, and therefore his veracity is pledged, and his power and infinite wisdom are secured for their fulfilment. *b.* Because they are all yea and amen in Christ; that is, he has rendered them by his work absolutely certain, having performed the condition on which they were suspended, and having received power to carry them into effect.

3. They are immutable. This is involved in their being sure. But it includes the special idea not only that God's purposes will never change, but that no contingency can interfere with their fulfilment. They do not depend upon any thing in us, in our fidelity, or the fidelity of the Church, considered as something outside the promise; for the promise is that God will keep us from falling, that he will keep us all faithful, and cause us to persevere.

VI. *How we are to derive the benefit of the promise.*

1. There are many causes of distrust and doubt, as, *a.* a sense of unworthiness; *b.* long delay; *c.* apparent failure. These are the common experience of the people of God. These are the means which Satan uses to deprive them of the benefit of the promises of God. But, *a.* they are not founded on our worthiness. *b.* The promises of God have been fulfilled after long waiting for them. *c.* The failures are only apparent. We misinterpret them, and because our interpretation fails, we think the promise fails.

2. What we have to do is—

a. To understand the promises and to this end to study them.

b. To secure an interest in them by faith in Christ, or by accepting them.

c. To live upon them.

XIV. The Wrath of God against Sinners.

[*Nov.* 13*th*, 1870.]

Meaning of the word when used of God. Anthropomorphism, *i. e.,* the doctrine that as man is the image of God, God is like man, is the foundation of Theism.

When we predicate intelligence, will and power of God, we mean and the Scriptures mean that God really possesses attributes analogous, *i. e.,* of the same kind as the faculties which that word expresses in us. So when we predicate of him, love, mercy, holiness and goodness, the same is true. In all these cases we must eliminate from the ideas which those words express when used of ourselves, every thing, when we apply them to God, which implies any limitation or imperfection.

In the Scriptures, wrath, anger, fury are attributed to God. These in man are perturbing, agitating, painful, states of mind, and generally more or less malignant. All these elements must be eliminated. What then remains? 1. A calm disapprobation, which is both a judgment and a feeling of which sin and sinners are the objects. 2. A determination to express this disapprobation. 3. This expression results in the banishment of the sinner from God. This is cutting him off from the source of all holiness and happiness, and consigning him to endless, hopeless, inevitable sin and misery. This is the death of the soul, the second death.

Hence it follows, 1st. That although the punishment of sinners is voluntary and judicial, it is nevertheless necessary ; that is, it of necessity flows from the character of God, from the necessary opposition between sin and holiness. 2d. That this punishment is inevitable. Because among men the infliction of punishment, being a voluntary act, may or may not be inflicted, or if inflicted may be remitted, men are apt to think the same thing is true with regard to God. Punishment at his hand is indeed voluntary, but God's will is determined by his nature, and therefore the one is as immutable as the other. As God's nature is of necessity opposed to sin, his will to punish it is also necessary, in the sense of being inevitable. As it is inconceivable that God should not love holiness, so it is inconceivable that he should not hate sin. And as it is inconceivable that he should not manifest his favor to the holy, so it is inconceivable that he should not manifest his disapprobation of the sinful.

3d. It follows that sinners cannot possibly escape the punishment of their sins. This is expressing the same idea in another form. But sinners while admitting that God is opposed to sin and that he will act accordingly, still hope to escape, either because they purpose to cease from sinning, or because they can atone for it, or because they hope that God will pity and forgive.

God has provided a way in which sin may be forgiven—a way which provides for the remission of its guilt and the removal of its pollution, and a restoration of the soul to the image of God. But to those who neglect or refuse to avail themselves of this method of salvation, there remains only a fearful looking for of judgment.

4th. The punishment of the impenitent sinner is necessarily endless, 1st. Because of the necessity of punishment. 2d. Because the ground of that necessity is permanent. The soul never ceases to be guilty and sinful, and therefore never ceases to be miserable. God has not only not revealed any purpose of bringing lost souls to repentance, but has revealed the purpose that they who reject Christ should perish forever.

5th. It follows that the punishment of the wicked will be inconceivably great. They are shut out from God and all good. They are given up to all the power of evil, which constantly increases. They must associate only with those like themselves. They have no hope.

1. We should think of these truths in their application to ourselves, and determine to avoid all sin and to flee to Christ for salvation. 2. These truths should fill us with burning zeal for the salvation of our fellow-men.

XV. Prepare to meet thy God, O Israel.—Amos 4: 12.

[*April 1st*, 1860.]

This as uttered by the prophet is a threat. It is equivalent to saying: prepare for divine vengeance. It is not in this light that it is to be now considered, but as an exhortation to prepare for judgment. It is parallel to those other exhortations: " Be ye also ready," etc.

All these exhortations assume,

I. *The moral government of God;* that he is to sit in judgment on the character and conduct of men, and reward or punish them according to their works.

1. This assumes not only the existence of God, but his omnipotence and his omniscience. He is assumed to take cognizance of human conduct and of all that determines human character.

This supposes not only the knowledge of all their external acts, but of the state of their mind and of all that determines it. The history of a single soul, as it must be known to God so as to be judged righteously, may be said in its acts, its states, in the circumstances that either aggravate or extenuate guilt, to present a field of knowledge too vast for any created intellect. What then must we say of the history of all the myriad millions of our race? It is plain that nothing less than omniscience could qualify any being to be judge of all the earth. If Christ is that judge he must be omniscient.

2. That this omniscient being is a judge, that he is one who administers law, who decides according to justice. The rule of judgment is justice; not pity, nor benevolence, nor expediency, but justice. This has claims paramount to pity, kindness or expediency. It is in this aspect that God is presented in the Bible as a judge, and therefore as deciding by rule, without respect of persons and with sole reference to the truth of the case.

II. *The subjects of this moral government are,* 1st. all rational creatures, because a rational nature is the ground of moral agency and of necessity places all rational creatures in the relation of responsible agents toward God. 2d. All men as they fall under the general category of rational creatures. Men as nations, as communities, as societies and as individuals; men in all the capacities in which they act and have moral character. Nations act as nations and have national character, and are therefore dealt with as nations. The same is true of any association. And of course, as every man stands before God, not as a member of a nation or family merely, but as an individual, so he is to be judged as such. And as this is far the most important relation in which we stand, so his judgment as an individual is far more important than any other.

III. *The ground of judgment, as already stated, is character and conduct.* This is true of nations and individuals. We as individuals are to be judged,

1. For every thing included under the head of conduct, all outward and inward acts, or acts of commission and of omission; for all feeling as well as for all volitions.

2. For every thing that falls under the head of character; not merely actual exercises, but abiding states.

IV. *Administration of his government.*

1. Over nations, it is by the providence of God in this world, for they exist as such only on earth. The moral conduct and character of nations are rewarded and punished with certainty and inevitably. This is illustrated by the history of the Jews, of other ancient and modern nations.

Hence follows the duty of individuals to take interest in political affairs.

The rule for Christians and ministers in this matter is, not the expediency, but the morality of national acts judged by the standards of the word of God.

2. Over individuals, this moral government is administered a. By established laws of nature which regulate the sequence of events and the connection of cause and effect. b. By God's special providence. c. Mainly in the future state, immediately after death and at the last day.

V. *How are we to prepare to meet God in judgment?* 1. Nations, either by national repentance and reformation or by making up their minds to bear the worst. 2. Individuals either, 1. By being prepared to present a faultless life and character, or 2. By taking refuge in the righteousness of Christ, in whom God can be just and yet justify the ungodly.

There is a sense in which believers, justified by the righteousness of Christ, are to be judged according to their works.

II.

CHRIST, HIS PERSON AND OFFICES.

XVI. The Advent.

[*December 24th,* 1854.]

The redemption of the world by Jesus Christ is the middle point in the history, not of our race only, but of the universe.

Reasons for believing this.

1. The nature of the event.

2. The declaration of the Scriptures that through the Church is the glory of God to be especially manifested. Hence follows the obligation of regarding this event as of all others the most important to be remembered.

The reasons why we should thus remember it and cherish a fixed sentiment of gratitude for this manifestation of love, are

I. *The infinite condescension and love which it displays;* the exaltation of the Son of God; and the depth to which he humbled himself in becoming man.

II. *From the benefits which we derive from it;* first, as individuals, and second, as a race.

First. As individuals. Under this head are 1. Pardon,—a deliverance from hell. 2. Holiness, or a deliverance from sin. 3. Reconciliation to God, or the enjoyment of his favor. Communion with him who is the infinite source of all good. 4. Exaltation; first as to our persons, in glory, dignity and excellence; and second as to honor and authority.

Second. As a race. Peace on earth and good will to men. Our world is redeemed. It is not to continue under the dominion of sin. It is not to remain the kingdom of darkness. Christ is to reign over the earth. Holiness, peace, happiness are to prevail universally. And in our redeemed race, exalted by union with the Son of God, is to be made the most wonderful exhibition of the glory of God.

Third. This is the third great reason why we should thus gratefully bear in mind the coming of God in the flesh. God is thereby to be honored in the highest degree, to all beings and to all ages. He is to be adored as the God of Redemption, even more than as Creator and Governor.

The two great duties which press upon every man who hears the gospel are, 1. To accept of Christ as his own Saviour, and 2. To make him known to others as the Saviour of men.

XVII. The Advent.

[*December 25th*, 1853.]

I. 1. The observance of Christmas is not commanded. Therefore it is not obligatory. The true Protestant principle is that what is not commanded cannot be enjoined. The importance of this principle as a protection from the burden of human authority. The Talmud and the traditions of Romanists are the two great monuments of the consequence of that principle being discarded. This is not to be confounded with the principle that what is not commanded is not to be tolerated. Against this, 1. The liberty of conscience. It is as much an assertion of authority to prohibit as to enjoin. 2. The uniform practice of the Church, and our own practice, national thanksgiving, &c.

2. The expediency of this observance. Much may be said for it and much against it. For it. *a.* The natural law of our associations. *b.* The analogy of the Old Testament. *c.* The sympathy and communion of Christians. *d.* A means of preserving and promoting knowledge. Against it are, *a.* The liability of abuse ; *i. e.*, its being made sacred, or considered of divine authority. *b.* The gradual superseding of the Sabbath. *c.* The worldly manner of celebration. These are things to be guarded against, and which should regulate the observance.

3. History of the observance.

It was not celebrated before the fourth century. Origen mentions only three festivals as generally observed, Good Friday, Easter and Pentecost. Augustine places Christmas in the secondary class of festivals. Chrysostom says in his time it was new. It had, he said, been introduced within ten years.

4. The day. Unimportant. It varied for a time.

II. *The uses, or the truths connected with the birth of Christ.*

1. The birth of Jesus is presented as a miraculous event ; as such predicted, as such recorded. The importance of this is that it conveyed our nature uncontaminated to Christ.

2. It is presented as the most wonderful event in its own nature. The Logos became flesh. The Son of God was born of a woman. He who was in the form of God was found in fashion as a man. He who was the brightness of the Father's glory, took part of flesh and blood.

3. It is presented as the most wonderful exhibition of condescension and love. God so loved the world that he sent his only begotten Son. God spared not his own Son. Herein is love, not that we loved God, but that he loved us, and sent his Son to be the propitiation for our sins. This is the great event of the history of the universe; the union of the divine and human natures in the one person of the Redeemer.

4. It is the most fruitful of consequences, of glory to God, of good to man.

a. Of glory to God. The angels shouted for joy. They cried glory to God in the highest. All eyes turned toward the manger in Bethlehem. Correggio's idea of a luminous infant is but a faint symbol of Christ shedding light throughout the universe. It is an exhibition (*a.*) of his love and condescension, (*b.*) of his wisdom and of his power.

b. Of good to man.

1. The means of reconciliation with God, of peace, of fellowship, of participation in his nature.

2. The means of peace in the union of the whole family of the redeemed, of the exaltation of our nature, of the establishment of that kingdom of which the Theanthropos, the God-man, is the head.

3. Of the triumph of God over Satan.

INFERENCES.

1. Gratitude.   2. Joy.   3. Obedience.   4. Devotion.

XVIII. Immanuel.

[*Nov. 9th*, 1862.]

The names of persons in ancient times, and especially among the people of God, were significant. When given by the parents they were expressive of what they the parents designed either to symbolize or to commemorate. When given by God, they were a mode of revelation. God's giving to the Son of the virgin the name Immanuel, was a revelation of the fact that God was to be with us.

I. *The sense in which God is said to be with his people, or with man.* 1. It expresses the general sense of nearness. God is, of course, every where, but he is said to be where he especially manifests himself as present. He is not far from any one of us, for in him we live, and move, and have our being. This kind of nearness is common to all creatures, and especially to all rational creatures.

2. It expresses the general sense of favor and assistance. When we say, "The Lord be with you," we pray that he would aid and sustain those whom we address. The Psalmist says of the Lord, "He is at my right hand, I shall not be moved," Ps. 16 : 8. This name of the Messiah

was therefore a promise that God would be with us in the sense of showing us his favor. What the angels afterwards announced, "Peace on earth and good will to men," was foretold in this prophetic designation.

All the ways and senses in which God for Christ's sake is said to be with us or favorable to us, it would be impossible to state. *a.* He is reconciled to us by the death of his Son. Christ has brought us to God. *b.* We are not only reconciled so far as his justice is concerned, but we are the objects of his love. *c.* He is everywhere present by his Spirit to aid, counsel and comfort. *d.* His providence is ever over us and watchful. The Lord is with us, at our right hand, around about us, near as a light, as protection, as strength, as consolation, as the infinite portion of the soul.

3. God with us, expresses that union which is effected by the incarnation; for it was because of the miraculous birth of this infant, more fully explained by the annunciation of the angel to the Virgin Mary, that the Holy Thing that was to be born of her was the Son of God. It was because the human and the divine natures were to be united in one person in that child that he was to be called Immanuel.

This union brought God and man into the most intimate fellowship in the person of Christ. But it did not stop there. It brought God into a relation to man such as he sustains to no other creature. *a.* It is such a relation that a divine person can say, we are one, *i. e.*, of one nature. *b.* That he can call us brethren. *c.* That he can sympathize with us. *d.* That what is done to us is done to him. *e.* That he lifts our nature above that of angels. *f.* That he forever remains in this relation, filial, fraternal, conjugal, with his people.

4. God with us, means that he dwelleth with us and is in us; παρ᾽ ὑμῖν μένει καὶ ἐν ὑμῖν ἔσται. Jno. xiv. 17. In virtue of the incarnation as a preliminary condition, and of the indwelling of the Spirit, Christ lives in his people. That is, he is the source of their spiritual life. The thoughts, feelings and actions which belong to that life are due to this peculiar relation between him and us. He is with us intimately, perpetually and everlastingly. It is a union nearer, dearer, and more lasting than any other.

Our great duty therefore is, 1. To live worthily of that union ourselves. 2. To endeavor to bring others to enjoy its blessings.

Consult the following passages and meditate upon them:—

"The Lord of hosts is with us." Ps. xlvi. 7.

"My faithfulness and my mercy shall be with him." Ps. lxxxix. 24

"As I was with Moses, so I will be with thee." Josh. i.: 5.

"Be not afraid, neither be thou dismayed; for the Lord thy God is with thee whithersoever thou goest." Josh. i.: 9.

"When thou passest through the waters I will be with thee." Isaiah xliii. 2.

XIX. For in him dwelleth all the fulness of the Godhead bodily. Col. 2: 9.

[*Nov.* 13*th*, 1864.]

God is the God of history and of the Bible. He guides the course of events and of revelation. All the books of the Scriptures are historical, *i. e.*, they have their place in history. In one sense they are the product of history. They were written not only in different periods of history, but they meet the wants of persons living in those periods.

Thus in two great parallel lines, as it were, of historical events and of divine revelations, controlled by the same hand, the whole of the great system of truths was gradually brought out. The books of the Old Testament were written to meet the wants of God's people before Moses, under Moses, and in the successive periods from Moses to the advent. The books of the New Testament, especially the epistles, were not written as essays or discourses, but as letters to particular congregations to meet their historical wants. But all, both under the old and the new economy, was so ordered that all truth necessary or desirable has been made known.

The epistle to the Colossians could have been sent appropriately to no other people and at no other time. They were exposed to the seductions of a peculiar class of heretics, such as never existed before or since. They were Jews, but Jewish Christians, who held much of the old system and much of the new. They acknowledged Christ to be the Messiah and the Saviour, but held to the necessity of circumcision, to the efficacy of rites, to the observance of months, days and years. In this, however, they did not differ from the Judaizing teachers by whom the churches of Galatia, Jerusalem, Antioch and Rome, had been corrupted and disturbed. The peculiarity of the false teachers in Colosse was that they were philosophers as well as Judaizers. They combined the theosophy of the east with the traditions of the Jews. They held to the elements of the Gnostic system, to emanation, to the existence of æons, to the evil of matter, to angel worship, and to the necessity of asceticism. They regarded Christ not as God, but as one of the higher æons, and therefore taught that we were not complete in him, that the believer needed more than he could give, and more than could be attained through his work and Spirit.

Paul's design in the epistle is to teach the all-sufficiency of Christ and the worthlessness of everything else, especially of the vain philosophy and the vain observances on which the Colossians had been taught to rely. He teaches therefore

1. That Christ is God, the Creator of all things visible and invisible; that all things are for him and by him.

2. That he is the head of theChurch, the source of its life, from whom comes all good, and union with whom is the indispensable condition of salvation.

3. That he is the Saviour of the Church. *a.* Because through the blood of the cross we are reconciled unto God, and *b.* Because from him through the Spirit, spiritual and eternal life is diffused by joints and bands, as in the natural body.

This being the case, they should beware lest any one had beguiled them and led them to look elsewhere than to Christ; or to depend on any thing except the merit of his death and the efficacy of his power.

If they had a divine Saviour, a Saviour truly God, what did they want besides? This is the main point. It is want of faith in this great doctrine in some form that leads to false dependence on something else, or something in addition to Christ and his work for salvation. It is Christ and Christ alone that we need. This is Paul's doctrine.

As we have Christ Jesus we should walk in him, be rooted and built up in him ; and beware lest any man should spoil us through philosophy or vain deceit. Why ? Because in Christ dwells all the fulness of the Godhead bodily.

The πλήρωμα τῆς θεότητος means the plenitude of the divine essence. It dwells in him σωματικῶς, not merely really or essentially, but clothed in a body. As in Luke iii. 22, the Holy Spirit is said to have appeared σωματικῷ εἴδει. If this be so then we *are complete*, πεπληρωμένοι, filled in him. Filled, not with the fulness of the Godhead, as Christ was and is, but with all the fulness of God, with the plenitude of all the good of which God is the author, and which flows from fellowship with him. We *are* thus filled ; we need nothing more. A divine Saviour as Christ, being truly God and God clothed in our nature, is all-sufficient.

1. Because he has in himself all that is necessary as an object of worship, and of supreme admiration and love. We are finite, but nothing short of what is infinite can satisfy the soul. It is because Christ is infinite in his being and perfections that he is a full and satisfying portion of the soul.

2. Because he is not only God but God clothed in our nature. Therefore, *a.* God is more perfectly known. *b.* He is more accessible. *c.* Who can have more intimate union and fellowship with us.

3. Because infinite merit thus belongs to his righteousness, and infinite efficacy to his blood ; superseding the necessity of all things else.

4. Because he is infinite in power, by his Spirit, to subdue our sins, to transform our souls into his likeness, to protect us from all his and our enemies, to deliver us from all evil, to bestow upon us all good.

5. Because in him are all the treasures of wisdom and knowledge. So that full provision is made not only for our wants as sinners and as religious beings, but for our minds.

6. Because he is everywhere present, so as to be always accessible, and eternal so as to save ἐις τὸ παντελές, both perfectly and always, all who come unto God by him, seeing he ever liveth to make intercession for them.

XX. The Unsearchable Riches of Christ. Eph. 3: 8.

[*April 4th*, 1858.]

The connection and the design of the passage.

What Paul was called to preach was the unsearchable riches of Christ. This may mean either the riches which belong to Christ— those things which make him rich—or the riches of which he is the author, the unsearchable treasures of grace and benefits which flow from him to both Jews and Gentiles. The former includes the latter, and is the natural sense of the words.

This passage is of special interest. First, as teaching us where we, in ourselves poor, may find true riches, and where only they can be found ; and, second, as teaching the precise or specific duty of the ministry. If they do what is here mentioned they do their duty ; if they do not this, whatever else may be done in promoting virtue, knowledge, or the well-being of man, they are unprofitable servants. What then are the unsearchable riches of Christ ? The word Christ here is a personal designation, not an official title. It is the historical person sometimes designated Jesus, sometimes Christ, sometimes Lord, the Saviour, etc., who is here intended. And therefore his riches are those things which rendered the Lord Jesus infinitely rich, and being in himself infinitely rich, therefore infinitely valuable and precious to us. These are,

1. The fulness of the Godhead, the plenitude of the divine perfections. In the constitution of his person, the divine nature was united with a perfect human nature, so that the one person known as Christ, possessed and possesses all the divine perfections. He is infinite, eternal, and immutable in his being, wisdom, power, holiness, justice and truth. Bring any man to the side of Christ, compare the intellect, the intelligence, the power, the goodness of the one with the other. Then we see how poor man is and how unsearchable are the riches of Christ. The highest angel sinks in like manner into absolute insignificance when brought into comparison with Christ. His preciousness to us as a portion, as an object of affection, and his value to us as Saviour depends on his being in this sense rich, rich to an unsearchable, *i. e.,* to

an infinite degree in all divine perfections. If they were taken away, what would be left? It is the great object of the ministry to preach the unsearchable riches of Christ, *i. e.*, to proclaim him as possessing all divine perfections in an infinite degree. If men are brought to see and acknowledge this, then are they converted and saved.

2. The unsearchable riches of Christ includes his infinite love, compassion, condescension and tenderness. These are divine attributes as belonging to his divine nature, and human attributes as belonging to his human nature ; they are distinct. Christ's love to us as the Logos and his love as a man, are as different as the divine and human. In Christ both are united, as the natures are, in one person. It is altogether impossible to trace out or to comprehend the value, the preciousness, the attractiveness, the suitableness, which results from this union of the divine and human natures in the person of the Lord. If simply God, he is too intangible, too august, too unapproachable; if simply man, he is nothing. But as God and man, he is all we can desire and possess. Our blessedness depends on our approaching and confiding in this infinite love, tenderness and compassion of our Lord. And our great business as ministers is to persuade men that these treasures of love and mercy are to be found in him.

3. The riches of Christ includes, *a.* His infinite merit. The efficacy of his blood to cleanse from all sin, the merit of his righteousness to satisfy the divine law. *b.* The inexhaustible fountain of holiness, *i. e.*, of sanctifying power which resides in him, and which flows out in ever increasing streams for the healing of the soul and for the healing of the nations. *c.* The infinite resources which he possesses to render his people blessed and complete in him.

OBSERVATIONS.

(1) He is ours by appropriating faith. (2) The sin and folly of neglecting this richness. (3) Duty and glorious privilege of offering and recommending him to others.

XXI. The Love of Christ.

[*No date given.*]

No words can express the varying states of the mind. We must use them in different senses, as the words, fear, repentance, belief. So of the word love. We love an infant and we love God. In all cases love includes delight in its object, and the desire for its possession and enjoyment according to its nature.

If human language cannot express what is in us, it must be still more inadequate when used of God. We speak of God being angry, of his hating the wicked, of his repenting, etc.

Two dangers : 1st. That we take these words literally. 2d. That we deprive them of all meaning. The true ground is, that the essential idea, what they express as removing all imperfection, is true of God. He is truly holy, just and good. He truly lives.

What is meant by the love of God, or of Christ?

1. Not mere benevolence. The distinctions between the two are universally recognized and must be observed.

2. Not mere philanthropy. But love in the true sense of the word. Now of this love it is to be noted,

1. That it is personal. Its objects are individuals. Christ loves his friends, his Church, his sheep. Paul says he loves me. There is the greatest difference between love that has a class of beings for its object, and love which fastens on particular persons. We know this from consciousness.

2. This love is mysterious. It is unaccountable. We are not only unlovely, but vile and offensive, and enemies. It is compared to the love of a mother for a child, which is independent of its character.

The love of Christ is therefore of the nature of grace. This is its peculiar character. This is insisted upon in the Scriptures. This is of the utmost practical importance.

3. It is infinitely great. *a.* The love of an infinite being. *b.* It led to the greatest sacrifice. *c.* It secures infinite blessings.

4. It is immutable. This is insisted upon in Romans v. and viii. This too is of great practical importance.

5. It is peculiar and exclusive. Compared to the love of a bridegroom to his bride. In this no one can share. This peculiarity of the love of Christ is dwelt upon in the Scriptures with great particularity. Thy Maker is thy husband. The Church is the bride of Christ. This is reciprocated.

6. It is the love of the Theanthropos, of the God-man. It includes all that is divine and all that is human.

This is the love of Christ. The wonder of wonders. The glorious mystery of redemption. The admiration of angels, the delight and blessedness of the saints.

The effects of this love on the soul.

When revealed by the Spirit, and shed abroad in the heart, it produces,

1. Wonder, astonishment.

2. The greatest humility.

3. It awakens love. We love him because he first loved us.

4. It leads to entire devotion, to consecration. The love of Christ constrains us.

5. It purifies and exalts.

6. It fills the soul with unutterable delight.

7. It supports under all trials and brings heaven down to earth.

XXII. The Death of Christ.
[*December 9th*, 1865.]

I. *Its Nature.*—Who was it who died? What is predicated of the body is predicated of the man. What is predicated of the humanity of Christ is predicated of his person. It was a divine person who died. It is right to speak of the death of God. As the death of a man is of more importance than the death of a brute, because he has a rational soul; so the death of Christ is as much more important than the death of a mere man, as his divine nature is higher than his human nature. It is therefore a stupendous event; the most important in the history of the universe, the central point of all history.

II. *Its Design*—was to save his people, and hence was

1. The most wonderful exhibition of love.

2. It was a full satisfaction of justice.

3. It satisfied the covenant; or, was a federal sacrifice.

4. It confirmed the truth.

5. It was the greatest exhibition of humility and of patience.

III. *Its Results.*

1. The actual salvation of the Church.

2. The destruction of the kingdom of darkness.

3. The development of angels.

4. The highest display of the divine perfections.

OUR DUTIES.

1. To embrace it as the foundation of our confidence towards God. There is no other. This is all-sufficient. It is freely offered to all, and therefore to us. The greatest guilt is contracted by our neglecting and despising it. The unpardonable sin is to trample under foot the blood of the Son of God. 2. To declare it. *a.* By the Lord's Supper. *b.* By making known all that is revealed concerning it. 3. To bring others to appropriate to themselves its blessings. 4. To recognize the obligations which it imposes.

XXIII. Death of Christ.
[*March 14th*, 1852.]

Its Nature,—who died.   II. *Its Design.*   III. *Its Relation to Us.* IV. *To the Universe.*

I. *Its Nature.*—1. What is death? It is the dissolution of the soul and body. It is departure from this world. 2. Christ experienced the

usual accidents of death. His soul left his body. His body was inanimate. His soul entered ᾅδης. His body would have returned to
dust. 3. But it was not the death of a man. It was the death of a
divine person—of the Lord of glory—of the Son of God—of God.
The divine nature as little affected as the human soul. To this is due
its infinite value and efficacy.

II. *Design.*—In general the redemption of man, including deliverance from condemnation and restoration to the image and favor of God.

This it effects:

1. By being a satisfaction to justice, a propitiation. 2. And hence
he becomes our ransom, by delivering us from the law and from Satan.
3. Presents us as righteous before God. 4. Secures the gift of the
Holy Ghost. 5. Secures access to God, and with his favor all the blessings of the covenant of grace.

III. *Its Relation to Us.*

1. It is our death. Because it was the death of our representative,
endured in our place. Proof of this.

2. Hence it is also our death effectively as well as legally. It involves a death to the law, a death to sin, a death to the world.

3. It becomes the source of life. The motive for avoiding sin. The
reason why we should live to God. The ground and source of our
joy.

IV. *Its Relations to the Universe.*

1. The great means of exhibiting the manifold wisdom, *i. e.,* the perfections of God.

  a. To fallen angels. *b.* To lost men. *c.* To good angels.

2. Hence to sustain the authority of God.

3. To promote the holiness and happiness of the kingdom of God.

INFERENCES.

1. The death of Christ should be the constant theme of our medita-
tions.

2. The ground of gratitude and devotion.

3. The means by which we should endeavor to convert the world,
i. e., by preaching Christ crucified, holding him up as having purchased
the world with his blood, and entitled to reign in and over all mankind.

XXIV. For where a testament is, there must also of necessity be the death of the testator.—Heb. 9: 16.

[*Dec. 9th*, 1866.]

Exposition of the passage.

Two views. 1. That διαθήχη (diatheke) here as elsewhere means a covenant. 2. That notwithstanding the context, it means a testament. In either case the passage teaches the same truths; first, the necessity of the death of Christ, and secondly, the benefits which it secures.

I. *The Death of Christ was Necessary.*—This necessity arises out of the nature of God. It is not a governmental necessity, or one of expediency, but absolute; because we are sinners and God is just. This is an important truth, teaching us that there is no other way in which men can be saved; that no other sacrifice is of any avail; that those who reject this have only a fearful looking for of judgment.

II. *The other truth is that the Death of Christ secures us great blessings.*

If viewed as a federal offering, it secures the blessings promised in the covenant. If viewed as the death of a testator, it secures to us the inheritance which he has acquired for us. If viewed as a sacrifice, it secures pardon and reconciliation with God.

These different views of the death of Christ are not inconsistent. The one does not exclude the other, as some theologians have assumed. They are only different ways of exhibiting the same truth.

The benefits which Christ has secured are,

1. Justification. 2. Sanctification. 3. Reconciliation to God. 4. A title to eternal life. 5. Consequently all the exaltation and blessedness of heaven. Viewed as the death of a testator it secures us these benefits, because this is an inheritance which Christ has acquired for us. Viewed as a federal offering it ratifies the covenant in which these benefits are promised to his people. And viewed as a sin-offering it is a full satisfaction to the justice of God, and not only removes the difficulties in the way of the gift of all these benefits, but renders them certain.

The first and most obvious duty of all who hear the gospel, is to avail themselves of the offer of these benefits. The neglect or rejection of them through indifference or unbelief is the great condemning sin of the world.

2. Gratitude and love to the adorable Redeemer, whose sufferings and death have secured to us such blessings.

3. The consecration of ourselves to his service. The abiding purpose of consecrating all we have to the advancement of his cause and kingdom.

4. Living conformably to the design of his, which was to save us from sin, to deliver us from the power of Satan and to make us fit for heaven.

5. The desire and effort to bring others to the knowledge and enjoyment of the benefits of Christ's death.

XXV. Who died for us, that whether we wake or sleep, we should live together with him. 1 Thess. 5: 10.

[*April 5th*, 1857.]

The Old Testament is filled with descriptions of the Messiah, of his work, and of his kingdom. This, the object of their expectation and longing, was ever present to the minds of the ancient people of God. When he came, his person secured the recognition and love of those who were called; but his kingdom, where was that?

It was not established under the anticipated form, nor in its glory. That was reserved for his second coming. The second advent therefore became to the early Christians the great object of longing expectation. With regard to this they made three mistakes. 1. That it was to occur soon. 2. That those of their friends who had already died would perfect their portion in that kingdom. 3. That they themselves, should they die before Christ came, would fail of salvation in its full sense. To correct these errors Paul tells 1. That the coming of Christ was to be unexpected, and subsequent to events not yet accomplished. 2. Those who had died before the advent, Christ would bring with him. 3. That as to themselves, they would be as fully saved, whether they should be alive or dead when Christ came.

The exhortation in the context is that Christians should live as children of the light, as members of the kingdom of light as distinguished from the kingdom of darkness. Light stands for knowledge, holiness and happiness. Darkness stands for ignorance, sin and misery. The exhortation therefore is, in its negative form, not to sink back into the world which belongs to the kingdom of darkness, *i. e.*, not to give themselves up to the opinions and practices of the world, and thus inevitably involve themselves in the ruin in which the kingdom of darkness must ultimately issue. It is an exhortation to act as became those who were members of the kingdom of Christ, *i. e.*, to exhibit the knowledge and holiness, especially in faith, hope, and charity which characterize those who belong to that kingdom.

The motive by which this exhortation is enforced is, that we are destined not to wrath but to salvation. And this salvation is secured by Christ who died, that whether we live or die, we should live together with him.

This teaches, 1. That the certainty of salvation is secured by the death of Christ. He did not die merely to render salvation possible, but to make it certain. This it does because it is a complete satisfaction of justice. It answers all the ends which our perdition could possibly answer, and therefore it renders that perdition unnecessary. Christ cannot fail to see of the travail of his soul. Those cannot perish for whom he died. That Christ died to render salvation not only possible, but certain, is true, secondly, because the salvation of his people was promised him in that covenant, in the execution of which he laid down his life.

This is the one great ground of consolation here promised. God has died for us. Let this truth operate on your mind. What effect does it produce? Suppose we bow our heads before God and hear him say that he loved us from eternity, and out of love he gave his Son for our salvation; that we hear the Lord Jesus say that to deliver us from the power and guilt of sin, to make us holy, to bring us back to the image and favor of God, he took on him the form of a servant, and was found in fashion as a man and humbled himself unto death, even the death of the cross; what effect would this have upon us? Would it lead us to carelessness, to the indulgence of sin, to live with the world, since we were not to perish with the world? This is not the effect such a conviction of the certainty of salvation would produce on the renewed heart; and such an effect would give clearest evidence that we were the children of the devil. But the renewed, those whose earnest desire is to be delivered from sin, and to live with Christ, and who know that redemption is deliverance from sin, these words would fill with peace, joy, patience, resignation, zeal, overflowing gratitude and love, and devotion to the service of Christ.

If these are the effects which we feel they would produce on us, then they are addressed to us, and we may take the comfort of them, and drink our fill of this fountain of pure and living water.

2. This passage teaches us the nature of salvation. First, it is life. We shall live. This is the common Scriptural designation of all that we include in spiritual and eternal life. All that is opposed to death is included in the idea. It is a holy, happy and immortal existence of the whole man, soul and body. Secondly, it is a life with Christ. This includes two things, association or communion, companionship with Christ, and also participation of his life, of its power, holiness, blessedness and glory. Thirdly, it is a life of all, ἅμα; we shall all, all the redeemed, all those dear to us who belong to Christ, all in every age and nation who love him, are to be associated and made the subjects of this life. Therefore comfort and edify one another.

XXVI. As Moses lifted up the serpent in the wilderness, even so must the Son of man be lifted up.

[*March* 19*th*, 1868.]

Nicodemus was a type of the better class of educated Jews. He believed in the Scriptures. He was devout and serious. He was solicitous to attain the knowledge of the truth. He was open to conviction and free from the self-righteous and proud spirit of the Pharisees. Yet he was in darkness. He had been brought up in Judaism, as then understood, a system which assumed that salvation belonged exclusively to the Jews. If men of other nations were to be saved, they must become Jews by being born again. The natural descendants of Abraham needed no regeneration. This he evidently believed, and yet he clearly was convinced that something more was necessary, than being a Jew and external conformity to the Mosaic law. He was more than a mere formalist. In this state of mind he came to Christ. His coming at all was a proof of his sense of ignorance, of his desire for instruction and of his candor; as also of his reverence for Christ. His coming by night was a probable intimation of his timidity, and of the weakness of his faith in Christ as one who had come from God. Our Lord met him with kindness, and adapted his discourse to his state of mind. The two fundamental errors of Judaism were, 1. That natural descent from Abraham, or at least external union with the chosen people was essential to salvation, and 2. That works,—what a man does and what he is, his inward state,—was the ground of his acceptance with God. Our Lord teaches, 1. That an inward spiritual change was essentially necessary to salvation, as much for the Jew as for the Gentile. 2. That the true method of acceptance or of justification was not by works but by faith; that men are to be saved in a manner analogous to that in which the Hebrews bitten by the serpents were healed.

The points of analogy are mainly these. 1. The serpent was lifted up, suspended on a pole in the sight of the people; so Christ was to be lifted up, suspended on the cross in the sight of all men. To be *lifted up* is not to be understood of Christ's exaltation, as some explain it in order to get rid of the idea of his sacrificial death. *a.* Because "to be lifted up" was in the Aramaic dialect and probably in the Hellenistic, almost as definite as the expression with us to be "hanged," or "crucified." Malefactors among the Jews were hung upon a tree, if not before, at least after death. *b.* The analogy forbids that interpretation. The serpent was not exalted in the sense of being honored. *c.* Christ elsewhere uses the word in the same sense. "I, if I be lifted up from the earth," signifying by what death he should die. The people understood him, and therefore said " We have heard out of the law that Christ abideth forever ; and how sayest thou, the Son of man must be lifted up?" That is, publicly put to death by suspension on the cross. Christ told Nicodemus that he was to be crucified, that as the serpent was lifted up, so was he to be publicly executed.

2. The design of the elevation of the serpent was the salvation of the people from temporal death, and their restoration to health and all the enjoyments of life. So the design of Christ's being lifted up was to save his people from perdition, and to secure for them eternal life.

3. In both cases the means was indispensable to the end. There was no other means by which the people could be healed but by the elevation of the serpent. This God had ordained. None other could be substituted in its place. To reject or neglect this was to reject the only means of cure. So Christ's death is the only means of salvation. If that be unknown, neglected or rejected, the soul perishes. Men have attempted a thousand substitutes, but all in vain. As they cannot see the fitness of the means to the end, they refuse to embrace it and so perish. If the Hebrews had asked how can a brazen serpent heal the bite of a living serpent, and refused to avail themselves of the means of life, until they could see the causal connection between the events, they would have died. And so it is with sinners.

4. The condition of cure was merely looking,—the simplest thing in the world,—adapted to all, to the old and to the young, to the ignorant and to the wise ; to the good and to the bad, to the rich and to the poor. This condition alone was required. Nothing subsequent, no pledge or engagement as to future conduct. So in the case of Christ. We have only to look, not with the eye of the body but of the soul. This includes, *a.* Knowledge or apprehension of the subject. *b.* Conviction of its being the appointed means of cure. *c.* Trust in its saving efficacy. This method of salvation is therefore adapted to all men, of every class.

5. The nature of the cure. The bitten Hebrew was freed from the venom of the serpent, rescued from death, restored to activity and life. So we are freed from the venom of sin, and from its condemnation, and receive a new, imperishable and eternal life.

This teaches us :

1. That the gospel method of salvation is perfectly gratuitous. It excludes all idea of merit.

2. It has its ground and source outside of ourselves.

3. It shows that no man co-operates in his regeneration or first reconciliation with God. It is not partly his work and partly the work of God.

4. No preparation for healing is possible or necessary. " Just as I am."

5. The Hebrew's cure was instantaneous and final. So, in one sense, is ours. But in another it is gradual. We need to look again and again, to keep always looking, and looking only unto Jesus.

6. We learn how we are to direct sinners.

XXVII. Christ is the Lamb of God.

[*October 14th*, 1866.]

Numerous designations are given to the Messiah. The Shiloh, the Seed of Abraham, the Branch, the Servant of God, a Light, the Sun of Righteousness, &c. All these are intended to set forth his character.

He is called the Lamb of God,

I. *Because He was a Sacrifice for Sin.*—The lamb in the Old Testament was the principal sacrificial animal. *a.* Because the freest from defects and the most attractive and pleasing of all domestic animals. *b.* Because harmless and gentle. *c.* Because unresisting, going dumb to the slaughter. In all these characteristics it was typical of Christ. It was especially the paschal lamb, and the lamb as used at the morning and evening sacrifice that the lamb was a type of Christ. He is our passover. And he is our perpetual sacrifice, needed not occasionally but constantly. Christ, as the Lamb of God, is declared to be our sacrifice, to be acceptable and divinely appointed, and constantly efficacious.

II. *In the Evangelists and the Epistles Christ is called the Lamb of God only three or four times and then always in reference to his sacrificial death.*—In the Revelation he is called the Lamb twenty times, and in different relations.

1. As a sacrifice. The Lamb that was slain. As he in whose blood the saints had washed their robes.

2. As the ruler of the Church and of the world, he is set forth as the Lamb. It is the Lamb who opens the seals, who is opposed by the wicked, and who overcomes them, who is the Lord of lords and King of kings, who is seated on the throne of God.

This teaches that the ruler of the Church and of the world, the Theanthropos, has the attributes of a lamb; and hence, *a.* That opposition to him is unprovoked and malignant. *b.* That his people may confide in his gentleness and tenderness. He is not like a ferocious, or even an austere ruler, but one whose sceptre is love, who rules by and in love.

3. As judge he is called the Lamb. The saints are enrolled in his book of life; and the wicked shall call upon the rocks to hide them from the wrath of the Lamb. This teaches that even in the administration of justice, Christ acts with the greatest tenderness and forbearance.

4. That as the Lamb he is the object of supreme worship to all orders of beings.   The elders, the living creatures, the redeemed, all bow down before him.   All ascribe salvation to him; all unite in worshipping God and the Lamb.

This teaches *a*. That the God-man, the Theanthropos is the proper object of worship.   A man, or a person, clothed in humanity is to be worshipped.   There is a difference between the ground and the object of worship.   *b*. It teaches that he is worshipped, because he is the Lamb of God.   It is because he has redeemed us that saints and angels worship him.   *c*. That although he is thus highly exalted he is still the Lamb, and may be approached with confidence and love.

5. That he as the Lamb is the source of the blessedness of heaven. The Lamb which is in the midst of the throne shall feed them and shall lead them unto living fountains of water, and God shall wipe away all tears from their eyes.   The pure river of water of life, clear as crystal, proceeds out of the throne of God and of the Lamb.   The Lord God Almighty and the Lamb are the temple of the holy city, New Jerusalem.   The city has no need of the sun, neither of the moon, to shine in it; for the glory of God doth lighten it, and the Lamb is the light thereof.   According to the Hebrew parallelism, these two last clauses are synonymous.

It is God therefore, not in his awfulness, not in his infinitude, not in his abstract perfection; but God as the Lamb, *i. e.*, as clothed with gentleness, with whom we are to have communion.

6. In his relations to the Church, he is called the Lamb. The Church is the bride, the Lamb's wife.   The consummation will be the marriage supper of the Lamb.

a. This expresses the relationship of Christ to the Church collectively and to each individual believer.   *b*. The nature of the relation is peculiar, intimate, tender and indissoluble; the strongest bond and the highest love.   *c*. The bridegroom of the soul and of the Church, although infinite in power, wisdom, goodness and truth, is a Lamb.   There is a world of consolation in that.

XXVIII. The blood of Jesus Christ, his Son, cleanseth us from all sin.   1 Jno. 1 : 7.

[*February 14th*, 1864.]

The operations of our moral nature are more mysterious than any other element of our constitution.   By the senses we are in communion with the external world.   By our reason we are in connection with truth, or with the intelligent world.   By our social affections, with our fellowmen.   By our moral nature, with God.   This, so to speak, is the point of contact between the soul and God. Here we recognize the idea of law, of responsibility, of liability to punishment. Of this department of our nature we can give less account than of any others. It is not under our control; that is, we cannot give it laws or decide how it shall act.

1. The conscience is not the will. We cannot will to approve or disapprove. We cannot will to feel remorse, or not to feel it, any more than we can will to suppress pain.

2. Neither is it under the control of the reason; that is, we cannot argue ourselves into the conviction that sin is not sin, and virtue is not virtue. We cannot persuade ourselves that we are not responsible for our character; or that the remorse which we feel is unreasonable or unfounded.

3. Though in this sense independent of the understanding, it can only act under its guidance, that is, ignorance of the moral law prevents its exercise. Without the law, sin is dead. Men live in sin without knowing the extent of their sinfulness. As this ignorance is never total, there is no man free from the sense of guilt; but the inactivity and insensibility of conscience is in proportion to that ignorance. Paul coveted without knowing it was wrong. He persecuted Christ, thinking thereby he did God's service.

4. The moral nature is the seat and source of the greatest blessedness and exaltation, and of the greatest degradation and suffering of which we are susceptible. Every man carries within, the elements of heaven or hell. We have within us principles of evil, which are like a nest of sleeping scorpions which may sting the soul to madness; and which a ray of light may excite to vigorous activity.

As we are sinful, and as sin includes guilt, pollution, and power; how can we be delivered from it?

1. Not by the power of the will. The will is totally powerless to remove guilt or its consequent remorse, or pollution; or to counteract the power of sin.

2. Not by the force of reason, not by knowledge, not by truth, and certainly not by error.

3. Not by self-inflicted penances or active observances.

4. Not by rites or ceremonies. Not by the power of the Church, nor by the influence of our fellow-men. No man can redeem his brother.

5. Not by the wisdom or power of angels. The angels doubtless deemed the pardon of sin and the restoration of a sinner as much an impossibility as undoing the actual, or recalling the past.

What is impossible with man is possible with God. What the law could not do, God has done by sending his Son in the likeness of sinful flesh, and for sin, and thereby condemned sin in the flesh. This teaches, 1. That the person sent was God, the Son of God, a divine person, and that it was necessary that he should be divine, if he were to do what no creature could do. 2. He was like sinful men, like them in being of the same nature and subject to the same infirmities. 3. That he came as a sacrifice for sin. That is, *a.* That he took our place. *b.* That our sins were laid upon him. *c.* That he bore the penalty due to them. 4. It teaches that this was a judicial condemnation of sin, *i. e.,* of sin in us.

This is the way in which the Scripture teaches that the blood of Christ cleanses from sin. It removes the guilt of sin, as it satisfies divine justice. And as it satisfies justice, it removes remorse, which is the clamoring of the conscience for the punishment of sin. And it removes *all* sin. No matter how numerous or how aggravated, there is no difficulty and no difference. We have all sinned and come short of the glory of God, and the difference between one sinner and another is, in this matter, of no account.

2. In cleansing from guilt it cleanses from pollution. By restoring us to the favor of God.

a. By restoring us to the favor of God, wherein is our life. *b.* By securing for us the Holy Ghost who regenerates and sanctifies the soul, so that it ultimately becomes as pure as the angels of God.

3. It destroys the power of sin, by introducing, or securing the introduction of a new principle of life, which being the life of God, is stronger than the principle of evil, and ultimately triumphs over it.

As the blood of Christ is the only means of cleansing sin, it follows, 1. That our first duty is to apply for its healing and cleansing power for ourselves, and that daily. 2d. That we should make known this fountain for sin and uncleanness to our fellow-sinners. In one form or other these are the inferences which flow from every subject which comes up for consideration.

XXIX. Christ our Priest.

[*Nov. 11th*, 1855.]

I. *The idea and necessity of a Priest.*

The holiness of God is his prominent characteristic. Hence he is opposed to sin. Hence he is inaccessible to sinners. Men are unholy. Holiness and sin are opposed not as two natural laws, or two elements, as fire and water, merely; nor as two principles, as justice and injustice; but as far as we are concerned, as persons, so uncongenial that association is impossible; and also, as far as the sinner is concerned, so guilty that God must forbid his approach.

As on the side of God there is infinite power, blessedness and excellence, this banishment from him involves on our part utter destruction. We cannot approach him. We must approach him or perish. All feel this. All this is symbolized under the Old Testament.

Hence the necessity of a mediator ; one who can approach and who can propitiate. These are the functions of a priest. This is included in the radical meaning of כֹּהֵן (Kohen) and ἱερεύς (hiereus) from ἱερός (hieros.)

II. *Christ is our Priest ;*—Christ, the person, the Theanthropos ; not as Logos, but as both, God and man ; Jesus the Son of God.

He is qualified for this work,

1. Because he has liberty of access.

2. Because he has somewhat to offer.

3. Because his infinite dignity gives infinite merit and efficacy to his work.

4. Because he ever lives.

5. Because he can be touched with a sense of our infirmities.

6. Because he is divinely appointed.

III. *What he does as our Priest.*

1. He actually atones. He renders God propitious. He expiates our sins.

2. He thus gives us access to God. This the old priests could not do because their sacrifices could not take away sin.

3. He makes intercession for us ; prays for our justification, sanctification and preservation, the supply of all our wants.

IV. *The duties we owe to Christ as Priest.*

The recognition of him in his office, not attempting to draw near to God without him, which unbelievers do, and the inquiring sinner so often and so fruitlessly attempts.

This recognition is not merely the acknowledgment of him as High-Priest, but the actual committing our souls into his hands to be atoned for, and to be introduced to God by him. This must be done not once, but constantly.

2. Confidence, *a.* In his willingness to act for us as our priest. *b.* In the efficacy of his blood and in the prevalence of his intercession. *c.* In his sympathy and tenderness. He is called a merciful and faithful, *i. e.*, trustworthy high-priest.

V. *Importance of this doctrine.*

1. To Christianity as a system of doctrine. Without this, the gospel is a mere philosophy. This constitutes the difference between Evangelical systems and Rationalistic, *e. g.*, Socinianism ; between Protestantism and Romanism.

2. To Practical Religion. Religion consists in intercourse with God. There is no intercourse except through Christ as priest. All our reli-

gious exercises therefore depend on our experimental recognition of this great truth.

XXX. Christ Our Passover.

[*April 1st,* 1855.]

I. *What was the Passover?*—1. The actual passing over by the angel of the doors of the Israelites. 2. The Lamb slain. 3. The festival.

II. *Points of resemblance between Christ and the Passover.*

1. The Passover was perfect.

2. It was crucified. 3. Exposed to the fire. 4. Must be eaten. 5. Its blood applied. 6. It effected deliverance.

III. 1. We are in danger of destruction. The angel of wrath has commission to destroy all the workers of iniquity.

This destruction certain, fearful, and will come as an angel of darkness at an hour we look not for him.

2. There is no other means of escape. We cannot bar our doors or windows against the entrance of this minister of wrath. We cannot propitiate him. We cannot resist him. We cannot bear up under his avenging stroke.

3. The blood of Christ, as it is the only means, is certainly efficacious. The angel entered no door sprinkled with the blood of the lamb.

4. That blood, however, must be applied. It is not enough that it has been shed. If men think themselves secure ; if they either think the angel will not come, or that they can by other means escape his anger ; or that the mere shedding the blood is enough, they will perish.

5. The application of this blood gives not only security but a sense of safety. Doubtless all degrees of confidence were felt by the Israelites. Some slept without anxiety ; others trembled at every sound ; others pressed their first-born to their bosoms and longed for the morning. So with sinners sprinkled with the blood ; all are secure, but the measure of their confidence is very different. The want of confidence arises from the want of faith.

6. The Passover secures not only preservation from death but deliverance from slavery and introduction into Canaan. So our Passover delivers us not only from death, but from the bondage of Satan, and brings us to the heavenly Canaan.

7. The Passover was to be commemorated as long as the old economy lasted. The death of Christ is also to be commemorated.

8. The Passover was celebrated with unleavened bread, with everything indicative of separation from the land of Egypt. So the death of Christ binds us to holiness. What would have been thought of a Hebrew who after such a deliverance, having for its object his redemption from the bondage of Egypt, had clung to his fetters.

This is the special application. We are bound to be holy; to make our life a Paschal feast, a perpetual season of devotion and service to God.

XXXI. Christ the end of the Law for Righteousness.
Rom. 10: 4.

[*January 28th*, 1855.]

The immutability of the law is a fundamental truth. This rests on its nature, and on the immutability of God. The evidence is found in the Scriptures and in conscience. This the Jews believed, and this truth lay at the foundation of their error, which was twofold. 1. That the law was to be fulfilled by their own righteousness. 2. That the form in which the law was immutable was the Mosaic law. This twofold error led to the effort, 1. To establish their own righteousness, and 2. To their making righteousness to consist in ceremonial obedience.

Paul taught, 1. That the law is immutable; as he asserts and proves. 2. That it cannot be satisfied by our righteousness, but is and can only be satisfied by the righteousness of God. 3. That Christ is therefore the end of the law for righteousness to every one that believeth. 4. Consequently the immutability of the law is consistent with its abrogation, because its abrogation is effected by its fulfilment. The law is immutable so far as it demands righteousness as an indispensable condition of justification. But it is abrogated so far as it says, do this and live, *i. e.*, so far as it requires our own righteousness.

There are different senses in which Christ may be said to be the end of the law. 1st. In the sense of its completion. But this is contradictory to the meaning of τέλος, which never occurs in the sense of πλήρωμα. 2d. In the sense of having made an end of it, abolished it. This he has done in two ways. *a.* In so satisfying its demands that it ceases to require our own personal righteousness as the condition of justification; and *b.* In putting an end to the Mosaic institutions, so that obedience to that law is no longer necessary to salvation. 3d. Christ is the end of the law in being its aim or object. This means either. *a.* That the end of the law is righteousness. Christ is the end of the law because he is our righteousness. The end or design of the law is secured in him. So that it is by faith and not by works that the end of the law is to be attained. This agrees with what follows. The law demanded what we could not do. The gospel requires simply faith. Or, *b*. Christ may be said to be the end of the law as he is the object aimed at in the law. It was designed to bring us to Christ. The law is a school-master. This is true of the moral and also of the Mosaic law. In any sense the great truth taught is that Christ protects us from the law, and is our righteousness. Whether this is taught by saying that he made an end of it, or that it loses itself in him as to its great design, so that what it contemplated is secured in him, matters little.

Out of Christ we are exposed, 1. To its inexorable demands. 2. To its awful curse. 3. To its slavish spirit.

In him, we are righteous. 1. We meet all the demands of the law by pleading what he has done. 2. We are free from the curse as he was made a curse for us. 3. We are delivered from the spirit of bondage again to fear and are filled with the spirit of adoption.

Hence, 1. As the apostle teaches, we have peace with God, and peace of conscience.

2. Assurance of eternal life, as no one can condemn those whom God justifies.

3. With this we have a principle of obedience, for until we are reconciled there can be no holiness.

4. We are made partakers of all the glory and benefits of his triumph. Having obeyed and suffered for us and as our representative, we share in all the blessings promised as his reward.

XXXII. The Intercession of Christ.

[*Oct. 27th*, 1861.]

The figurative representations of Scripture are intended not to impress the imagination but instruct the understanding. They must therefore be interpreted so as to convey definite truth. They are not to be understood literally ; nor is the analogy which they suggest to be pressed too far. Nevertheless they are never to be explained away as mere figures of speech. As the intercession of Christ is represented as the ground of confidence and a source of consolation, it must be understood to express, 1. The relation in which Christ stands to his people. 2. The nature of one part of the work which he discharges on their behalf.

I. *The relation which Christ as intercessor sustains to his people;*— or, the relation which is implied in the work of intercession. It is that of an advocate to his client. The former personates the latter; puts himself in the client's place.

It is while it lasts, therefore, the most intimate relation. The client does not appear. He is not heard. He is not regarded. He is lost in his advocate, who for the time being is his representative. This is the relation in which Christ as our advocate stands to us. He appears before God for us. We are lost in him. He, not we, is seen, heard and regarded. It is not necessary that the client be personally present. His advocate supplies his place. Christ thus assumes our position.

II. *The work of an advocate is twofold.*

1. It is to vindicate an accused person from the crimes laid to his charge, to secure for him the verdict of not guilty. In other words, it is to save him from the infliction of the penalty with which he is threatened.

2. It is to establish the claims of his client, to secure for him the quiet enjoyment of his inheritance or property.

When Christ therefore is said to be our advocate or intercessor, it means that he performs for us these two offices. He secures for us the verdict of not guilty. He obtains our justification, at the bar of God. And he secures for us the enjoyment of all those blessings to which we are entitled according to the terms of the covenant of grace. These are not only our justification, but the gift of the Holy Ghost, which secures regeneration, sanctification, knowledge of the truth, consolation, guidance and perseverance in grace unto the end; together with that measure of temporal blessings which shall best minister to our holiness and usefulness; and finally the consummation of the work of salvation in heaven.

III. *The qualifications for an advocate are,*—1. The right to appear in court. This does not belong to every one. It must be admitted by competent authority. And this admission is founded on evidence that the applicant or candidate professes the requisite qualifications. Thus we have no right to appear before God. Christ was appointed by God for this office. And his appointment supposes that he has the requisite qualifications. He has the right of entry to the courts of the Lord, as the representative of his people.

2. Knowledge. *a.* Of the law; of the demands of justice; of the administration of the government to which the court belongs. *b.* Complete knowledge of his client's case. *c.* Knowledge of the way in which his case can be properly presented and urged. This knowledge on Christ's part is omniscience. It is coupled with sympathy both divine and human.

3. An adequate plea. No advocate is competent to plead a client's cause successfully unless he has a sufficient plea to offer in his behalf. Christ has this plea in his own perfect righteousness, and in the promise of God. On these grounds he secures our justification and the bestowment on us of all the blessings of redemption.

IV. *Characteristics of Christ's intercession.*

1. He is the only mediator or advocate. There is no other who is authorized or qualified to act in our behalf. And no other is necessary.

2. His intercession is perpetual. He ever maketh intercession for us.

3. It is successful. It has never failed and it can never fail.

4. It is freely offered to all and freely rendered.

V. *Duties of a client to his advocate.*

1. He must commit his case into his hands without reserve, and not depend on himself or any one else.

2. Trust and confidence. He must rely on his ability to conduct his cause, and not attempt to take it out of his hands.

3. Gratitude and love.

This, therefore, is a perpetual and everflowing source of consolation.

XXXIII. And if any man sin, we have an advocate with the Father, Jesus Christ the righteous. And he is the propitiation for our sins. 1 John 2: 1.

[*December 4th*, 1859.]

I. *Sin is always represented in Scripture as a very great evil,*—as degrading the soul, as producing all misery, as separating us from God, as justly deserving his wrath and curse.

Viewed in the light of our own judgment, it is seen to be all that the Scriptures declare it to be. As seen by God, it is proportionately offensive in his sight. The opposition of his nature to sin is inevitable and necessary. It is infinitely great; and his justice renders the condemnation of the sinner inevitable.

II. *All men are sinners.*—We, of course, are among the number. Our sins are numerous, inexcusable and greatly aggravated. We cannot deny them. We cannot cancel them. We cannot atone for them. We are in a state of hopeless condemnation. Hopeless, because just.

III. *We therefore need an advocate;*—that is, one who has a right to appear before God for us, and who is qualified to plead our cause at his tribunal. No one can do this for himself. No man can do it for his fellow-man. No creature can do it for his fellow-creature.

IV. *We have an advocate, Jesus Christ the righteous.*—He is qualified for this office, 1. Because he is the Son of God; a divine person; entitled to appear before God, whose intercession must be right and sure to be heard. His divinity gives infinite dignity and worth to his work, and efficacy to all he does in our behalf.

2. He is the Son of Man; clothed in our nature, and therefore able to obey and suffer in our stead, and to sympathize in our infirmities.

3. He is righteous and a propitiation for our sins. He has done all that justice and holiness require in order to our pardon and acceptance. The plea which he is thus enabled to present is a sufficient one. It is not only sure to be heard, but it must be heard. It cannot be right-eously disregarded. This plea is not only effectual for some, but for all in whose behalf it is urged. It is of force for all who come unto God. So that no man has a right to say there is no ground for his acquittal, though there may be ground for the acquittal of others. Christ's righteousness is not only of infinite value, but is equally avail-able or suitable for all mankind.

4. This advocate, so exalted, so tender, furnished with an availing plea, with such solid reasons why those for whom he pleads should not be condemned, ever lives to make intercession for us. His advocacy is uninterrupted, and will never fail. He never can be absent from the court in which our case is to be decided.

5. He is always accessible. We can at all times go to him, at all times find him, no matter where we are or what may be the emergency.

This doctrine is presented by the apostle not as an encouragement to sin, but as a ground of consolation for those who desire to forsake their sins.

He acts for those who come to him for pardon, sanctification and salvation. For those who desire to continue in sin, he does not act unless it be to bring them to apply to him for help.

XXXIV. The Presence of Christ with his Church.

[*Jan. 6th*, 1867.]

The promise is, " Lo, I am with you alway, even unto the end of the world."

I. *To whom is this promise addressed, and what is its purport?*

Both the points are embraced in the Romish theory, which assumes, 1. That the promise was to the apostles and to their successors in the apostolic office. 2. That it was a promise to be with them as apostles. *a.* To impart to them the necessary gifts, first, for teaching, and second-ly, for ruling. *b.* To render them infallible in their official acts. *c.* To enforce their decisions and sustain their authority.

This is a beautiful theory. It would to human view be a blessed thing to have a succession of apostles, *i. e.*, of holy men, infallible in their judgments, to settle all points of doctrine, to remove all doubts, to solve all questions of conscience, and to rule with undeviating right-eousness over the whole Church.

And when to this is added, on the assumed primacy of Peter, and of his successor, the Bishop of Rome, as the representative of Christ, we have the beau ideal of a theocracy for the Church and ultimately for the world.

But in proportion as this theory is good if true, it is destructive if false. If the prelates are not apostles, have not their gifts, their infallibility or authority, then for sinful, erring, wicked men to claim their prerogatives is ruinous. To be under the guidance of a good angel is a blessing; but to be under the guidance of Satan, in the guise of an angel of light, is destructive.

That this view is not true is plain, 1. Because the promise is not addressed to the apostles exclusively. 2. Because the apostleship was not perpetual. 3. Because the Romish prelates do not claim individually but only collectively those endowments. 4. They do not show the signs of apostles. 5. History proves them to be false apostles.

II. *The promise was not made to the apostles as ministers of Christ and to their successors in the ministerial office, but to the whole Church.*

This is plain, 1. Because others than ministers were present when the promise was made. 2. Because the same commands and the same promise are elsewhere given to believers. 3. Because the presence of Christ, as realized, is with all his people.

III. *The sense in which Christ is present with his Church.*

The Speaker is not God, not the Spirit, but Christ. The thing promised is therefore specifically his presence and not merely the presence of his Father, or of the Holy Ghost. It is true that where the one is, there are the others; and therefore the forms of expression interchange.

The presence promised is, 1. Not a corporeal presence. 2. It is not a mere dynamical presence, as though a new energy, power, or life had been infused into humanity, which was to develop itself by its own forces. A certain school teaches that in every organism, such as the Church is assumed to be, there is, *a.* An underlying substance, principle, life, or force. In this case, it is the life of Christ. *b.* This principle contains in itself all that is evolved from it. *c.* The evolution is according to a law peculiar in itself. *d.* The evolution is constant and progressive. *e.* The whole is one, the underlying potential basis and all that is evolved from it, as in the germ and they that spring from it. This is a mere philosophical theory, without support from Scripture, and contrary to its facts. It takes Christ from us. It gives us nothing of him but what we have in ourselves.

3. The presence of Christ is not merely a presence to the thoughts and feelings as in the case of an absent friend. 4. It is a personal presence. It is not merely God, or the Spirit, or the Eternal Logos, but Christ, who is ever present with his people. And this presence of

Christ is not merely or exclusively as to his divine nature, but as to his whole person. That is, Christ, as God-man, is *a.* Near to us so that we can speak to him, praise him, confess to him, avow our love to him, pray to him with the assurance that he hears us. *b.* He is near to us in the sense that he always sees us. Knows our temptations, trials, our inward state, our outward circumstances, our weakness and wants. *c.* He is present in that he can and does hold intercourse with us, revealing to us his glory, assuring us of his love, and guiding us in the way in which we should go. *d.* He is present with us not only thus to instruct and comfort us, but to strengthen for duty, to support us under trial, to console us and to render our efforts in his service successful. *e.* He is with us as he was with the apostles, not only in their inward spiritual life, but in their work, guiding them; giving them words which their adversaries could not gainsay or resist; rendering their preaching effectual, confirming its truth and vindicating its authority. And thus he will be with his church to the end of the world.

XXXV. How is it that thou wilt manifest thyself unto us and not unto the world?—John 14: 22.

[*Sep. 21st*, 1862.]

The manifestation spoken of is, 1. Peculiar to believers. 2. Common to all believers, and therefore not that made in the body after his resurrection.

The great truth therefore here taught is: an inward spiritual manifestation of Christ to the souls of his people. He reveals himself to them so that they may be said to see him, to have intercourse or communion with him. As to this, it may be remarked, 1. That we are surrounded by a material world which reveals itself to our senses and acts upon them. And we are surrounded by a spiritual world, *i. e.*, by the souls of other men, by spirits good and bad, by God.

2. We know that these spirits reveal themselves to us and act upon us. Our fellow-men address themselves to us in words, looks, and acts. Evil spirits we know act on the soul, as in the case of Satanic temptation and in the case of demoniacs. So God thus acts. This is the doctrine of natural religion and of all Christians.

3. This manifestation of God's presence in his providential agency, is analogous to that made by the soul of a man on the control and government of the body.

4. But the manifestation which he makes to his people is peculiar not only as to the mode in which it is made, *i. e.*, by the Holy Ghost, but also as to what is revealed. God reveals himself to the wicked as an

avenger, as a consuming fire. To his people he reveals his glory and his love.

5. The scriptural doctrine is distinguished on the one hand from the Deistical or Rationalistic doctrine, in that God's revelation of himself is only mediate, that there is no intercourse between the soul and God; and on the other hand from mysticism. This system teaches,

a. The immediate communication and contact of the soul with God. *b.* That thus new truth is revealed and guidance granted. *c.* That the soul is ultimately merged in God. *d.* That this beatific vision is attained by passivity and abstraction. In opposition to both these errors, the Scriptures teach, as above stated,

1. That God has intercourse with the soul, not merely through his works and by his word, but immediately by his Spirit. 2. That the effects of this manifestation are, *a.* Vision, we are said to see him. *b.* Knowledge. *c.* Holiness; we are transformed into his image. *d.* Assurance of God's love. *e.* Hope of his glory. *f.* Joy unspeakable. 3. That the subjective conditions of this manifestation are love and obedience. We must be first reconciled to God through Christ. But this may be with little or no intercourse between the soul and God, as in infants and children. And when reconciled we must have the soul in the requisite state, free from unholy and disturbing passions, and the conscience purged from dead works. 4. That this manifestation is not a matter of consciousness, only its effects. But this is true of all spiritual manifestations.

INFERENCES.

1. As intercourse with God is possible and is productive of such incalculable benefits, we should most earnestly desire it and assiduousl cultivate it.

2. We should be on our guard against either denying or abusing the doctrine.

XXXVI. Christ our Life.

[*Sept. 4th*, 1853.]

What is meant by life? The word is very comprehensive. It includes, 1, appropriate activity; 2, happiness. The life here intended is *a.* Not natural life. *b.* Not intellectual life. *c.* But spiritual and eternal life.

Christ is our life in that he is its author, its object, and its end.

I. *Christ the author of life.*

1st. He saves us from death, *a.* By his atonement, which satisfies the law. *b.* By delivering us from the power of Satan.

2d. He is the author of inward spiritual life. *a.* Because he procures for us the gift of the life-giving Spirit. He has redeemed us in order that we might receive the promise of the Spirit. *b.* Because he not only merits, but sends or imparts the gift of the Holy Ghost. He baptizes with the Holy Ghost and with fire.

II. *He is the object of life.*

1. The exercises in which the spiritual life consists terminate on him.

2. The happiness involved consists in fellowship with him. He is our life, as he is our joy, our portion, our everlasting inheritance.

III. *He is the end of our life.*

It is Christ for us to live. While others live for themselves; some for their country, some for mankind, the believer lives for Christ. It is the great end and design of his life to promote his glory and to advance his kingdom.

INFERENCES.

1. Test of character. The difference between the true and nominal Christian lies here. The one seeks and regards Christ as his life, only as he delivers from death. The other, as the end and object of life.

2. The true way to grow in grace, or to get life, is to come to Christ.

3. The happiness and duty of thus making Christ our life.

XXXVII. I am that Bread of Life.—John 6: 48.

[*April 11th,* 1869.]

Occasion of this discourse. Christ had fed the multitude. The people flocked to him because they did eat of the loaves. He exhorted them not to labor for the meat that perishes, but for that which endureth unto everlasting life, which the Son of man shall give unto them. That meat was himself. " He that believeth on me hath everlasting life. I am that bread of life. Your fathers did eat manna in the wilderness, and are dead. This is the bread which cometh down from heaven, that a man may eat thereof and not die. I am the living bread which came down from heaven ; if any man eat of this bread he shall live for ever; and the bread that I will give is my flesh, which I will give for the life of the world. . . . . Whoso eateth my flesh, and drinketh my blood, hath eternal life."

The truths taught in this connection are:

First. That Christ is the source of life. The life spoken of is called everlasting life. It is not physical life, but spiritual and eternal life. The life of the soul. The opposite of spiritual death. It includes holiness, blessedness, glory in the highest measure man can enjoy those blessings.

This eternal life can be obtained in no other way. Not from ourselves; not from any external rites or ceremonies; not from external privileges and special prerogatives, such as belonged to the theocratical people of old, who ate of the manna and died. Those who are without Christ; those who reject him; who refuse to recognize him as the source of life, or receive and appropriate him, shall perish. There is no life but in and through Christ.

Second. That Christ is the life-giving bread; not his doctrine, not his law, not his example, not his influence or moral power, not the form of religion which he introduced, not the Church which he established, but Christ himself, his person and his work.

Third. Christ is, or becomes our life, by giving himself for the life of the world. " The bread I will give is my flesh." He gave himself, his flesh, his body, his blood, as a sacrifice for the sin of the world. Thus he is the life of the world, 1. Because it saves us from the sentence of death. 2. It restores us to the favor of God. 3. It secures the indwelling of the Spirit, which is subjectively our life, eternal life in us.

Fourth. It is not enough that Christ gave himself; not enough that manna fell in the wilderness; not enough that bread should be provided; not enough that a sacrifice should be provided. The manna must be gathered and eaten. The bread must be appropriated and used. The sacrifice must be applied to each soul to be of benefit to the soul.

Fifth. This appropriation of Christ is expressed in different terms in the context, 1. By coming to Christ. All that the Father giveth me shall come to me. And I will raise him up at the last day.

2. By eating his flesh and drinking his blood. This all means the same thing, for the same effect is attributed to each.

Sixth. Eating Christ's flesh and drinking his blood, does not mean, 1. Receiving the substance of his body and blood, as Romanists and Lutherans say. 2. Nor the dynamic influence of his glorified body as Calvin says is done in the sacraments. 3. Much less does it mean the mere moral influence of his sufferings and martyr death. 4. Nor his theanthropic life. 5. But, as giving his flesh for the life of the world is dying for the world; and dying for man is dying as a sacrifice, so eating his flesh and drinking his blood is appropriating to ourselves his flesh as broken and his blood as shed.

As he had spoken of himself as bread, and the act of appropriating as eating; and as he had said the bread was his flesh, so appropriating his flesh as a sacrifice is called eating.

The grand truths are,

1. That Christ is the only source of life.

2. That every man must receive and appropriate him for himself.

XXXVIII. Christ our Example.

[*December 3d*, 1856.]

God himself is set before us as an example in the Scriptures. But Christ as possessing our nature, subject to our infirmities, temptations, and sufferings, brings before us not merely divine, but human perfection as a model for our imitation. We are therefore commanded to be followers or imitators of Christ.

We should thus imitate him,

I. *In his piety or devotion to God, in the constant reference to God's glory;*—constant confidence in his promise; constant obedience to his commands; constant submission to his will; and in the frequency, fervor and attendance on the other means of grace, for he fulfilled all righteousness.

II. *In his benevolence, his disinterested devotion to the good of others.*—He sought not his own. He went about doing good. Neither his own honor nor advantage was the end which he pursued. Let this mind be in you which was also in Christ Jesus. Let the governing principle of your life, the end for which you live, *be what his was.*

III. *In his manner of resisting temptation.*

1. He never placed himself in danger. He refused to tempt God.

2. He resisted the first suggestions of evil.

3. He appealed to the authority of the Scriptures, or used them as the sword of the Spirit.

IV. *In his endurance of injuries.*—Never was such ingratitude, disrespect, indifference, malice, contempt and scorn, heaped on any other head; and that head encircled with the radiance of divine perfection, and the crown of universal dominion. Yet, 1. There was no resentfulness. He did not call down fire from heaven on his enemies. He did not return evil for evil. He did good for evil and prayed for those who shed his blood. 2. He did not threaten. In this there is a strong contrast between him and many of the martyrs.

V. *His faithful rebuking of sinners.*—1. Here it was sin he rebuked, and his censures were the expression of his hatred of sin. 2. It was fearless and impartial. 3. It was with authority.

VI. *Christ as a teacher.*—1. Adapted his instruction to the state of his hearers. 2. He seized every occasion and gave his lesson a character of being especially applicable. 3. He spake as a witness.

VII. *Christ as a sufferer.*—1. He did not manifest stoical indifference. 2. He was meek and resigned. 3. He looked to the end, the glory that should follow.

XXXIX. Christ our Physician.
[*January 27th*, 1861.]

I. *We are all laboring under the malady of sin.*—This malady is, 1. Universal. 2. It pervades our whole nature. 3. It is attended by great suffering, degradation and loss of power. 4. It will issue, if not arrested, in eternal death.

II. *No man can cure himself.*—This is proved, 1. By consciousness. 2. By experience. All efforts at self-cure result in failure or self-deception, or, at best in mitigation of the symptoms.

III. *No man, or set of men can cure others.*—This has been attempted, 1. By educators. 2. By philosophers. 3. By ascetics. 4. By ritualists. The world is filled with charlatans or quack pretenders to the power of healing the disease of the soul.

IV. *Christ is the only physician.*

1. He secures the right of applying the only effectual remedy by propitiating the justice of God, and securing liberty of access to the soul for the Holy Spirit.

2. He sends that Spirit as the Spirit of life and strength. As the constitution is radically affected, a radical cure is necessary, and this can only be effected by a life-giving spirit.

3. This cure is a long and painful process. The soul is not at once restored to a state of perfect health. It must pursue a protracted course of regimen. It must submit to self-denial, and to the use of the prescribed remedies.

4. But if we submit to his directions, the cure is certain and permanent. It results in immortal vigor, beauty and strength; to the restoration of our nature to a far higher state than its original condition.

5. Christ is not only the only physician, and one able to heal with certainty all our maladies, but he is accessible to every one and at all times. It is not any one form of spiritual disease, or any one degree of it, but all forms and all degrees. Any one in the last stage of spiritual death may come to him with the certainty of being received and cured. He demands no conditions. He asks no terms. He requires no preparation, and will receive no recompense.

6. He is not only thus infallible and thus accessible, but he is tender, patient and forbearing. He has all the attributes of a good physician in infinite perfection.

INFERENCES.

1. The duty of every one to apply to him for cure.

2. The one reason why we or any are not cured must be in us, not in him.

3. The duty of making this physician known to others.

XL. Christ the Bridegroom.

[*Jan. 8th,* 1854.]

The relation of Christ to the Church is variously presented. 1. He is the head of the Church, as his body. 2. He is the vine. 3. The foundation or corner-stone. 4. He is her prophet, priest and king. 5. He is her shepherd. 6. *He is the Bridegroom.*

This is intended to express,

1. Intimate union. *a.* Sameness of nature. *b.* Common life.

2. Peculiar love. *a.* This love is exclusive. It has no other such object. *b.* Peculiar pride, delight. *c.* Strength of affection.

3. He adorns the Church with graces; clothes her in the robe of righteousness and the beauty of holiness; honors and exalts her, making her partaker of his own glory.

4. He cherishes, provides for and protects her from dishonor, from misery.

5. He enriches the Church. Not his honor only, but his possessions are shared with her. This is variously and frequently presented in the Scriptures. This wealth includes, *a.* The Holy Ghost. *b.* All needed means of grace and good. *c.* Heaven, or eternal life.

6. He uses towards her the language of endearment, 'gives and requires assurances of love. He has communion with her, not as a stranger, nor as a δοῦλος (slave), but an intimate associate.

7. He takes her to his Father's mansion with great honor and rejoicing, and abides with her in an indissoluble union forever.

Her duties.

1. Love. This again must be exclusive and supreme, without a rival, without an associate.

2. Obedience. His will must be her law, because it is his will. This obedience should be, *a.* Cheerful. *b.* Universal. *c.* Constant. *d.* Self-sacrificing.

3. Fidelity. The want of this violates and vitiates the union. The transfer of affection to any other object is the greatest sin against the relation which can be committed.

4. Dependence. She must look to him for protection, for support, for happiness.

5. Delight in his presence, longing for the manifestation of his love.

6. Zeal for his honor. Identified with him, what honors him honors her.

XLI. The Transfiguration.

[*March 29th,* 1863.]

Different modes of interpretation. 1. The historical. 2. The naturalistic. 3. The symbolical. 4. The mythical. The first is the only one which can be admitted. The character of the narrative and the character of the gospel history forbid any other explanation.

I. *The facts of the case.*—1. Not a change of figure, but a change of state and appearance of the same figure.

2. Not a mere illumination of Christ's body, but a change in it, from its ordinary to an extraordinary state, so that it was refined and glorious as the sun. It was not a change of substance. Charcoal and diamond, flint and glass, are examples of the different states of same substances.

3. His garments themselves were changed, or merely illuminated.

4. Moses and Elias were really present in body, and they really talked with Jesus audibly and intelligibly to others.

Theophanies and manifestations of angels under the Old Testament dispensation. Mode of presence. Why they rather than others.

5. The cloud and voice, and what the voice uttered.

6. The effect on the disciples.

II. *This was not a dream;* nor a vision such as the prophets had. Much less a mere illusion, such as the sights seen in delirium, or in a somnambulistic state. But a real occurrence. Christ, Moses and Elias were actually present.

III. *Cause of this change and of these occurrences.*—Not natural causes alone. Not divine power through second causes. But the immediate efficiency of God.

IV. *Design of this manifestation.*

1. To prove that Christ had power over his own life. To him death was not a necessity of nature. His sacrifice was a voluntary one.

2. To prepare his disciples for the great trials which were before them.

3. To manifest his glory and attest his divine mission.

V. *What this solemn scene teaches.*

First, Concerning Christ.

1. His divinity. *a.* As a manifestation of his glory. Peter says, "we were eye-witnesses of his majesty." Μεγαλειότης, (megaleiotes) the word for majesty, is used in the New Testament only of God, with the single exception of being once applied to Diana in a heathen sense. It proved Christ to be God. *b.* This proved also by the recognition of him as the Son of God by the voice out of the cloud.

2. The unity of his person. It was the Θεανθρωπος (Theanthropos) ; God manifested in the flesh.

3. It teaches and attests his divine mission.

Second, Concerning the intermediate state. It teaches the conscious individual existence of the soul after death. Moses and Elias appeared as individual men.

2. It seems also to teach that the souls of the departed have a knowledge of the state of the Church in this world, and are interested spectators of its progress.

Third, As to the future life.

1. It is a revelation of the nature of the resurrection body, which is to be glorious, identical with the present body and capable of recognition.

2. That there can be and will be in the future life not only recognition but intercourse.

The two great duties which the Transfiguration of Christ should impress on us are,

1. To regard and reverence Jesus Christ as the Son of God, as God and man, infinitely, glorious and lovely. 2. To obey him. Hear ye him. Receive as true all he says. Believe his doctrines. Rely on his promises. Obey his precepts.

XLII. The memory of Christ and the reason why it should be cherished.

[*March 9th*, 1856. *Communion Sunday.*]

Distance, absence and the past, form a dark region into which the eye cannot penetrate. Where are the Patriarchs, Adam, Enoch, Methuselah, Noah, Abraham, Moses, Isaiah, and all the prophets? Not absolutely forgotten because they are historical, but thought of as shadows, shades only.

There are three classes of persons hidden in the past. 1. Those who have lived and died as the leaves of the forest, and left no trace. Such are the vast mass of men. 2. Those whose names are inseparably connected with the history, and who can never be forgotten as long as history is cultivated. 3. Those who not only have accomplished great things in their generation, but the effects of whose lives and acts continue and determine the condition of the present generation. To this class belong all men who are the authors of great revolutions and of permanent institutions, or of systems of doctrine or of philosophy which consciously determine the opinions or conditions of succeeding ages. Such were the men of our Revolution, Mohammed, Luther, Calvin.

Christ constitutes a class by himself. He is not only an historical personage, as Sesostris or Numa. He is not only the author of a system of doctrine embraced by one-third of the human family; not only the founder of the Church, which determines the form of modern civilization, and therefore, in that sense, cannot be forgotten, as his name is mentioned many millions of times every day, and in every part of the world. All this is true, but all this is too little.

To remember is not merely to recall the past, as the object of present knowledge. It is also to estimate, appreciate and duly consider. When we remember God, we remember our obligations, our privileges, and the promises which were made to us. There is recognition of the truth, and an appreciation of the effect which it ought to produce, which is implied and intended.

To remember Christ is therefore not merely to call to mind the facts of his life; nor to acknowledge our obligations to him as the teacher of the gospel and the founder of the Church, as Mussulmans may remember Mohammed; but besides all this, it is to consider and appreciate our present relation to him. It is to cherish the lively consciousness that he is our life. 1. Our deliverer from death, the judicial death to which we were exposed, and from which we are preserved only by him. We are to remember the hand which holds us up from Hell every moment. A man floating on the ocean might as well forget the plank which sustains him; or the man suspended over an abyss, forget the rope which holds him up, as we, to forget Christ.

2. We are to remember, *i. e.*, be always mindful of the fact that it is not we that live, but Christ that liveth in us; that all right thoughts, all just purposes, all holy affections, all good acts, are the product of his continued agency in our hearts. Shall the branch forget the vine? The earth the sun?

3. We are to remember that he is the author of all happiness, of peace of conscience; the source of God's favor, of our access to God, of communion with him, of all temporal and social blessings, of security from our spiritual enemies by whom we are surrounded, principalities and powers. Can a man forget the source of all his present joys? Can he forget his food, the air he breathes, the light of heaven, the all-sustaining power in which he lives and moves and has his being? Neither can the believer forget Christ.

4. We live not only in the past and in the present, but also in the future. We have an eternity before us. Christ is our life, not only in having delivered us and in now sustaining us, but in being to us, *a.* The principle of eternal life. *b.* In being its object, *i. e.*, to know him, to be with him, to be like him, to be engaged in his service, fills all our future with light and glory.

We cannot look back without seeing Christ. We cannot look beneath, above, or around us in the present, but he fills the whole horizon. We cannot look forward but he is the effulgence which sheds its glory on our eternal career. To remember Christ, therefore, is all our duty, for it is to live on him, to live for him, and to live with him.

XLIII. The grace of our Lord Jesus Christ be with you all.—Rev. 22: 21.

[April 22d.—Year not given.]

Grace.—The primary meaning of Χάρις (charis) is, that which gives joy. And as nothing is such a source of joy as love, grace means love. And as love of a superior to an inferior is specially gratifying, such love is with emphasis grace; and as love towards the unlovely, the ungrateful, the sinful, the guilty is of all other forms of love the most powerful and effectual in rendering blessed, so this is the distinctive idea of grace in the Scriptures,—*undeserved* love.

The secondary meaning of the word is gift, benefit, undeserved benefactions; and especially divine influence.

II. *Whose grace or love is here invoked ?*

1. Of a divine person. It is the love of the Second Person of the Trinity. Therefore it is divine. The love of God is *a.* infinite, *b.* immutable, *c.* the sufficient and certain source of all good. If we are the special objects of this infinite, immutable and unmerited love of God, we are just as sure of receiving all we need, if we do his will, as a child is of receiving the care and protection of a parent.

2. This love of Christ is a human love. It is the love of a person who has human affections, human tenderness, human sympathies, human yearnings, just as truly and in the same sense that we have.

3. It is the love of a Lord. This includes *a.* The idea of possession. It is the love of one to whom we belong, as we belong to no one else; one who has bought us, bought us with his blood; to whom we are precious; whose heritage, whose reward, whose crown and glory we constitute. *b.* Lordship includes also the idea of authority. *c.* Of rightful power. *d.* Of actual protection.

The grace of our Lord Jesus Christ is the undeserved love of a divine person clothed with our nature, whose love has all the attributes of sinless human love; the love of one who owns us, who is invested with absolute dominion over us and who is our protector and preserver.

III. *What is meant by this love being with us.*—When one sends his love to another, it is only the assurance of his love. So when we say the love of Christ be with you, we mean, 1. May Christ actually love you; may you be the object of his love. 2. May you have the assurance of that love so as to be able to enjoy it and rejoice in it. 3. May you have the manifestation of that love. 4. The communion of loving intercourse, such as that between intimate friends. 5. All the benefits which flow from the love of Christ, not only the inward joy, fellowship and delight, but the supply of our wants, assistance, protection, support and final deliverance which the love of an infinite Saviour can secure.

Now this assumes that Christ is present with us.

1. We have no such communion with an absent friend as Christians are assumed to have with Christ. We have no communion with the dead, *i. e.*, no intercourse with them. We can't communicate our thoughts, our feelings, our wants to them, nor can they communicate with us or help us. He is present with us in the sense in which a friend is present, with whom we can converse, with whom we can constantly communicate.

2. It implies that Christ is present with us as to his human nature. There are different kinds of presence. *a.* Local in space as opposed to distance. *b.* A presence of power and influence and manifestation, as the sun.

In this sense Christ's human nature is present, *i. e.*, the love of Christ is of a person who has the attributes of humanity, and therefore his love which is with us is a human love.

This conference this afternoon has special reference to the Senior Class. It is the invocation of their professors and their fellow-students that the grace of the divine human Saviour, whose they are, whom they serve and who is their protector and master, may be with them; that is, that they may always be assured of his love enjoyed by them, and thus be sustained, assisted, supported and comforted by it to the end.

XLIV. Jesus crowned with glory and honor. Heb. 2:9.

[*Dec. 14th*, 1862.]

The interpretation of Scripture, especially of the prophecies, is to be determined, 1. By the *usus loquendi*. 2. By the facts of Scripture and history. 3. By the authoritative expositions found in the Bible. The declaration of the Psalmist concerning the exaltation and dominion of man would seem to mean nothing more than that man is to be the head or lord of this creation, *i. e.*, over the irrational creatures inhabiting this globe. We learn from the Scriptures and from the exaltation of Christ, that this is but a drop of the bucket compared to its full meaning. The language of the Psalmist had its fulfilment in the exaltation of Christ. The passage is applied to him and interpreted in the same way in 1 Cor. xv. 27 and in Heb. ii. 8, which, by the way, is a strong collateral proof that Paul wrote the epistle to the Hebrews.

I. *The subject of the exaltation here spoken of.*—This is not the Logos, nor is it the human nature of Christ, but it is the Theanthropos. The union of the divine and human did not of itself necessitate this exaltation. Our Lord from his birth to his resurrection was a man of low degree, a δοῦλος, (doulos). There was nothing in his appearance to command the recognition of his divinity, or make him the object of admiration or fear. His exaltation was declared to be something given. The Logos, as one with the Father, would have had his divine excellence and blessedness; but as one with humanity, might have remained as He was here on earth.

II. *The ground of this exaltation is twofold.*

1. The possession of a divine nature. It is a principle in the Scriptures that no one is exalted to an office without the qualifications for it. The power exercised flows from what is inherent. Christ could not have been exalted to equality with God in dominion and glory, had he not been equal with God in all excellence. It is because he is the brightness of the Father's glory and upholds all things by the word of his power that he is seated at the Father's right hand.

2. His humiliation, suffering and death. This is taught in Heb. i: 4; ii: 9; Phil. ii: 6–11, and often in other places.

III. *The nature of this exaltation.*

1. Christ is made the head or ruler of all creatures. All divine authority is exercised through him. This was never so before.

2. He is the object of adoration. The central person in the universe. The invisible God is visible in him. Better known, comprehended, and therefore loved.

3. He is the head of his Church. His people, their salvation and blessedness, is a large part of his reward. Christ is the immediate sovereign to whom the allegiance, the love, the loyalty of all creatures, especially of his redeemed ones, belong.

IV. *The effect of this exaltation.*

First. On Christ himself, *i. e.,* on his human nature.

1. It was not destroyed. It does not cease to have the substance and the attributes of humanity. It does not possess divine perfections. It is not infinite in reference to space, nor to power, nor to knowledge. 2. It does not destroy the individuality of that nature. He is still Jesus. Not only has he a true body and a reasonable soul, but the very body and the very soul which he assumed and wore on earth. 3. It does not destroy the marks of this identity. Those who knew him on earth, knew him on the mount and in heaven. His person in heaven bears the impress of his sufferings on earth. These are the things to be denied. What is to be affirmed is simply what the Bible teaches us, viz.: that his humanity is made so glorious that he cannot now be looked upon by mortal eyes. Those who saw him became as dead men. His body is glorious, incorruptible, powerful and spiritual. The humanity is included in the personality of the Logos. It is the same I who said:

" Before Abraham was I am " and " I thirst." The manifestation of his hypostatic union has been made since to all creatures. Before, it was seen imperfectly and only by the few.

Second. Its effects on other creatures.

1. It greatly increases their knowledge.

2. It enlarges the sphere of their activity.

3. It increases their blessedness.

Third. Its effects on his people.

1. It exalts human nature above all creatures. What the Psalmist said is true not only of Christ, but in its measure of his people. They are exalted above the angels in some things.

2. It brings them therefore into a participation of Christ's kingdom. Its effect is that we reign with him ; we partake of his glory ; we judge angels.

V. *Inferences.*

1. As we are to be like Christ, we should purify ourselves even as he is pure. We should live worthy of this destiny.

2. We should consecrate our whole soul, and life, and power to his service.

3. We should be content and happy. It is enough for us that we are one with Christ.

XLV. The Coming of Christ.

[*December 21st,* 1856.]

I. *Nature of it.*—Christ came. He comes. He is to come.

1. He came in the flesh. The long lines of predictions from Adam to Malachi were accomplished at last, after long delay and anxious expectation.

2. He comes continually. *a.* In the extraordinary manifestation of his presence and power, whether for judgment or mercy. *b.* In the special manifestation of himself to his people.

3. He is to come. *a.* Personally and visibly. *b.* With power and great glory. *c.* The dead shall rise, the just and the unjust. *d.* The judgment will then be held. *e.* The world destroyed. *f.* The kingdom of God shall be consummated.

The consequences of his advent to his people will be. *a.* Their redemption ; that is, their final deliverance from the power of death. *b.* Their complete conformity to the likeness of Christ. *c.* Their perfect enjoyment of that kingdom prepared for them from the foundation of the world.

II. *As to the time of the Second Advent.*

1. It is unrevealed. 2. It is to be unexpected. 3. It will not be until the conversion of the Jews, and the calling in of the Gentiles. Did the Apostles expect him in their day? 1. They regarded his coming as they regarded the coming of death. 2. It was at last revealed to them that there was to be a falling away first. We must distinguish between their personal expectations and their teaching. The latter alone is infallible.

III. *Points of analogy between the first and second coming.*

1. Both long predicted.

2. Long and anxiously expected.

3. The people indulged in many speculations as to the time and mode of his coming.

4. They were greatly disappointed as to the one and the other.

IV. *The state of mind which the doctrine of the Second Advent should induce.*

1. A firm belief in the revealed fact that he is to come. This faith should not be shaken by long delay. How long Abraham waited and died without the sight.

2. Earnest desire. The hopes of the ancient people were concentrated on the coming of the Messiah. This led them to bear patiently what they had to suffer. To set their hopes on the future and not on the present. The same effect should be produced on us.

3. Watchfulness and anxiety, lest that day should overtake us as a thief in the night. We should have our lamps trimmed and our lights burning. It would be a dreadful thing, should Christ come and find us immersed in the world.

4. Prayer and waiting. "Waiting for the consolation of Israel."

5. Solicitous efforts to prepare others for his coming, and to prepare the way of the Lord. He will not come to the individual nor to the Church until the way is prepared. This includes, 1. Taking out of the way obstructions to his coming. 2. The accomplishment of the appointed ingathering of his people.

III.

THE HOLY SPIRIT AND HIS OFFICES.

XLVI. The promise of the Spirit. Gal. 3: 14.

[*September 21st, 1856.*]

The doctrine of the Trinity is everywhere recognized as the foundation of religion. The Father elects, the Son redeems, the Spirit sanctifies. The Son came in execution of the covenant of redemption. Having fulfilled its conditions, he was entitled to its promises. One of those promises was the gift of the Spirit, Acts 2: 33. "Therefore being by the right hand of God exalted, and having received of the Father the promise of the Holy Ghost, he hath shed forth this which ye now see and hear." Accordingly the gift of the Holy Spirit was the great Messianic blessing promised and predicted; and as John said, the Holy Ghost was not yet given because that Jesus was not yet glorified; and Christ promised that he would send them another comforter.

I. *The first great truth on this subject is that the Holy Ghost is secured for the Church only by the mediation of Christ.* It is due to his work that he is sent. His influence and presence is the great blessing secured by the death of Christ.

This does not imply that those living before the advent were not partakers of the Spirit, because all the benefits of Christ's death were enjoyed from the beginning. It is not the less true however that he died to secure those blessings

II. *The second great truth is that Christ is the immediate giver of the Holy Spirit.* He sends him to whom he pleases, and bestows through him what blessings he pleases. Therefore men must seek the Spirit specially from Christ, as our mediator.

III. *The third great truth is, that election by the Father and redemption by the Son avail only in virtue of the Spirit's work.* Until the Spirit is received, the elect do not differ from the non-elect, the redeemed from the unredeemed. Hence our obligations to the several persons of the Trinity are the same. We owe as much to the Father who chose as to the Son who redeemed, and no less to the Spirit.

And as the Son acted voluntarily in redeeming those whom the Father chose, so the Spirit is voluntary in applying the redemption purchased by the Son.

This is consistent with the Father's sending the Son, and with the Son's sending the Spirit. Hence our love, gratitude, reverence and obedience are as much due to the Spirit as to the Father and the Son. This is not always remembered.

IV. *The work of the Spirit, i. e.,* his inward subjective work, is,

1. To renew or quicken those dead in sins.

2. To illuminate. To reveal the glory of Christ, the holiness of God, the justice and extent of the law, the evil of sin, the certainty of judgment, and the truth and authority of the word of God.

3. To work repentance and faith, *i. e.,* turning from sin and turning to God.

4. Constant guidance into the knowledge of truth and duty.

5. To qualify for special duties and offices.

6. To sanctify.

7. To comfort.

8. To glorify the soul and body. All this we owe to the Spirit.

V. *The dependence of the individual and of the Church on the Spirit is absolute.* Nothing can be experienced and nothing done but by him. Analogous to the dependence of the creatures on the Creator ; *a.* for existence ; *b.* for faculties ; *c.* for activity ; *d.* for the results or success. But not in any one of these cases is our activity superseded, and in them all the need of effort and exertion is the same.

VI. *Election, redemption and sanctification are inseparably connected.* Those whom the Father elects, the Son redeems, and the Spirit sanctifies. And consequently whom the Spirit does not sanctify, the Son has not redeemed and the Father has not elected.

Hence 1. The folly and wickedness of Antinomianism.

2. The only evidence of redemption and election is sanctification.

XLVII. Dependence on the Holy Ghost.

[*March 1st*, 1857.]

Three forms of life in man : the sensual or corporeal, the intellectual and the spiritual. The first and second are sustained by the providential efficiency of God. The latter by the work of the Spirit.

I. *The first is carried on according to material laws, i. e.*, the laws which control the operations of matter. The second according to the laws which determine the operations of mind. These are natural. The spiritual life is supernatural. That is, 1. It does not belong to our nature since the fall. 2. It is not produced by any natural process as in the case of our corporeal and intellectual life. In matter the appropriate combinations always produce the same results. So of intellectual life; men may be trained or educated to any form of mental exercise. But there are no means which will produce spiritual life or sustain its exercises. You cannot produce faith, love, repentance, hope, joy, or heavenly-mindedness by any possible combination of agencies or by any possible exercise of efficiency. The analogies and illustrations of Scripture take this for granted. Men are said to be born of the Spirit, to be created, to be raised from the dead.

3. It is supernatural, (positively) because its existence is due to the direct agency of God through his Spirit; an agency not only distinct from the operation of all natural causes, but also from all the influences of the means of grace; neither the truth, nor the sacraments, nor priestly ministrations can impart life to those spiritually dead.

II. *Although spiritual life, in the sense stated, is not natural, neither is it unnatural.* 1. It is not incongruous to our nature. It is not incongruous that we should love God, worship Christ, exercise faith, repentance and all other forms of spiritual life. Our nature in its perfection would have these exercises, and all our rational, moral and emotional powers enter into them and form the basis, so to speak, of them. It is unnatural for a beast to speak, but not for one born dumb. 2. It is not unnatural in the sense of being magical, produced and sustained by occult causes, which have no relation to the effect produced. If washing with water, anointing with oil, or making the sign of the cross, produced holiness, it could be only by some magical influence. As when magicians by spells, amulets or incantation pretend to work wonders. There is nothing of this kind in the case of spiritual life. It is not in this sense unnatural. On the contrary, the means of grace are appropriate to the ends for which they are used. The truth concerning God, Christ and ourselves is adapted to produce the exercises of spiritual life where we are not dead. Just as heat, light and moisture would produce vegetation and growth in a seed if the seed be not dead; or as the powers of the mind are called forth by and developed by the appropriate moral training.

III. *These are the two great truths taught us in the Scriptures on this subject.* First. Spiritual life is not natural. Second. It is not unnatural.

From the former of these truths it follows,

1. That we are in a far higher sense dependent upon God for spiritual life than for corporal or intellectual life. For the latter we are indeed dependent; but they are communicated and continued according to fixed laws, while our spiritual life is not. It cannot in any way be produced in ourselves or communicated to others without a direct intervention of God. It is in this point analogous to a miracle. And we should feel our impotency to change our own heart, or to convert others as sensibly, and recognize it as being as absolute as it is to give sight to the blind or to raise the dead. And this is one of those truths which the Spirit forces men to acknowledge.

He never converts them unless they feel they cannot convert themselves; and he never makes them the instruments of converting others, until they feel that they cannot do it; that their skill in argument, in persuasion, in management, avails nothing. This is a pregnant truth, which should govern all our endeavors. We must feel it as men, as ministers and as a Church. The Spirit must be honored by this sincere and heartfelt recognition of dependence.

2. A second inference from this truth, or a second form of our dependence is, that the influence of the Spirit cannot be merited. We cannot place God under any obligation either as a matter of justice or as a matter of promise to give us the Holy Ghost, or to attend our labors with his divine influence. He has made general promises; general purposes have been announced. But the man who seeks repentance and faith, (and many seek to enter in who shall not be able,) has no right, should he fail, to complain. Divine influence is a grace. The man that preaches the gospel at home or abroad ever so long, or so faithfully, must be contented to acknowledge that success is a favor, not a debt. This is the second great truth which we must acknowledge.

3. Another inference is that this blessing is absolutely necessary, and yet may be withheld; that it must be sought with earnest importunate prayer. The sick in the days of Christ could not heal themselves. He was under no obligation to heal them; therefore they sought his help as a necessity and as a favor.

These are the inferences from the doctrine of the supernatural character of divine grace, or from the fact that it is not natural. The inferences from the doctrine that it is not unnatural are,

1. That we must not depend on rites and ceremonies, or outward institutions or ordinances.

2. That we must not expect the results without the diligent use of the means. This is true of ourselves. We mock the Spirit when we pray that he would sanctify us, and do not use the means. And no less when we pray for the conversion of others without using the means.

The doctrine of dependence produces,

1. Humility.   2. Gratitude.   3. Confidence.

XLVIII. Dependence of the believer and the Church on the Holy Spirit. Psalm 51 : 11.

[*Sept. 4th*, 1859.]

The old saying that what is false in philosophy is true in theology is a contradiction in its obvious sense. It amounts to saying that the true may be false. Yet there is a sense in which the saying is true ; or rather, there is a truth which at times was expressed by that paradox. That truth is, that what we know to be true on the testimony of God and experience, may appear to be false, or at least irreconcilable to other truths, to the understanding.

There are two sources of conviction : The one is the discursive understanding ; the other, intuitional consciousness. These are always in accord in the sound or normal state of the mind, but often in conflict in the present disordered state of human nature ; and we must make our choice between them. If we follow the former we shall become skeptics ; if the latter, and we be the children of God, we shall know and believe the truth.

There is no subject on which this conflict of the understanding and of the inward consciousness is more apt to occur than the relation of God to the world, the dependence of the creature upon the Creator, the consistency of the controlling agency of God with the agency of the creature. The Scriptures and experience teach that there is such a dependence, and that it is absolute. But it is different in different cases.

1. The dependence of inanimate matter on God.

2. The dependence of sensitive living creatures on God.

3. The dependence of rational creatures on God.

4. The dependence of the soul for all the exercises of the spiritual life on God.

This is the subject of consideration. As to this point it is to be remarked,

1. That it is peculiar to fallen beings. As animals have a life of their own which is not the life of God, and as rational creatures have such a life, so it may be presumed that unfallen holy beings have a spiritual life of their own ; so that their dependence on God for their spiritual life is analogous to their dependence on him for their rational life.

2. This dependence is not to be confounded with our dependence on God as creatures for our rational life. But it is a dependence on the Spirit of God.

3. It assumes that we are dead, and that a new kind of life is produced by the Holy Ghost and sustained by him. So that without him we can do nothing.

4. We are thus dependent for knowledge, for holiness, for consolation, for perseverance and growth in grace.

5. This dependence, although absolute, does not supersede the use of means, or our obligation to exert ourselves. The promise of assistance is to those who strive and are faithful.

6. What is true of the individual believer is true of any company of believers, and therefore of such institutions as this and of the Church. Here we are absolutely dependent on the Holy Spirit. So is the ministry. So is the Church.

INFERENCES.

1. This relation to the Holy Spirit should be inwardly recognized and openly acknowledged.

2. We should abstain from everything which tends to separate from him. These things are, first, a spirit of self-dependence; secondly, every thing which offends the Spirit as unholy.

3. Earnest longing and prayer.

XLIX. He will reprove (convince) the world of sin, because they believe not on me.—John 16: 8, 9.

[*Sept. 20th*, 1863.]

I. What is conviction of sin? II. What is the sin of which men must be convinced? III. How is the Spirit the author of that conviction?

The word κόσμος (kosmos) means 1. Order, proper and harmonious arrangement. 2. The universe as thus arranged. 3. The earth. 4. The inhabitants of the earth, mankind, men. 5. The wicked, unrenewed, as opposed to the Church or believers. Here it means men, considered as unrenewed; not all men, but the class or order who are the subjects of this conviction.

I. *What is conviction of sin?* The word ἐλέγχειν means, 1. To reprove, censure, or upbraid. 2. To convict, prove to be guilty. 3. To render manifest. Here it is used in the two latter senses. The people of the world are to be convicted at the bar of their own conscience of being sinners. That act is to be manifest to their own consciousness; and as sin includes two elements, viz. : guilt and pollution, the one expressing the relation of sin to justice and the other its relation to holiness, conviction of sin includes, *a*. The conviction of just exposure to the wrath of God on account of our character and conduct. And this includes the conviction that we deserve punishment, and secondly that we ought to be punished, and thirdly that we certainly shall be punished, unless in some way our guilt be removed. *b.* The conviction of moral defilement or pollution : that is, that we are in fact and in our own eyes offensive, degraded, and the proper objects of loathing.

The effects of conviction flow from these two sources, and are, *a.* Terror or dread of the wrath of God. *b.* Self-condemnation. *c.* Remorse, which includes both the consciousness of ill-desert, sorrow for the offense, and craving after satisfaction. It is stilled by punishment or adequate atonement. *d.* Self-abhorrence. *e.* Shame and confusion of face. There is nothing holy in all this.

II. *The sin of which men are to be thus convinced is the sin of not believing on Christ.*

This presents three points : 1. What is it to believe upon Christ ? 2. What is included in the conviction of the sin of not thus believing? 3. Why is unbelief so great a sin ?

First. What is it to believe on Christ ? This includes, 1st. The belief that he is what he claimed to be, viz. : the Son of God, or God manifest in the flesh ; the Messiah ; the Prophet, Priest and King of his people, and therefore the Redeemer of men. This involves the recognition or the conviction and acknowledgment of the truth of all his doctrines. This faith, to be genuine, must not rest merely on external evidence, but on the revealing and testifying influence of the Holy Spirit. 2d. It includes reliance on Christ, in his propitiation, on his saving, sanctifying and protecting power. 3d. It includes, not exactly in its nature as faith, but as its inseparable adjunct and necessary effects, adoring love for his person, zeal for his glory, devotion to his service, and submission to his will. As we cannot separate in fact, or even in consciousness, the apprehension of beauty from the delight in it, so we cannot separate from faith in Christ, love, zeal, devotion and submission. The want of all these is unbelief. And men are convinced of sin when convinced that want of faith in Christ deserves the wrath and curse of God, and degrades and pollutes the soul.

III. *Why is unbelief in Christ, or want of faith in him so great a sin and the greatest of all sins ?*

That it is so is directly asserted in John iii. 18. "He that believeth not is condemned already, because he hath not believed in the name of the only begotten Son of God," and elsewhere as is distinctly implied in this verse. It is so great a sin, 1. Because it is the manifestation, exercise and effect of the greatest depravity. The disbelief of speculative truth is not sinful except where some moral obligation is violated in rejecting the evidence by which it is supported. But the rejection of moral truth is in its nature sinful because it implies moral blindness and perversion of moral feeling.   To call evil good and good evil, to approve of those who do evil, implies greater corruption than the mere commission of sin.   Unbelief of the moral truth differs in the degree of its sinfulness according to the importance of the truth and the amount and kind of evidence with which it is attended.   That the heathen are sinful and without excuse because they do not believe God as revealed in nature, is asserted by Paul.   But this sin is slight compared with those who rejected God as revealed in the Old Testament, and their guilt again is small, compared to that of those who reject Christ.   He is God in the clearest and most attractive revelation ever made of the Divine Being.   The rejection of him implies the greatest blindness and depravity.   It is therefore the greatest of all sins, and implies Satanic blindness of the eyes.

2. Because it involves the greatest conceivable ingratitude.   It is not only the rejection of God, but it is the rejection of God humbling himself to be found in fashion as a man, and becoming obedient unto death, even the death of the cross, out of love to us and for our salvation.

3. Because it involves a preference and deliberate choice of evil instead of good, of Satan and the kingdom of darkness instead of the kingdom of God.   " He who does not bow to Christ, has bowed to me," as the Poet makes Satan say.

4. Because it is the rejection of eternal life for ourselves, and doing what we can to render certain the perdition of others.

IV.   *The Holy Spirit alone can convince men of this sin.*

1. It is certain that human reason or our own nature, as it is, will not do it.   2. That flesh and blood cannot do it.   3. The Holy Spirit alone can do it because he alone can open our eyes to behold the glory of God in the face of Jesus Christ.   4. It is his office to take the things of Christ and show them unto us.

INFERENCES.

1. That it is our first and greatest duty to repent of this sin and to believe on Christ in the sense above stated.   2. Our next great duty is to labor to convince the world of this sin, (for the Spirit produces this conviction through the truth), and to lead them to receive, acknowledge, love, worship, serve and trust the Son of God.

L. The necessity of the Spirit's teaching in order to the right understanding of the Scriptures.

[*Sept. 20th*, 1868].

There are two kinds of knowledge, of faith, of repentance.   Simon Magus believed and remained in the gall of bitterness.   Paul believed and became a Christian.

In both cases there was a persuasion of the truth. Simon believed when he saw the miracles wrought by the Apostles: Paul, when Christ was revealed within him. Judas repented when he saw the evil consequences of his treachery; Peter repented when he saw his conduct in its true character. So there is a simple intellectual knowledge of the truth, and there is a spiritual knowledge and discernment.

How are these related; that is, how do they agree and how do they differ? 1. The things known are the same. 2. The act of knowing is the same. 3. But the spiritual excellence of the object is not apprehended in the one case, while it is in the other.

This may be illustrated by the case of the discernment of beauty. Now with regard to the knowledge of the Scriptures, there is no reason why the unrenewed man, without any special aid of the Spirit, should not acquire that knowledge as well as the knowledge of any similar volume. Of course, however, it must be under the same conditions. 1. He must study assiduously. 2. In the right method, and in the use of the right means. 3. He must be impartial and honest; not endeavor to establish a theory, but simply to ascertain the true sense.

Now, although this is possible, it is in reference to the Scriptures difficult and rare, because of the opposition of the heart to the doctrines of the Bible, and because the judgments of men are so largely determined by their feelings.

Therefore, for the attainment of this intellectual knowledge, there is great need of the Spirit's guidance to produce, 1st, Docility. 2d. To prevent opposition to the truth blinding the mind.

For spiritual knowledge the case is plain. On this subject the Scriptures teach, 1. The absolute necessity of divine teaching. No man cometh to me except he be taught of God. The natural man receiveth not the things of the Spirit of God: for they are foolishness unto him: neither can he know them, because they are spiritually discerned. No man can call Jesus Lord but by the Holy Ghost. He that confesseth that Jesus Christ is come in the flesh, is of God. Besides, the Bible abounds in prayers for this divine teaching. And Paul declares all external teaching in vain without it.

2. The Scriptures say that the cause of this ignorance, blindness and inability to know the things of God, arises from two sources; first, our depravity. We are natural, carnal, the opposite of the spiritual, and cannot by any possibility discern that which is spiritual. And secondly, Satan, the god of this world, blinds the eyes. His influence is great and general. He persuades men to reject the truth. He raises objections, and excites the enmity of the heart.

It is a solemn fact, therefore, that those and those only who are led by the Spirit, come to the knowledge of the truth. This is the great office of the Spirit. This is to be recognized, and his guidance sought and submitted to.

Correct speculative knowledge and spiritual knowledge experience teaches do not admit of protracted separation. There can be no spiritual knowledge without speculative knowledge, but there may be the speculative without the spiritual.

But orthodoxy will not last without piety. An unconverted ministry forsakes the truth. This all history proves. Hence the great importance of this subject. The salvation of men largely depends on the ministry preaching the truth. That ministers should preach the truth, depends on their being converted and taught by the Spirit. Therefore, whether you are to be blessings or curses to the Church depends on your being taught of God.

LI. The indwelling of the Spirit.

[*November 26th, 1854.*]

I. *The meaning of the expression, God dwells, is that he specially and permanently manifests his presence.*—Thus he is said to dwell in heaven; among the children of men; in Zion; among his people; in believers.

The Spirit is said to dwell in his Church, which is thus the temple of God; in believers individually, they are severally his temple; in the body of believers, so that it also is the Temple of the Holy Ghost.

II. *It follows that where the Spirit dwells his presence is indicated by certain specific effects.*—These are, 1. Either gifts ordinary or extraordinary, 2. or, graces, *i. e.*, the fruits of the Spirit, 3. activity, 4. guidance, 5. consolation. The graces are, 1st. Knowledge. This is one of the chief ends for which the Spirit was promised by the Saviour to his disciples. This knowledge includes correct intellectual convictions and spiritual discernment. To this are due orthodoxy and love of the truth, and adherence to it under all circumstances. To this source also are we indebted for the unity as well as the preservation of the faith. This is a ground of conviction beyond the reach of scepticism and unassailable by infidelity.

2d. Holiness in all its forms, of faith, confidence in God, in his word, promises, favors, etc. Love to God, Christ and the brotherhood, and to all men. Temperance, meekness, long-suffering.

3d. Hope, joy and peace. The consolations of the Spirit which sustain the soul under all sorrow, whether from conviction of sin or from afflictions.

4th. Other effects or manifestations of the Spirit's presence, are activity in resisting sin and in doing good. He is a source not only of inward spiritual life, but also of outward acts of devotion and obedience to the will of God.

5th. Another effect is guidance. This guidance of the Spirit is, *a*. By the word. *b*. By the inward operation on the mind, guiding its thoughts, shaping its conclusions and exciting right feelings; and not by impulse, and suggestion, or any magic methods.

Duties which flow from this doctrine.

1. To cherish the conviction that we in a special sense belong to God.

2. To reverence and cherish, and to obey the admonitions of the indwelling Spirit.

3. To preserve our soul and body pure as the temple of the Holy Ghost.

4. An humble, grateful sense of the unspeakable blessing thus conferred upon us, and of the dignity which belongs to all believers as the temples of God.

LII. The Spirit giveth life. 2 Cor. 3: 6.

[*January 8th*, 1865.]

These words taken by themselves express a general proposition containing a comprehensive truth. By Spirit is meant the Spirit of God. It is not mind as opposed to matter, or life as opposed to form. The truth is not the philosophical dogma that all force, all power of life is a manifestation of Spirit, that the external or material is purely dead and powerless. But the scriptural truth that the Spirit] of God is the source of all life. He is the Spirit of life.

1. Of the external world. 2. Of the animal world. 3. Of the rational world. 4. Of the spiritual world. In other words he is the source of spiritual life. We are dead. We are quickened by the Spirit. He dwells in us as the source of life, working in us both to will and to do. So that all just thoughts, right feelings, and holy conduct are to be referred to him, as all his gifts.

This is very different from the true meaning of the words in their connection. In other words, that is not the truth which Paul here intends to express. The meaning of the words is to be determined, first, by the drift of the apostolic discourse; secondly, by the explanatory or equivalent phrases which occur in the context.

Paul is here contrasting the law and the gospel, the old covenant and the new covenant. God, he says, had made him a minister of the new covenant. And then he goes on to show the glory of that ministry as contrasted with the ministry of the law. By the Spirit; therefore he must mean the gospel.

2. This is plain from the antithesis. Not of the letter but of the Spirit. The letter is explained to be that which was written on stone, *i. e.*, the law; the decalogue, which was the substance of the Mosaic law, or its foundation. As opposed to that the spirit means the gospel.

3. The letter is called the ministration of death; the Spirit the ministration of life. The one slays, the other gives life. In saying he was a minister of the Spirit, he says the same thing. So in Gal. iii: 3, he says, "having begun in the Spirit, are ye now made perfect by the flesh?" *i. e.*, having begun with the gospel, are ye made perfect by the law? The reason why the law is called the letter is plain. The reasons why the gospel is called the Spirit are, 1. Because it is antithetical to the letter. 2. Because the gospel is spiritual as opposed to what is literal, ceremonial and external. 3. Because the gospel is the organ of the Spirit. 4. Because the effusion, presence and power of the Spirit constituted the great characteristic of the Messianic period, or of the New Testament. In saying that he was a minister of the Spirit, the apostle says he was the minister of that covenant in and through which the Spirit, the source of all life, was given.

The sense therefore in which Paul intended us to understand the words, the Spirit giveth life, is determined by the sense in which the letter giveth life.

1. The letter or the law kills because it denounces death.

2. Because to convince and to condemn is all the law can do.

3. Because it awakens the sense of sin and helplessness, and slays all hope.

4. Because it excites sin and cannot either justify or sanctify. The Spirit or the gospel giveth life.

1. Because it declares the way of life. It reveals a righteousness which delivers us from the law and frees us from the sentence of condemnation.

2. Because it is that through which the Spirit is communicated as a source of life. Instead of a mere outward exhibition of truth and duty, it is a law written on the heart. It is a life-giving power.

3. Because the state of mind which it produces is life and peace. The Spirit is the source of eternal life.

The effects which this view of the subject produced on Paul were,

1. It filled him with a high sense of the dignity and glory of his vocation. It was in his estimation the highest of all works.

2. It made him humble under a sense of his insufficiency.

3. Yet confident, for God had rendered him able, or sufficient.

4. It determined him to use great plainness of speech, not to veil the truth as Moses veiled his face.

LIII. The Spirit's Intercession. Rom. 8: 26.

[*Dec. 11th*, 1864.]

Salvation is entirely of grace. The fall has brought us into an estate of sin and misery. From that estate we do not deserve to be delivered. And from it we cannot deliver ourselves. We must be redeemed. We are the subjects, not the agents of that work.

There are two distinct parts of redemption. One is referred to Christ, the other to the Spirit. Christ acts as our prophet, priest and king. The Spirit applies the redemption purchased by Christ. He convinces of sin. He renews, enlightens, sanctifies, leads and comforts. He dwells in us and constantly works in us to will and to do. He is in us the source or principle of spiritual life.

The work of intercession belongs both to Christ and to the Spirit. Although the word is the same, the work is different. Christ intercedes as a priest; the Spirit as an advocate. This latter word is so comprehensive that it expresses both the work of Christ and that of the Spirit. Christ is our helper. So is the Spirit. But the help they afford is not the same. The help of Christ is that, as just said, of a prophet, priest and king. That of the Spirit, so far as expressed in this passage, is that of an advocate whose office it is to put pleas and words into the mouth of his people. Christ intercedes by pleading for us, presenting his own merits and claims. The Spirit does not supplicate, but he teaches us and supplicates in us, in our name: so that the desires, the thoughts, the words, are his, *i. e.*, due to his suggestion and agency, and not to the operation of our own minds. This is the difference, or one difference, between the intercession of Christ and that of the Spirit.

They differ, as we have seen, 1. In that Christ presents his own merits and claims. This the Spirit does not. 2. Christ himself asks, and asks in his own name. This the Spirit does not. 3. The Spirit does what he causes us to do. We pray under the dictation of the Spirit, and thus he is in us who utter the prayers, not as his, but as our own.

As to this intercession, it is, 1. According to the will of God, *i. e.*, the desires and thoughts which arise in the mind and the petitions we utter are agreeable to his will, and that in two senses. *a.* Agreeable to his preceptive will. They are such as he approves. *b.* They are according to his purpose. The desires the Spirit excites are for things which it is in accordance with God's purpose to bestow.

2. This intercession finds expression often in groans, or desires which we cannot clothe in words. It is not necessary to the efficacy of prayer

that it should be clothed in articulate language. The Lord knows the mind of the Spirit, *i. e.*, the state of mind produced by the Spirit.

3. Such prayers are certainly efficacious. It is said of Christ, "Him the Father heareth always." His intercession cannot fail. This is no less true of the Spirit. The desires and prayers which he puts into the hearts of his people are sure to be answered, because, 1st. It is derogatory to the Spirit to assume the contrary. 2d. Because the apostle declares them to be according to the mind, *i. e.*, the will and purpose of God.

4. If it be asked how we can distinguish between desires and petitions which are the dictate of our own hearts and those which are dictated by the Spirit, it may be answered in general that it is analogous to the question, how can we in any religious exercise determine whether it is gracious (spiritual) or not? How can we tell whether our sorrow for sin, our fear of God, our love of Christ, etc., are natural or gracious affections? This cannot be determined by any distinct consciousness we have of the Spirit's influence. It can only be told, 1. By the objects of these affections. 2. From their nature. 3. From their effects.

And so with regard to these prayers; if they are for objects which we know are right and in accordance with the will of God; if they are pure and spiritual, not selfish or mercenary in their nature; and if they produce in us the fruits of peace, submission or resignation, we may infer they are from the Spirit.

As the Spirit does not reveal to us what is according to the purpose of God, we must in our holiest aspiration say, "not my will but thine be done." 5. This intercession of the Spirit is a great ground of confidence and source of consolation.

Duties. 1. We should keep ourselves as far as in us lies in the fellowship of the Holy Ghost.

2. We should feel our dependence and obligations in regard to the Spirit.

3. We should adore the mystery of the Trinity, as the several powers of the Godhead co-operate in our salvation.

LIV. As many as are led by the Spirit of God, they are the sons of God. Rom. 8: 14.

[*Date not given.*]

I. *By the Spirit of God is of course meant the Holy Spirit.*—The Spirit is everywhere present. He controls all the operations of nature. He operates on the minds of men, endowing and controlling them. He specially operates on the souls of the children of God. 1. In renewing them. 2. In imbuing them continually with new life. 3. In determining their inward and outward life.

II. *What is meant by being led by the Spirit?*

1. It is not by blind suggestions or impulses. It is not by a miraculous or abnormal operation, directing what text the eye shall fall upon. The general statement is that just made. The Spirit is the determining principle of the inward and outward life of the believer. So it is not they which live, but Christ, *i. e.*, his Spirit which liveth in them. This leading of the Spirit is, 1. Consistent with our rational nature, liberty, and responsibility. 2. It is not a matter of consciousness. His influence mingles with our consciousness and determines it, but cannot be distinguished from it. 3. The guidance of the Spirit is not always or necessarily irresistible. We may yield to it or we may oppose it. Hence men are said to resist, to grieve, to quench the Holy Spirit. In all true believers the Spirit will in the end, according to God's promise, overcome all opposition and render them obedient. Nevertheless, it is true that, to their great detriment and loss, they may refuse to be led by him. So much for the nature of this leading.

III. *As to the result of it, or the ends to which the Spirit leads us, they are,*

1. The knowledge of the truth. This is not by revelation, or inspiration, but by illumination. There is thus spiritual teaching apart from the outward teaching of the word, as is proved from the Scriptures and by experience.

2. To the love of the truth, or the conformity of our hearts, our affections to the standard of God's will. That is, we are made to love God, Christ, the people of God, the service of God. We are led to all right exercises of faith, penitence, meekness and every Christian grace and virtue.

3. To the conformity of our outward life to the will of God. It leads to the government of the tongue, to the control of the passions, to the ordering of our life. It gives right views and right motives to determine our conduct in all the emergencies of life. Hence the Spirit leads one man to the ministry, another to some other profession, another to the missionary field.

IV. *Why are those who are led by the Spirit, and they only, the sons of God?*

1. What is meant by the sons of God?

a. Those who partake of his nature, by regeneration.

b. Those who are adopted into his family and are thus made the objects of his parental care and love, and the heirs of his kingdom.

c. Those who are governed by a filial, as opposed to a slavish spirit; who love, reverence, obey God as his children and are zealous for his glory.

There are three reasons why those who are led by the Spirit are the sons of God.

1. Because this submission to the Spirit of our whole inward and outward life is the only evidence of our regeneration and adoption, in other words, of our sonship.

2. Because the Holy Spirit is in his nature a Spirit of adoption. He is not a servile Spirit. It is the Spirit of the Son, and therefore it is sent to those who are sons. Those and those only who are actuated by this filial Spirit are the sons of God; that is, are such in their inward character and temper.

3. Because in so far as the sonship, or being the sons of God, involves the idea of exaltation, dignity, glory, dominion, power or blessedness, the indwelling of the Spirit and his controlling power is the immediate source of all these distinctions and excellences.

V. *The necessary conditions on our part in order to this guidance.*

1. We must renounce our own guidance, the right, the ability or the desirableness of guiding ourselves. This includes the renunciation of the guidance of our own understanding, of our own will, or of our own desires.

2. We must renounce the guidance of men. *a.* Whether of the world, or of individual men, *b.* or of the Church.

3. We must under a sense of our dependence, and in full faith in the Spirit's office, resign ourselves to his guidance and submit to it.

LV. The Spirit itself beareth witness with our spirit that we are the children of God.—Rom. 8: 16.

[*Dec.* 21, 1862.]

I. The thing testified to. II. The nature of that testimony.

I. *The thing testified to,* is that we are the children of God, τέχνα θεοῦ. There is the same difference between τέχνον and ὑιὸς as there is between *child* and *son;* the former applies to either sex, and is the more tender. We are born of God, *i. e.,* produced by him. 1st. This does not refer to us as creatures, nor as rational creatures, but as regenerated, born again. So that we are partakers of the divine nature.

2d. It expresses the relation in which we stand to him, *a.* as objects of his love; *b.* as loving him, *i. e.,* regarding him as a father. This filial spirit on our part includes, 1. Confidence in his love to us. 2. Reverence. 3. Zeal for his glory. 4. Devotion to his service.

3d. The word expresses or indicates the privileges arising from this relation to God. We are the heirs of God, the partakers of all those benefits and blessings which he has provided for his children. In testifying to our being the children of God, the Spirit testifies, that we are born of God, that we are the objects of his paternal love, and that we are heirs of the inheritance of the saints in life.

II. *The nature of his witnessing.*—It is not involved in our filial feelings, for the Spirit is said συμμαρτύρειν, to testify with, *i. e.*, with our own hearts.

But, 1. It is direct or immediate. The Spirit assures us, just as he produces the assurance of the truth. 2. It is mysterious or inexplicable, just as much and no more than other operations of the Spirit are. And these in their turn are no more mysterious than the action of mind on matter, or matter on mind, or one created spirit on other such spirits. 3. It is self-evidencing. That is, it reveals itself as the witness or testimony of God. Just as the voice of God in the Heavens, in conscience, in the law, in the gospel, reveals itself in his word; so when the Spirit speaks to the soul it is known to be the Spirit.

4. It is infallible testimony, and produces assurance. This is not inconsistent with doubt and anxiety, first, because this witnessing is intermittent more or less; and secondly, because this voice of God may vary from the slightest, almost inaudible whisper, to the most clear and articulate enunciation.

5. It is sanctifying. That is its nature. It produces that effect just as fire burns, or light dispels darkness. It is never given where it is not true. And where it is true, where the soul is regenerated, then to banish doubt and fear and anxiety, is to infuse new life and vigor. It is to give peace and call out all graces. 1. We are to guard against self-deception in this matter. 2. We should cherish the Spirit, that he may testify with our spirit.

LVI. Who hath also sealed us, and given the earnest of the Spirit in our hearts. 2 Cor. 12: 2. See also Eph. 1: 13; 4: 30; 1 Tim. 2: 19.

[*No date given.*]

The object of attaching a seal to any thing is,

1. To authenticate it, as when a man signs and seals a deed. Thus, John vi: 27, our Lord was sealed, sealed or proved to be the Son of God. 2. To preserve either from inspection, as when a letter or book is sealed, or from violation or injury. The sepulchre was sealed to preserve it from violation. Any person or thing is in the Scriptures said to be sealed when preserved from destruction. 3. To indicate ownership, 2 Tim. ii: 19; "having this seal, the Lord knoweth them that are his," etc.

So in Revelation the people of God are said to be sealed or marked as belonging to him. See Ezekiel ix: 4.

When therefore it is said that God hath sealed us, one or more, or all the above ideas are intended. In some passages one, and in others another, of these ideas is rendered the most prominent. All, however, are included. Those whom God seals, on whom he impresses his seal, he authenticates as his people, he secures from destruction, and he makes them as his own. They are known by that seal to be his. Any man therefore who has the seal of God impressed upon him is thereby proved to be one of his children ; he is secure from destruction and is marked as belonging to God, claimed by him as his own.

II. *What is the seal of God?*

It is the Holy Spirit. His presence in the soul authenticates it as born of God, secures it from apostacy, and marks it as the property of God, the purchase of the Redeemer's blood. Hence the two expressions, " hath sealed us " and " hath given to us the earnest of the Spirit," are explanatory, the one of the other.

Any one, therefore, in whom the Holy Ghost dwells, knows thereby and is thereby known by others to be a genuine child of God.

Because the spirituality or holiness induced by the presence of the Spirit is, in its nature, affinity with God ; or sonship, in one of the principal senses of that term.

Again he is assured of ultimate salvation. Not that he has no doubts or fears on that point. But he has the grounds of assurance and confidence, greater or less. The Holy Ghost secures the salvation of those in whom he dwells, because he is the purchase of the Redeemer's death. His continued indwelling is secured by the covenant of grace. And he conveys to the soul, in whom he dwells, this sense of security, because the Scriptures teach that those in whom the Holy Spirit dwells can never perish ; because the feelings of which he is the author involve hope, joy, confidence, assurance of the love of God ; and because he witnesses with our spirits, that we are the children of God ; and if children, then heirs. That is, by his communion with our spirits he awakens confidence in the fidelity of God just as he awakens the feeling of humility and penitence.

Again, as the different orders of knighthood or nobility among men are indicated by certain badges, so the believer by the indwelling Spirit is marked as belonging to the order of the sons of God. As such they are reverenced and waited on by angels, and as such they know and rejoice in each other as members of the same royal family.

Such being the doctrine on this subject, it follows : —

1. That the more distinct the impress of the seal of God is on the soul, the more will it experience of the benefits and blessedness which flow from being thus sealed. Ancient seals sometimes, as now, had figures and sometimes sentences engraved upon them, 2 Tim. ii. 19.

The figure may be so slightly cut, or so incrusted by foreign substances as to be scarcely distinguishable. The figure, so to speak, on the seal of God is the likeness of Christ. If that image is enstamped on the soul clearly, then all recognize it; but if it be feeble and indistinct, then the soul itself is forced to study it out carefully, and often is at a loss to determine whether it is the seal of God or not; and others are in the same state of suspense. Hence if we would experience the benefits of being sealed, we must grow in grace and in conformity to Christ. There is no peace to the wicked nor to those who live so near to the confines of sin that they cannot tell to which kingdom they belong.

2. The whole tendency of this doctrine is to humble, to elevate, to wean from the world, to render us content with our lot, and to induce us to live as becomes the children of God. No matter how poor, how despised or how afflicted a man may be, if he bears on his forehead the seal of God, he is a king and a priest.

LVII. The Holy Ghost as the Paraclete. John 14: 16.

[April 8th, 1860.]

Circumstances under which the promise of the Spirit as our Paraclete was made. Its design was to encourage the apostles and to sustain them under the loss of Christ's presence.

The promise had special but not exclusive reference to the apostles. The Spirit was to do for them a two-fold work; one which contemplated them as believers, the other which contemplated them as apostles.

I. *The meaning of the promise.*

The word παράκλητος, as an adjective, means *called* for; as a substantive, one called upon for aid, as an advocate, called to one's side. The most comprehensive meaning of the word is *helper.* The Holy Ghost is our helper.

II. *His qualifications.*

1. He is omnipotent. 2. He is Almighty. 3. Infinite in wisdom. 4. Infinite in love. 5. Ever accessible and willing to help. 6. He is the Spirit of Christ, united to him and to his people, and in one sense is the principle of life in both.

III. *How the Spirit acts as our helper.*

A. TO THE APOSTLES.

1. In bringing all things to their remembrance.

2. In rendering them infallible.

3. In conferring upon them the peculiar gifts of office, courage, παῤῥησία (boldness of speech,) patience, zeal, &c.

4. In co-operating with them miraculously, so as to confirm their divine mission and authority.

5. In attending their preaching with power, so as to render it effectual.

B. TO BELIEVERS, INDIVIDUALLY.

1. As a teacher leading them in the knowledge of the truth. *a.* By regeneration, imparting life and the power of vision; *b.* By illumination; *c.* By aiding them in their mental operations; *d.* By bringing things to their remembrance and thus acting as a counsellor.

2. As a source of strength. *a.* Strengthening the principle of life by his constant communications. He strengthens our faith, love, &c. *b.* By giving the requisite qualifications for duty. For private, social and official duties. *c.* By sustaining us under discouragements and trials.

3. As a comforter. This is specially prominent because this is what the apostles specially needed, and what all believers as an afflicted people ever need. *a.* The Spirit comforts by assuring us of the love of God. *b.* By revealing to us the infinite glories and blessedness in reserve for us. *c.* By calming our agitations and shedding abroad in our hearts the fear of God. *d.* By calling into exercise those Christian graces which in themselves include true blessedness.

4. As an intercessor. *a.* He brings to God. To whom through Christ we have access by the Spirit. *b.* He indites our petitions. *c.* He excites desires which cannot be uttered in words, but which God understands and hears.

5. As the revealer of Christ. He takes of the things of Christ and shows them unto us. *a.* He reveals the glory of Christ. *b.* He reveals to us his work and offices, and our relation to him. *c.* He reveals Christ's love to us.

C. TO THE CHURCH.

1. As the bond of union. They are one body through the Spirit. 2. By causing them to recognize, love, serve and help each other. 3. By making the word, sacraments and preaching means of grace, and of the conversion, enlarging and edifying of the Church. 4. By calling to the ministry, and giving the gifts for the office.

IV. *Our special duty to the Spirit as the Paraclete.*

1. To feel and acknowledge our entire dependence. 2. To desire and earnestly seek his aid. 3. To avoid every thing by which he can be grieved or his influence quenched.

LVIII. Grieve not the Spirit.

[*September 15th*, 1861.]

I. *Principles on which the language of Scripture is to be interpreted.*

1. We must not attribute to God the imperfections or limitations which belong to our own natures. When God is said to love, to be angry, or to be grieved, we are not to suppose that God is subject to any agitation, much less to any painful emotion.

2. We must not leave the language vague or meaningless. To speak of an unconscious power or principle or law being angry or grieved, would be either a positive personification or meaningless. Such language when used of God is intended to give us definite knowledge, and such knowledge is trustworthy. All that it necessarily implies is to be received as certainly true.

II. *The subject above announced implies,*—1st, tnat the Holy Ghost is a person; that he is intelligent, self-conscious, and as such, not only an agent but the object of agency. That he is capable of being loved, obeyed, or disobeyed; that his approbation and favor may be won or lost.

2. It implies that the Spirit stands in an intimate relation to us, so as to be the object of our action; not only cognizant of our conduct, but so to speak affected by it in so far as his agency or operation toward us is measurably determined by our character and conduct.

3. This language implies or assumes what is elsewhere explicitly taught in the Scriptures, viz.: that the Spirit of God is the source of all life and activity in the universe. And more especially of all spiritual life. He is not only omnipresent and everywhere active in the world of mind and of matter, but he dwells in every believer individually and in the Church collectively, as the source of life and of all good. Consequently we are ever in his presence, and he is ever present with us. He knows our thoughts. He feels our emotions. He takes cognizance of every word, act and look.

III. *Such being the nature of the Holy Spirit and the relation in which he stands to us, it follows that any thing inconsistent with his nature or which tends to oppose his works in us or others must grieve him*—That is, it is, on the one hand, so far as we are concerned, an offence of the same nature as grieving a parent, a benefactor, would be; and on the other, it determines him to act towards us as an offended and wounded love leads a wise and holy parent to act towards a child. He withdraws his influences. He leaves us to ourselves. This dereliction, if final and entire, would be eternal perdition. As the Holy Ghost in his relation to us is set forth as the Spirit of truth, of holiness, of love, of consolation, and of glory, it follows,

1. That what is contrary to truth grieves the Spirit of truth. Not only what is opposed to veracity in word or act, but especially what is opposed to the truth as revealed by God. *a.* Want of faith, or submission to the truth in our own minds, all unbelief or scepticism. *b.* All endeavors to pervert the truth in the minds of individuals. *c.* All heresy and false doctrine in the Church.

2. Everything impure or unholy; cherishing impure or unholy feelings in our hearts; exciting them in the hearts of others. This is represented as a sacrilege or desecration of the temple of God.

3. All irreverence, ingratitude or disobedience toward God, and all malignant or unamiable feeling or conduct toward our fellow-men, all disposition or conduct which tends to disturb the peace of the family, of the community, of the Church, or of the world, is opposed to the Spirit of love, who is thereby also the Spirit of peace.

4. So all that tends to produce misery or distress is opposed to him who is the Comforter.

IV. *We should not grieve the Spirit,*

1. Because he is a divine person. 2. Because we are so greatly his debtors. 3. Because he loves us and all his purposes and activities regarding us tend to our good. 4. Because we are absolutely dependent upon him for truth, holiness, and salvation. If he depart from us we perish forever.

IV.

SATAN AND HIS INFLUENCE—SIN AND SINS.

LIX. Satanic Influence.

[*Nov. 24th*, 1861.]

I. *There is such a thing.*

That the Scriptures speak of such a being as Satan, and attribute a certain influence to him is certain. This is not to be understood as a figurative mode of speaking of the principle of evil in the world and in the hearts of men, nor is it an accommodation to Jewish notions and forms of opinion.

1. Because of the principle that we must understand the Scriptures according to their historical sense.

2. Because the rule of interpretation which gets rid of the doctrine of Satan and his influence, if carried out, would blot all the peculiar doctrines of the Scripture from the Bible. It has been so applied, to explain away the doctrines of sacrifice, justification, heaven and hell.

3. Because the attributes and acts of a personal being are so ascribed to Satan as to render it certain that the sacred penman did believe him to be a personal being.

II. *What the Scriptures teach concerning the sphere of his power.*

1. They ascribe to him great power and authority over other fallen spirits.

2. They ascribe to him power in the world and over the world. He is the god of the world. This means, *a.* that he controls the men of the world. *b.* That the aims, ends and agency of the world tend to the promotion of his kingdom. *c.* That this service and subjection, although unintentional and ignorantly rendered, are of the nature of homage. Paul thus teaches that idolaters are worshippers of demons. The things which they sacrifice they sacrifice to devils.

3. They ascribe to him a power over the souls of men, controlling in

the children of disobedience, harassing and impeding in the children of God.

4. That the whole power of Satan over spirits, over the world and over the souls of men, is exerted against God and his kingdom. It is exerted in promoting evil and counteracting good. In individual men, in promoting error, in blinding the mind to the truth, in fostering unbelief, in exciting evil passions, in tempting to sin, as in the cases of Judas and Ananias; and in leading to despair.

III. *As to its nature.*

1. The Scriptures declare it to be exceeding great. 2. It is in the highest degree subtle, as in the temptation of Eve and in the temptation of Christ. He transforms himself into an angel of light.

3. It is inscrutable as to its mode, as we know not how one spirit operates on another.

4. But it must be congruous to the nature of the soul. *a.* Because it is described as a deceiving, as a seducing, as a tempting. *b.* Because it can be resisted. *c.* Because it is never represented as lessening the guilt of his victims.

5. As it is the power of a creature and of his subordinates, it is not almighty; neither is it ubiquitous. We know not the relations of spirits to space nor what limitations are placed on their activity. We only know that Satan is finite and therefore not everywhere.

IV. *This power of Satan should be resisted.*

1. Not in our own power, but in the power of the Lord. This means *a.* That the power of resistance is derived from the Lord. *b.* That it is the Lord's own almighty power exerted through us, as in miracles.

2. The means of resistance are not our own weapons, but the armor offensive and defensive of God. *a.* The breast-plate of righteousness. *b.* The girdle of truth. *c.* The shield of faith. *d.* The helmet of salvation. *e.* The sword of the Spirit. All are made available and brought into exercise by incessant prayers.

V. *The issue of the conflict is not uncertain.*—Christ has bruised Satan under our feet. If we resist in the strength of the Lord and in the use of his armor, we shall conquer. If we do not resist, or if this resistance is in our own strength or with our own weapons, we shall perish.

LX. Temptation.

[*Nov. 30th,* 1862.]

Its nature; its sources; the means of resistance; its uses.

I. *The nature of the temptation.*

To tempt is to try. We tempt a person when we put him to the test. This may be done, 1. To see what he will do, as when men tempt God. They put his patience, his power, his fidelity to the test; or call upon him for proof of his being what he is. 2. To show what is in the person tempted, as when God tempts man. Thus God tempted Abraham and is represented as trying his people, to bring their faith or patience into exercise and to render them conspicuous for the benefit of others. 3. This tempting may have for its object to lead into sin, as when Satan tempted Eve, Christ, and the wicked at all times. It is this latter kind of temptation: viz: solicitation to evil, that attention is now to be directed.

II. *Sources of such temptations.*

These, according to Scripture, are the world, the flesh and the devil.

1. The world, which includes men and all earthly things. First, the world presents the objects of our natural affections and desires. Secondly, it presents objects to excite inordinate or unholy affections and desires. It holds up to wealth its honors, its pleasures for our pursuit, and by them the great majority of men are led into perdition. Thirdly, the world tempts as much by its threats as by its solicitations. It threatens contempt, neglect, persecution, hatred. Fourthly, the men of the world seduce by their example and their principles, by their arguments and persuasions, by their denunciations and wrath.

2. The flesh, *i. e.*, our corrupt nature, the evil heart, the remains of sin. This is the impelling power, the proximate power which leads to sin. So far as the world is concerned it has little or no power, except so far as it tends to excite what is evil. This is not intended to intimate that a holy nature may not be tempted, as were Adam and Christ. But simply that the power of what is outward to lead into sin depends mainly on the evil that is within. Every man is tempted when he is drawn away by his own lust and enticed. This term, lust, includes, 1st, the desires or appetites of the body; 2d, the evil dispositions of the mind, pride, envy, malice, vanity, &c.

3. The devil. He is the great tempter. He tempted our first parents, David, Judas, Christ, Ananias and Sapphira. He tempts the children of disobedience and the people of God. They are cautioned against his devices and called upon to resist his machinations. With regard to the temptations of Satan, it is certain, first, that he does tempt the children of men; all men; us as well as others. Secondly, how he does this we do not know. Thirdly, we cannot distinguish between his temptations and the suggestions of our own evil hearts, any more than we can between the leading of the Spirit and our own exercises. Fourthly, the temptations of Satan are subtle, powerful and greatly to be dreaded; not to be despised or made light of. Most men are led captive by him at his will.

Besides these general sources of temptation common to all men, there are others peculiar to particular times of life—youth, manhood and age; to particular seasons, as of prosperity and of adversity; to particular professions, etc.

III. *Means of resisting temptation.* These are not the precepts of Philosophy, which prescribe the means of cultivating virtue. They are all supernatural or divine.

1. Watch and pray lest ye fall into temptation. Exercise the utmost care against the occasions and the beginnings of evil, and constantly look to God to protect you from being tempted, and to deliver you when temptation comes. He has taught us to say daily, Lead us not into temptation.

2. Another means is instant resistance. Let there be no dallying with evil. This is applicable to all kinds of temptation.

3. Faith in Christ, *i. e.*, believing appeals to him as our Saviour, our King to protect us from all our spiritual enemies.

IV. *Uses of temptation.*

1. They teach us our weakness and reveal the depravity that is within us.

2. They teach us to depend on God.

3. They exercise and strengthen our graces.

4. They qualify us to sympathize with others and to aid them.

LXI. Indwelling Sin.

[*March 4th*, 1855.]

I. *Importance of the subject.*

Redemption is deliverance from sin. Hence, the theory of redemption is determined by the theory of sin. 2. The practical application of redemption is determined by the sense of sin. That is, both our theology and our religion are determined by our views of sin.

As to theory. If there is no sin then there is no redemption. 2. If sin consists merely in action and is easy or possible to be avoided, then, redemption is a small matter. 3. But if sin is a great, certain, universal and unconquerable, and incurable corruption of our nature, this redemption is the work of God.

As to practice. It is a matter of fact that the religious experience of every man is determined by his view of sin. It is his sense of guilt and pollution which leads him to look to God for help, and of course the kind of help he seeks, and is willing to accept, depends upon his views of his sinfulness. All genuine religious experience consists in the conformity of our convictions and feelings with the truth of God.

II. *Nature of indwelling sin.*

1. What the Scriptures teach on this subject is the entire and universal corruption of our nature.

2. That this innate inherent, hereditary corruption manifests itself in all forms of actual sin, as a tree is known by its fruits.

3. That regeneration consists in creation of a new principle, a germ of spiritual life, and not in the absolute destruction and removal of this inherent corruption.

4. That consequently in the renewed there are two conflicting principles, sin and grace, the law of sin and the law of the mind.

5. That this remaining hereditary corruption, as modified and strengthened by our actual sins, is what is meant by indwelling sin.

III. *The proof of this.* 1. The plain declarations of the Scriptures, which everywhere teach not only that the renewed fall into actual sins, but also that they are burdened and polluted by indwelling corruption.

2. Our own consciousness and experience, which reveals to us the existence of this abiding evil; conscience upbraiding us not only for actual sins but also for the permanent, immanent state of our hearts in the sight of God.

3. The recorded experience of the Church in all ages; so that we must separate ourselves from the experience of God's people to deny this.

IV. *The great evil of indwelling sin.*

1. It is in itself of greater turpitude than mere individual acts. Pride is worse than acts of haughtiness or arrogance; so of malice, want of love of God, unbelief, the absence of love and of all right affections. It is this abysmal evil which humbles, burdens and oppresses the soul and forces it to look to Christ for deliverance.

2. It is a fruitful source of actual sins.

3. It is beyond the reach of the will and can only be subdued by the grace of God, in the use of the divinely appointed means.

V. *These means are the Word, sacraments and prayer.* By the assiduous use of these means the principle of evil is weakened and the principle of grace is strengthened.

2. By acts of faith on Christ, who is said to dwell in our hearts by faith.

3. By mortification; not asceticism, but refusing to gratify evil proensities and keeping under the body.

LXII. Indwelling Sin.

[*Sept. 17th*, 1866.]

No subject is more difficult than that of sin. Concerning no other have there been so many controversies. And in none other have those controversies been so persistent. They are renewed with every generation.

There are two ways of looking at the subject, two guides assumed in the study of it. The one, philosophy or human reason, the maxims of morals; the other, the Scriptures, with which Christian experience always concurs. Often men adopt a principle in the philosophy of morals which seems clear to the understanding, which they find does not accord with their experience, and which the Scriptures do not recognize. And they feel they must renounce one or the other guide.

I. *Sin, as determined by the Scriptures, and by experience of Christians, is want of conformity to the standard of right.* That standard is the nature and law of God. Sin, or sinfulness may be predicated,

1. Of acts; 2 Of feelings; 3. Of volitions, specific or generic; 4. Of dispositions; 5. Of innate and immanent states of the mind.

II. *Indwelling sin belongs only to the fourth and fifth classes.* That is what is meant by indwelling sin is the original, inherent, hereditary corruption of our nature, and those modifications of this natural corruption induced by the habits of the individual. Or, it may be said to be inherent corruption as it exists in any individual.

III. *The Scriptures teach,* 1. Not only that all men sin; not only that all are under influences which render their sinning certain; but that the nature itself is corrupt or sinful. It is not such as God made. It is not conformed to his nature and law. It is not such as it ought to be.

2. That Regeneration consists in the production, not of new acts, nor of new views, feelings and purposes, but of a new principle antagonistic to the principle of depravity.

3. That Regeneration does not destroy the principle of evil, which remains, although weakened and counteracted.

4. That these two principles, the flesh and the Spirit, the law of the mind and the law in the members are in constant conflict.

5. That the new principle is generally victorious, constantly increases in strength and constitutes the character. It has on its side God, his Word, his Spirit, reason, conscience and the will. Against it are arraigned the world, the flesh and the devil.

6. That the new principle does not always prevail as to specific acts, and never as to complete conformity to the will of God.

7. That the final and complete victory of the new principle is certain. We are not engaged in a doubtful or hopeless conflict.

8. This victory is due not to us, not to the strength of the new principle, but to Christ by his Spirit, who works in us to will and to do.

IV. *This victory is conditioned on our part,* 1. By constant watchfulness. 2. By constant effort directed and guided by the word of God.

3. By constant penitence. 4. By constant faith. 5. By constant use of the means, including the whole panoply of God.

V. *The practical conclusion is* that we are infected with a mortal disease which can be kept in check and ultimately eradicated only by the most assiduous care and by the faithful adherence to the prescriptions of the Great Physician. But with care and through his power and skill we are sure to be restored not only to the paradisiacal health and beauty but to the full conformity to the image of Christ, and crowned with the wreath of victory. Those who are thus crowned are those who come out of great tribulation and conflict.

LXIII. The Deceitfulness of Sin.

[*April* 3*d*, 1853.]

Either the latter, sin, qualifies the former, *a being deceived*, which is sinful, *i. e.*, for which we are guilty; or, the first word qualifies the second, *sin that is deceitful.* Compare the expressions, deceitfulness of riches, of unrighteousness, of lusts. The latter is the better sense. The subject for consideration is the characteristic of sin as deceitful.

I. *Sin is not an act but a power, a principle, something innate, indwelling, permanent and active,* an enemy of the most dangerous kind, not only because it is within and ever on the alert and powerful, and has so many allies, but also because it is so treacherous.

II. *How is sin deceitful?*

1. It deceives us as to what is sinful, as in the case of Adam. So also in the case of thousands.

2. It deceives us as to its demands. It promises to be satisfied with a limited indulgence. So the slothful, the negligent, the sensual, the avaricious. *It is the first step that costs.*

3. It deceives as to the pleasure it promises. Adam expected to be like God.

4. It deceives us as to the true motives which determine our conduct. Ministers, missionaries, as well as others are thus deceived.

5. It deceives us as to its effects and to the degree of impunity with which it can be indulged.

III. *The effects of sin as thus deceitful.*

1. It hardens. That is, *a.* as to the will it renders it stiff and fixed. It becomes settled in evil. *b.* As to the feelings it renders them obdurate. Motives cease to affect, the conscience to warn or reprove, and the result is a reprobate mind.

2. It slays or destroys the soul. *a.* In destroying its sensibility. *b.* In destroying desire and hope of amendment. *c.* In bringing it fully under the power of the law.

IV. *Means of safety.* The preliminary conditions are, 1. A sense of danger. 2. A sense of weakness. The means are, 1. Committing ourselves to Christ and his Spirit. To be guided by his wisdom. To regard nothing as innocent or harmless which he condemns.

2. To resist the beginning and first suggestions.

3. In doubtful cases always to go against what may be evil.

LXIV. The Sin of Unbelief.

[*March 4th*, 1866.]

There are three general forms of unbelief.

1. That of scepticism, either doubting or rejecting the truths of religion and morals in general, or the divine origin and authority of the Bible in particular. Such persons are called sceptics or infidels.

2. Want of faith and confidence in God, in his promises and providence, which may and often does co-exist with a speculative belief of the Scriptures.

3. The rejection or failure to receive the Lord Jesus Christ as he is revealed and offered in the Bible, as when our Lord said the Spirit would convince men of sin, because they believe not on him.

These several forms of unbelief, although they have their common source in an evil heart, have, nevertheless, their specific causes and their peculiar form of guilt.

I. *Scepticism.* This arises,

1. From pride of intellect; assuming to know what is beyond our reach and refusing to receive what we cannot understand; setting ourselves up as capable of discerning and proving all truth.

2. From the neglect of our moral nature and giving up ourselves to the guidance of the speculative reason.

3. From the enmity of the heart to the things of God; or opposition in our tastes, feelings, desires and purposes, to the truths and requirements of the things of religion.

4. From frivolous vanity; or the desire to be thought independent or upon a par with the illuminate.

The sinfulness of this form of unbelief is manifest; first, as pride, self-exaltation is sinful and offensive in such a feeble insignificant creature as man.

Secondly, as the habitude of the moral nature which makes it possible to believe a lie, is evidence of moral degradation.

Thirdly, as opposition to the truth, is opposition to the God of truth. It is alienation from him, in which all sin consists. Hence unbelief is the generic form of sin. It is the general expression of aberration, and the opposition of our nature to his. It is, therefore, the source of all other sins.

II. *Unbelief, or want of confidence in the doctrines, the promises and providence of God.* This may exist in even the hearts of believers. It is a matter of degree. It arises either—

1. From the entire absence or from the low state of the religious life.

2. Or from the habit of looking at ourselves and on difficulties about us rather than at God. 3. Or from refusing to believe what we do not see. If God does not manifest his care, does not at once fulfil his promise, then our faith fails.

The sinfulness of this state of mind is apparent, 1. Because it evinces a low state of the divine life. It is the evidence and effect of spiritual weakness and disease. 2. Because it dishonors God, refusing to him the confidence due to an earthly friend and parent; which is a very heinous offense, considering his greatness and goodness, and the evidences which he has given of his fidelity and trustworthiness. 3. Because it is a manifestation of the same spirit which dominates in the open infidel. It is unbelief in a form which it assumes in a mind in which it has not absolute control. But it is in all its manifestations hateful to God.

III. *Unbelief in reference to Christ.*

This is a refusing to recognize and receive him as being what he claims to be. 1. As God manifest in the flesh. 2. As the messenger and teacher sent from God. 3. As our atoning sacrifice and priest. 4. As having rightfully absolute proprietorship in us and authority over us. This is the greatest of sins. It is the condemning sin. Its heinousness consists, 1. In its opposition to the clearest light. He who cannot see the sun, must be stone blind. He who cannot see the glory of God in the face of Jesus Christ must be blinded by Satan. This blindness is moral, religious, and spiritual deadness.

2. It is the rejection of the clearest external evidence, which evinces the opposition of the heart.

3. It is the rejection of infinite love, and the disregard of the greatest obligation.

4. It is the deliberate preference of the kingdom of Satan before that of Christ,—of Belial to Christ.

LXV. Doubting in Believers.

[*Jan. 25th,* 1857.]

Doubting is hesitation in believing. It implies uncertainty. It is therefore opposed at once to unbelief and to assurance.

I. *Believers are often in this state of mind.*

1. As to the truth which God has revealed. *a.* For example, as to the divine origin of the Scriptures ; or admitting that, the inspiration of the Word of God. *b.* Or as to some one or more of its doctrines, the divinity of Jesus Christ, the constitution of his person, the nature of his work, the personality and work of the Spirit, the divine providence, etc., etc.

2. They are often doubtful, *i. e.*, distrustful of the divine promises, either in reference to themselves or others.

3. Or they are doubtful as to his providence, afraid to commit themselves to his care.

4. They are often doubtful as to their good estate. These doubts are sometimes reasonable and sometimes unreasonable.

II. *They are reasonable, when there is real ground for doubt.* So long as a believer is in a state which affords little evidence either to himself or others of his reconciliation, it is only right that he should doubt. To be without doubts under such circumstances is carnal security. Such doubts are unreasonable and offensive to God,

1. When they arise from a self-righteous spirit. That is, when they arise from the impression that something to be done or experienced by us is necessary to our acceptance with God, or is required as a condition to be fulfilled before we can venture to believe.

2. When they arise from a distrust of the entire freeness of salvation. This is only stating the same cause in another form.

3. When they arise from a distrust of the merit of Christ, as though our sins were too great to be forgiven.

4. Or from distrust of the love of God to us. We can believe that God's grace is sovereign ; or that he loves others, even sinners, but for some reason we cannot believe that he loves us. This, however, is the precise thing which we are required to believe.

5. A very common source of these doubts is the disproportionate influence of the subjective truths of the gospel, as compared to the objective truths, the anthropological as distinguished from the soteriological doctrine.

The former relate to man's nature before conversion and after it. If a man is always pondering over what is in himself instead of looking to Christ; if his hope rests on evidence of regeneration which he can see in his own heart rather than on the work of Christ, he will of necessity often be in doubt. This is illustrated not only in individuals but in churches or communities.

III. *The cure of these doubts.*

1. As to sceptical doubts, the cure is to be found, *a.* In a due practical understanding of the true ground of faith. If a man believes only what he understands, what he can vindicate from objections, what

he can clear up to his own mind and prove to be true, he will never have any peace. Faith does not stand in wisdom but in the power of God. We must bring ourselves to believe simply on the authority of God, *i. e.*, on the testimony of his Word and Spirit. *b*. We must remember that faith is a grace; something supernatural; something which we are to receive and not achieve for ourselves. And therefore we must seek it as an undeserved favor.

2. As to doubts in the promises and providence of God. The only cure is to be sought in *growth* in grace, which will give strength to the inward principle of faith. That particular principle may be cherished by the prayerful study of God's word, observing the abundance of wisdom which it affords of his faithfulness and care. And as to distrust of Providence, as it commonly arises from undue solicitude about our comfort in this world, the cure for it is to be satisfied with heavenly things.

3. As to doubts of our personal salvation. They arise, *a*. From the fact not only that we are so imperfect, so unworthy, so cold, so remiss, (these should produce sorrow and humility, but not doubt), but that we deliberately sin; that we do things which our conscience condemns and continue to do them. This being the case there can be no rational or scriptural peace or hope, unless we renounce those sins.

b. From mistakes of the evidence of regeneration or from having our attention directed to ourselves rather than to Christ.

c. From obscure views of the plan of salvation. The cure is to be sought in cherishing correct views on this point.

LXVI. Hardness of Heart.—Ps. 31: 12; Rom. 2: 5.

[*Nov. 10th*, 1861.]

The Scriptures do not teach philosophy, but a philosophy underlies them. Philosophy is only the scientific explanation and arrangement of the facts of consciousness and the laws of our constitution which those facts reveal. The Scriptures, coming from the author of our constitution, are consistent with those facts and assume those laws. The Scriptures, therefore, recognize the soul as one. They have no name exclusively devoted to the several faculties. The same word is used of the intellect and of the seat of the affections.

The thoughts of the heart, the blindness of the heart, are familiar representations. The heart therefore here is the soul. Its obduracy is a state, not of one faculty, but of all. The same word is sometimes translated to blind and sometimes to harden. As there are two words πῶρος (poros,) a stone, and πώρωσις (porosis,) blindness or hardness. Mark iii: 5; Rom. xi: 25.

II. *The hardness therefore of which the Scriptures speak is,*

1. Not mere callousness or insensibility of feeling.

2. But also the blindness of the mind.

3. Fixedness of the will in opposition to God and his truth.

It is of course a matter of degrees. *a.* Disobedience and secret opposition to the truth. *b.* Zealous opposition and hatred of it, manifesting itself at length in blasphemy and persecution.

III. *This hardness is a sinful state.*

1. From its very nature.

2. In its higher form it is the state or character of the lost and of Satan.

3. It is self-induced; *a.* As it is the natural result or effect of our depravity. *b.* As it is the consequence, *i. e.*, the natural consequence of the indulgence of sin. As the natural consequence of the cultivation of virtue, is virtue; of kindness, is kindness; of tenderness, is tenderness; so the natural consequence of the indulgence of sin is-sin,—a sinful hardness of heart.

IV. *It is none the less a divine judgment and a premonition of reprobation.* Any degree of it is reason to fear such reprobation. The higher forms of it are direct evidence of it.

1. It is attributed to God who is said to harden the hearts of men, as we attribute the results of an agent's acts to the agent himself. We say a father ruins a child. By this we mean that the ruin is the natural effect of the father's conduct. It need not be intended.

In case of God, let it be observed,

1. That God exerts no efficiency in hardening the hearts of sinners, as he does in working grace in men.

2. But it is a punitive withdrawing of the Spirit; the inevitable result of which is obduracy. God determined to let Pharaoh alone, and the result was what it was.

V. *This hardness is,*

1. Beyond the reach of argument, or motive, or discipline, or culture.

2. It is beyond our own power to cure or to remove. It is, therefore, *a.* To be greatly dreaded. *b.* It is to be withstood and operated against. *c.* It is to be prayed against. *d.* It is to be avoided by avoiding grieving and quenching the Holy Spirit.

LXVII. Pride.

[*December 4th*, 1853.]

I. Its general nature. II. Its different forms. III. Its guilt. IV. Its causes and cure.

I. *Its general nature.*

It is an overestimate of ourselves; our own powers, merit or importance. It is a sentiment or feeling. It designates a state of mind and not of the outward bearing. The manifestation of pride in look, language or deportment, is arrogance. Vanity is nearly related to pride, but is very different. It is the desire of admiration. It is something light and trivial, as its etymology indicates. The vain man is often amiable: the proud man is malignant.

II. *The different forms of pride.*

1. When it arises from some outward distinction, as ancestry, title, office, wealth.

2. When it arises from mental superiority, real or supposed. This is intellectual pride, which may be manifested towards God, or is evinced in an undue reliance on human reason and an unwillingness to submit to the mysteries of divine revelation. Of this the apostle speaks when he says every proud thought and high imagination must be brought low to the obedience of the faith. And our Saviour speaks of it when he says, we must be converted and become as little children. This intellectual pride is the characteristic of the Greeks, of Rationalists, of philosophers, and one of the great evils which beset every student of the Bible.

3. When it arises from an undue estimate of our own goodness. This is spiritual pride. We have its type in the Jews, especially the Pharisees, who regarded themselves as so much better than other men, and said, "Stand by, for I am holier than thou!" It lurks in every heart. We are disposed to compare ourselves with others and think ourselves better than others, more conscientious, more faithful, more holy. Even our most sacred experiences are apt to be attended by a rising feeling of self-complacency, and pride gathers food even from humility, and makes self-abasement a means of self-exaltation.

III. *Its moral hatefulness and guilt.*

1. It is a lie. It is a falsehood, *i. e.*, false estimate of ourselves.

2. It is irreligious in its essence. It is the substitution and exaltation of self in the place of God.

3. It is diabolical, both because it was the sin of Satan, and because it allies us to Satan. The most Satanic men are proud, malignant men.

4. It is essentially selfish, making self supreme, exalting it above our equals and superiors, and even above and against God.

5. It is on all these accounts specially hateful in itself and in the sight of God, as is evinced: *a.* By the frequent and severe denunciations of it in the Bible. *b.* By the opposite state of mind being made essential to salvation. *c.* By the whole plan of redemption in its provisions and administration being designed to abase the pride of men.

IV. *Its causes and cure.*

1. It arises from ignorance and apostacy from God, and from false standards of excellence.

2. Its cure is, *a.* A due sense of our insignificance and dependence. *b.* A due sense of our unworthiness. *c.* Being filled with due apprehensions of the glory of God.

Subordinate means. 1. Always humble yourselves, *i. e.*, never seek exaltation or honor or praise.

2. Do not dwell on your own superiority, real or imaginary.

3. Condescend to men of low estate.

4. Seek not your own but the things of Jesus Christ, and how you may do good to others.

LXVIII. Spiritual Pride.

[*October* 16*th*, 1864.]

I. *Pride is undue self-estimation.* It is thinking of ourselves more highly than we ought to think. Vanity is the disposition to seek applause, to delight in it. The one excites condemnation; the other, contempt.

This undue self-estimation may be manifested and cherished on various grounds, as, 1. Personal advantages. 2. Intellectual superiority. 3. Social position. 4. Correctness of conduct, of opinion, or religious attainment.'

That form of pride which is called spiritual is so called not because it has its seat in the spirit or soul, as distinguished from what is sensual; much less because it arises from the Spirit, but because it relates to spiritual things.

There are two forms of this evil. The one is Pharisaism; the other is assumption of superiority in spiritual attainments. These agree in that under both forms it leads its subjects to say, "Stand by, for I am holier than thou." "Lord, I thank thee that I am not as this publican." But they differ essentially in their grounds and in their character.

The spiritual pride of the Pharisees rested on the assumption that they, irrespective of their personal character, in virtue of their descent and their membership in the theocracy, were the favorites of heaven. Where an order of nobility exists, those who belong to it feel superior to other classes of society, and are recognized and looked up to as such, not because of their personal qualities, exterior, intellectual, or moral, but simply because they belong to a privileged class, to a higher order of men than the masses.

So the Pharisees held that because they were the children of Abraham, and of the commonwealth of Israel, they were the favorites of heaven, secure of pardon, exaltation, dominion and eternal life. They were holy; other men were common, sinners, profane, in no respect worthy of being placed upon an equality with themselves. They were not to be admitted to their peculiar privileges. They were but dogs, who should be satisfied to eat of the crumbs which fell from the tables of the Jews.

In like manner, those who regard the Church as an external society, of a given organization, to which the promises of God exclusively belong, as is done by Romanists and Anglicans, regard themselves in virtue of membership in that Church the favorites of God, the exclusive and certain heirs of the blessings of salvation. All other men are out of the ark, out of the pale, left to uncovenanted mercies, having no assured portion in the blessings promised to the Church. This is High Churchism.

It is to be remarked, however, that the sense of superiority founded on the external relations, always generates the belief of inward personal superiority. The noble feels that he, as a man, is a higher order of man than the plebeian. The Pharisee or Jew felt that he was personally holier and better than the Gentile. And the Churchman has the same conviction with regard to the dissenter and the schismatic.

II. *The other form of spiritual pride is not founded on the external relations of its subject, but primarily on his outward state.* It is the assumption of personal superiority in the spiritual graces to other men. It is accompanied on the one hand with self-complacency and self-approbation; and on the other with depreciation and undervaluing of their fellow Christians or their fellow-men.

This may be nothing more than that false estimate which a man makes of his own character and his own merits, when unconvinced of sin. In this sense, every man who does not feel the need of a better righteousness than his own may be called spiritually proud and self-righteous.

But the term is more frequently used in reference to religious men, men who profess to be religious and who assume that their attainments in religion render them superior to their brethren and justify them in cherishing self-complacency in view of their spiritual state, and in looking down upon others.

In all its forms spiritual pride is one of the most offensive of sins. Christ placed the Pharisees below publicans and harlots. Their sin was of a higher order. It was a test of character. It formed a more fatal barrier to their entrance into heaven. This teaches that spiritual sins, as pride and malignancy, are more evil than mere sins of the flesh.

The reasons why pride is thus offensive are, 1. Because it is an utter falsehood. It is a false estimate.. It supposes that to be true which is not true. It supposes that we are what we are not.

2. Because it is founded on ignorance of God, of his law and of its requirements.

3. Because it is the opposite of the state of mind which becomes our true character and our true relation to God.

4. Because it is in its own nature offensive and disgusting for the loathsome to assume that it is attractive, the impotent that it is strong, the evil that it is good, the revolting that it is beautiful.

5. Because it is the source of malignity, contempt, cruelty and injustice.

LXIX. Ambition.

[*March 22d,* 1857.]

I. *What is it?* II. *Proof that it is evil.* III. *Means of cure.*

I. *Ambition is to be distinguished from the desire of excellence.* It is not to be confounded with the desire of approbation. Nor is it of the same nature with the simple desire of praise. It is specifically the desire to be first, to be above or before others, to be in fact better than they, to know more, to be able to do more, and to have that superiority known and acknowledged. This is only another form of the desire that others should be inferior, *i. e.,* below us in knowledge, in ability, in goodness, in station or power.

This principle is well nigh universal. It is manifested in all states of society and by all classes of men, in matters trivial and in matters of importance. Men are accustomed to speak of a holy ambition, or of a noble ambition, when the object for the mastery of which men strive is elevated and not evil or trivial. This desire being thus universal is natural. It is also, in one sense useful, *i. e.,* it is productive of incidental benefits, just as the desire for wealth leads to diligence, enterprise, frugality, self-denial, etc. But a principle may be both natural and incidentally useful, and yet evil.

II. *That ambition is evil in its nature, and therefore degrading in its influence, is evident,*

1. Because it is inconsistent with our relation to God as creatures. We are utterly insignificant in comparison with God, and even in the scale of creation. It implies a great deal of ignorance, a forgetfulness of what we are, to cherish this desire of pre-eminence. In this aspect ambition is ridiculous. It exposes us to the contempt of all intelligent beings.

2. It is inconsistent with our relation to God as sinners. A genuine sense of sin, a conviction of our guilt and pollution in the sight of God,

of necessity, leads to self-abasement and self-abhorrence. In this aspect ambition is disgusting.

3. Because Christ always reproved this desire of pre-eminence. He always taught that those who desired to be first should be last and least. This he did on various occasions; as when the two disciples, James and John, came to him to ask that they might sit at his right hand and at his left; and when there was a contention among them, who should be greatest.

4. This trait of character did not belong to Christ. He did not glorify himself. And we never conceive of him as animated by an ambitious spirit. He is the standard. To his image we are to be conformed. He was the meek and lowly Jesus.

5. We always approve of the opposite temper, whenever we see it manifested. The instinctive judgment of the mind condemns all self-seeking.

6. It is inconsistent with our being governed by right motives and affections. The love of God, the glory of Christ, the good of men, are the motives which should control the Christian; and just in proportion as we allow other and lower selfish motives to rule in our hearts, are we degraded and defiled.

III. *Means of cure.*

1. Cultivating a sense of our insignificance and unworthiness. The more we grow in grace and in the knowledge of ourselves, the more truly humble should we be.

2. Having our hearts filled with Christ. The more we know of him, the more we appreciate his excellence and claims, the less shall we desire to be great in ourselves.

3. By constantly refusing to yield to this evil desire, refusing to cherish it or to obey its dictates. By uniformly avoiding to seek the honor which comes from men.

LXX. The Sacrifice of the Wicked is Abomination.
Prov. 21: 27.

[*Oct. 2d*, 1864.]

A sacrifice is properly something slain and presented to God as an atonement for sin, or to propitiate his favor; then, any thing offered to God or done for him. What is here said is that the most sacred, solemn, and even commanded things, are an abomination when rendered or performed by the wicked. Not merely their indifferent actions (as ploughing), but their best actions; those done in obedience to God, out of a sense of religion or desire to secure forgiveness or favor, are hateful in the sight of God.

Abomination is that which excites loathing and disgust. It is applied to moral acts or character, that which excites a high degree of disapprobation and revulsion of mind.

By the wicked is often meant the immoral. But the word means the guilty, those worthy of punishment. It is opposed to the righteous. And as the Scriptures divide all men into the righteous and the wicked, those who do not belong to the one class belong to the other. The wicked are all the guilty, all who are unreconciled to God, who are still under his wrath and curse due to them for sin.

There are two great truths involved in the passage :

I. *That no outward service, however enjoined, is acceptable to God when the heart is not right.* The principle that God requires to be worshipped in spirit and in truth, is peculiar to the Bible. It does not belong to paganism, nor to corrupt forms of Christianity.

1. It stands opposed to all the religions of the heathen, in which the external act is alone regarded. The worship, the ritual, the discipline, are all a series of outward acts, which are assumed to be acceptable for their own sake ; as a gift relieves the poor by whomsoever or from whatsoever motive given.

2. It condemns the ritual worship of the Romish Church, its penances, its works of merit, all which are assumed to have a value independent of the views and feelings of the worshipper.

3. It condemns all formalism. That is, it teaches that we offend God when the service which we render him is rendered only from custom, from regard to public opinion, or is a mere service of the lips.

4. It shows how vain are the hopes of sinners who attempt to propitiate God by acts of benevolence even on their death-beds ; and also how vain the hopes of those who are inquiring the way of life and seeking salvation, when they rely on their prayers, or their efforts or their own works, in any form, as a means of propitiating God. All service rendered for a wrong object, from a bad motive, or in the abuse of a right frame of mind is an abomination to God. 1. As a God of truth, because the service professes one thing, and the one who renders it professes another. Or, what he does is of the nature of a lie, and of a lie to the God of truth. 2. As a God of holiness. Such hypocritical, insincere service is in its own nature offensive, as the professions of esteem, friendship or love to a fellow-creature, when they are insincere.

II. *The other great truth involved in this passage is the one expressed in the parallel proverb, " The ploughing of the wicked is sin."*—Sinfulness attaches to all they do. Not merely their transgressions of the law of God, not merely things in their own nature wrong, but acts in their own nature indifferent, are in their case sins, *i. e.*, acts offensive to God. Such are the representations of the Bible, and therefore in the sense intended, they must be true. Such representations, however, do not mean that indifferent acts are moral acts, that things which have no moral character have a moral character. This would be a contradiction in terms, and would offend the moral judgments of men. Such declarations of the Scriptures are intended to teach us, 1. That acts in themselves indifferent become sinful, or rather the agent sins in performing them, when he has not the right state of mind. There is no sin in eating when hungry, nor in ploughing. But a man sins in eating, and while he eats, if he does it without a sense of gratitude to God, the giver of all good. There is no sin in ploughing; but the man who ploughs or sows his field without a sense of his dependence on God, sins while he ploughs.

2. They are designed to teach us that a man out of favor with God, in rebellion against him, is judged and estimated by his abiding character, and not by his individual acts. A profligate son, or a rebel against his sovereign, is a wicked son or subject, whether he eats or sleeps, or whether he ploughs or sows. He is always, while persisting in his rebellion or disobedience, a just object of disapprobation and condemnation. So the sinner until reconciled to God is a sinner in all he does, whether his acts are in themselves indifferent, or in themselves right; whether they be acts of justice, benevolence, or religion. They are the acts of a sinner, and offensive to God.

This principle is often perverted. Men have taught that it was wrong for sinners to pray. This is absurd. It is better for an unconverted farmer to plough than not to plough. He would sin far more in the latter case than in the former. What he should do is to plough with the right spirit. So of prayer.

LXXI. Every idle word that men shall speak, they shall give account thereof in the day of judgment. Matt. 12: 36.

[*Nov. 4th*, 1860.]

The great truth here presented is that the words of men reveal their character and shall furnish the criterion by which that character is to be determined.

The word ἀργός (argos), rendered idle, is properly, unfruitful, useless, and by implication, evil. Our Lord had said that a word spoken against him should be forgiven, but he that speaketh against the Holy Ghost should never be forgiven. What was spoken determined character and destiny. Because a good tree bringeth forth good fruit, and an evil tree, evil fruit. So out of the abundance of the heart the mouth speaketh. For your words, therefore, ye shall be judged. The truth taught, therefore, is not the sin of frivolity. But, first, that the words of a man come from within, out of the heart. Secondly, for every evil word we shall have to render an account and shall be judged by them.

I. *Words reveal the character because they are determined by it.* The relation between words and thoughts is such that it is doubtful whether we can think without the use of words. They are the measure of thought. No nation and no individual rises above the language which it or he uses. A rude people have a rude language, so far as its vocabulary is concerned. If of nations, so also of individuals.

Not only does language reflect thought, but it is much the vehicle of feeling and is determined by it.

Words of blasphemy or irreverence; words of malice, of satire, of contempt; words of pride and vain-glory; words of impurity; words of falsehood and treachery; words of folly and nonsense;—all these reveal what the man is. They determine his character. They are to the man what foliage, flowers, fragrance and fruit are to plants.

II. *For these he shall give account.* Men are not to have their destiny determined by their birth in this or that nation or church, as the Jews thought. They are not to be judged only for or by their acts or works. It is not only the drunkard, murderer or thief who is to be condemned, and not only the man who does what is right and benevolent who shall be justified; but words are as true an index of character, and therefore as proper a ground of judgment as outward acts. The Saviour doesn't mean that words are the ground on which a man shall be justified, but they are evidence of his character. It is ἐκ τῶν λόγων σου, *out of thy words* shalt thou be justified or condemned. "Out of thine own mouth will I judge thee." The words spoken were not the ground of judgment, but the evidence of guilt.

III. *The vast importance of our words.*

1. Because they are determined by our character and therefore reveal it.

2. Because they react on character and confirm it. Hence the importance of the use of words in prayer and praise.

3. Because they are clothed with a mysterious power for good or evil on our fellow-men.

Men are represented as temples of the Holy Ghost, and of Christ. Every idle word we utter in their hearing tends to defile that temple whether they be words of error or words which excite evil thoughts and feeling.

1. The greater part of our influence for good or evil is due to words. The apostle James said that if a man offend not in word, he is a perfect man. The tongue governs. The tongue is a world of iniquity. It defileth the whole body. It sets on fire the course of nature. It is set on fire of hell.

2. The tongue is unruly. All holy men set a guard upon their lips, that they offend not with their tongue. We have two great duties to form.

1. To destroy the principle of evil.

2. To prevent the manifestation of evil.

We must make the tree good.

In spiritual things to prevent the manifestation of a principle tends to destroy it. He who never utters words of anger, destroys the disposition. He who will never speak falsehood destroys the disposition to deceive. So of malevolence, detraction, etc.

LXXII. Cleanse thou me from secret faults. Ps. 19: 12.

[Oct. 19th, 1856.]

The scriptural idea of sin is the want of conformity of any act, state or feeling with the law of God. This assumes ;

1. That the standard of judging is not reason, nor expediency ; but the law of God, and that law, not as it exists in our knowledge, or in our misconceptions, but as it is in itself.

2. That in order to sin, there is no necessity of an intention to sin; that is, of a purpose to go counter to the will of God. These would be presumptuous sins.

3. That it is not necessary that we should know that a thing is sinful, in order to its being sin in us. The sinfulness of anything depends upon its nature. A thing is not true, or false, simply because we so regard it. Are all righteous who think themselves righteous? The maxim that the character of an act depends on the motive with which it is performed, is true only of acts in their own nature indifferent. Giving bread to the hungry, inflicting pain, depend on the motive. But hating God, cursing God, are evil without regard to the motive.

4. That not merely the omission of required acts, but the absence of required states, any want of conformity to the law of God is sin, the want of zeal, of faith, of gratitude, of love. The standard is absolute perfection. Any and every thing short of it is sin. This is the testimony of God's Word, as also of reason and of conscience.

5. That the law and not ability is the measure of obligation. The maxim that a man is not bound to do what he cannot do, like most other errors, is a half-truth. It is true with regard to intellectual and to outward acts, but not to internal moral acts and states. If a man hates his brother, it matters not whether he can help it or not, he does hate him, and malice is evil. If he loves him, whether he can help loving or not, the feeling is good.

The question, however, what is sin, admits of being presented in two lights. I. *What is the nature of sin?* II. *What comes under the category of sin?*

I. *What is sin, is a question which admits of no other answer than such as may be given to all primary ideas.* Sin is moral evil. What is moral evil? It is the opposite of moral excellence. Right and wrong are simple ideas, like pleasure and pain. We have in our constitution a susceptibility to pleasure and pain, to beauty and deformity, to right and wrong. Sin is what is opposed to holiness, to the infinite holiness of God.

II. *What comes under the category of sin?* Any want of conformity unto, or transgression of the law of God. Hence;

1. The standard is the law of God.

2. Intention is not necessary to constitute that sinful which the law forbids. 3. Knowledge is not necessary. 4. The mere absence of good is evil. 5. Ability is not the measure of our obligation.

III. *As the gospel is a scheme for deliverance from sin, our views of redemption must be determined by our views of sin.* If the latter is limited or defective, so also must be the former. Augustinianism, Pelagianism, Arminianism, all begin with varying views of sin, and hence all other difference. With these theories their experience and form of religion correspond. Hence the importance of the question, what is sin, in both its aspects.

IV. *Such being the nature of sin, what are secret sins?* 1. Not mere sins secret to others. Many men indulge themselves in sins which are unknown, and they trouble the conscience little because they are unknown. Let a man ask himself how he would feel if all his secret acts were known, his thoughts and feelings, his inward pride, vanity, malignity to his fellow-men.

2. But sins not known to ourselves.

1st. Things which we are mistaken about, and which we regard as either indifferent or as good, *a.* as persecuting zeal; *b.* bigotry; *c.* censoriousness; *d.* sanctimoniousness, such as that of the Pharisees; *e.* the desire of pre-eminence; *f.* certain professional and business habits.

2d. Things which escape our notice, or which we fail to recognize as sinful. *a.* The negation of God, the absence of proper affections towards God, Christ, and our fellow-Christians and fellow-men. *b.* Neglect of duty, the failure to do the good which we might have done.

INFERENCES.

1. Our sins infinitely transcend our knowledge. Who can understand his errors?

2. The utter impotency of man to save himself.

3. The need of a redemption which cleanses from all sin.

4. Our need of the enlightening and sanctifying work of the Holy Ghost.

5. Our obligations to the mercy and forbearance of God.

LXXIII. Backsliding.

[*Oct. 1st*, 1865.]

There are two kinds of backsliding mentioned in the Scriptures. 1. that of professors; and 2, that of the true people of God. To the former class belong the backslidings of the Israelites, which consisted in their falling away from the worship of God and the observance of his law, and in their worship of idols and following the customs of the heathen.

Such backsliding was in their case generally, so far as individuals were concerned, final, and ended in their destruction.

To the same class is to be referred the backslidings of Christian churches and communities. The Eastern, Latin, the English, Scotch, Holland, German, Swiss churches have all experienced such backsliding. In some there is a perpetual apostacy, in others, a temporary one. To the same class belongs the backsliding of professors of religion ; persons who have experienced more or less of the power of religion, and have regarded themselves and been regarded by others as true converts, and have joined the full communion of the church and subsequently gone back to the world, given up their profession, and in many cases become immoral or sceptical. The last case of such persons is worse than the first. In some cases it is impossible to renew such persons unto repentance. Heb. vi : 6–10 shows how great may be the attainment and how varied and deep the religious experience of such persons, and how awful and hopeless may be their fall.

II. *The backsliding of the people of God.*

This for a time may not be distinguishable from the former. It is possible that a true child of God may so fall away that he may lose all evidence within of his being a true Christian, and he may fail to exhibit such evidence to others. There is, however, all the difference between these two cases that there is between a swoon and death. In appearance the two are alike. But, 1. In a swoon there is still a dormant principle of life. 2. It is sure to revive. Whereas, in the other, the principle of life is absent and revival is out of the question.

In the backsliding of the people of God, there is, 1st. A decline in the power of the inward principle of spiritual life, and 2d, a decline in all its normal manifestations. These go on increasing. *a.* The neglect of fellowship with God. *b.* Neglect of the more private duties of religion. *c.* Neglect in watching the heart, the thoughts, and words. *d.* Neglect of outward duties. *e.* Conformity to the world. *f.* Commission of open sin.

Decline merely in fervor of feeling, whether penitential or joyful, is not an evidence of backsliding. Our feelings depend on many circumstances. They sometimes vary with the hours of the day, with the weather, with the season of the year, with the state of the body, or with the period of life. The young are full of emotion. The old are calm. People often distress themselves unnecessarily. The true test is to be founded in the power of the principle of piety to determine our faith, our habits and our conduct.

III. *Danger of backsliding arises,* 1. From its insidiousness. 2. From its tendency to become worse and worse. 3. From its offensiveness to God, as a great sin. 4. From the certainty that it will end in perdition, if not arrested. There is nothing in us to stop its progress, or in anything around us, or in others, Christians, ministers or means of grace. It depends alone on the purpose of God. 5. It necessarily involves much suffering and loss, and entails great disgrace on the cause of Christ.

IV. *Its cure.* Those who are conscious of having backslidden must, 1. Repent; 2. Do their first works.

Their repentance includes, 1. A just apprehension of their true condition, and their guilt as connected with it. 2. A settled purpose to renounce everything inconsistent with a holy conversation. 3. Humiliation and sorrow for the sin they have committed, and the evil they have done.

Doing their first works, includes their return to God by the very means and steps by which they first found his favor.

1. They sought earnestly with tears and supplications, long, continual and persevering.

2. They sought it through Christ, and by application to his blood; or, by the exercise of faith in him.

3. They sought it in the diligent use of all the means of grace.

4. In humble dependence on the undeserved and forfeited aid of the Holy Spirit.

LXXIV. The Unpardonable Sin.

[*Oct.* 23d, 1864.]

The doctrine of the Trinity is the foundation of Christianity, both as a system of doctrines and as a religion. We stand in special relation to the several persons of the Trinity. The Father is the fountain of law and the author of the scheme of redemption. He devised the plan, he elects and calls. The Son redeems. The Spirit applies the redemption purchased by the Son. We disobey the Father; we disbelieve the Son; we resist, grieve, blaspheme the Holy Ghost. All sin as against the Father or the Son may be forgiven, but the sin against the Holy Ghost can never be forgiven.

I. *Its general character.* On this subject it may be remarked, 1. That there is such a sin which is unpardonable. 2. It is an open sin, not a sin merely of the heart. It is blasphemy. It requires to be uttered and carried out in act. 3. It is directed against the Holy Ghost, specifically. It terminates on him. It consists in blaspheming him, or doing, despite unto him.

II. *Its specific character.* This includes, 1. Regarding and pronouncing the Holy Ghost to be evil; ascribing the effect which he produces to Satan or to an evil, impure spirit. 2. It includes the rejection of his testimony, as false. He testifies that Jesus is the Son of God. The man guilty of sin, declares him to be a man only. He testifies that Jesus is holy. The other declares he is a malefactor. He testifies that his blood cleanses from all sin. The other that it is an unclean thing, and tramples it under foot.

3. It includes the conscious, deliberate, malicious resistance of the Holy Spirit and the determined opposition of the soul to him and his gospel, and a turning away from both with abhorrence.

This sin supposes, 1. Knowledge of the gospel. 2. Conviction of its truth. 3. Experience of its power. It is the rejection of the whole testimony of the Spirit and rejection of him and his work, with malicious and outspoken blasphemy.

It is by a comparison of Mat. xii: 31 and the parallel passages in Mark and Luke, with Heb. vi: 6–10 and x: 26–29 that the true idea of the unpardonable sin is to be obtained.

III. *The consequence of this sin is reprobation, or a reprobate mind.* This may evince itself in stolid unconcern. Utter indifference to God and his declarations. Or, it may evince itself in great horror of mind, in the upbraidings and scorpion stings of conscience, and in a fearful looking for of judgment. Every thing which the lost experience, the man guilty of this sin may experience. But nothing experienced by the people of God or by those with whom the Spirit still strives, can be experienced by one thus reprobated.

IV. *Importance of clear views of this subject.*

1. Because erroneous views prevail, as, *a.* That every deliberate sin is unpardonable, as the apostle says, He who sins wilfully. *b.* Any peculiarly atrocious sin, as denying Christ by the lapsed. *c.* Post-baptismal sins.

2. Because people of tender conscience often are unnecessarily tor-

mented with the fear that they have committed this sin. It is hard to deal with such persons, for they are generally in a morbid state.

3. Because as there is such a sin, every approach to it should be avoided and dreaded. All making light of religion, all speaking against the truth, or the work of the Spirit; all resisting his operations on our own hearts or on the minds of others.

4. Because we owe specific reverence to the Holy Ghost on whom our spiritual life depends.

V.

CONVERSION—ENTRANCE UPON THE CHRISTIAN LIFE.

LXXV. Salvation by Grace.

[*March 20th*, 1853.]

I. *Reason is neither the source nor the standard of divine truth.* Yet all truth commends itself to enlightened and sanctified reason, *i. e.*, to reason in holy persons. The religion of the Bible, in other words, accords with the consciousness of men. Two truths are universally admitted by unrenewed men; viz.: their own ill-desert and helplessness. The only religion therefore suited to convinced sinners must teach salvation by grace.

II. *Salvation includes,*

1. Pardon, or deliverance from the curse of the law.
2. Deliverance from the dominion of sin.
3. The blessedness of heaven.

III. *This salvation is by grace.* 1. As to pardon. It is entirely free and undeserved. It is not founded on any thing we can do or have done. The source of it is the love of God. The ground of it is the merit of Christ.

It is of free grace that one man and not another is pardoned. It would not be gratuitous if this were not the case. Not many wise men after the flesh, not many mighty, not many noble are called; but God hath chosen the foolish things of the world to confound the wise; and God hath chosen the weak things of the world to confound the things which are mighty; and base things of the world and things which are despised, hath God chosen, yea, and things which are not to bring to nought things that are; that no flesh should glory in his presence.

2. As to sanctification. *a.* The power by which it is effected is not nature, not rites, but entirely the Spirit of God. In regeneration the Spirit does everything. In sanctification, he excites and aids and gives efficacy to the means.

b. The gift of the Holy Spirit is a matter of grace. God gives his Spirit not according to our merit, not because of any peculiar susceptibility in one rather, or more than in another, but simply according to his own good pleasure.

3. As to the blessedness of heaven.

This is also entirely gratuitous. It is the reward of Christ's work, not of ours. Though according to our works, yet those works are themselves a part of our salvation and the gift of God. Those whom he most blessed here, he blesses most hereafter.

Salvation therefore is entirely of grace. 1. That God provided salvation at all. 2. That he saves some and not others. 3. In its application, *i. e.*, in the points above mentioned, vocation, justification, sanctification, heaven, it is all of grace.

INFERENCES.

1. This trait is the leading characteristic of the gospel. Everything that detracts from this attribute mars the gospel. Therefore it is a test of doctrine.

2. Religious experience, so far as genuine, is the accordance of our experience with the truth of God. Therefore, our subject affords a test of religious experience.

3. It furnishes the only guide to inquirers. This is the truth which they need, without which they grope in darkness. Guilt and helplessness and gratuitous salvation go together.

LXXVI. The Value of the Soul.

[*February 7th*, 1864.]

The question, What is the soul, is not easily answered. 1. The answer of the materialist, who ignores the distinction between mind and matter, would refer to the functions of matter all the phenomena of the world, whether physical, vital or mental. Life is the result of organization, and not its cause. Thought and intelligence are mere functions of the brain. But this doctrine destroys the soul's individuality and also its value.

2. The pantheistic answer is that it is a form of God; a mode in which the general agency of God is manifested in connection with a given organism. This destroys moral character, responsibility and personal immortality. There is a dangerous approximation to this doctrine which refers all the operations of second causes in nature to the immediate agency of God. If it is God who burns when fire burns, why is it not God who thinks when the mind thinks? The difference

between matter and mind may be arbitrarily assumed, but it cannot be proved on this hypothesis.

3. The answer of the Realist is that the universal principle of humanity is manifested in connection with a corporeal organism. The difference between this and Pantheism is, that it assumes the existence of a distinct substance called humanity (of which there is no evidence). If this substance is a unity, then there can be no individuality of the soul, any more than there is of magnetism, or electricity, or vegetable life. If it be said that each individual soul is a separate part of this common humanity, then humanity and the soul must be material and capable of division. No man would say that his hand or foot was or contained a part of his soul. It is difficult to see how this realistic doctrine can be reconciled with the individuality or personal immortality of the soul.

4. The common doctrine of men, of the Scriptures, and of the Church is, that the soul is a distinct individual subsistence, a substance having personality. This doctrine underlies all the representations of the Scripture, and is alone consistent with individual responsibility and immortality.

In determining the value of the soul, we must,

1. Determine the class of beings to which it belongs. There are various orders, organic and inorganic, sensible and insensible, vegetable and animal, rational and irrational, mortal and immortal. The soul, as it belongs to the highest general class of beings, that of rational and immortal spirits, has a very elevated position in the scale of being.

2. Although it may be lowest in that class, and therefore its absolute value less than that of the higher order of spirits, yet its inherent value, as determined by its capacities, by what it can know, enjoy or suffer, and by what it effects, is above all estimate. By this standard it is more valuable than all the irrational creatures combined. Less would be lost if a material globe, teeming with animal and vegetable life, should be blotted out, than if a single soul should perish.

3. Its value is not determined, however, merely by the powers which it possesses, but by the unending duration which belongs to it. If it was to exist but for a few years, here on earth, or for a few centuries, or for millenniums hereafter, it would be comparatively worthless. It is because it is to exist in constant activity forever, with the capacity of unlimited development in sorrow and enjoyment that its intrinsic value does not admit of being estimated.

4. The soul has in its moral and religious nature a higher element of value than that which belongs to its mere rational nature or capacity for joy and sorrow. It is because it is capable of partaking of the nature of God, of bearing his image in knowledge, righteousness and holiness, that its worth is unspeakably greater than it otherwise could be.

5. As the great end, and therefore, the value of the creation is to manifest the glory of God, the value of any part of the creation is to be estimated by its adaptation to that end; and as it is in rational, holy, and immortal beings that the glory of God is most clearly revealed, they are, therefore, unspeakably the most valuable portion of his works.

6. The estimate which God makes of the value of the soul is shown in the provision which he has made for its salvation.

The considerations above mentioned relate to the absolute or intrinsic value of the soul. They do not concern its relative value, that is, its value to us. This we can only muse upon. We cannot argue about, or estimate what is infinite.

1. If we compare the soul to anything else, the world and all it contains, we see the two do not admit of comparison. The one is infinitely less than the other. The relation of a grain of sand to the material universe, of an insect to all animated nature, of a new-born infant to the whole intelligent creation, or a single moment of pleasure, a draught of cold water to a long life of the highest blessedness, fail utterly to indicate the disparity between the value of our souls to us, and all other things.

2. If instead of comparing the soul with anything else, we try to estimate its value by what it may enjoy in heaven, or by what it must suffer in hell, if not saved, we are lost and overwhelmed.

INFERENCES.

1. Work out your own salvation. 2. Labor for the salvation of others.

LXXVII. The Conversion of Paul.

[*Oct. 28th*, 1866].

I. *Its circumstances.*

1. It was without any preliminary preparation, or special instruction.

2. It was without human instrumentality.

3. It was attended with a miraculous display of light, and sound of words.

4. The physical effects of these displays; blindness and prostration.

II. *Nature of his conversion, or that in which it essentially consisted.*

A sudden and entire change in his views of Jesus Christ. He had previously regarded him, *a.* as a mere man; *b.* as a bad man, unfaithful to the religion of his fathers and a perverter of the people; *c.* as an impostor, one falsely pretending to be the long promised Messiah. Honestly, that is, really entertaining these views, he thought it a duty which he owed to God to persecute the followers of Christ, and to do all he could to arrest the progress of the new religion. This was very wicked.

First, because the views which he took of the Old Testament Scriptures and their predictions of the Messiah were due to a carnal state of mind. Secondly, because the evidence of the divine mission of Christ was such that none but a wicked person could reject it. Paul therefore considered himself the chief of sinners because he persecuted Christians, a clear proof that honesty of conviction does not exonerate.

These false views of Christ were instantly rejected. He saw him to be the Lord, *i. e.*, a divine person, the Son of God. This is taught in Gal. i: 16. Secondly, he saw him to be God manifest in the flesh. He believed that Jesus, a man, was the Son of God. Thirdly, he saw he was the promised Messiah. That was the truth that he at once preached, *i. e.*, that Jesus is the Christ.

III. *Agency by which this conversion was effected.*

1. Not by the outward circumstances.

2. Not by the revelation of Christ to his sense of vision. The wicked at the last day shall see Christ in his glory and flee from him.

3. But by the immediate power of God, Gal. i : 16. So our Lord said to Peter, "Flesh and blood hath not revealed it unto thee, but my Father which is in heaven."

4. It was the special work of the Holy Spirit.

IV. *Effects of this change.*

1. Entire submission and devotion, a willingness to renounce everything, and to do anything which Christ required at his hands.

2. This supposes the recognition of him as God. So Christ became at once to him the supreme object of worship, of love, of zeal. It was Christ for him to live. These were the inward effects. From despising, hating, opposing, he came to adoring, loving Christ with his whole soul. The effect on his life was that he consecrated his whole strength and resources to endeavoring to persuade men to be Christians in the sense in which he was a Christian.

3. It made him one of the greatest, and best and happiest of men.

4. It secured him a place among the redeemed in glory.

This subject should lead us to examine ourselves to see whether our conversion was like Paul's; like it in its nature; like it in its effects.

LXXVIII. Conviction of Sin.

[*February 3d*, 1861.]

What is sin? Sin is any want of conformity unto, or transgression of the Law of God. The Law of God is the eternal rule of rectitude. It is a revelation of what is right, of what rational creatures should be and do. It has supreme excellence and supreme authority.

It is not merely a revelation of what is right and reasonable, but what we are bound to be conformed to. All sin has reference to God. It is contrary to his will, and therefore includes the ideas of guilt and of defilement. Of course, as sin has relation to law, our views of sin will be determined by our views of the law. If the law is only the law of reason, sin is simply unreasonable. If the law is limited, so is sin. If the law is perfect, then all want of perfection is want of conformity to law.

II. *Conviction of sin is therefore a conviction of want of conformity to law.*

This includes, 1. the want of conformity of the heart; 2. of conscious states of the mind; 3. of particular acts. Conviction of sin under the gospel is specially of unbelief, as a sin against Christ. Conviction includes the consciousness of this as guilt, *i. e.*, as justly exposing us to the condemnation of the law. This includes the conviction that we can never make atonement for our guilt. This is constantly attempted, but never with success even to the satisfaction of conscience.

Conviction, again, regards this want of conformity, as not only guilt, but also defilement, as that which renders us morally offensive, the objects of disapprobation, of disgust, and of abhorrence. This stands opposed to self-complacency, or self-approbation. It may go a great way and yet be ineffectual.

III. *The necessity of this conviction arises out of the fact that the gospel is a plan for the salvation of sinners.* It is designed for sinners. If we are not sinners, we do not need the gospel. If we do not feel that we are sinners, we do not feel our need of the gospel and will not embrace it. If we do not feel ourselves guilty, we will not look to Christ for pardon. If we do not feel ourselves to be polluted, we will not look for nor desire cleansing. We must therefore be convinced of sin in order to be saved.

IV. *But what kind or degree of conviction is necessary?* Or, what are the evidences of genuine conviction?

1. Every human being is convinced of sin, in a certain sense and measure. But only in such measure as is consistent with indifference or carelessness.

2. Others are so convinced as to create great anxiety and to lead to long, continued and painful efforts to save themselves.

3. Others are so convinced as to be thoroughly persuaded that they can neither atone for their guilt nor deliver themselves from defilement, or make themselves holy. This is the result to be desired.

This may be attained at once, or it may be long delayed. It is not determined by mere pungency or depth of feeling or terrors of conscience. There may be much or little of all this. The main thing is,

1. That we should be led to renounce ourselves, self-justification, or excuse, and self-righteousness. 2. That we shall be made ready to fall at the feet of Jesus and say, Lord, if thou wilt thou canst make me clean ; Lord, save me, or I perish.

LXXIX. Conviction of Sin.

[*Nov. 18th,* 1855.]

I. *Its nature.* It is expressed by ἔλεγχος (elenchos) and ἐπίγνωσις (epignosis). It includes,

1. Knowledge of what sin is. Paul says he had not known sin, but by the law, and had not known lust, except the law had said, Thou shalt not covet ; and that by the law is the knowledge of sin. So long as ignorance continues and so far as it extends, there can be no conviction. Multitudes live in sin, without knowing it. What they really do is sin, though not so in their consciousness. So Paul indulged concupiscence, and persecuted the Christians. Such is generally the case with heathen, such with men of the world. The first necessity therefore is that the mind should be enlightened by the law.

2. It includes the sense of sin, the conviction that we are personally chargeable with it. This includes a sense of guilt or sense of just exposure to punishment ; with which is connected more or less an apprehension of the righteous judgment of God, and also a sense of pollution or unworthiness which is the opposite of self-approbation and complacency. Remorse and self-loathing are included in this sense of sin.

3. It includes a sense of helplessness. There is an intimate persuasion, *a.* That we can never atone for our sins, or free ourselves from guilt. *b.* That we can never cleanse ourselves from pollution. The deaf, the blind, and leprous were thus convinced of their deplorable and helpless condition before they applied to Christ for relief.

These are all natural feelings. They may and often do precede regeneration. They are often experienced by those who never are renewed. They are nothing more than a higher measure of what every sinner from the constitution of his nature more or less experiences.

II. *Conviction of sin, though no evidence of conversion, is necessary to it.*

1. Because the gospel being a provision for the relief of the guilty, it cannot be embraced by those who do not feel their guilt. The degree to which this is to be felt is not to be determined by liveliness of emotion but by its effects. It must destroy the disposition to self-justification. It must destroy reliance upon our own works or modes of

satisfaction. It must convince us that without the righteousness of Christ we perish.

2. Because the gospel, being a provision for sanctifying the unholy, those who are not sensible of pollution will not apply to this source of relief. Here again, it is not the liveliness of the feelings of remorse or self-loathing, but the effect, the persuasion that we need to be cleansed by the power of the Spirit.

3. Because the gospel being a provision for the helpless, those who think they can help themselves will not come to Christ, and cannot accept him.

There is no point as to which souls are more distressed than this. They feel that they have never been sufficiently convinced. The difficulty arises from assuming a wrong standard; viz., feeling instead of the effect upon the life.

III. *Means of obtaining conviction.* 1. It is the work of the Holy Spirit. Even in the unconverted it is the effect of his common grace. He is sent to convince the world of sin. The reprobate, those whom God has abandoned, have the conscience seared. They are ἀπηλγηκότες (apelgekotes), and therefore commit sin without restraint.

2. The Spirit convinces of sin through the law. Therefore we must bring ourselves to that standard and not judge ourselves among ourselves, or compare ourselves with ourselves.

3. It is specially by the revelation of the holiness of God, by the glory of God in Jesus Christ, by the manifestation of the love of God in Christ, that this conviction is produced.

Whatever tends to darken the mind, as false theories of the nature of sin, false views of the divine law, false doctrines as to man's responsibilities, tends to hinder genuine conviction. So also whatever tends to harden the conscience, to render the heart callous, as the commission of sin, self-palliation, etc., has the same effect.

IV. *This conviction should be permanent.* It is not felt once for all. All our experience is modified and determined by our sense of sin. Hence the difference between Christians and churches.

LXXX. Repentance.

[*Feb.* 26th, 1865.]

This in a religious sense is the turning from sin unto God. When genuine it is a fruit of regeneration, and a gift of the Spirit. In the wide sense in which it is used it includes the whole process of conversion. That is, it includes the exercises or acts of the soul which have sin for their object, and those which have Christ for their object It is in this sense it is used in our Catechism, where it is defined to be a saving grace, whereby a sinner, out of a true sense of his sin and apprehension of the mercy of God in Christ, doth, with grief and hatred of his sin, turn from it unto God, with full purpose of, and endeavor after, new obedience. The essential act is turning from sin to God. This turning is characterized, first, by its attending circumstances; secondly, by its motives; thirdly, by its effects.

I. *Its means.* It is,

1. From a due sense of sin. This includes, *a.* a knowledge of sin; *b.* a conviction of our own sinfulness. *c.* A proper sense of our own guilt and pollution. The knowledge of sin supposes proper views of the holiness of God, of his justice, and therefore of the greatness of the evil of sin. A conviction of our own sinfulness includes, *a.* a conviction that we are guilty, *b.* that we are polluted, *c.* that we are helpless, or absolutely at God's mercy.

2. It is with apprehension of the mercy of God in Christ.

Repentance is not possible as long as we think we are without hope. For despair precludes repentance. We must apprehend, *i. e.*, believe,

a. That God is merciful. *b.* That he can consistently exercise his mercy. *c.* That we are or may be its objects. *d.* That this is through Christ, because out of Christ, conscience and Scripture teach that he is a consuming fire.

II. *The attending circumstances are grief and hatred of our sins.* 1. Grief, *i. e.*, sincere sorrow for having committed them. This includes, *a.* Remorse. *b.* Self-abhorrence. *c.* Self-condemnation. *d.* Shame. All arising out of a due sense of the evil of sin.

2. Hatred includes disapprobation and disgust.

III. *The act itself.* Turning from sin. Turning from the approbation, from the indulgence, from the promotion of sin. Turning to God, *a.* As an object of excellence. *b.* As an object of enjoyment.

IV. *The effects of Repentance are purpose and endeavor.*

Purpose, a decision of the will to obey God in all things. Endeavor to do so, continued, sincere and effective.

LXXXI. Except ye be converted and become as little children, ye shall not enter into the kingdom of heaven. Matt. 18 : 3.

[*Nov. 19th,* 1865.]

I. *The occasion of this remark was the manifestation of a desire of pre-eminence.* As to this principle or desire, it is universal; it is powerful; it is productive of great good, apparently, as well as great evil; it is generally recognized as laudable, or at least, as lawful.

Nevertheless, it is evil. 1. Because it is selfish. Self, and not Christ, is the end.

2. Because it is an inferior motive to the love of God. 3. Because Christ always condemns it. 4. Because we feel that it would degrade our idea of Christ, had he acted from this principle. 5. Because we instinctively exalt the man who is free from it, over the man who is governed by it.

It is to be distinguished ; 1. from the desire of excellence; 2. from the desire of honor.

II. *The nature of conversion.*—It is evidently a change not of outward conduct merely, nor of mere acts of the mind, but of the character, *i. e.*, of the inward principles which control the inward and outward life. This change is declared to be necessary.

III. *The evidence of it is the disposition of a child.*

1. A disposition which is the opposite of an ambitious spirit. The children of the rich and poor, of bond and free, if left to themselves, play together as equals. The stronger, the brighter, the superior are recognized as such independently of their external distinctions. Children are humble.

2. A child is confiding. It trusts its parents.

3. A child is submissive. We must submit our understanding, our circumstances and destiny to the hands of God. A child led by the hand of its parent in the dark, follows him without hesitation or doubt.

IV. *Why this change is necessary.* Because the disposition of a child is the only one that agrees with our relation to God. This will apply, 1. to our ignorance, 2. to our weakness, 3. to our guilt and pollution.

V. *The blessedness of this disposition.*

1. The peace it gives.

2. The security it affords. God cares for us.

3. It places us in our normal relation to God. 4. It secures our admission into the kingdom of God, of which Christ is the head and the centre.

LXXXII. The sorrow of the world and sorrow after a godly sort. 2 Cor. 7: 10, 11.

[*April 20th*, 1856.]

I. *Happiness is an element of life.* It is one of the conditions for the healthy development of our nature. This is an important principle in education, even in the training of animals.

II. *Sorrow of the world worketh death.*

1. The sorrow of the world is that sorrow which worldly men experience, whether from ordinary calamities or on account of their sins.

2. Such sorrow works death. *a.* It has no tendency to make men better. This is often overlooked. Men look to suffering as a means of sanctification. *b.* It makes men worse. It makes them rebellious. It

exasperates. It hardens. The proof of this is in experience, and in what the Scriptures teach of fallen angels and of the lost. The death which the sorrow of the world produces is spiritual and eternal. It is moral and physical. It makes worse and it makes miserable.

III. *The sorrow,* χατὰ Θεόν *(kata Theon,) is godly sorrow.* It is the form which sorrow assumes in a pious mind, and which, in its causes, measure and exercises, is agreeable to the will of God.

The effects of this sorrow are,

1. Repentance. 2. Salvation. By repentance is meant a turning from sin to God. Salvation is its consequence. What brings us to God, brings us to salvation, for our life is fellowship with God.

IV. *Effects and evidences of repentance.* These are the same in a community as in an individual. Paul is here describing the effects of repentance in a congregation for the offense of one of its members and for their own remissness and neglect of discipline. But what he says is applicable to the experience of every penitent. The eleventh verse enumerates six particulars, after the general one, as effects of godly repentance; but they are reduced to three, as two are in each case united.

The first and most general effect of repentance is σπουδή (spoude), solicitous concern as opposed to listless indifference, which the unregenerated manifest. Sin is nothing to them. But to the penitent, it is a matter which awakens solicitude and attention. This, however, is not all.

2. 'Απολογία (apologia) and ἀγανάχτησις (aganaktesis). That is, apology and indignation. The former does not mean palliation or excusing one's self, but the effort to rid one's self of the guilt and turpitude of sin. The latter means the indignation which we feel against ourselves for our sins, the contempt which the folly and wickedness of sin excite.

3. Φόβος (phobos) and ἐπιπόθησις (epipothesis), fear and vehement desire. Fear of God's displeasure or of any falling into sin. Earnest desire after God's presence and favor.

4. Ζῆλος (zelos) and ἐχδίχησις (ekdikesis), zeal and revenge; zeal against our sins, and a desire to destroy them.

LXXXIII. Strive to enter in at the strait gate.

[*At the College, May 14th, 1856.*]

There are two modes of representation which run through the Bible, apparently at variance with each other. According to the one, the plan of salvation is represented as simple. Believe and be saved, touch and be healed, look and be made whole.

According to the other, salvation is represented to be very difficult. We must strive to enter in at the strait gate. We must work out our salvation. We must run as in a race where the prize is our life. We must fight the good fight. Many who seek shall not enter in. Even the righteous are scarcely saved.

Both these modes of representation are of course correct. They refer to different things. The former relates to the meritorious and efficient cause of salvation. We have not to work out a righteousness of our own, nor are we to attempt the work of regeneration or sanctification in our own strength. The whole work of meriting salvation has been done for us. We have nothing to do but to accept the righteousness which is offered to us, to trust in what Christ has done.

So, too, with regard to sanctification. It is the work of God. We are renewed by the Spirit after His image. It is not a natural process carried on by natural laws, but by the power of God, attending the use of the appropriate and appointed means. In one sense we are the passive recipients of salvation. On the other hand, however, the difficulty of bringing our hearts to a simple, constant and entire reliance on Christ, and the difficulty of avoiding the grieving and resisting the Holy Ghost, is unspeakably great. So that the experience of believers is in accordance with the Scriptures, that it is hard to be saved.

The Bible says expressly that no drunkard, or unclean person, or covetous man, no one who loves the creature more than the Creator, no one that is carnally-minded, no one who is not converted and made as a little child, can enter into the kingdom of God. To these and other forms of destructive evil we are impelled,

1. By the corruption of our own nature.
2. By the allurements of the world.
3. By the influence of evil companions.
4. By the temptations of Satan.

These are formidable enemies, not to be overcome without effort.

Therefore, 1. Lay it to heart that salvation is a difficult work. You cannot float into heaven.

2. That a constant use of the means of grace, of secret and social prayer, of public worship, the reading of the Scriptures, and the use of the sacraments is absolutely necessary.

3. That constant watchfulness against sin, avoiding temptation, company, associating with the people of God, are all necessary.

4. That constant effort to advance in piety is the only way to avoid declining, and declension leads to apostasy.

5. That with all these means should be united a constant sense of danger and constant dependence.

6. At the same time, the spirit of the gospel is not a fearful despond-

ing spirit, but a spirit of filial confidence and joy. The great thing is to remember that safety is only to be found in a lively and growing state of piety in the heart.

LXXXIV. Coming to Christ.

[*December 7th*, 1856.]

Come unto me all ye that labor and are heavy laden, and I will give you rest, Matt. xi: 28. Ye will not come to me that ye might have life, John v: 40. All that the Father giveth me shall come to me, John vi: 37. No man can come to me, except the Father which hath sent me draw him, v: 44. If any man thirst, let him come unto me and drink, John vii: 37. Them that come unto God by him, Heb. vii: 25. Let him that is athirst come, Rev. xxii: 17. He that cometh to God must believe that he is, etc., Heb. xi: 6.

I. *To those who come to Christ rest is promised.* All given to him shall come unto him. He will reject none who come. He that comes shall never hunger. Hence it follows:

1. That coming to Christ is essential to salvation. 2. That it is the thing, and the precise, definite thing which the awakened sinner should be exhorted to do. He is not to be directed to submit, nor to make choice of God, nor to change his purpose. These are duties, but not the duty any more than giving alms, or attending Church.

II. *What is meant by coming?* This is often an anxious question. Those exhorted to come do not know what to do. The reasons of this difficulty are, 1. The simplicity of the things to be done.

2. The reluctance to do what is involved in the command.

To understand what it is to come, we need only refer to the case of those who came to Christ, literally, *i. e.*, the blind, deaf, leprous, the sick, etc. What did they do? Negatively, 1. They did not remain contented as they were. 2. They did not resort elsewhere for help. 3. They did not postpone application to Christ when the opportunity offered.

Affirmatively. 1. They went to him. But so did others. 2. They went for the purpose of being healed. 3. They went expecting to be healed. 4. They, therefore, made actual application to him. To do this, it was necessary, 1. To feel that they needed healing. 2. That they could not heal themselves, and that help could be obtained from no other quarter. 3. That Christ could and would heal them. 4. That he would heal not only others, but them, and that too when they applied.

This teaches us, first, What in reference to the coming of the soul to Christ is necessary before we come. 1. A sense of want. A conviction that we need spiritual healing, *i. e.*, pardon and deliverance from sin. 2. That we cannot save ourselves. 3. That no one else can save us. 4. That Christ can and will. He that cometh unto God must believe, *a.* That he is. *b.* That he is a rewarder of them that diligently seek him. So we must believe, *a.* That Christ is what he is, the Son of God, the Saviour of sinners. *b.* That he will save all who come to him.

Secondly, What is meant by coming.

1. It is to draw near to Christ as the ever present Saviour, with the desire and expectation of being pardoned and sanctified by him.

2. It is actually to apply to him for salvation, believing that he will do it, trusting to his assurance that he will save all who come to him. The evidence of coming is that we receive what we come for. Those who came to Christ on earth received the gift of sight, hearing, speech, health, etc. So if we come, we get rest, pardon, eternal life.

III. *Who are to come?*

1. Not merely sinners who never came before. 2. But also his people, in all times of emergency.

Two additional truths are revealed by Scripture on this point.

1. The unwillingness of men to come, and consequently the guilt of not coming. 2. The necessity of being drawn by the Spirit.

The Scriptures teach,

1. That all are invited to come.

2. That all the elect do come.

3. That coming is essential.

4. That it is the very thing to be done.

5. That none who come shall be cast out.

6. That the reason why men do not come is their unwillingness.

7. That divine assistance is necessary.

LXXXV. Come unto me, all ye that labor and are heavy laden, and I will give you rest. Mat. 11: 28.

[*January 10th,* 1869.]

I. *The promise.*—The rest spoken of includes two ideas; first, relief from every thing that is burdensome and grievous; and second, rest or complete satisfaction of the soul, that state in which all the powers are appropriately exercised, and all the desires and aspirations are satisfied, and all capacities of the soul completely filled.

Nothing short of this can give a rational and immortal being rest. This implies knowledge for the understanding; excellence, subjective excellence, so that there should be inward harmony; and love and fellowship adequate to our nature and capacities.

II. *The persons to whom the promise is addressed.*—It is to all. There is no distinction or limitation. It is not to Jews, as such, or to Gentiles, to young or to old, to learned or to unlearned, to good or to bad. But it is whosoever, every one, all. These are the terms used in the Scriptures. The promise therefore is to men of all classes, of all nations, and of all generations to the end of the world.

As there is no limitation as to the class of persons addressed, so there is none as to the kind of burden under which they groan. It may be sickness, poverty, sorrow, responsibility, opposition, injustice, oppression, care of any kind.

It is specially intended, doubtless, for those who are burdened with a sense of guilt and consequent exposure to the wrath of God; those heavily laden with a sense of the power of their own evil hearts; those who have specific inward trials or temptations, whether from scepticism or any other source.

III. *The person who makes the promise.* Considering the nature and the universality of its address, it would be a mockery if made by any creature. No angel and no man could have the effrontery to utter such words as these. They are only suited to the mouth of God, to him who is present in all times and all places, who has all knowledge, who is omnipotent, and whose power extends to the soul as well as over outward events. They are the words of him who has in himself all the resources to satisfy all the wants of men and to free them from all their evils.

The speaker, however, is not God as God, nor God the Father, nor the Son, as such, nor the Spirit, but Christ, *i. e.*, God as manifest in the flesh, the Theanthropos. It is the promise of one who has all the resources and attributes of the Godhead, and yet is bone of our bone and flesh of our flesh ; who has suffered as we suffer; who has borne all the burdens we have to bear and all the sorrows we have to endure, save only those which flow from an evil heart.

The promise is from him who came into the world with the very purpose of delivering men from all the evils of the fall, of securing peace on earth, peace with God, and inward peace or rest for the soul.

It is the promise of one who has not only all the power requisite for its fulfilment, and all the love and tenderness which secure the exercise of that power, but of one who has made full provision for the supply of the wants which he proposes to relieve, provision for our justification, sanctification and complete salvation.

IV. *The condition on which the promise is suspended is coming.* To those who have no sense of need, no faith in Christ's willingness or power to give rest, or who, while admitting all this, still exclude themselves and fail to embrace the promise, it is of no avail.

Coming is simply believing. Not speculating but actually appropriating the offer of Christ as made to us personally. This is a transient act not to be repeated. It is a permanent state of trust and a repeated exercise of faith, in every emergency.

LXXXVI. My Son, give me thy heart.—Prov. 23: 26.

[Oct. 5th, 1862.]

I. *What is meant by the heart?*

Human knowledge precedes science. Many of the facts of electricity were known, before electricity was discovered. The heart was known as the seat and source of life, before the circulation of the blood was thought of. In the earliest books of Scripture the word is used as freely for the inward life as it is at present. We can now see the propriety of the figure better, but it is not more intelligible. As the bodily organ receives and sends forth the blood to every part, bearing heat, life, activity, through the whole body; so the power which drives the current of thoughts, feelings, affections, desires and volitions, all that constitutes our inward life, is called the heart. The Scriptures therefore speak of the thoughts and purposes of the heart as well as of its desires. The word includes the whole inward life. The heart is therefore the man's interior and real self, and the demand, give me thy heart, is a demand for the whole soul.

II. *What it is to give the heart to God.*

1. It is to make God the end of our lives. The object for which we live should not be self, the world, the creature in any form, but the glory of God, *i. e.*, that God should be known, worshipped, loved and obeyed.

2. It is to make his will the rule of our life. Not our own desires, nor reason, nor conscience; but his revealed will. Not expediency, or the supposed good of others, but what God has declared to be right and obligatory.

3. It is to make God the delight of our life. That is, that we should not seek our happiness in the creature, but in God; assured that his favor and fellowship are our blessedness. This is what God demands of us. It is a reasonable demand,

1. Because of his infinite greatness and excellence.

2. Because our happiness and excellence depend on it. If we give our hearts to the creature, we thereby and therein give ourselves to perdition.

III. *The objection that our hearts are beyond the control of the will.*

1. This objection is not peculiar to this particular command. It lies equally against all the requirements of Scripture and conscience. The fact of inability is a fact of consciousness.

2. It is no less a fact of consciousness that this inability does not destroy, or even weaken our obligation.

3. While we cannot change our hearts or in our own strength turn to God, we can acknowledge our weakness and seek help from God, as did the blind and the deaf.

4. There is much that we can do. So far as the will is concerned we can determine that. And we can determine our outward acts. Those who thus persistently act, God draws to himself.

LXXXVII. Submission to God.

[*Dec.* 11*th*, 1853.]

There are two great kingdoms in the world; that of God and that of Satan, of truth and of error, of light and of darkness, of holiness and of sin. All men are the subjects of the one or the other. There can be no neutrality. Not to submit to the one, is submission to the other. The exhortation of the Apostle is to submit to God and to resist the devil.

I. *The nature of this submission.*

1. In general, submission is the practical recognition of the rightful authority of God over us as our sovereign. Subjects are required to submit to magistrates, wives to their husbands, children to their parents, servants to their masters. In every case the nature of the submission is determined by the nature of the relation. Our relation to God requires that our submission to him should be absolute, without reserve, without hesitation, and without limitation.

2. This includes submission of the understanding to the truth of God. It may be assumed as certain that no revelation of God in his word can contradict the revelation which he has made of himself in our nature. Obedience to the laws of belief implanted in our nature, is only one form of submission to God, and therefore forms no limitation of the submission of our understandings to his truth. The intuitive principles of the mind are very few and limited, and therefore give us only a small amount of truth. God's word is the great storehouse of truth. To that and to all it contains we are to submit. It contains nothing inconsistent with the laws of our nature, or it would not be his word, and therefore to everything it contains we are to submit our understanding. This is the obedience of faith, a difficult duty, yet not to be evaded. It is the only security, the only ground of peace and assurance.

3. It includes, specially, submission to the plan of salvation. The Jews would not submit themselves unto the righteousness of God, Rom. x : 3. This is the specific thing required to be done in order to sal-

vation. This, however, is very different from that doctrine of submission which requires only submission to the sovereignty of God. Such submission can only hang together with a perverted theory of religion.

4. It includes submission to the will of God, however manifested, as to our duty, where we shall go, what we shall do, and what we shall be, submission to our trials and afflictions. This is often the severest test of our subjection to God.

5. Submission includes becoming his subjects, so that God not only rules over us, but in us; so that all the powers of our mind, all the resources of our nature, all the members of our bodies, all our acquisitions and possessions should be given up to him and to the protection of his kingdom and glory.

II. *Reasons or grounds for submission.*

1. For general submission. *a.* God's right as our Creator; *b.* as our preserver; *c.* and his infinite superiority.

2. For submission of the understanding. *a.* Our own feebleness of intellect. *b.* God's infinite wisdom. *c.* The certainty of error in refusing to submit to God's teaching.

3. Submission to the plan of salvation. *a.* We have no righteousness of our own. *b.* That of Christ alone is all-sufficient. *c.* Our salvation depends on it. *d.* Perfect peace is the fruit of this form of submission.

4. Submission to the providence of God is founded, *a.* On faith that he does thus govern the world. *b.* On faith in his love. *c.* Faith in his wisdom. *d.* Willingness that he should do what seems to him to be good.

5. Subjection and devotion to his service rest, *a.* On his right to us. *b.* On our obligation to him. *c.* In this way only can we attain the end of our being.

LXXXVIII. Work out your own salvation with fear and trembling. Phil. 2: 12.

[*April 6th*, 1856.]

I. *The end to be attained.* II. *It is to be attained by working.* III. *The encouragement given to exertion.*

I. *The end to be attained is salvation.* This includes, 1. Pardon. 2. Sanctification. 3. Eternal life. In other words, the whole benefits of redemption.

II. *Salvation is to be attained only by working.* This teaches, negatively, 1. That it is not a matter of course that men are saved because Christ has purchased redemption for them.

2. That salvation is not a benefit which others can confer upon us. We must work out our own salvation, and each man, his own. No priest can save us.

3. That it is not an easy work. Κατεργάζεσθε (katergazesthe) is a strong expression, and this working is to be with fear and trembling, i. e., with solicitude and anxiety, lest we should after all fail. This shows that we are engaged in a work which requires our utmost exertion. This is taught in various ways in the Scriptures. It says, strive to enter in at the strait gate. The kingdom of heaven suffereth violence.

The Israelites, to gain possession of Canaan, had to fight long and hard. No cross, no crown.

Positively, this teaches that working must be directed to a right end; not to making atonement for our sins; not to meriting salvation by our good works. These are the two great errors of all false religions. Men laboriously endeavor to work out their salvation, that is, to accomplish these ends, and they never make any progress. The end of our working is to obtain an interest in Christ and to bring our hearts and lives into conformity with the will of God. This is a great work, and one absolutely necessary. If a man thinks it enough to believe in Christ and then live as he pleases, he turns the grace of God into licentiousness, and lays up wrath against the day of wrath. We have to subdue the flesh, i. e., our corrupt nature, the world and the devil.

2. Our working is not only to be directed to the right end, but it must work, not in accordance with natural religion, or asceticism, or enthusiasm, but in accordance with the gospel. If God has devised and revealed a plan for saving men, it is only by conforming to that plan we can be saved. Therefore our working must recognize, a. The work of Christ, as Prophet, Priest and King. b. The work of the Holy Ghost. c. The efficacy of all the means of grace, none of which are to be neglected.

3. This working is not only to be directed to the proper end and according to the proper plan, but it must be assiduous, unremitting and laborious.

III. *The encouragements.*

The work is so great and we are so weak that, if left to ourselves, we should fail and might despair. God has not left us comfortless.

1. The encouragement is that God can, does and will aid us. 2. That this aid is not merely outward, giving us the means and opportunity, but inward and efficacious, giving us strength and will. 3. There is, therefore, a divine *concursus*, a co-operation promised, analogous to the working of God in nature and in those cases in which He gave strength to the palsied or to the lame.

4. This divine co-operation is congruous to the nature of the soul, though it is not sensible of it and does not feel coerced. 5. As it is absolutely necessary, it should be sought and relied upon.

LXXXIX. Work out your own salvation with fear and trembling. Phil. 2: 12.

[*September 18th*, 1853.]

I. *Salvation, the greatest of all blesssings, without which everything else is lost.*

1. Deliverance from the punishment of sin.

2. Deliverance from its power.

3. The eternal enjoyment of God.

II. *Work out your salvation,*

1. Does not imply that we can merit it;

2. Nor that we can effect it;

3. But that we have an important agency in its accomplishment. As illustrations of such agency, we have the examples of Christ's putting clay on the eyes of the blind man and telling him to wash in the pool of Siloam; Naaman commanded to bathe in the Jordan, etc. The sick may be assured of restoration, but they are exhorted to use diligently the appointed means.

What is the work? And how is it to be done?

The work is obedience. 1. To the gospel. 2. To the prescribed means of grace. 3. To all the commands of God.

How is the work to be done? With fear and trembling. This implies,

1. The general, conscientious, and earnest desire to attain the object.

2. Apprehension of failure through neglect.

3. Conviction of the need of effort and labor.

It is opposed, 1. To indifference. 2. To security. 3. To antinomian neglect.

III. *The motive.*—It is God which worketh in you both to will and to do of his good pleasure, Phil. 2: 13. We are not to despair, nor be discouraged, because the work is so great. We have an Almighty Helper. 1. God does assist men. 2. His assistance consists in or is rendered by his working in us. 3. He works τὸ θέλειν καὶ τὸ ἐνεργεῖν (to thelein kai to energein). The former includes, *a*, right feelings; *b*, right determinations. The latter, right actions. He gives strength to carry out our wishes and determinations.

Of this working of God it is taught, 1. That it is internal and not merely outward and objective. 2. That it is efficacious. 3. That it is sovereign and gracious.

Here as everywhere the divine and human are reproduced in their true relation.

1. Both are indispensable.

2. They are perfectly harmonious.

3. The human is subordinate and instrumental; the divine, controlling and efficient.

XC. Regeneration.

[*March 12th*, 1854.]

I. *The natural state of man.*

1. It is a state of spiritual death.

2. As to the understanding, it is a state of blindness.

3. The affections are alienated from God and fixed on the creature.

4. The life or activity is devoted to things seen and temporal.

II. *The translation from this state into a state of spiritual life is regeneration.*

It is called in Scripture by different names, such as new birth, resurrection, new creation, change of heart.

With regard to this change, it is,

1. Not an outward one.

2. It is not a natural one.

3. It is not an essential one, or a change of essence.

4. But it is supernatural, both as to its nature and its origin.

5. It is not a mere change of purpose, or of opinion, or of feeling.

6. But it is the infusion of a new spiritual principle.

III. *Its author is God.*

It is a divine work. It is a work of power.

IV. *The means of regeneration are the word and sacraments.*

In what sense are they means?

1. That without them the effect is not produced.

2. They are not efficient of themselves.

3. They are not uniformly successful.

4. It is with and by the word that God effects the change. Illustrations: the healing of Naaman; the clay on the eye of the blind.

V. *The evidences of regeneration are of three kinds:*

1. The nature of the exercises of the new life. Holy affections contain in themselves the evidence of their own nature.

When sufficiently strong, there is no doubt entertained as to their character. There is great difficulty, however, in arriving at a satisfactory conclusion in this way.

a. Because these exercises are often weak.

b. Because it is so difficult to discriminate between gracious and natural affections, *e. g.*, sorrow for sin may be from fear, or it may be a mere natural remorse, or it may be a spiritual apprehension. So our love to God may be mere natural reverence and gratitude. Our regard for Christ may be either natural or spiritual. So of faith.

c. Because the affections are not in exercise when submitted to examination.

No one can tell a good tree from a bad one by stripping off its bark, and submitting its organism to the microscope.

2. The witness of the Spirit.

a. There is such a witness.

b. It is different from the exercise of filial or gracious affections.

c. It is not of the nature of a revelation.

d. But is the production of a confidence in our own acceptance produced by the immediate agency of the Spirit, the effects of which are joy, peace, gratitude, love, obedience and devotion to the glory of God.

3. The third class of evidences is the effects produced. These are of three kinds:

a. There is a kind of knowledge which is the fruit, and therefore the evidence of regeneration. This knowledge is not speculative. It is not intuitive, but it is spiritual discernment, a divine illumination which includes (1) the apprehension of the truth whether concerning sin, or ourselves, or Christ, or the plan of salvation, or the moral law, or things unseen and eternal. (2.) The apprehension of the excellence of all that God approves. We see the glory of God, the beauty of holiness, the evil of sin, the face of God in Christ.

b. There are affections which are the effects and evidence of regeneration. That is, we seek our happiness in new objects. We prefer God's service to the world. We prefer Christians to other men. We find the duties of religion a delight.

c. There is a new life consequent upon regeneration. There is a worldly life, a scientific life, there is a philanthropic life, and there is a religious life. That is, one whose object is not self, not the world or creatures, but God. The definite fixed purpose is to glorify him. And the whole outward life is devoted to his service and regulated by his will.

XCI. Evidences of Regeneration.

[*September* 22*d*, 1860.]

I. *What is Regeneration?*

1. It is not any outward reformation.

2. Nor any change of external state or relation.

3. Nor any change, though inward ; of belief.

4. Nor any change in the substance of the soul.

5. Nor any mere change in its acts or exercises. But a change of nature, *i. e.*, of that inward immanent disposition or spiritual state which is back of all voluntary or conscious activity, and which, in the things

of God, determines that activity. It is the change from spiritual death to spiritual life.   It is the work of the Spirit, and not of the subject of it, or of one man on the soul of another operating through the reason, conscience or the feelings.   It is due to the immediate Almighty power of God, and therefore belongs to the class of supernatural events.

II. *The question whether we are regenerate or not, is a question whether we are the children of God or the children of the devil,* whether we are alive or dead, whether we belong to the kingdom of darkness or the kingdom of God's dear Son, whether we are saved or lost.   Such being the nature of the change, and such the interests involved, two things would seem to follow.

1. That no man can rationally be indifferent to the question whether he is regenerated or not.

2. That a change so radical and so great must reveal itself.   It cannot be a doubtful matter whether a man is alive or dead.   Yet many true children of God are in doubt, from one or the other of two causes.

1. The life though present is so feeble.   It is often doubtful whether a man in a swoon or cataleptic state is alive or not.

2. What is the more common cause, taking a wrong standard of judgment, assuming the necessity of evidences which they do not find in themselves.

III. *What are then the evidences of regeneration?*   The negative side of the question at least is clear.   That is, there are certain things which are clear evidence that we are not regenerated.

1. Infidelity, or the wilful rejection of the leading doctrines of Scripture.

2. Conscious aversion to Christ, his ordinances, or his people.

3. The purpose carried out in our lives to make self the end and rule of life, not only refusing to submit to the restraints of the law, but the refusal to submit ourselves to Christ and to live for his glory.

The positive side is no less clear, at least as a matter of theory.

1. As regeneration is the work of the Spirit, as it consists in the Holy Ghost entering the soul and there abiding as a principle of a new life, it follows that evidence of his presence is the natural and inevitable effect of the presence of a source of light, of love, of power, of holiness, peace and joy.

2. Hence, where the Spirit dwells there will be light.   The soul will see truth to be truth, to be excellent, lovely and divine.   Especially will it see the record concerning Jesus to be true, that he is the Son of God and Saviour of the world.   It will have love to God, to Christ, to the Scriptures, to the Church, to the people of God.

3. There will be power to believe, to overcome the world, to conquer sin, to obey God, to make his will the rule of our life and his glory its end.

4. There will be peace and joy. Despair is inconsistent with spiritual life. Doubt and despondency are hostile to it. The question therefore whether we are regenerated is not to be decided by a metaphysical or microscopic examination of our emotions or affections. The character of these from the mere revelation of consciousness we cannot determine. But rather,

1st. From the general and habitual conformity of our mind to the mind of God.

2d. From the habitual conviction that Jesus is the Son of God, such a conviction as secures his being practically God to us.

3d. From the habitual purpose and endeavor to overcome all sin and to live for Christ's service and in obedience to his will.

XCII. Confession of Christ.

[*Jan. 23d*, 1854.]

I. *Confession, i. e.*, ὁμολογεῖν (*homologein*) *is*,—1. To say the same thing with others. To agree with. 2. To promise. 3. To acknowledge, to declare a person or thing to be what he or it really is.

II. *To confess Christ is therefore to acknowledge him to be what he really is and declares himself to be.*

1. To be the Son of God.

2. To be God manifest in the flesh.

3. To be the Saviour of the world.

4. To be the Lord.

III. *Nature of this confession.*

1. It is not enough that we cherish the conviction in our hearts, or confess it to ourselves or to God, to friends who agree with us.

2. It must be done publicly, or before men, friends and foes; amid good report and evil report; when it brings reproach and danger, as well as when it incurs no risk.

3. It must be with the mouth. It is not enough that men may infer from our conduct that we are Christians. We must audibly declare it.

4. This must be done, *a.* In our ordinary intercourse. *b.* In the way of God's appointment, *i. e.*, by Baptism and the Lord's Supper.

5. It must be sincere. Not every one that saith, Lord, Lord, shall enter into the kingdom of heaven. It is only when the outward act is a revelation of the heart that it has any value.

IV. *The advantages of confession.*

1. It strengthens faith. *Credo.*

2. It is proof of regeneration, because it supposes the apprehension of the glory of God in the face of Jesus Christ.

3. It is an indispensable condition of salvation. How is this?

a. Because God requires it. *b.* Because not to confess is to deny.
c. Denial implies want of faith or want of devotion.

4. Christ will acknowledge those who acknowledge Him. He will
do it publicly, before the angels of God, with His mouth, and to our
eternal salvation.

V. *The duty of confessing Christ.*

1. It is not merely a commandment.

2. It is the highest moral duty to acknowledge the truth, and
especially to acknowledge God to be God.

3. It is the most direct means we can take to honor Christ, and to
bring others to acknowledge him.

Matt. x: 32, "Whosoever therefore shall confess me before men,
him will I confess also before my Father which is in heaven."   Luke
xii: 8, "Whosoever shall confess me before men, him shall the Son of
man also confess before the angels of God."   Mark viii: 38, "Whosoever therefore shall be ashamed of me and of my words in this
adulterous and sinful generation, of him also shall the Son of man be
ashamed when he cometh in the glory of his Father with the holy
angels."   Rom. x: 9, 10, "If thou shalt confess with thy mouth the
Lord Jesus, and shalt believe in thine heart that God hath raised him
from the dead, thou shalt be saved.   For with the heart man believeth
unto righteousness; and with the mouth confession is made unto salvation."   2 Tim. ii: 12, "If we deny him, he will also deny us."   1 John
iv: 2, "Every spirit that confesseth that Jesus Christ is come in the
flesh is of God."   1 John iv: 15, "Whosoever shall confess that Jesus
is the Son of God, God dwelleth in him and he in God."

XCIII. Lord, what wilt thou have me to do?

[*January 18th*, 1852.]

I. *As an introduction, give an account and explanation of Paul's conversion.*   II. *The state of mind expressed by this prayer.*
III. *The cause of it.*

I. *Paul's conversion.*

1. It was an improbable event.

2. It was a miraculous event, in its circumstances.

3. As such, it is a proof of the gospel.

a. Because no rational solution, other than that he gives, can be
given for it.   It was not a delusion.   It was not a deception.

b. Because it proves Christ's resurrection, and thereby the whole
gospel.

c. Because it authenticates Paul's doctrine as a supernatural revelation from Christ.

4. Though miraculous in its circumstances, it was normal in its essentials:

a. As to the nature of the change.

b. As to the means by which it is effected.

c. As to the evidences of its sincerity.

II. *State of mind expressed.*

1. It included an entire abnegation of self. He sought not, *a.* his own advancement, *b.* or his own enjoyment, *c.* or his own improvement.

2. It included absolute submission to Christ's authority. *a.* Not his own will; *b.* nor that of friends, rulers, or the world; *c.* but Christ alone had authority to determine and direct his course.

3. It included entire consecration to the service of Christ. *a.* Readiness to do his will. *b.* A willingness that he should determine not only the service, but the field and the circumstances.

III. *Means by which it was produced.* It was the revelation of Christ.

1. The nature of this revelation.

a. It was external and adventitious. Yet this was not all, for he was thus revealed to thousands.

b. It was a revelation to the reason. A rational conviction was produced.

c. It was a spiritual revelation, effected by his Spirit, and consisting in spiritual manifestation.

2. The truth revealed was the Divinity of Christ.

a. Because called Lord.

b. Because, in Gal. i : 16, he says: "It pleased God to reveal his Son in me."

c. Because of the analogy between this revelation and that in the Mount of Transfiguration.

d. Because Paul makes conversion consist in this knowledge of Christ.

e. From its effects, which were an entire turning from self, an entire submission to Christ, and entire devotion to him.

IV. *Application.*

1. Have we this state of mind?

2. In order to have it, we must have Christ revealed to and in us as Paul had.

VI.

CHRISTIAN EXPERIENCES, CHARACTERISTICS, AND PRIVILEGES.

XCIV. If any man be in Christ, he is a new creature.
2 Cor. 5: 17.

[January 19th, 1862.]

Paul had been a proud, self-righteous, malignant, persecuting man, hating Christ and Christians. He became just the opposite. That is, he became a new creature. This is not, 1. A mere change of opinion or of faith. 2. Nor of mode of life. 3. Nor of ecclesiastical connection; but an inward, radical change of character; a change of course for the better, as καινός (kainos) itself teaches, and as the nature of the case demands.

The prominent points in this change, as presented in the context, are, 1. A change in his views of Christ. He once regarded him κατὰ σάρκα, (kata sarka). He had no faith in him as the Messiah, as the Son of God, or as his Saviour. He had no reverence for him even as a good man, much less as a divine person. He had no love for him and no zeal for his glory or for the advancement of his kingdom.

2. A change in his governing motives and in the object of his life. He was selfish. He regarded his own happiness and interests as the first and dearest object. The motive which governed him was the desire to advance his own interests as connected with those of the nation to which he belonged. The object of pursuit with him was worldly, a worldly church, a theocratical kingdom which differed in nothing from the kingdoms of this world, save that God was its ruler and the immediate author of its security and grandeur.

From this state of mind he was so converted that, 1. His views of Christ were changed. He came to regard him as God manifest in the flesh, to reverence and love him supremely, and to desire above all things his glory and the advancement of his kingdom.

2. His object now was not self. He no longer lived for himself but for Christ. The motive which governed him was not self-love, but the love of Christ, not to him, but his love to us.

This is a portraiture of conversion drawn by an inspired man. It must be, therefore, correct. It is not individual, peculiar to one case. It is declared to be general, *i. e.*, designed to set forth what is the experience of every Christian. The converse of the proposition contained in the text must be true. If a man is not a new creature, he is not in Christ, and if not in Christ, he is none of his, has no part in his salvation. How then, brethren, is it with us? Let us not deceive ourselves. It is easy to say, Lord, Lord; to profess his name; his doctrines; to live so as to escape the discipline of the Church, and even the condemnation of men. But are we new creatures? Does the love of Christ constrain us? Is the governing motive of life with us, love for him? and the great object for which we live the glory of his name and the advancement of his kingdom.

We may be amiable, just, benevolent, correct, devout, without being Christians. The only evidence of our being in Christ is that we live for him who died for us, and because he loved us and gave himself for us.

Great things are said of those who are in Christ.

1. They are reconciled unto God. There is no condemnation to them. 2. They are the sons of God. 3. They are made in the righteousness of God. 4. He is their wisdom, righteousness, sanctification and redemption. 5. They are partakers of his life, of his kingdom and glory. 6. They are new creatures.

Union with Christ therefore determines not only our relations, but our subjective state, not only our relation to the law and justice of God, and our external circumstances, but our inward character and life. This of itself proves that being in Christ cannot be anything merely formal or outward. Union with him must be of such a nature as to account for all these wonderful and glorious effects. What then is it to be in Christ?

1. It is to be in him by covenant, to be of the number of those given to him from eternity, for whom he assumed our nature, obeyed and suffered, and thus satisfied in their behalf all the demands of justice. Thus they are made righteous and heirs of his kingdom.

2. It is to be in him as a branch is in the vine, so that they are partakers of his life, *i. e.*, of the Holy Spirit, who is the source of all life.

3. It is to be in him by faith, conscious of our covenant and spiritual union. From the second flows our holiness, and from the third especially, our joy and peace.

The method of salvation, therefore, is not, 1. Reformation. 2. Nor merely turning unto God. 3. Nor turning from self-love to loving the universe. 4. Nor making God our portion. All these leave Christ out of view. It is simply receiving Christ, becoming united to him, embracing him. If we do this, then it is proof that we are in him by covenant and by the indwelling of his Spirit.

We can do this as well as we can do anything else which is said to be necessary, turning to God, making ourselves a new heart. It is all we can do. We must fall into the arms of Christ. If not willing to do this, it is our own fault. If we do this, we are saved.

XCV. The Christian Race.

[*March 29th*, 1857.]

There are many forms in which the Bible teaches the doctrine that the attainment of salvation is a difficult task.

1. It is directly asserted that few are saved; that the way is narrow and the door strait; that the kingdom of heaven suffereth violence; that the righteous scarcely are saved.

2. The comparison of a laborer. We are to work out our salvation. We are compared to servants with whom the master is to reckon.

3. To soldiers engaged in a deadly struggle with numerous and powerful enemies.

4. The Bible abounds with exhortations, warnings and directions, implying the difficulty and the danger of the work.

5. We are compared to men called upon to run a race.

I. *The main thing designed to be inculcated by all these modes of instruction is the necessity of exertion and effort in order to salvation.*

If a laborer sits idle all the day, his work will not be done and he will lose his reward.

If a soldier neglects to watch or refuses to fight, his enemy has him in his power.

If a man called to run a race saunters along and puts forth no effort, he will not win the prize. And just as surely, if we take religion thus easy and make no strenuous exertion, we shall fail of eternal life.

II. *The special truths meant to be taught by this figure of a race are*

1. That we must renounce our sins. The man who ran a race divested himself of all encumbrances, his flowing robes. He laid aside every weight. So we must lay aside our own sin which is a clog, and which easily besets us. It gets in our way. What fetters would be to a runner, sin is to the Christian. It must be laid aside. It not only puts us to disadvantage and makes the race more difficult, but it renders success impossible. We must choose between giving up sin and giving up the race.

2. The necessity of self-denial. This includes a great deal more than casting off sin. It includes self-control. The refusal to indulge in any thing however lawful, which under the circumstances may be injurious. The subjugation of the appetites of the body, the affections of the heart, the habits of the life to the strict demands of duty and the exigencies of the case. This is illustrated by the apostle when he refers to the discipline of the combatants in the Grecian games.

3. The necessity of perseverance to the end; the exertion must be kept up to the last. What would it avail that a man should run one-half or two-thirds of the course and then give up? His failure would be as complete and as ignominious as though he had never started. This is the case with multitudes. "Ye did run well," says the apostle, "who did hinder you?"

4. The necessity of fixedness of purpose and of aim. A runner must keep the goal in view. He must go directly towards it. He must not turn aside for any thing, however alluring or however important. If he does he will certainly fail. So, brethren, we must run our race as our great business to which every thing is subordinate. We must look away from the attractions of the world. It is not the question whether they are right or wrong, but whether they further or hinder us in our Christian race. We must look to Jesus, *a*. As our example. *b*. As the giver of strength. *c*. As himself our exceeding great reward.

III. *The encouragements are proportioned to the difficulties of the race.*

The reward is infinite. The evil of failure is infinite. A defeated combatant slinks away from notice, mortified, disgraced, unhappy, but what were his sufferings compared to what we must endure. We shall be banished from God and Christ and all holy beings, and consigned to outer darkness forever and ever.

XCVI. Justification by faith.

[*February 10th,* 1867.]

The relation of God to fallen men. God is holy, man is polluted. God is just, man is guilty. God is infinite in all his attributes. His acts, or all his manifestations, in relation to his creatures are determined by his nature. He can no more act contrary to his holiness and justice than contrary to his reason. He, therefore, as holy repudiates the unholy, and as just he condemns the guilty. His nature is opposed to them. He is to them from his nature a consuming fire. There is nothing in the nature of God to render it necessary that he should save sinners. Not in his infinite love, for he has allowed the angels to perish without redemption. That God can pardon the guilty, that he can restore the unholy to his favor, cannot be learned, therefore, from any knowledge we have of his nature; nor from any thing which we find revealed in ourselves. Much less is the fact that he will receive and pardon sinners, a matter of human discovery or knowledge, but purely of supernatural revelation.

1. It was revealed simply that God could and would receive and pardon the guilty.

2. The method was perhaps made known from the beginning, so far, at least, as it was to be, *a.* In a way consistent with the character of God. *b.* And, therefore, in such a way as would secure satisfaction to justice; *c.* That this satisfaction was to be rendered for us, not by us. In the course of time all this was more clearly made known as it is now in the gospel.

1. That the eternal Son of God assumed our nature. 2. That he took our place. 3. That he fulfilled all righteousness in our behalf, satisfying both the justice and the law of God. 4. That this righteousness is freely offered to all who will receive and trust in it. 5. That those who do thus believe are justified, *i. e.*, it is declared that so far as they are concerned, justice is satisfied, and they are restored to the favor of God.

The effects of this justification are declared to be, 1. Peace with God and peace of conscience. 2. Freedom of access to God. 3. The enjoyment of his favor and gift of the Spirit. This secures sanctification. 4. Security from the accusation of the law, from the power of Satan, from apostacy, from any cause of evil. 5. Participation with Christ in all the benefits of his redemption. We become the sons of God, and if sons, then heirs.

Justification and sanctification are therefore inseparably connected. And the objection that this doctrine leads to licentiousness is declared by the apostle to be self-contradictory. It proceeds on an entire mistake of our relation to Christ, through which our justification is secured. We are justified by his righteousness only because we are united to him, but if united to him, we are partakers of his life; and if partakers of his life, we live as he lives. It is impossible, therefore, that any unholy person, *i. e.*, any one who determines to live in sin, or who does not strive to die unto sin and to live unto God, can have any scriptural hope of justification. God justifies only the members of Christ's body. Their sanctification is not the ground, but it is the evidence and effect of it.

This doctrine has been the corner-stone of the Church in all ages. It stands opposed,

1. To the rationalistic and Pelagian doctrine that men are justified by their own moral character.

2. To the doctrine that they are justified in virtue of the works done under the power of the Spirit or from a renewed heart.

3. To the doctrine that we are justified by obedience to the demands of the gospel as a lower rule of duty.

4. To the doctrine that justification is a subjective change in the man himself. All these views are inconsistent with Scripture, and effectually destroy the grounds of the sinner's hope, and are unfriendly to morals and holy living.

XCVII. Sanctified by faith that is in me.—Acts 26: 18.

[April 7th, 1867.]

In this verse the words "by faith" do not qualify the preceding clause, but indicate the means by which the inheritance among the sanctified is to be obtained. Nevertheless as we are sanctified by faith, and as that is the subject intended for consideration, it may be best to consider the passage as teaching that doctrine. 1. What is sanctification? 2. How it is by faith. This latter includes two points: first, what is here meant by faith; and, second, how sanctification is by faith.

I. *Sanctification morally, is cleansing, a cleansing from sin.* And as sin includes guilt and pollution, sanctification includes both. The sanctified are those whose sins are pardoned, and whose souls are renewed.

Sanctification, therefore, includes far more than moral reformation. It includes the removal of guilt by expiation, or satisfaction of justice, and the renovation of the whole soul after the image of God. It is a radical change of nature, involving the death or crucifixion of the old man and the putting on the new man, which is renewed after the image of God, in knowledge, righteousness and holiness.

II. *The faith here intended is not* 1. A mere belief that God is, that we are his creatures, dependent upon him, and accountable to him. It is not faith in the great principles of religion and morals. 2. Neither is it simply faith in the Scriptures. 3. Nor faith in the fact that Jesus is the Messiah. *But it is*, 1. Faith of which Christ is the specific object. 2. Which includes belief of the record which God has given of his Son, viz.: that he is all that he is set forth in the Scriptures as being, God manifest in the flesh, the Saviour of men, the prophet, priest and king of his people. And this faith is not a mere conviction of the understanding, not a speculative, heretical or moral faith, but a conviction founded on the demonstration of the Spirit. 3. It is not only this assent to the truth but confidence in Christ, reliance upon him as a teacher, as an atoning priest, and as an Almighty ruler, full of grace and truth.

III. *This faith sanctifies*—i. e., it secures deliverance or cleansing from sin. How this is, so far as the guilt of sin is concerned is familiar to all. The forgiveness of sin and imputation of Christ's righteousness are promised to all who thus believe. The law demands perfect obedience and satisfaction of justice. This Christ has rendered. Those who renounce their own righteousness and believe that Christ has made a full satisfaction in their stead, and put their trust in what he has done, are immediately absolved from all guilt and accepted as righteous in the sight of God. Thus they are cleansed from guilt by faith in Christ.

As to the relation of faith to the spiritual cleansing of the soul from the presence and power of sin, the Bible teaches,

1. That the favor of God is the source of spiritual life. So long, therefore, as men are under the law and consequently under the curse, they must be under the power of sin.

2. When redeemed from the law and restored to the favor of God, they are immediately brought under the influence of his love and fellowship. When a man is condemned and confined to a dungeon, he is in darkness and misery. When pardoned and brought out into the light, he is brought under all the influences which are essential to his physical well-being. So it is with those who are translated from the kingdom of darkness into the kingdom of God's dear Son.

3. The effect of faith is union with Christ. The effect of union with Christ is the participation of his life and of his Spirit. We are in him as the branch is in the vine. And this is the indispensable condition of holiness. And not only the condition, but the cause or source of holiness.

This is one of a series of Scripture representations on this subject. There is another, very different, although consistent. What has been said relates, so to speak, to the passive effects of faith, i. e., to the effects produced upon us on the condition of faith. If we believe, we are justified, restored to God's favor, receive his Spirit, are united to Christ, and he dwells in us. But the Bible also presents another view of the subject, or, so to speak, the active effects of faith; how it acts in promoting our sanctification.

1. Faith is spiritual knowledge, or includes spiritual discernment. The effect of spiritual discernment is holy affections. 2. Faith is the evidence of things not seen. It brings us under the influence of the things unseen and eternal. It raises us above the world and makes us to walk with God and live in heaven, and therefore renders us spiritually-minded.

3. It is a shield by which we quench the fiery darts of Satan.

4. By faith we maintain constant intercourse with the Lord Jesus;

seek his aid, his direction, the supply of his grace.   We subdue sin by these acts, and call into exercise love, patience, meekness and all other holy affections.

XCVIII. They that are Christ's have crucified the flesh with the affections and lusts.—Gal. 5: 24.
[*Nov.* 11*th*, 1856.]

I. *They who are Christ's.* 1. Those who belong to Christ, who are really his, the subjects of his redemption. 2. Those who are his people, his sheep, the members of his body.

II. *They have crucified the flesh, i. e.*, they entirely, finally, and effectually (though not perfectly) died to sin. They have renounced it, determined not to cherish or obey it. This is a change which they not merely desired or professed or hoped, but which they had experienced. The chapter treats of the principle of evil in man and of the counter principle of spiritual life. The works of the flesh and of the Spirit are enumerated. And the Apostle asserts that they who are Christ's, and they only, are delivered from the dominion of evil, and are under the control of the Spirit. No one therefore who is not free, of whom this is not true, has a right to regard himself as a Christian.

By flesh is meant our corrupt nature. It is the root of which evil passions and desires are the fruit. The Scriptures constantly recognize the existence and power of a principle of evil in our nature which is the cause or source of all conscious or active manifestations of sin.

III. *The truth asserted is therefore the freedom of believers from the dominion of sin, and their being under the control of the Spirit of God. But why is this?*

This is also taught in these words, as it is more clearly and fully elsewhere.

1. It is because the design of Christ's death was to destroy the works of darkness, to redeem his people from their sins, to bring them to God, to sanctify them as a peculiar people. Such being the design of his death, it fails of its object, unless this deliverance be actually accomplished in those that are his.

2. Because in virtue of the union between Christ and his people, his death was their death. His death satisfied the demands of the law, freed his people from condemnation, and restored them to the favor of God. The Scriptures teach that those under the law are under condemnation, *i. e.*, under the wrath and curse of God, and do nothing but sin, because his favor is the life of the soul. The source of all holiness as well as of all happiness. Those therefore who are Christ's are being restored to the favor and fellowship of God, and are brought under his life-giving influence.

3. Because such is the nature of the union in question, those who are Christ's are partakers of his life. It is not a mere external or federal union, nor a union of sentiment and feeling, but such a union as exists between the branches and the vine, the members and the head of the body. As therefore the members of the body partake of the life of the head and cease to be members as soon as this ceases to be the case, so they are Christ's, that partake of his life. They are not his members, they are not his unless this be the case.

It is only saying the same thing in other words to say that the Holy Ghost is given to all who are in Christ, to effect this deliverance from the power of sin. The Spirit descends from Christ to us, and Christ dwells or lives in us by the Spirit.

INFERENCES.

1. The folly of those who profess to be Christians and hope that they are so, if they are servants of sin. That is, if in point of fact they are not delivered from its reigning power. They must not only desire and strive against it, but they must more and more overcome it.

2. The obligation which rests on us to live agreeably to our relation to Christ. If we live in the Spirit, let us walk in the Spirit.

3. The unspeakable blessing of being Christ's. The duty of love, gratitude and devotion to him, and of endeavoring to bring others to this life-giving Saviour.

XCIX. Mortify the deeds of the body.

[Nov. 17th, year not given.]

In the natural man there is but one principle of life. In the renewed man there are two principles. These in Scripture are called flesh and spirit; the law of the mind and the law of the members, the new and the old man.

By principle is not meant any act or purpose or state of conscious feeling. It is something which is the source of acts, purposes and feelings, and which determines their character. It is a law in the sense of an abiding force.

The natural man is under the dominion of the flesh, i. e., his nature as it is since the fall. He can be under the dominion of nothing else, for there is nothing else in him. The word does not designate the sensual as opposed to the rational, the social or the moral principles of his nature, but it includes them all, as they exist since the fall. The work of regeneration is the production of a new nature, or a new principle of life, not to the exclusion or immediate destruction of the old, but in juxtaposition or co-existence with it. In the Scriptures this new principle is sometimes represented as something immanent in the mind, as when it is called a law, or grace (habitual). Sometimes it is said to be the Holy Spirit as dwelling in us. These modes of representation differ only in form. The Holy Spirit is the source of this new life, and he is its source, not merely by a transient act, as in the creation of a rational creature, but as his abiding presence is the cause and condition of this new principle of life. So that it is one and the same thing whether we say the one principle contends against the other, or whether we say that the antagonistic forces are, on the one side, the flesh or corrupt human nature, and on the other the Spirit of God.

When these principles exist, as they are antagonistic, the consequence is strife. 1. This strife is necessary or unavoidable. 2. It is deadly. It must be carried on until one or the other is destroyed. 3. If the flesh triumphs the result is death. If the Spirit triumphs the result is life. By death is meant all that is included under the categories of spiritual and eternal death; and by life all that is included under those of spiritual and eternal life.

In Scripture, we are sometimes represented as the spectators of this conflict; we are the prize for which the combatants contend; the one striving for our perdition, the other for our salvation. More frequently we are represented as the combatants. The battle-field is not around us but within us. The opposing forces are the conflicting principles of our own nature as renewed.

Now it is implied in all this, 1. Not only that we are deeply interested in the issue of this struggle, but, 2. That we must take an active part in it. We must take sides with the one or with the other party. We cannot be neutral; we cannot be inactive; we cannot change from one side to the other. If we take either of these courses we perish. Our only safety is in taking the side of the Spirit. Unless we are successful in actually slaying, putting to death the evil principle, we shall perish eternally.

I. *How is this to be done?*

It is by mortifying the deeds of the body. The principle itself is beyond our reach. So far as we are concerned, our business is with its acts. No plant can live unless it is allowed to grow. If what reveals itself above ground be cut down as often as it appears, the root itself will die. This with noxious weeds is often a tedious process, but if persevered in, it must finally succeed. So with the old man, or the principle of sin. If its acts, or actings are prevented or destroyed, the principle itself will grow weaker and weaker, until it finally dies.

II. *It is to be accomplished,*

1. By the use of all rational means. That is, by those means which human wisdom and experience suggest. As for example, *a.* The deter-

mination not to allow any such exercise to abide in the mind. *b.* By constant watchfulness against their manifestation. *c.* By carefully avoiding the occasions for calling them forth. *d.* By keeping the body under, *i. e.*, by withholding all aliment to the principle of evil. This is the opposite of pampering the body and our evil passions.

But these means are all inefficient. They are necessary as subsidiary means and methods, but are of themselves powerless. And therefore,

2. It is by the Spirit. This means,

a. By the strength derived from the Spirit.

b. By the continued indwelling and co-operation of the Spirit with the feeble spiritual principles in our hearts.

c. By the use of all those means which the Spirit has ordained as the channels of his divine influence; faith in Christ, the word, sacraments and prayer.

C. Living by Faith.

[*Feb.* 16*th*, 1862.]

I. *What is faith?* There are two senses of the term which it is at least convenient to distinguish: a principle or state of mind, and an act. When it is defined as the evidence of things not seen, etc., or when used as antithetical to sight, it is the former. When we are commanded to believe, it is an act which we are required to put forth. These two things run into each other. When we trust, we perform an act, and we call into exercise an abiding principle. So when we believe in God or Christ, it is not merely a transient act, but an abiding principle which is called into exercise.

II. *Living by faith.*

Life includes all our activity as rational, moral and religious beings. Living by faith is to have our whole activity, inward and outward, permanently and characteristically determined by faith. It matters not whether we take this to mean by the objects of faith, or by the principle of faith. For the conscious exercise of the principle is on the objects.

All the things which call forth, regulate and determine our activity, our acts inward and outward, may be divided into two classes: objects of sight and objects of faith. The former includes all that we know of ourselves, *i. e.*, the knowledge of which we attain by the exercise of our own powers, and the conviction of the reality and truth of which rests on sense or reason; the latter includes all we know, only because it has been supernaturally revealed to us, and our conviction of whose truth and reality rests on the authority of God.

It is true that these two classes of objects are not entirely distinct. They overlap each other. There are some things which we know of ourselves which God has revealed. So that the same object may be an object of faith, and an object of knowledge. But, 1. This is true only of some of the objects of faith. 2. What is known is only imperfectly known, compared to what is revealed.

3. The real practical conviction which controls the life is not that which rests on knowledge, but that which rests on testimony.

Under the head of the objects of sight, therefore, fall, 1. All the objects of sense, all things material. 2. All the truths of science. 3. All the truths of philosophy. The negative fact with regard to Christians is, that their life is not determined and controlled by this class of objects. They are not the supreme objects of their attention, desire or pursuit. Under the head of objects of faith fall all those truths which have been supernaturally revealed. They are called in Scripture the things not seen, the things of God, the things of the Spirit. They embrace all the great truths of Theology, Anthropology, Soteriology, Eschatology, which are presented in the Scriptures, and our knowledge and conviction of which rests on the testimony of God. That testimony is not merely objective, not external as by human inspired lips, nor by miracles, but inwardly by the Spirit, which reveals the nature as well as the reality of these truths. Hence these things do and must control the life of the believer. They have a governing power over him. They command his attention, his affections, and they call forth his efforts.

This is the comprehensive sense of a life of faith. And we are commanded thus to live, and to do this we must, 1. Abstract ourselves from all undue, abnormal converse with the things of sight. We must not devote ourselves to them beyond what is necessary or what is due to their real, though subordinate importance. 2. We must keep our minds and hearts in contact with things unseen, the objects of faith, that they may exert their due influence on us. 3. Seek by prayer and the use of all appointed means the aid and fellowship of God's Spirit.

The Scriptures, however, speak of living by faith in another sense. We are said to live by faith of the Son of God. This means that our whole religious life is sustained, guided and controlled by faith in the Lord Jesus. That is, by believing what the Scriptures have revealed, 1. concerning his person; 2. concerning his relation to us; 3. concerning his work for us. This is the form under which, and the means by which the more general life of faith is maintained. It is vain to be religious in the general, to have faith in the general truths of Scripture, unless we have this specific life of faith in Christ. He is our life.

When a blind man is led by the hand, he walks by faith, not by sight. This is not a less safe mode of walking, not a less confident one, but it is a blind, dependent one. So a man is who is guided in a strange land. Thus the believer who is led by the hand of God into the knowledge of truth, the way of duty, the journey of life, and the path to heaven. He submits to be blindly led.

CI. Walking with God.

[*Jan. 7th*, 1855.]

I. *What is it!*

Walking with any one is a familiar Scripture phrase for fellowship or communion. Walking with God, therefore, is habitual communion with him. 1. This includes a sense of his presence, a belief that he is, that he notices us, and is cognizant of our state and acts.

2. A sense of his favor, a conviction that he is reconciled to us, and that he loves us.

3. A continued reference to him in our inward and outward conduct; an outgoing of the heart and thoughts towards him in prayer, thanksgiving, love, reverence and confidence; and the consequent desire and effort to accommodate ourselves to his will, and to please him.

4. The believing reception of his communications to us. God dwells with his people. He manifests himself to them as he does not unto the world. He reveals to them his glory. He sheds abroad his love in their hearts. He by his Spirit brings his word and promises to mind, and thus maintains a constant intercourse between himself and the souls in whom he dwells.

II. *The necessary conditions of thus walking with God are*

1. First of all, reconciliation through the blood of Christ. Men are under God's wrath and curse. There can be no friendly intercourse until they are reconciled. And there is no reconciliation but through the blood of Christ.

2. Regeneration and the indwelling of the Holy Spirit. Without holiness no man can see or have fellowship with God. Unless, therefore, we be renewed in the temper of our minds, so as to desire and delight in God, we can have no fellowship with him.

3. Keeping the conscience free from guilt, and the mind from pollution. God will not come into a heart in which unholy affections are deliberately cherished. Pride, malice, envy, jealousy and all uncleanness must be banished, and the graces of the Spirit kept in lively exercise, in the use of all the appointed means of grace, if we would walk with God.

III. *The advantages of walking with God are*

1. That it purifies and elevates the soul. It tends to depress and weaken, and to strengthen all the principles of grace. It makes us like God.

2. It is the source of peace, it is the life of the soul, the highest form of its activity, and the perennial source of blessedness. It is independent of all external circumstances. It may be enjoyed in solitude, in sickness, in poverty. It satisfies and fills the soul, and renders it blessed,

so that no other good is desired.   " Whom have I in heaven but thee, and there is none on earth that I desire beside thee."

3. It gives strength to do, to resist temptation, to bear trials and sufferings.   It gives us power for good over our fellow-men to a greater extent than anything else.   It cannot be imitated or feigned or assumed, any more than a cold body can appear hot.   The power emanates from the reality, not from the semblance.   A painted flame gives no heat.

REMARKS.

1. This walking with God is not inconsistent with activity in outward duties.   It does not require monastic seclusion.   2. It is absolutely necessary in order to prevent outward duties and forms of activity in religious works degenerating into mere heartless formality or worldly business.   A man may conduct missions as he would conduct a mercantile enterprise.

CII. Dying unto Sin, and Living unto Righteousness.

[September 10th, 1876.]

So far as we know, the redemption of man, i. e., delivering him from the guilt and power of sin—is the greatest work in the history of the universe—the greatest as a manifestation of the glory of God.

It is greatest also as to the difficulties to be surmounted.   These difficulties were objective and subjective, i. e., those outside of man and subject of redemption, and those arising from the natural state of man.

The objective—From the justice of God—from his holiness—from his benevolence.

The subjective—i. e., the destruction of the evil principle and the control of the good principle.

The Bible teaches concerning this,

1. That it is a continuous process—not like justification.

2. It is a difficult process.   It is a work—it is a conflict—a race—a dying—a long and painful process.   A man in a fever or in consumption is often months and months in dying.   So the believer is not months but years and years in dying to sin; i. e., in becoming free from its influence, as those in their graves are dead to the world.

3. This is our work.   We must repent, and believe.   It is we that must renounce the world, the flesh and the devil.   No man wins a battle or a race without exertion, neither does he gain the victory over an enemy sitting still.   He has his part to do in working out salvation, etc.

4. It is a supernatural work.

This means, a. That it is not a process of moral culture.   b. It is a work for which the power and ability comes from above. *c.* It is a work carried on by supernatural means, as taught in Eph. vi.

5. It is by faith. We are sanctified by faith. How? *a.* By accepting Christ as reconciling us to God. *b.* By believing in the love of God. *c.* By deriving our strength from Him. *d.* By continually looking to Him.

6. It is an absolutely necessary work.

CIII. Living hope through the resurrection of Christ.
1 Pet. 1: 3 .
[*Sept.* 16*th,* 1855.]

It is not easy to put ourselves in the place of the apostles. As Jews their knowledge of a future state was imperfect. Their conceptions of Christ's kingdom, earthly. Their hopes bounded very much to what was to be expected from the Messiah in this world. His death disappointed and confounded them, etc. His resurrection introduced a new era.

1. It proved the fact of a heavenly future state, and far more clearly than Scripture or reason had before revealed it.

2. It revealed the nature of that state, or of Christ's kingdom. It proved that it was not of this world. That it was not to consist of earthly advantages. It was future—in the unseen world. It was discovered to be an inheritance incorruptible, undefiled, that faded not away, and one reserved in heaven.

3. It not only revealed the nature of that heavenly state, but it produced the hope of attaining it. It imparted the assurance that it was reserved in heaven for us.

It did this, *a.* Because it was a tangible, palpable proof of its existence.

b. Because it proved Christ to be the Son of God, and authenticated all his claims and all his teachings.

c. Because it was the public acknowledgment, on the part of God, that his mediatorial work was accepted; that his sacrifice was sufficient, and therefore that God was reconciled. Our debt was paid, our ransom was accepted. The price of the inheritance was paid.

The apostles could not doubt the fact of the resurrection, and therefore they could not doubt what the resurrection proved to be true.

1. They could not doubt the resurrection, because they had seen, felt, looked upon and handled the Son of God after he had risen from the dead. They had seen him repeatedly and under circumstances which forbade the idea of delusion.

2. Because he had himself foretold his resurrection, as they now came to see, or,

3. Because the resurrection explained what they before could not understand.

4. Because God bore continual testimony to the fact by the gift and influences of his Spirit; by signs and wonders and divers miracles, which they themselves were enabled to work.

The hope of heaven, therefore, founded on the resurrection, was a *lively* hope, ἐλπὶς ζῶσα, a living hope. This means:

1. An animating vigorous, active hope; not a dull, lifeless, lethargic dubious expectation—such as was begot by reason, or even by the obscurer revelations of the Old Testament, and,

2. An abiding hope, as opposed to a fitful hope, interchanging with doubt and fear; and what the resurrection was to the apostles, it is to us.

1. The evidence in proof of its occurrence has not diminished, but rather increased. It is as certain to us as it was to them.

2. Secondly, what it proved to them it proves also to us.

3. And, therefore, the hope it begot in them, it should also beget in us.

The effect which this hope should produce is:

1. A patient endurance of all present trials; a contented, happy spirit.

2. An earnest desire and longing for the coming of Christ, when this salvation shall be revealed, and,

3. Heavenly-mindedness—negatively freedom from worldly-mindedness—and positively a pure, elevated, spiritual frame, arising from the expectation of such an inheritance.

CIV. Now abideth Faith, Hope, Charity; but the greatest of these is Charity. 1 Cor. 13; 12.

[*Jan. 26th*, 1862.]

The design of this chapter is to show the superiority of graces to gifts; of what determines the inward character and assimilates it to that of God, to what merely elevates the powers of man. The apostle teaches that a man may have the highest intellectual abilities, the largest stores of knowledge, and the greatest amount of power, and yet be a reprobate. Therefore the knowledge of the truth; the ability to present and enforce it, will avail us nothing, without inward piety. As the Corinthians coveted those gifts which most attracted the admiration of men, as the gifts of tongues, and of miracles—so now we are apt to covet eloquence, intellectual ability and knowledge, things which in our day attract admiration, and secure popular favor. What Paul taught the Corinthians, he teaches us. He teaches us:

1. That all gifts, however great, valuable in themselves, without love are of no avail. They will not sanctify or save our souls.

2. That we should not seek ourselves, our own exaltation, nor covet gifts which tend to that result, but should seek the good of others and gifts by which we may edify one another.

The apostle classifies spiritual gifts on three different principles. 1. Their relation to our own inward character. He teaches that those which involve moral and religious excellence are immeasurably above those which imply intellectual superiority and power. 2. Those which are permanent are more important than those which are temporary. 3. Those which are useful, are, in that point of view, the greater.

In other words he divides them, 1. As to their effect on the character. Some have no effect in rendering men better, as the gifts of tongues, of miracles, and prophecy. Love, however, has in it all that is morally and spiritually good, as a man may have the former and yet be nothing without love.

2. As to their permanency. Some have relation to our present state alone, as tongues, miracles, prophecy (or knowledge), others as, faith, hope and charity, are permanent. Not only as lasting through all ages of the Church, while miraculous gifts were soon to cease, but as abiding forever.

3. As to their relative usefulness. Prophesying was better than speaking with tongues; and love is better than either faith or hope. The latter relate to ourselves; the former to others. As he that spake with tongues edified himself, while he that prophesied edified others, therefore says Paul, Greater is he that prophesieth than he that speaketh with tongues; so in like manner love as tending to the good of others is greater than faith and hope, which are purely subjective and personal in their effects.

Three classes of gifts.

1. Those which do not determine the religious character, as distinguished from those which do. Tongues, prophecy, gifts of miracles belong to the former; love to the latter.

2. Those which pertain to the present state of things and those which are permanent.

3. Those which edify ourselves and those which edify others.

Judged by the first principle—love is immeasurably superior to intellectual gifts.

Judged by the second, the same result.

Judged by the third, love superior even to faith and hope.

The Corinthians sought those who exalted themselves. Paul teaches them, 1. That all intellectual gifts are worthless without love.

2. That they should not seek themselves, but the good of others.

Remember the historical character of the Books of Scripture. We must therefore place ourselves in the position of those to whom they were addressed to understand them. During the apostolic age spiritual gifts were abundant and various. They were not confined to Church officers. They became objects of emulous competition. Those intrinsically and the least important, the most desired.

Paul classifies on three principles.

1. Their inherent character.
2. Their permanence.
3. Their usefulness.

1st. Some not sanctifying. 2d. Some (often the same) not permanent. 3d. Some even of those permanent, not useful to others.

He teaches the Corinthians, 1. That they might possess all those gifts which imply simply knowledge and power, and be reprobate.

2. That they should regard not themselves but others, and therefore covet those gifts which would edify the Church.

CV. Unbelief (or doubts) in Believers.—Matt. 6: 30; Mark 6: 6.
[*Dec. 18th*, 1858.]

I. *Its nature.*

Unbelief is of course the opposite of faith. Faith is the conviction of the truth contained in the word of God founded on the testimony of the Holy Ghost. This faith may have reference either to the doctrines or to the promises of the word of God. If to the latter, it may refer either to the promises, or to our interest in them.

It is essentially a holy exercise. It supposes holiness, and it is itself holy.

Unbelief, its opposite, is either (as found in the renewed) a weakness of faith, or a faith, beset with doubts or alternating with them. It may have reference to the truths or to the promises of God. It is unholy. It is a fact in Christian experience that the believer has to contend with unbelief. He is often troubled with doubts, as to the truth of God's word, or of some of its doctrines, or of his interest in the promises.

II. *As to the source of these doubts.*

1. In general it is an evil heart. In the unrenewed this precludes faith, and as the Christian is imperfectly sanctified, the evil of his heart produces unbelief. If perfectly holy, we should have no doubts. This should be impressed upon us, that we may feel our guilt, and not cherish doubt as a manifestation of humility. The reason why holiness precludes doubt, or tends thereto, is 1. The evidence of the truth is abundant, and that it is addressed to the spiritual understanding. So that if that is unclouded, our apprehensions would be clear and our

convictions strong and constant. This is the general source. The more specific causes of doubt are:-

2. Looking for, demanding, and relying on wrong kinds of evidence. Those who look for or demand "wisdom," *i. e.*, proof addressed to the reason, instead of testimony, will always be in doubt. Some men do this from undue regard to their own ability. They lean on their own understanding, grapple with authors and arguments too strong for them. With regard to the promises, doubt often arises from looking for wrong evidence of our interest in them. We have the idea that we are entitled to believe only if we feel aright. Right feeling comes from faith.

3. Grieving the Spirit. As all true faith is founded on the testimony of the Spirit, whatever tends to grieve the Spirit leads to a suspension or withdrawal of his witnessing to the truth, and to our spirits. Hence God is said to give the wicked up to believe a lie.

4. Sometimes these doubts, especially desponding ones, have their source in the physical temperament, or in the state of the body. This should be known both to the people, and to those who have the care of souls.

III. *The effects of this unbelief.*

1. It is in general to destroy the power of the truth. The truth becomes clouded, and cannot operate with full effect on the soul. Hence unbelief produces,

2. Sin. What arises from evil produces evil. It leads to separation and alienation from God, whose truth is his image, through which we have fellowship with him. Hence Paul says it leads to apostacy. No matter whether it have reference to the truths or to the promises of God, it alienates from him, prevents intercourse and thus spiritual death.

3. Of course it destroys peace of mind. Peace is the fruit of faith, whether that peace be the quiet of the mind which arises from freedom from conflicts with doubt and acquiescence in the truth, or whether it be that peace which passes all understanding, which flows from the assurance of the divine favor.

4. It necessarily weakens us for all duty, and dries up the sources of all spiritual consolation. Nothing more miserable than a sceptic unless it be the man whose understanding and conscience witness for the truth which his heart rejects, or which he is unable to appropriate to himself.

IV. *The cure of unbelief and doubts.*

Much of the physician's skill in the care of his patients is evinced in telling them what not to do. So here the negative part of the prescription for the cure of unbelief is no less important.

1. Do not grieve the Spirit of God.

2. Do not rely on our own understanding for faith.

3. Do not grapple with sceptical books unnecessarily.

4. Do not take false views of the plan of salvation, overlooking the grace of the gospel.

On the other hand,—

1. Look to God for faith.

2. Live in communion with God, in the use of the means of grace.

3. Allow the truth to operate freely and fully, by frequent reading and meditation.

4. Be active in the service of God. Obeying produces believing.

CVI. Contentment. 1 Tim. 6: 6.

I. *Its nature.* It is the opposite of dissatisfaction. It is, therefore, a quiet acquiescence in the allotments of providence with regard to ourselves. Not self-sufficiency as αὐτάρκεια might seem to mean, nor self-satisfaction, nor listless unconcern, as to what we are, and what happens to us, but it has reference not to what we are, or what we can do, but to what God does. It is quiet acquiescence in the share of good which he assigns us,

Whether this relates 1. To our wealth or outward estate. Some rich, some poor, some of every grade between, 2. or to our position in society. In point of fact there are grades. Some are above us, some below us. In other countries this relative position is determined by birth, and by the laws of the land. Here by fortuitous circumstances. Nothing more pitiable than discontentment with our social position. It leads to envy, subserviency, extravagance, contempt of the poor and all uncharitableness.

3. Or to personal advantages, of health, strength, mental endowments, or advantages of education.

4. Or to our success in life, the degree of honor, or usefulness, God may see fit to assign us.

II. *The grounds of this state of mind.* It is as a Christian grace one of the fruits of the Spirit. Nothing short of his power can so mortify our natural desire for enjoyment and pre-eminence, as to make us cheerfully to acquiesce in being poor, suffering, of little account and of little esteem.

This state of mind arises out of, 1. A deep and abiding sense of guilt, insignificance and pollution. If this conviction is strong, we shall never cease to feel, that any thing short of utter condemnation is a mercy.

2. Faith in the universal providence of God, the conviction that all

things are ordered by his power and wisdom, that all circumstances are determined by his will.

3. The assurance of our reconciliation to God; that not only are our circumstances determined by his wisdom but by his love. If it were better for us to be richer, happier, more eminent or powerful, he would make us so. It would be to act as children who cry for poison, to be craving after forms of good which God denies.

4. The conviction that not only our good, but God's glory, is most promoted by our lot being what it is.

5. A peculiarly Christian character is given to these considerations, when we remember that it is our own Lord and Saviour, who is the God of Providence, and who determines the bounds of our habitation.

6. The great ground of contentment is that God is our portion. The apostle remarks ευσέβεια with αυταρχεια because they are so intimately related. The one flows from the other. This complex state of mind, where ευσέβεια and αυταρχεια are combined, is the union of heaven and earth. As when the sky melts the horizon, or when the placid lake reflects a placid heavens. In looking on such a lake, we see the quiet of earth and the sublimity of heaven united. It is, therefore, a great gain. It is better than wealth or fame, a surer source of happiness, and a higher means of good.

CVII. Submission.

[*May 3d,* 1857.]

I. *What is submission ?*

In general it is acquiescence in the teaching, the will, or acts of another.

Submission to God is,

1. Acquiescence in his authority; a cordial recognition of his right to do what he will with us. It is an unresisting subjection to him and his authority, as manifested in all the dispensations of his providence, in his assigning us our position in the world, our talents, health, wealth, means of happiness. It stands opposed, *a.* To discontentment. *b.* To envying or repining at the good of others. *c.* And still more, to open murmuring and rebelling against the will of God. So much as concerns ourselves.

Submission, however, moreover implies acquiescence in the providential dispensations and arrangements of God, with regard to the ordering all events in the world and in the church. We are disposed to be disturbed at the course which things take in the state or in the church, and it is our duty to do what we can to give them a right direction; but if they are guided into other courses than such as we would choose, we must submit to the will of God, without repining or despondency.

2. Submission includes the subjection not only of our will to the will of God, but of our reason to his instruction. That is, we must receive as true whatever he has revealed on the ground of his authority. We must be converted and become as little children. This is opposed, *a.* To ignoring the revelation of God. *b.* To refusing to receive what he has revealed because it clashes with our preconceived opinions. *c.* To the principle that we must understand whatever we are required to believe.

3. So far as concerns the method of salvation, submission is, not a willing to be damned for the glory of God, which is contradictory and impossible; nor is it a mere submission to his authority, but it is a submission to the method of salvation which he has revealed. This includes, 1. A rejecting of our own righteousness and submitting ourselves to the righteousness of God. 2. A cordial acquiescence in the teaching of his word as to our helplessness and dependence, and a willingness to be saved in the way which he has prescribed, and for his glory.

II. *Grounds of this submission.*

1. The infinite superiority of God. The fact that he is infinite in wisdom, power and goodness is reason enough why his will should be acquiesced in, why his teaching should be received, and why his plan of redemption should be received and acquiesced in, without debate or opposition.

2. Opposition of our will to God's, of our intellect to his, of our method of securing salvation to his, can only result in our destruction. If we oppose our will to his as to our external circumstances, how does that alter our condition? Will it give us health, wealth, or happiness? If we oppose our intellect to his, will that bring us to the knowledge of the truth? Has any system of philosophy ever stood the test of time? Or; if we insist on being saved in some other way than that revealed in the Bible, will our salvation be thereby secured? Do we obtain righteousness by refusing to submit to the righteousness of God? Do we gain grace by refusing to admit that God is a sovereign in the gift of his Spirit, by asserting our right to be converted, sanctified or saved?

3. Our whole happiness and well-being depends on our submitting ourselves to God. If we are in harmony with him, with his will and purposes, and allow him to execute his plan, and rejoice in the sovereignty of his will, then all things will work together for our good, and the end to which infinite wisdom and love conducts all things, will include our supreme and everlasting blessedness. If we submit our reason to his teaching we shall be preserved from all fatal and hurtful

error, and guided more and more into the knowledge of the truth. And if we are willing to acquiesce in his plan of salvation, then it will take effect in our case.

CVIII. Parable of the Rich Man and Lazarus.
[*April 22d*, 1857.]

This parable presents the picture of a rich man arrayed in splendid garments, and faring sumptuously, and at his gate a poor man, nearly famished, and covered with sores. The one the object of respect, if not of envy, the other of commiseration and contempt. In a moment the scene changes. The poor man is seen in the bosom of Abraham, and the rich man in hell.

What was this meant to teach?

1. Not that the rich because rich go to hell, and that the poor because poor go to heaven. This would be to contradict the great principle of the Bible, that character and not external circumstances determine our destiny before God. It would contradict the facts recorded in Scripture, as many rich men, as Joseph and David, Abraham and Isaac and Jacob, were the children of God—many poor men were wicked. It would no less contradict our daily experience. It would lead us to distrust all who are rich, and tempt the vicious poor to claim heaven as a compensation for their suffering in the present life.

2. Neither was the parable designed to teach us the danger of riches. It is hard for a rich man to enter into the kingdom of heaven. But so it is for the poor. It is difficult to say which condition presents the greatest obstacles to salvation.

3. It is doubtful even whether it was designed to teach us the end to which an abuse of wealth inevitably leads. But it does teach:

1. That what is highly esteemed among men, is an abomination in the sight of God. It is intended to teach that God knows and judges the heart; that his estimate and judgment is not founded on appearances or on external circumstances, but on the inward state. And therefore, *a.* we should adopt the same rule, and not honor men for wealth and rank, but for their excellence. *b.* We should remember that the same rule of judgment will be applied to ourselves.

2. Another great lesson taught is, that God's providential blessings are not distributed according to the merit of their recipients. He gives wealth, and rank, and honor, and privileges to those whom he means shall perish, and sends poverty and sorrow to those whom he means to save. We should not, therefore, envy the prosperous, or repine at afflictions.

3. A truth incidentally taught is, that the state of the soul is deter-

mined immediately after death. There is no sleep of the soul. No intermediate state between heaven and hell. No state either of probation, or of purification.

4. The condition of the soul after death is unalterable. There is an impassable gulf between heaven and hell.

5. That the sufferings of the lost are extreme and without mitigation. Even a drop of water was desired. The recompense or enjoyment of the righteous is also great beyond all present conception.

6. That repentance is necessary in order to escape final perdition.

7. That the want of evidence is not the reason why men do not repent and believe.

This includes two things, *first*, that no amount of external evidence can produce repentance. This proved, *a.* Because repentance involves a change of heart, which such evidence cannot effect. The only effect of such evidence is speculative conviction, but speculative conviction has no power over the affections. *b.* The example of the Israelites proves the same thing. *c.* So also does the example of those who saw the miracles of Christ. This should stop our mouths, as it shows that our impenitence and unbelief has a deeper foundation than the want of evidence.

The *second* thing included is that the Scriptures are the best adapted means to repentance, so that those who do not repent and lead a holy life under their influence, would resist all other means. Repentance implies, 1. A knowledge of sin. 2. Conviction of sin. 3. A turning from it with grief and hatred unto God.

Now the Scriptures are adapted, 1. To give us this knowledge, and to produce this conviction. 2. They are adapted to lead us to return to God, *a.* By the exhibition which they make of his character and love. *b.* By revealing to us the way of return through Jesus Christ. *c.* By presenting all the motives to repentance which can influence a rational being.

INFERENCES.

This parable should lead us to be content with our lot. We may be rich and perish, we may be poor and yet be saved. It was a small matter to Lazarus because he had suffered so much while on earth.

2. It should teach us that we are within a hairs-breadth of heaven or hell every moment, and therefore should live in fear and trembling, and that others are in the same predicament, and therefore we should endeavor to awaken them to a sense of their danger.

3. It should teach us that now is the day of salvation, and that as we have the means of salvation, if we perish, our blood will be on our own head.

CIX. Growth in Grace.

[*October 29th*, 1854.]

I. *Use of the word grace in the Scriptures.*

1. An inward disposition.

2. Any favor, especially divine influence.

3. The inward effects of that influence, the Christian graces. These are gifts of the Holy Ghost. They are the fruits of a renewed heart, the abiding principle of spiritual life, which itself is grace, a gift.

II. *What is the growth of grace?*

It is another form of expressing the idea of the increase in the power of religion in the soul. It is an increase at once of the principle itself and of all its manifestations, *e. g.*, Faith, Love, Submission, Patience, Meekness, Zeal, Diligence, etc.

With this is connected increase in the knowledge of our Lord and Saviour Jesus Christ, *i. e.*, of Christ as our Lord and our Saviour.

III. *What is it to know Christ as our Lord?*

Knowledge is speculative and experimental.

Both forms of knowledge must be united. The object of this knowledge is Christ, as Lord and as Saviour.

As Lord, it includes his divinity and his incarnation, as it is the Theanthropos whom we recognize as Lord.

Increase in this knowledge includes,

1. Clearer apprehension of his glory.

2. Of his exaltation and dominion.

3. Increase in the inward feelings belonging to the relation which we bear to him as Lord, who rules in us, reigns over us, and subdues all his and our enemies.

IV. *What is it to know Christ as our Saviour?* It includes, 1. Knowledge of what he does for us in this character. 2. Inward experience of his saving work on our own souls.

V. *Means of growth in Grace.* The necessary conditions of all growth are light, food and exercise.

1. Light and warmth. This is, so far as spiritual life is concerned, the favor of God, the assurance of it, the experience of it. We must bring our souls under the influence of the love of God. The more this is done the more life shall we have. It must be in the way the gospel prescribes. The assurance must be evangelical. If unfounded, it will promote only evil.

2. The food of the soul is truth.

a. This must be pure, *i. e.*, scriptural.

b. It must be daily received.

c. It must be appropriated, and applied.

3. The exercise of grace. This includes, *a.* All acts of worship. *b.* All exercises of faith and love, etc. *c.* All outward duties performed in obedience to God and to promote his cause.

VI. *Evidence of growth in grace, is*

1. Not fervor of feeling. 2. Nor enjoyment. 3. But increase in, *a.* Our acquiescence in the truth. *b.* In our conformity to Christ. *c.* In our power to resist sin and to do and to bear the will of God.

CX. Growth in Grace.

[*October 2d*, 1859.]

Growth is incident to life. In all its forms, life is progressive until its end, or perfection is attained. If there is no end to the power of expansion, there is no end to the growth. What is true of other forms of life is no less true of the divine life. The nature of growth, however, is different.

1. In plants and animals growth is a natural and involuntary process. It goes on without effort, and by a law of natural development. This is true also of the growth of the body in man. All that is necessary is that the proper conditions of nourishment, heat, light and air be present, then growth is not only involuntary but necessary.

2. In intellectual life this is only partially true. There is little growth in knowledge or intellectual power without conscious effort. It is true that men are so surrounded by the occasions and necessities of intellectual exercise that there is a necessary and almost unconscious increase from infancy to age. But beyond this limit, there must be effort in order to secure increase.

In the divine life, the case is different. It does not owe its existence or its continuance, and much less its increase, to any law of nature. It will not grow of itself, as does the plant or the animal. Therefore the exhortation, grow in grace. We cannot exhort a young animal to grow. This, therefore, is a preliminary truth, the conviction of which should be graven on our hearts, that our religion will perish, if let alone. It will wither and die, unless by the use of the appointed means, it is caused to grow.

II. *The means of growth.*

1. This growth cannot be secured by any arbitrary process; not by an act of the will; not by a mere desire; or by the use of unappointed means. It is a divine life as to its nature and origin, and so also in its support and increase. It can be sustained and increased only in the use of the means of God's appointment.

In order to growth, two things are necessary. 1. The increase of the vital force. 2. The necessary conditions for the exercise and development of that force. You may do what you please to a dead tree; you may spread around it the richest soil, plant it by rivers of water, and let in upon it the brightest light, and spread about it the purest atmosphere, yet it remains as dead as ever. So the most appropriate and abundant supplies may be given to a diseased or dead being, without producing life, or securing growth. There is wanting the indispensable preliminary condition of vital force. It is so in the divine life. The most abundant supplies of light, the freest access to all that is adapted to its nourishment may be supplied, and there can be no growth without the inward principle. Now this inward principle is the Spirit of God, or Christ. This inward principle is communicated, and maintained, and increased in power only by the word, sacraments and prayer. We may do what we may. We may preach, exhort, go about doing good, all to no effect. These are like exercise which invigorates where there is inward life and strength, but exhausts if that principle be feeble and decaying.

2. But supposing the inward communications granted, then there is no less necessarily the constant exercise of that principle, *i. e.*, the constant exercise of faith, love, meekness, humility and benevolence in promoting the spiritual welfare of others. This is another mistake. Growth in grace is not promoted by a life of seclusion and asceticism.

III. *Evidence of growth.* 1. Not fervor of feeling. The young have more of this than the old. 2. But increase of knowledge.

3. Increase of strength to do and to suffer.

4. Increase of firmness and fixedness and singleness of purpose.

CXI. Blessed are the Poor in Spirit.

[*March 3d,* 1861.]

The great question when Christ was on earth was, to whom did the kingdom of heaven belong? Who were to enjoy its prerogatives and blessings? By the kingdom of heaven is meant the Messianic kingdom, that which Christ came to establish.

Its blessings were not of this world, nor temporal, as consisting in wealth, honor, or power; but justification, adoption, sanctification and eternal life. These were the μέλλοντα ἀγαθά (mellonta agatha) which Christ came to secure and to bestow. To whom did they belong? Who were to receive them?

1. Not the Jews as Jews. Not all the descendants of Abraham.

2. Not the rich and prosperous, the wise, the noble, as a class.

3. Not the poor as poor and because poor. Poverty is not the condition of membership in this kingdom. Its blessings are not bestowed as a recompense for the evils of poverty.

4. Not those who are voluntarily poor. The Romanists may so interpret the passage in favor of monastical vows.

5. Not those who, although rich in this world's goods, feel themselves to be poor. That is, those who buy and yet possess not. Not those who do not make riches their portion and trust.

But the poverty intended is a poverty as to the spirit. This of course is not to be understood as something derogatory. Poor-spirited is a term of reproach. It expresses the absence of manly virtue, of courage, strength of conviction and of will.

The poor in spirit are those who are conscious of their spiritual poverty. They stand opposed to those who falsely assume and assert that they are rich and know not that they are wretched and miserable, and poor and blind and naked.

Poorness in spirit includes therefore,

1. A sense of ignorance and a willingness to be taught. It stands opposed to pride of intellect and to confidence in the conclusions of our own understandings. Where this state of mind prevails, this intellectual blindness is the consequence. Those who profess themselves to be wise become fools. It is only those who are sensible of their ignorance and of their insufficiency to discover truth and who are converted so as to be as little children, who have the Holy Ghost, who is the source of all true knowledge and one of the great blessings of the kingdom of God.

2. A sense of unworthiness, as opposed to a spirit of self-righteousness. It is a consciousness of guilt and ill-desert in the sight of God which leads the soul to cry, God, be merciful to me, a sinner. So long as a man thinks that the law of God does not condemn him who cherishes the persuasion that he has never done anything worthy of death, so long is he left in his delusion. But when he is made sensible of the enormity of his guilt, and when he trembles at the wrath of God and renounces his own righteousness, then he receives the righteousness of Christ and becomes rich indeed.

3 A sense of pollution, as opposed to self-complacency or a disposition to admire our own excellence and to regard ourselves as attractive in the sight of others. To this is opposed a sense of vileness, which leads us to abhor ourselves and lay our mouths in the dust before God. To those who are thus poor in spirit, the Spirit comes and adorns them with all his heavenly grace.

4. A sense of helplessness. This is opposed to the conceit of our own power to change our hearts, to subdue sin, to secure holiness of

heart and life. Those who have this conceit God leaves to their own resources, either to perish in their delusion or to convince themselves of their utter impotence, because then they are endued with power from on high.

So when they think they have power in themselves to accomplish any good work in the Church, God leaves them to try. It is only those who are poor in spirit whom He helps.

5. Poverty of spirit is a sense of wretchedness, *i. e.*, of the utter incompetency of the world to fill the desires of the soul. Those who think themselves rich because possessed of this world's sources of happiness, and desire nothing more, God leaves in their contentment. But those who are sensible of their poverty, who hunger and thirst after God, He fills with Himself.

CXII. Conscience.

[*September 22d*, 1861.]

I. *The facts of conscience.*

1. We have a discernment of the difference between right and wrong.

2. We approve of the one, and we disapprove of the other, as of good and bad laws.

3. We condemn ourselves for what conscience disapproves in our states and acts.

4. We are impelled by conscience to do what is right, and deterred by it from what is wrong. Conscience therefore is not a simple faculty. It is a collective term for those exercises of our rational nature which concern moral good and evil. It includes cognition. It includes a judgment of approbation and disapprobation, which is a complex state of mind, including feeling as well as decision. And it is an impulse, as desire and affections are. It is not a mere decision as to truth.

II. *Of this mysterious power, the obvious characteristics are,*

1. That it is independent of the understanding and of the will. No man can force himself by a volition to approve of what he sees to be wrong. Nor can conscience be perverted by mere sophistry of the understanding. If a man honestly thinks a thing which is wrong to be right, his conscience will approve his doing it. But no man can argue his conscience out of its convictions. Nor can it be silenced. It will be heard in spite of all we can do.

2. It is authoritative. It asserts the right to rule, to control our hearts and lives. And this authority we cannot deny. We may disregard it and rebel against it; but we must admit it to be legitimate.

3. It does not speak in its own name. The authority which it exercises is not its own. The vengeance which it threatens is not its own

displeasure. It is the representative of God. It brings the soul before His bar.

4. It is avenging. It is made so by God. Remorse is a state produced by conscience. It includes self-condemnation, self-abhorrence, regret and apprehension of wrath. It can be opposed only by what satisfies justice.

III. *Our duty in regard to conscience.*

1. To enlighten it. It is not infallible in its judgments. It is in this respect on a par with reason, for it is in fact only a function of reason. We find men, therefore, differing widely as to what is right and wrong. Our thinking a thing right does not make it right. It is of the last importance to have an enlightened conscience, as opposed to a perverted conscience, to a scrupulous or a seared one.

2. To obey it. No man is better than his conscience. No man is as good. Although he is liable to error, yet he must obey his conscience in all cases in which its decisions are not contrary to a higher law.

3. Not only to obey it in particular cases, but to have a fixed and governing purpose to permit it to rule. That is, that we will not act from impulse, self-interest, from mere feeling or inclination, allowing ourselves to be determined by what is agreeable or disagreeable, and in small matters as well as great. He that is faithful in that which is least will be faithful in that which is much, etc.

The ground of this obligation to obey conscience is—

1. The authority of God in whose name it speaks. In resisting conscience we resist and disobey God. This is to be understood with the limitations above mentioned.

2. Respect for our own dignity as rational and moral beings. Self-degradation and ruin are the consequence of disobedience and the habit of it.

3. The greatest happiness flows from an approving conscience, and the greatest misery from a wounded conscience.

CXIII. Conscientiousness.

[*December 5th*, 1869.]

I. *What it is.* It is acting from a sense of right, as opposed to acting from considerations of expediency, or for self-indulgence.

II. *There are three classes of men.* 1. The conscientious, who always ask, what is right? 2. The mass of men, who do what is agreeable or what promotes their interests. 3. Those who on great matters are conscientious, but not in small matters.

III. *Difficulty of being conscientious.* 1. Because of the strong opposing principles within. 2. Because of the opposing influences from without; the influence of friends; of party; of example. 3. Because of the moral courage and firmness of character it requires.

IV. *Your duty.* 1. Be conscientious in your religious duties in the closet and in keeping the heart. 2. In your special duties of study recitation, etc. 3. In your ministerial duties, in preparing for the pulpit, in visiting the people, in care for the young. 4. In church courts.

V. *Aids.* 1. A fixed purpose. The power of the will is great. 2. Living near to God. 3. Habit. 4. Prayer.

VI. *Advantages.* 1. We are doing right. 2. It purifies the heart. 3. It gives power, because it secures influence and respect.

CXIV. Diseased Conscience.

[*December 19th,* 1852.]

I. *What is conscience?*

There are certain phenomena of our moral nature of which all men are conscious. 1. The perception of moral distinctions. 2. A sense of moral obligation. 3. A feeling of approbation and disapprobation (entirely distinct from admiration and contempt) of the acts of others, or of self-approval and self-condemnation. Whether and how far these exercises belong to the cognitive faculties, and how far to the susceptibilities (reason and feeling), is hard and perhaps useless to determine. They are rational in so far as they suppose a rational nature and involve the exercise of reason. But every cognition when its object, moral or æsthetic, is not an act of the pure reason, but of a rational soul, involving feeling as well as knowledge. It is here, as in the perception of beauty, and even in our sensations, which are different in us from what they are in a brute. It is hard to distinguish these elements in our perceptions, affections and moral judgments.

II. *The attributes of this moral sense or conscience.* 1. It is universal. 2. It is innate. 3. It is representative. 4. It is independent. 5. It is authoritative. 6. It is indestructible.

III. *Conditions of a healthy conscience.*

1. Knowledge, which is light. Conscience needs this just as reason needs knowledge, or as taste needs correct principles. Some knowledge is original and intuitive, other is acquired.

2. Due susceptibility. Men differ much as to this point. It may be excessive or deficient, but for a healthful conscience is necessarily due susceptibility. So that moral distinctions do not concern light matters, or trifles give as much concern as serious matters. *a.* Before acting. *b.* In applying the rule to doubtful cases. *c.* In the subsequent state.

3. Strength to constrain obedience. Sickly sentimentality is very different from a sound healthful conscience.

III. *Diseases of conscience.*

1. Perversion. This is due either to wrong principles, or to prejudices and passion. The cure is to be found in knowledge, objective and subjective.

2. Obduracy. Cause, ignorance and crime; cure, *a.* Knowledge again. *b.* Regeneration and sanctification.

3. Scrupulosity, cause, either weakness of conviction or undue sensibility, not really moral, but a sensitiveness analogous to false shame, bashfulness, etc. Cure, growth in strength. " Be strong in faith."

4. Wounded conscience. The only cure is, *a.* The blood of Christ. *b.* Confession. *c.* Restitution. *d.* Reformation.

The immense importance of this subject. On it depend, 1. Our excellence. 2. Our happiness. 3. Our usefulness.

CXV. Spiritual-mindedness.

[*Dec.* 10*th,* 1854.]

I. *Its nature.* 1. The word φρονεῖν (phronein) is used of all inward acts, thinking, willing and feeling. Let this mind be in you that was also in Christ Jesus. Set your affections on things above. Minding the things of the flesh. So φρόνημα (phronema) is used either for state of mind, or for thought, feeling, or volition. To mind the things of the flesh, therefore, is to make them the object of thought, desire and pursuit. And the things of the flesh are those things which are adapted to our nature considered as corrupt. The things of the Spirit are those things which the Spirit reveals as the proper objects of thought, desire and pursuit. And to mind them is thus to make them the object of our meditation, desire and pursuit. And the φρόνημα τῆς σαρκός (phronema tes sarkos) is either the inward carnal disposition or the actual pursuit, desire and thought of which the flesh is the object. And so of the phrase φρόνημα τοῦ πνεύματος (phronema tou pneumatos). Spiritual-mindedness, therefore, is that state of mind which manifests itself in making the things of the Spirit the great object of thought, desire and pursuit. The things of the Spirit are God, Christ, truth, holiness, the interests of Christ's kingdom and heaven.

To the spiritually-minded these objects are, 1. The great subjects of their thoughts. Their minds are occupied with them. They are in communion with them. They dwell upon them in meditation. They study them. They spontaneously think of them by the way, and in the watches of the night.

2. They are also the great objects of desire or affection. Their hearts are set upon them. They are the sources of their peculiar enjoyments.

3. They devote themselves to the enjoyment or promotion of these objects. This supposes, of course,

1. That these things appear to the spiritually-minded as true. They are not the objects of sight or knowledge, but of faith. But they are real and true in their apprehension.

2. That they are most lovely and excellent. The state of mind in question arises out of the perception of the glory of the things of the Spirit, *i.e.*, out of spiritual discernment.

3. That they are seen to be of infinite importance. The things which are seen are temporal, but the things which are not seen are eternal.

II. *The effects of spiritual-mindedness.* To be carnally-minded is death. It not only leads to death, but is death. That is, death consists in the degradation, the corruption, and the misery which are involved in this state of mind. To be spiritually-minded is life and peace. That is, the life and blessedness of the soul consist in the elevation, the holiness and happiness involved in being spiritually-minded.

The reason of this is that God is the true life of the soul, the source and object of life. The former state of mind is separation from him; the latter involves fellowship and communion. Sin is separation from God, and therefore death. Holiness is union with God, and therefore life. This death and life are here inchoate; hereafter they are to be complete.

III. *Method of attaining spiritual-mindedness.* 1. Reconciliation to God through Christ. This is the first condition of union. 2. Participation of the Holy Spirit as the gift of Christ. 3. Constant use of the means of grace and strenuous self-discipline, extending to the thoughts, feelings and outward life.

IV. *Fruits.* These are excellence, happiness and usefulness.

CXVI. To be carnally-minded is death; but to be spiritually-minded is life and peace.

[*March 6th*, 1865.]

The analogy between matter and mind is so great and obvious that terms expressive of the state and acts of the former are used to express those of the latter. This is a principle on which all languages are constructed. To see, to perceive, to apprehend, all express bodily actions, but they also express acts of the mind. This is not arbitrary. When we see a thing, we know that it is and what it is. So when the mind knows that a thing is and what it is, it is said to see. The invisible things of God are said to be seen. This usage, of course, pervades the Scripture. Hence, as we might expect, the words, death and life, are transferred to the soul.

In relation to the body, death implies,

1. Entire ignorance or the want of power to perceive the things of sense. It neither sees, hears nor feels.

2. It is shut out from all enjoyment.

3. It decays and becomes offensive.

4. It is absolutely powerless. All this is included when we speak of the death of the soul.

1. It is ignorant of the things of God.

2. It is incapable of enjoying them.

3. It is corrupt and offensive.

4. It is perfectly helpless.

On the other hand, life is the opposite of all this. The life of the body supposes its capacity to apprehend the objects around it, to enjoy them, the absence of decay and the possession of activity, etc. The life of the soul in Scripture language includes.

1. Knowledge, or right apprehension of divine things.

2. The enjoyment of them.

3. Holiness or purity.

4. Activity and power in the sphere of the spirit.

What the apostle asserts is that the carnal mind is death in the sense stated, and the spiritual mind is life.

The carnal mind φρόνημα τῆς σαρχὸς (phronema tes sarkos) means that state of mind which is the effect of our apostacy or the product of our corrupt nature. In other words, our corrupt nature manifests itself,

1. In ignorance.

2. In alienation, hatred, want of capacity to enjoy the things of God.

3. In moral corruption, or the exercise of all unholy thoughts and feelings.

4. In utter inability to alter this state of things. Whereas the φρόνημα τὸυ πνεύματος, the state of mind produced by the Spirit, includes a. Knowledge. b. Love and happiness. c. Holiness. d. Activity and power.

1. This is the simple and comprehensive truth here taught. The first remark suggested by it is that men mistake in regarding punishment and reward too much as positive inflictions; that is, something imposed or given from without. The death of which the Bible speaks as the wages of sin is mainly a subjective state. No greater misery is possible or conceivable than that which would follow from a sinner being left to himself. His inward state includes all the elements of misery; just as Milton makes Satan say, "Myself am hell."

It is true that the circumstances of the righteous, their associates and their surroundings minister to their blessedness. So doubtless will it be with the impenitent in the opposite way.

2. The wicked, those who are carnally-minded, are lost. They are now in a state of perdition, not hopeless and final in this world, not left to themselves; but still they are in that state which, if not radically changed, will issue in eternal death. So, on the other hand, believers, the spiritual, are saved. They *have* eternal life. The Holy Spirit in them is a source of spiritual and eternal life.

3. The decision of which of these two classes we belong to is not determined by anything external, our being in or out of the Church, our professing this or that faith, our outward deportment, or the reputation we have in the world, but simply and solely by our inward state. If the things of the flesh, *i. e.*, adapted to our sensuous, physical or corrupt nature; if, in short, the things seen and temporal, the things to be professed and enjoyed in this life are the things which engross our thoughts, fix our desires and fill our hearts, we are in a state of spiritual death, from which nothing but the power of Him who can raise the dead can deliver us. On the other hand, if the things of the Spirit—God, Christ, heaven, the kingdom of the Redeemer, the spiritual interests of men—engross our minds, then we are spiritually-minded. This is a matter on which it is vain to attempt to deceive ourselves. We cannot make death life.

4. From what is said above, will appear the duty both of the carnally-minded and of those who hope they have the Spirit.

CXVII. Spiritual Discernment. 1 Cor. 2: 15.

[*April 8th*, 1855.]

I. *The epithet* πνευματικός (*pneumatikos*), *as applied to believers, is one of the most significant and comprehensive.* It does not mean rational as opposed to sensual, but is applied to one under the influence of the Spirit. It is the indwelling of the Spirit that gives character to the believer. The Spirit has an illuminating power, so that new discernment is imparted to the soul. This does not arise from light shed upon the object, but from the effect produced on the mind. Its faculty of vision is restored; its eyes are opened. Before, it was blind, not rationally, so as not to perceive truth in its logical relations, nor morally, so as to be insensible to moral distinctions, but spiritually, so that it cannot discern the things of the Spirit. The case of the Jews in their judgment concerning Christ is an example. They saw that he was a wise man. They understood his words. They saw he was just, benevolent and kind. But they had no such discernment of his character as enabled them to see the glory of God as it shone in him. The effect, therefore, produced in the mind is the ability to discern the things of the Spirit.

II. *Hence, first, there is a coincidence of judgment between the believer and God.* What God declares to be true the believer sees to be true.

He acquiesces in the judgment of God as to sin, the method of salvation, the person of Christ, the doctrines of grace, and the reality and importance of eternal things. So also in his judgments of men. Those whom God approves the believer approves.

This is the ground, 1. Of the unity of faith among believers. 2. Of the unity of fellowship ; so that all Christians recognize each other. 3. It is the ground of the authority of the Church as a teacher, and of the only legitimate authority of tradition. 4. It is the ground or reason why schism is a sin.

Hence, secondly, there is not only this coincidence of judgment as to truth, but also of feeling. That is, the spiritual love what God loves ; they hate what God hates. They love those whom God loves, and so far as their character is concerned, they hate those whom God hates. The friends of God are their friends. This is the ground of the unity of communion between Christians. It is the reason why they have a common experience, and why they love each other as brethren.

Hence, thirdly, there is a conformity in the life of the believer with the will of God. He does what is in accordance with the mind of the Spirit. This is the ground of the community of worship. They all walk by the same rule. They all worship the same God and Saviour.

Hence, fourthly, all believers are united so as to form one body, the temple of God and the bride of Christ. Because they are πνευματικόι (pneumatikoi) they are united to Christ, conformed to his image, and rendered glorious and blessed. For the Spirit is not only the source of knowledge and holiness, but also of consolation and of glory.

If we are Christians, we are πνευματικόι. We believe the truth. We agree with the Scripture and with our fellow Christians. We are united to them in love. We love the brethren. We shall be united to them forever in heaven.

CXVIII. Spiritual Consolation.

[*Feb. 17th,* 1856.]

Man is a child of sorrow. Though possessed of numerous sources of enjoyment and much happiness, there is no man who has not to drink of the cup of sorrow. The sources of sorrow are numerous. 1. Bodily pain and infirmity. 2. Pressure of external circumstances, poverty, disappointment, loss of reputation, and of confidence of friends. 3. Bereavements. 4. Sin in others, more or less nearly connected with us. 5. Sin in ourselves. Its power and its effects on the conscience. Its effect on faith and hope, and therefore despondency and fear of reprobation or final condemnation. From all these sources, man is certain to be more or less affected.

There are three sources of consolation. 1. The world. 2. Satan, who comforts his children with false hopes, with unbelief, and with sinful pleasures, as the drunkard drowns his sorrows in the bowl.

3. The Holy Ghost. He is set forth in the Scriptures as the Comforter.

II. *The Holy Ghost as Comforter.* The word παράκλητος (paraclete) means indeed more than Comforter, but it includes that idea. It was when speaking of the sorrow of his disciples that Christ promised to send them the Holy Ghost.

1. The need of a divine comforter arises, first, from the insufficiency of man for himself. He has no adequate resource in himself of knowledge, holiness or happiness. He must go out of himself for all these forms of good. Secondly, from the insufficiency of the creature. The world can never give the good we need. The soul of man, formed for God, can only be holy or happy in communion with God.

2. The way in which the Holy Ghost acts as our Comforter is, therefore, first, by bringing us to God, as the overflowing source of all good. Christ has opened the way, but we have access only through or by the Holy Spirit. This is the first great work of the Spirit.

Secondly, it is by taking the things of Christ and showing them unto us. That is, by revealing to us the glory of the Son of God. He thus fills the soul with a new affection, causes it to overflow with such admiration and delight, in view of Christ, that all our sorrows are lost in that sea of joy. This is a matter of daily experience. A man has been sadly afflicted by the sense of evil, when the accession of a far greater good has caused him to forget his sorrow in his joy.

Thirdly, by revealing and applying the truth to the heart and conscience, and giving us faith to embrace and appropriate it. Thus the convinced sinner is consoled by a view of Christ as a sacrifice and priest, and by having faith given to embrace him. Thus the soul, harassed and discouraged by the power of sin, is comforted by the promise, "My grace is sufficient for thee." Thus those who are weighed down by outward afflictions are comforted by the Spirit enabling them to see that these afflictions will work out for them a far more exceeding and eternal weight of glory. This is often carried so far that the believer glories in infirmities. It can be made so great that the stake itself has no terror.

Fourthly, by giving the soul such views of heaven as to render all earthly things inconsiderable.

Fifthly, by shedding abroad the love of God in the heart, and testifying with our spirit that we are the children of God. Christ by his

Spirit nourishes and cherishes, ἐκτρέφει κὰι θάλπει, (ektrephei kai thalpei) his people as a tender mother her infant, Eph. v : 29.

III. *How to enjoy these consolations.*

1. We must not seek consolation elsewhere. If we turn to the world, God will leave us to the world. It is only by looking to the Spirit, we can enjoy the consolations of the Spirit.

2. We must be careful not to grieve the Holy Ghost, by whom we are sealed unto the day of Redemption.

CXIX. The Spirit of Adoption.—Rom. 8:15.

[*February 10th*, 1856.]

I. *Meaning of the expression.*

1. That Spirit which brings us into the relation of sons to God, that is, the Holy Ghost.

2. The spirit of adoption may mean a filial spirit, the spirit which sons have ; that spirit which makes us feel toward God as children toward a father. The Holy Ghost is the Spirit of adoption, for two reasons: 1. Because he brings us into the relation of children to God. 2. Because he produces in us the feelings appropriate to that relation, a filial spirit.

II. *What is that relation ? or, What is it to be the children of God ?*

1. The general idea of sonship is participation of nature. In this sense Christ is, κατὲζοχήυ, the Son of God. In this sense Adam and all mankind are God's children. And in this sense, the regenerated, who are brought to be partakers of God's nature, are specially his children. They are renewed after the image of God in knowledge, righteousness and holiness. Those partaking of God's nature are of course like God. This is the fundamental fact which conditions all the rest.

2. Objects of special favor. In this sense the Israelites were God's children. This is the consequence, or rather an adjunct of the former. Those whom God loves, and towards whom he acts as a Father, are his children.

3. Sonship is heirship. The one is included in the other. The sons of Abraham are the heirs of Abraham. The sons of God are the heirs of God.

III. *The spirit of adoption as a filial spirit means that spirit or disposition towards God which is appropriate to this relation.* 1. It is a spirit of reverential love, of admiration, of gratitude and delight. 2. A spirit of confidence, founded on this relation and on the assurance of God's love and care. 3. A spirit of zeal for his glory, jealousy for his honor, and desire to see that honor promoted. 4. A spirit of obedience and resignation. A willingness that his will and not our own should be done.

IV. *The outward conduct becoming this relation to God and which is the effect of a filial spirit.*

1. A life regulated by his commands and devoted to his service. A life of holiness.

2. A life elevated above the world, not immersed in its pleasures and not devoted to its possessions. A life which has its end and consummation in heaven.

3. A life of inward intercourse and fellowship with God.

4. A life of joy and cheerful anticipation of the time when we shall see him as he is; when shall occur the manifestation of the sons of God.

Paul compares in Galatians the condition of believers under the law to that of νήπιοι (nepioi) and that of believers now to that of υἱοὶ (huioi). So we may compare our present state to that of νήπιοι and the state of believers after the second coming of Christ to that of υἱοί. Then and not before will it be known what it is to be the sons of God.

INFERENCES.

1. The great sin and folly of Antinomianism, which separates the external privilege from the internal character of the sons of God. No man is the son of God in the sense of being an heir who is not a son in the sense of participation of nature.

2. Our infinite obligation to Christ; for we are the sons of God only in him and by virtue of faith.

3. How are we to become the sons of God? This is answered by what precedes. It is by faith in the Son of God. To as many as received him to them gave he power to become the sons of God. It is furthermore by the indwelling of the Holy Ghost. Because ye are sons, God hath sent forth the Spirit of his Son into your hearts, crying, Abba, Father.

CXX. As many as are led by the Spirit of God, they are the sons of God. Rom. 8: 14.

[Oct. 18th, 1874.]

There are two classes of men in the world, the ψυχικόι (psychicæ), and the πνευματικόι; the natural and the spiritual; those who are controlled by their own nature, and those who are controlled by the Spirit of God. The former are governed as to their thoughts, opinions, feelings and outward life, by the principles of human nature in its present state. These principles are numerous and complete, some evil and some good. Reason, conscience, regard for their own interest, natural fear of God, are among the principles which control the inward and outward life of the majority of men, who are not openly and avowedly wicked. Such men never rise above the sphere of the natural. They look at the things which are temporal. They live for the present.

The spiritual are those in whom the Spirit of God dwells and reigns. The Bible teaches that God is immanent in the world, preserving and controlling all the physical causes, and the immediate author of all organic structure indicative of design. In like manner the Spirit of God is immanent in the souls of believers. He controls the operations of their minds and hearts as God controls the operations of nature. And as God does not violate natural laws, so neither does he violate the laws of our rational and moral constitution, nor does he disregard them. He does not say: Let it rain, let it snow, let there be a harvest; but he controls natural causes to produce those effects. So neither does he govern his people by blind impulses. He works in them to will and to do. In acting thus, he uses appropriate means.

1. He leads them into conformity with the mind of the Spirit, so that they receive and see to be true what the Spirit reveals to be true, to approve what the Spirit approves.

2. He controls their affections, so that they love what the Spirit sets forth as the proper objects of love, God, Christ. He leads them to set their affections on things above.

3. He leads them to endeavor to subdue all evil in their hearts, to be humble, long-suffering, benevolent, to live for others rather than for themselves.

Those led by the Spirit are conformed to the Spirit in their judgments and feelings ; and to his will as to their mode of life.

Whether we are natural or spiritual is not a matter of profession or belief, but of fact. If led by the Spirit, we are the sons of God. If not so led, we are not sons of God.

If sons, then, 1. We have the nature of God ; 2. We are the objects of his special care and love ; 3. We are heirs of his kingdom.

CXXI. The liberty wherewith Christ hath made us free.
[Feb. 23d, 1862.]

The nature of this liberty is determined by the nature of the bondage from which we are delivered.

I. *It was a bondage to the law, to the obligations to fulfill all its precepts as a condition of salvation.*

Secondly, to satisfy its penalty or the demands of justice for its violation. Thirdly, an inward spirit of bondage inseparable from this condition and relation.

II. *It was a bondage to sin.*—The power of sin as a law in our members.

1. This power exists. It is a real controlling influence which determines the character and conduct.

2. It cannot be broken or overthrown by any effort of our own. It is a real and fearful bondage.

3. It cannot be overthrown or destroyed by any human or any creature power. From this servitude Christ redeems us.

III. *It was a bondage to Satan.*

1. This subjection is real. Satan does rule over men. They are his captives. He controls them at will, so far as God permits.

2. They are unable to free themselves from his dominion. They are no match for him, and he has them at a disadvantage.

3. This dominion is the dominion of evil, and ends in eternal perdition. From this Christ has made us free by destroying the power of Satan by his own death.

IV. *It is a bondage of their reason and conscience to human authority.*

1. In fact what men are to believe and what they are to do, has always been determined either by the priesthood or by public opinion.

2. From this subjection men cannot deliver themselves.

3. It is a degrading and ruinous subjection. From this Christ has freed us, *a.* By destroying the grounds of that subjection which were the consciousness that we could know what we must believe and do in order to be saved. *b.* By substituting his own authority for all that which is illegitimate. He teaches us by his word and Spirit what we are to believe and do.

V. *It is a bondage to human despotism.* 1. There is no real liberty but where the gospel reigns.

2. The reign of the gospel secures civil and religious liberty, not only by restraining the power of rulers within legitimate bounds, but also by making the people act on the principle that they must obey God rather than man.

VI. *The liberty wherewith Christ has made us free consists of freedom from all illegitimate authority, and of subjection to truth, reason, and God, and final deliverance of his people and of " the whole creation " from the bondage of corruption.*

CXXII. He that is called in the Lord, being a servant, is the Lord's freeman.—1 Cor. 7 : 22.

[*September 16th, 1867.*]

The ideas of liberty and slavery are antithetical. They therefore explain each other. We cannot understand the liberty spoken of until we understand the bondage. The reverse is true. We cannot understand the nature of the bondage without understanding the nature of the liberty.

Liberty is not freedom from restraint or authority. This cannot be predicated of any creature. All rational beings are under the authority of reason and right. And as these are in infinite perfection in God, all creatures are under absolute subjection to him. And this subjection is the highest liberty. In renouncing subjection to God, man lost his liberty. He became:

1. The slave of sin. This Christ declares. This subjection to sin is true bondage. a. Because it has no right to rule. It does not belong to our normal state, and is inconsistent with the end of our being. b. Because it is independent of the will. We cannot throw it off. This is a matter of consciousness and experience.

2. The slave of the law. He is under the obligation of satisfying its demands or of bearing its penalty. a. This obligation is inexorable. b. It reveals itself in the conscience. c. It produces the most intolerable bondage. d. It produces a slavish spirit. e. Fear and anxious looking for of judgment.

3. This subjection to sin and the law involves subjection to Satan. We are in his kingdom. We are in his power. We are under his control.

4. This subjection to sin and the law leads to subjection to men in various ways.

a. It destroys the balance and power of the soul. Not being subject to God and being unable to guide itself, it submits to the world, to public opinion, to authority in some form. And especially does it lead to subjection to the priesthood and to the church.

Now, as Christ is a Redeemer, as he came to preach deliverance to the captives, to proclaim the acceptable year, i. e., the year of jubilee; as he is the author of our liberty; as they only are truly free whom the Son makes free, he must deliver his people from all the forms of bondage above referred to. This he does in the following way and order: 1. He frees us from condemnation. Until this is done nothing is done. A man in prison under sentence must be freed from death or he cannot be delivered from other evils. How Christ frees us from condemnation we know.

2. He frees from the law or the obligation of fulfilling its demands. How this is done we know.

3. He frees us from the authority and power of Satan. How we know. Heb. ii : 14, 15.

4. From the reigning power of sin.

5. From a slavish spirit.

6. From all undue subjection to men. a. By bringing the reason

under subjection to his truth, we are freed from their authority as to doctrine. *b.* As we are subject to him alone, as to the conscience, we cannot be subject to any other authority in deciding what is morally right or wrong. *c.* As we have through Christ deliverance from condemnation and acceptance with God, we are free from the priesthood. *d.* As all we do is done in obedience to him, subjection to men is part of our liberty.

So a slave may be truly and perfectly free. He is the Lord's freeman. And this is the reason why Paul exhorts slaves to regard their bonds as of little account.

No tongue can tell our obligations to Christ, as our Redeemer, from the awful bondage into which we were brought by our apostacy from God.

CXXIII.   Ye believe in God, believe also in me.

[Date not given.]

The discourses of Christ were designed for and indirectly addressed to all believers. This discourse was immediately addressed to the apostles, when they were about to experience a great trial and to enter on the discharge of a great duty. It was designed therefore to comfort and to encourage them.

Here are three things presented for our consideration; the duty enjoined, to believe; the object of faith, believe in me; the truths concerning Christ which we are to believe.

I. *What is it to believe?* Faith includes two things, assent and trust. It includes, therefore, first, the submission of the reason to all Christ has revealed; and, secondly, trust in all that he has promised. Both of these are difficult duties. To receive as true what we cannot understand on the testimony of God is declared to be irrational. But two things are to be remarked, first, that faith is rational; and, secondly, that the testimony of God is informing. It gives light.

To trust is no less difficult. To trust that we shall be pardoned, saved, preserved, is hard for our unbelieving hearts.

II. *The object of faith is Christ.* That is, the things to which we are to assent are truths concerning Christ, and the things in which we are to trust are the promises of Christ. Christ is here distinguished from God. The faith which the apostles were required to exercise was faith in Christ. This is the only form in which we can exercise faith in God. If we believe not God as seen, how can we believe in him as not seen.

III. *But what are we to believe concerning Christ and what are the promises that we are to trust?*

First. We must believe that he is the way, *i. e.*, that he brings us to God. There are three senses in which we are absent from God, or separated from him.

1. By our ignorance. Christ brings us near to God as an object of knowledge. He is the Logos or Revealer. He is God; God in our nature, God in fashion as a man.

2. By our guilt. Christ brings us near to God by reconciliation through his blood. He atones for our sins. We are enabled to draw near to God with hope of acceptance.

3. By our pollution or enmity. Christ by revealing the knowledge of God and by reconciling us to him, removes our enmity. Believe that I am the way, that God in me is revealed to you, brought nigh to you, that he is reconciled, that you through me are brought to love him.

Secondly. We must believe that he is the truth. This means,

1. That he is real; the true God. That he is the true prophet, priest and king.

2. That in him is all truth, religious, moral and scientific.

3. That in him is all excellence. For truth is goodness. Christ is the absolute good; a sea of excellence and glory.

Thirdly, that he is the life.

1. The source of universal life.

2. Of intellectual life.

3. Of spiritual and eternal life. It is not we that live, but Christ that lives in us.

What promises are we to trust to? The promises of the Spirit.

1. That his presence is permanent and internal.

2. That he will reveal Christ.

3. That he will be our Paraclete.

CXXIV. Ye are bought with a Price.—1 Cor. 7: 23.

[Sept. 14th, 1856.]

We, in common with others, sustain different relations to God. 1. As our Creator. We owe to him our existence, our faculties, and we are sustained by him. 2. As our Father, that is, as the objects of his care, of his beneficence. He gives us every thing that we possess, and is the source of all good. 3. As our moral governor, whose will is the rule of duty, to whom we are responsible, and who will reward us or punish us according to our works. These are relations common to all men. They belong to us as rational beings. They are not peculiar to us as Christians. Our peculiar relation to God as Christians is that we are his redeemed ones.

I. *What is redemption?* II. *By whom we are redeemed.* III. *At what price?* IV. *To what end?*

This redemption is peculiar to us not only as distinguished from other men, but from all other creatures. No angels, no other order of beings are the subjects of redemption.

I. *What is redemption?*

It is deliverance from captivity or bondage, or death, by purchase.

1. We were in captivity to Satan. He could do with us what he pleased; we were in his power, hopelessly and helplessly under his control.

2. We were in bondage to sin; to its power, from which no resources of our own, or of any creature, now or in eternity, could deliver us. To be forever sinners was all that we could expect.

3. We were in bondage to the law, subject to its demands, and to its penalty, which is eternal death. There was no possibility of escape. To be redeemed is to be delivered by a ransom from this captivity to Satan, this bondage to sin, and this condemnation. It is not to have the offer of deliverance, or to have it rendered possible, but it is actual deliverance.

II. *Who is the redeemer?* "The only Redeemer of God's elect is the Lord Jesus Christ, who being the eternal Son of God, became man, and so was, and continueth to be, God and man, in two distinct natures, and one person forever." Our eye does not rest on any angel, nor on the throne of God, but on the Incarnate Son. As he did not undertake the redemption of angels, so he did not assume their nature.

To God we stand in the relation of creatures, of children, of subjects; but to Christ, as redeemed. We are his property. We belong to him. We are the δοῦλοι Χριστοῦ (servants of Christ). This is our distinguishing peculiarity. It involves two things: (*a*.) That our relation is to Christ. (*b*.) That it is that which arises from redemption, that is, by purchase; so that we are his, and are bound to make his will the rule of our conduct, and his service the business of our lives. This all the redeemed must and will do.

III. *The price of redemption was himself.* He gave himself for us. It involves, 1. His incarnation. 2. His subjection to the law, to fulfil all righteousness. 3. To its curse, including all the miseries of this life, the painful death of the cross, and the wrath of God.

IV. *The end of redemption.*

1. The proximate end is our holiness and happiness; that we should glorify God in our bodies and spirits which are his; that is, that we use our bodies, all their members and all their powers, and all the resources of our spirits, to his glory, *i. e.*, so as to cause him to be

honored. This is to be done in honoring him ourselves, and in causing others to honor him. We glorify God when we worship, love and serve him, and also when we cause others to do the same.

CXXV. Who are kept by the power of God through faith unto salvation, ready to be revealed in the last time. 1 Pet. 1: 5.

[*September 17th*, 1854.]

The salvation of the renewed is secured by the power of God, and through faith.

1. Those here addressed are elected unto obedience and sprinkling of the blood of Jesus Christ.

2. They are renewed.

3. They have a living hope.

4. They have an inheritance incorruptible, undefiled, and that fadeth not away.

5. They are kept by the power of God.

The attainment of salvation is difficult. The dangers arise,—

1. From our own corruption.

2. From the temptations of the world.

3. From the power and malice of Satan.

Yet salvation is certain,—

1. Because they are elected.

2. Because they are renewed.

3. Because they are kept by the power of God. How are believers kept by the power of God? There are two forms under which the power of God expresses itself, viz.: his providence and his grace. The one is outward, and the other inward.

Providence includes all the oversight and guarding which God exercises over his people.

1. In ordering their circumstances.

2. In protecting them from their enemies and persecutors.

3. In restraining and conquering Satan.

Grace includes all the inward operations of the Spirit.

1. In teaching and revealing truth.

2. In sanctifying and consoling.

3. In sustaining under temptation, and thus preserving from apostacy.

How are believers kept through faith?

Faith is used in two senses, or two kinds of exercises are included under the term.

1. Acts of credence in the truth, an abiding conviction of the truth of God; a persuasion, *i. e.*, of the truth of the gospel, and all that it reveals.

2. Acts of confidence in Christ. (*a.*) Confidence in his being what he is declared to be. (*b.*) Confidence in his protection. (*c.*) Confidence in his merit, and in the prevalence of his intercession. The soul may repose itself securely, assured that it is guarded as in a citadel. This protection is to be continued until the end. The salvation of believers begun here, is continued at death, and consummated at the Second Advent. Then their bodies are to be raised, and then the whole number of the redeemed are to be united.

INFERENCES FROM THIS DOCTRINE.

1. The duty of patience, even in the midst of trials.
2. The duty of being hopeful.
3. The duty of being holy as God is holy.
4. The duty of brotherly love.

CXXVI. Security of Believers.

[*Sept. 2d,* 1856.]

I. *In what sense they are secure.*
1. From the condemnation of the law. 2. From the power of temptation. 3. From the dominion of Satan. 4. From everlasting death.

II. *The grounds of this security.*
Negatively. 1. It is not their own righteousness. 2. Not their own strength. 3. Not their own prudence. 4. Not their own fidelity. 5. Not the efficacy of the means of grace. 6. Nor the security of the asylum, *i. e.*, the church, to which they have betaken themselves.

Positively. 1. It is the covenant of Redemption. 2. The work of Christ. 3. The indwelling of the Spirit. 4. The fidelity of God.

III. *Inferences.*

1. Not that we may live in sin and yet be saved; because the security of believers is a security from sin. This is the great distinction between the doctrine of perseverance and Antinomianism. As it is a contradiction to say that God saves the lost, so it is a contradiction to say that he preserves those who indulge in sin.

2. Not that we may neglect the means of grace. For the security promised is as much a security from negligence as from any other evil. The promise of God is to save his people from sin, to purify unto himself a peculiar people zealous of good works, to make them diligent and faithful in the discharge of all duty; but,—

3. This truth 1. Is adapted to fill the heart with abounding gratitude and love to God. The doctrine that believers may fall from grace and perish, supposes an entirely different theory of the gospel. It supposes

that Christ makes salvation possible; that whether or not a man is saved, depends, (a.) on whether he chooses to believe, and (b.) on whether he will persevere in his faith. Both depend upon himself. The other theory supposes that the work of Christ secures the salvation of his people; that faith is God's gift, and that its continuance depends simply on God's fidelity. The one supposes that God loves us because we love him, and so long as we love him. The other supposes that his love is gratuitous and infinite; that we love him because he loved us; and that having loved us when enemies, he will continue to love us as friends. The practical effect of this doctrine is, therefore, to promote holiness.

2. It is adapted to produce peace and a filial spirit. The man who is under a legal system, who stands in the relation of a slave to God, who feels that his standing depends on his good behaviour, of necessity has a slavish spirit. Whereas he who is under grace, who is a child of God, who feels that God's love is founded on something else than good conduct, that he loves us because we are his children, and that holiness is the result and not the ground of adoption, by a like necessity has a filial spirit, and that spirit is a joyful, confident, peaceful spirit. He who thinks that his soul is in his own keeping, and that no promise of God secures its safety, must be in continual anxiety and doubt.

3. The third effect of this doctrine is to produce alacrity in the service of God, and in working out our own salvation. The greater the doubt of success, the less the motive to exertion. If there is no hope, there is no effort; on the contrary, the greater the hope, the greater the cheerfulness and diligence. You assure a man that he will become rich or become great by the faithful and diligent use of certain means, and he will be faithful and diligent. If you tell him that he will be rich whether he uses them or not, or that there is a bare probability of success, you destroy in a good degree the motive to exertion. The case of the individual believer is analogous to that of the Church. What motive would there be to preach the gospel at home, or to carry it abroad, if we had not the assurance of the ultimate triumph of the Redeemer?

IV. *How can we attain a sense of security?*

As the Scriptures teach that whom God predestinates, them he calls, the only evidence of election is vocation, and the only evidence of vocation is holiness. Everything else is a delusion and fanaticism. It can only be by keeping ourselves in the love of God, that we can have a present sense of his favor, and the assurance of salvation.

CXXVII. Ye are complete in him. Col. 2: 10.

[*October 27th*, 1872.]

The false teachers in Colosse were Jews, but not Judaizers. They were philosophers. They designed to substitute philosophy for Christianity, not by denying the latter, but by explaining it. They distinguished between faith and knowledge. Faith was for the people, knowledge for the educated few. The objects of faith were the historical and doctrinal statements of the Bible. The objects of knowledge were the speculative truths underlying those statements, and into which they were to be sublimated. Paul's object in this epistle is to prove two things.

I. *That philosophy was an utter failure.* He pronounces it a vain deceit: that is, (*a.*) Void of truth. (*b.*) Void of reality. (*c.*) Void of all worth and power. It was κενός (empty, vain) in all those senses. And moreover, it was a deceit. It disappointed all our expectation, and betrayed those who trusted to its guidance. This was no slight matter. He warned his readers lest any man in this way should make a prey of them to their utter destruction.

II. *That all the objects which philosophy vainly attempted to accomplish, were effectually and completely accomplished in Christ.*

1. As to the first proposition, viz., that philosophy is a vain deceit.

It is important to determine what Paul means by philosophy. This is not to be decided arbitrarily. Some would say he means heathen philosophy, as opposed to Christian philosophy; others, that particular system which prevailed in Colosse, the Gnostic. Every one would say, false and not true, yours and not mine. There must be some way of deciding this question. The apostle decides it for us,

First, by what he says of the system which he opposes. By philosophy he means systems of that nature.

Secondly, by the arguments which he uses against it. He includes under the term philosophy, every system against which his arguments legitimately bear. What then was the nature of that system? It undertook to determine *a priori*, and from the principles of reason, 1. The nature of God, or of the absolute Being. 2. His relation to the world, or what the world is in relation to him (or rather it). 3. What the origin, nature and destiny of man. 4. What Christ is, and how he effects the restoration of man.

Such is the system. The arguments which Paul urges against it are, 1. These are matters about which, from the nature of the case, we know and can know nothing. They are matters of revelation. "Eye hath not seen, nor ear heard, neither have entered into the heart of man, the things which God hath prepared for them that love him. But God hath revealed them unto us by his Spirit; for the Spirit searcheth all things, yea, the deep things of God. For what man knoweth the things of a man save the Spirit of man which is in him? even so the things of God knoweth no man, but the Spirit of God" (1 Cor. ii: 9, 10, 11). "No man hath seen God at any time; the only begotten Son which is in the bosom of the Father, he hath declared him." (John i: 18).

2. He shows that God, in the Scriptures, hath declared the wisdom of this world to be folly. "Where is the wise? Where is the scribe? Where is the disputer of this world? hath not God made foolish the wisdom of this world?" (1 Cor. i: 20).

3. Experience has proved that the world by wisdom knows not God.

4. God has determined to save man, not by philosophy, but by the gospel.

Paul does not depreciate reason. The senses have their sphere. Reason has its sphere. But there is a supernatural or spiritual sphere into which reason cannot enter. We might as well judge of a syllogism by the tongue. This conclusion is sustained by consciousness. What do you know? There lies the grave! Where does it lead to? What lies beyond it?

We see, therefore, that Paul, by philosophy does not mean, 1. Exclusively the oriental philosophy; for what he says here, he says to the Corinthians. 2. Not natural philosophy. 3. Not mental and moral philosophy. But 4. Any attempt to solve the great problems above mentioned, *a priori.*

III. *All that philosophy vainly pretends to do is accomplished in Christ.*

1. As to knowledge. This is necessary; even knowledge of these supreme problems. In Christ are all the treasures of wisdom and knowledge, and he is the only source of knowledge. The knowledge which he gives is sure, satisfying, sanctifying. This we know.

2. Redemption. It is, first, objective, pardon and reconciliation. This is accomplished by Christ's atoning work. Second, it is subjective, delivery from inward sin and restoration of divine life. This Christ does, because in him dwells the fulness of the Godhead bodily. We are filled with God in him.

3. Restoration to our former status, to the kingdom of light; it is exaltation. This is done by being made partakers of the glory of Christ. All this depends on our union with him. This union is (*a.*) Representative. (*b.*) Spiritual. (*c.*) Voluntary, by faith.

The great lesson is,

1. That we are not to trust to our own reason or that of other men for instruction on these great points.

2. That we have sure knowledge in the gospel, and to reject it is certain perdition.

CXXVIII. Priesthood of Believers.

[*Feb. 8th*, 1857.]

Priests and kings are the two highest classes of officers among men, *e. g.*, Moses and Aaron, David and the High Priest, the Pontifex Maximus among Romans. To say that believers are priests and kings may be a figurative expression, declaring their dignity and exaltation. More however is meant.

I. *The nature of the priesthood.*

It includes properly, 1. The right of access to God. 2. The duty of offering sacrifices for sin. In the strict sense, therefore, there is under the New Testament dispensation, no other priest than Christ. This is one of the greatest differences between Romanists and Protestants, which supposes a radically different theory of the gospel.

II. *The sense in which all believers are priests, is.*

1. That they all have liberty of access to God. This is the main idea. This is the great distinction and blessedness intended to be expressed by the term. 2. They offer to God the sacrifice of a broken heart, the incense of prayer, the thank-offering of praise. They minister before God, and are in this sense priests. 3. They make intercession for others.

III. *The qualifications for the priesthood.*

1. No man taketh the priesthood on himself. This is true both of the official priesthood and of the general priesthood of believers. A priest must be selected and constituted such by God. 2. This appointment must be signified and certified; the external priesthood by external forms, the spiritual priesthood by internal anointing. 3. A priest must have something to offer. What was a priest without a sacrifice? What are we without a contrite spirit? Without a believing and grateful heart our priesthood would be merely nominal. The external priesthood had its external dignities, emoluments and prerogatives; but the spiritual priesthood has only spiritual advantages. The latter is indeed as much higher than the former, as the things of the Spirit are higher than the things of the flesh; but the want of these spiritual gifts is more fatal in the latter case than in the former. 4. As a priest acts not for himself only, but for others also, he must sympathize with them. This is taught with regard to the priests of the Old Testament, with regard to our blessed Lord, and it is no less true with regard to us. 5. A priest must be holy in two senses. (*a.*) As to his person-

al character. Under the Old Testament it was required that the priest should be free from all blemish of body and deficiency in intellect. Under the New, we cannot draw near to God unless we are pure in heart. The Old Testament priests were required to abstain from all defiling contact with external things. We are to abstain from the pollutions which are in the world. They could not approach, unless ceremonially clean; we cannot, unless inwardly sanctified. (b.) In the second place, a priest must be holy in the sense of sacred, set apart, or consecrated. The Old Testament priests were a distinct class, separated from the people. They could not engage in ordinary avocations, nor seek support in the ordinary way. Those who ministered at the altar were partakers of the altar. In like manner, Christians are a people separated from the world, and consecrated to God. They cannot belong to the world, seek its objects, or enjoy its pleasures. 6. A priest must be faithful. This includes, (a.) The assiduous discharge of all his duties, as opposed to negligence. (b.) Trustworthiness. The people should be able to rely upon them as being what they professed to be, and really possessing the qualifications of their office. So we as priests should be faithful in drawing near to God, in offering sacrifices, and in interceding; and all should have reason to confide in us as being indeed the priests of God.

IV. *The prerogatives and privileges of the priesthood.*

1. Access to God. This is the end of redemption. It includes all its blessings. When the people saw the High Priest enter the most Holy place, they felt that he was the most honored of mortals.

2. The favor of God. The priest was highly distinguished.

3. Power with God. The power of the priesthood has ever been higher than that of kings. Believers have power with God. Their prayers control the world.

CXXIX. Priesthood of Believers. (No. 2.)

[*April 12th*, 1863.]

Exaltation and honor tend to make men worse,

1. When assumed as a right. 2. When sought and enjoyed for selfish ends. 3. When consisting in external prerogatives and advantages.

They have a contrary tendency

1. When felt to be undeserved.

2. When regarded as designed for God's glory and the good of others.

3. When what is outward is merely accessory to inward excellence. All the distinction and glory promised in the Scriptures have these conditions, and therefore tend to humble and purify. Believers are represented as a priesthood.

I. *The priests were a separate class of the people.* The people generally were not priests, and no man could become a priest by his own will. He must be called of God. In this respect believers are like them. They are a separate class of men; they are chosen and called of God.

II. *They were an elevated and honored class.* Kings and priests were the highest order of men. The one governed the body, the other the soul. The one had regard to the world and the things of this life, the other to the things of eternity. The sphere of the latter was higher, and their actual power greater. The two offices were united in Melchizedek, Christ, and in believers. In saying that believers are priests, it is meant that they are a higher order of men, exalted above their fellows in all that elevates and ennobles.

III. *The priests were a sacred class.*

1. They were consecrated with peculiar solemnity. They were washed, anointed, and clothed with pure garments; and victims of expiation and consecration were presented in their behalf.

2. They were required to be personally holy. *a.* Free from bodily defects. *b.* Free from vice. *c.* Free from ceremonial defilement. *d.* Many things lawful to others were not lawful to them.

3. They were sacred in their occupations; that is, they were not to engage in worldly occupations, but minister in holy things. In like manner believers are a sacred class of the community. They are consecrated to God in baptism. They are washed, anointed and purified with atoning blood. They are to keep themselves unspotted from the world, and live not for the world, but for God.

IV. *Priests were not an idle, useless or merely ornamental class of the community.* They had most important functions to perform.

1. They approached God for the people. There was no access to God but through them, no pardon, no acceptable worship, no enjoyment of God's favor. This is the distinctive idea of a priesthood. It is a class of men who have access to God for the benefit of others. Believers have this access; no other men have, and therefore believers are priests.

2. The priests offered sacrifices of worship, of expiation, of thanksgiving. Believers offer true worship, and they only. They present and plead before God the sacrifice of Christ, in their own behalf and in behalf of the unconverted. They offer the constant sacrifice of thanksgiving, and the incense of praise. They are the priests of the earth. What the Jewish priests did for the Jews, believers do for the world. What would the Jews have been without their priests? And what would the world be without believers? No acceptable worship would ascend from earth to heaven, and no blessings descend from heaven to earth.

3. The priests were the instructors of the people. Their lips kept knowledge. It was their business to teach the law in its doctrines and precepts. When they were ignorant or apostate, the people perished. So believers are depositaries of the truth. They have the great prerogative of presenting and extending it. The church is the pillar and ground of truth.

V. *The priests were a dependent class.*

1. They had no portion in the land. They depended on the contributions of the people.

2. Their services were not for themselves. They were not the end.

3. They were designed to promote the knowledge and glory of God, and the good of the people.

So believers do not live for themselves. They are saved and exalted to this dignity not to honor themselves, but to honor God, and to do good to their fellow-creatures.

Great honor, great sanctity, great responsibility are involved in belonging to the royal priesthood of believers.

CXXX. Who is he that overcometh the world, but he that believeth that Jesus is the Son of God? 1 John 5: 5.

[*March* 22d, 1863.]

I. *Who is the conqueror,* ὁ νιχῶν, *but the believer,* ὁ πιστεύων? The word world in the Scriptures means, 1. The material universe. 2. Our earth. 3. What they contain, and all that they contain. 4. Their rational inhabitants, and when spoken of the earth, mankind. 5. The wicked as opposed to the Church. 6. What characterizes the world, *i. e.*, men, the lust of the flesh, the lust of the eyes, and the pride of life. 7. Things seen and temporal; all things, the fashion of which is passing away.

II. *Overcoming the world is therefore a very comprehensive work.* It includes, 1. Successfully resisting the influence of the things of the world, as seductions to sin, its wealth, its pleasures and its honors.

2. Raising ourselves above all under the influence of the things seen and temporal, and living under the influence of the things unseen and eternal.

3. Taking the word "world" to mean men, and especially the ungodly, to overcome the world is to overcome their undue and pernicious influence over our opinions and over our conduct. The force of public opinion and passion is almost irresistible. The dominating influence of the philosophy, of the maxims and customs of the world, is of all things the hardest to overcome.

4. The world is the kingdom of darkness; it is Satan's kingdom. To

overcome it, is to overcome error, ignorance, vice, evil, in short, in all its forms. This, therefore, is a stupendous work. Think of a solitary soul —and in one sense every soul is solitary, it is isolated, having its own life, consciousness and character—think of such a soul in a world, in a universe of evil, operated on by all things sensible, by all other souls, itself corrupt, its own nature in alliance with its enemies, and it will be seen that to overcome the world is indeed a work exceeding all human power.

III. *How is this work to be accomplished?*

1. Not by asceticism. 2. Not by philosophy. 3. Not by the power of reason, conscience, or the will. 4. Not by Theism. 5. Not by faith in the word of God in the general. 6. Not by the Church, its rites, its ministry, or its worship. But, 7. By believing that Jesus is the Son of God. What does this mean? and why does this faith secure us the victory over the world?

What is it to believe that Jesus is the Son of God? (1.) That the man Jesus, the person who appeared and was recognized under that name, was the eternal Son of God; that he was God manifest in the flesh. This includes faith in his divinity and incarnation. (2.) It is not only the person but also the work of Christ that is here intended. His relation to us is expressed by the name Jesus, his relation to God, by his title, Son of God. As to us he is a Saviour, as to God he is his equal. The truth believed then, is that we have a divine Saviour, therefore an almighty, an all-sufficient, an everywhere present Saviour.

How does faith in this doctrine overcome the world? 1. Not by the mere moral power of the truth believed. It is not merely because the doctrine of the incarnation is a more exalted and powerful doctrine than the doctrine of God; it is not that God as manifested in the flesh is more intelligible, more accessible, more lovely, more congenial than God as an infinite Spirit. All this is true. But all this is true to devils, as well as to thousands who are the slaves of the world.

2. It is (*a.*) Because those who believe this doctrine are reconciled to God. This is the first step. So long as the soul is an outcast, an unpardoned criminal, incarcerated in the prison of God's justice, the object of his displeasure, he is of the world, he is a member of the kingdom of darkness. It is only when he is delivered from God's curse, reconciled to him by faith in Christ, that it is possible for him to resist or overcome the influences by which he is surrounded, and by which he is thoroughly pervaded. (*b.*) But secondly, those who believe that Jesus is the Son of God are born of God. They are partakers of a new life. The life of Christ is communicated to them. The principle in them, antagonistic to the world, is no longer mere feeble darkened reason, a scared conscience and perverted and rebellious will, but the

indwelling God, the Holy Ghost. It is therefore an almighty, indestructible, permanent power, which is imparted to them, and which manifests itself in them by raising them above the world. "Because I live," says Christ, "ye shall live also." (c.) Thirdly, the spiritual, not the moral power of the truth that Jesus is the Son of God, is made by the Holy Ghost the proximate means of our overcoming the world. (1.) The glory of God in the face of Jesus Christ is made so clear that we are ravished by it, absorbed by it, delivered thereby from the love of sin and of the world. (2.) The constraining influence of the love of this incarnate God, leads us to renounce all things for his sake. (3.) Zeal for his glory, for the advancement of his kingdom is enkindled in the soul, and overcomes all other motives to action. The great lesson taught is, that it is not by ourselves, nor by human means that we can be delivered from this present evil world, but only by believing what the Scriptures teach concerning Christ.

CXXXI. Ye are Christ's. 1 Cor. 3: 23.
[*March 10th*, 1861].

The two ideas of dependence and possession are here expressed. "We are Christ's," means that we are dependent on him, and also that we belong to him. In the preceding verse the apostle had said, "All things are yours;" that is, all things are designed and overruled to promote your welfare, and all things are comprehended in that dominion or kingdom to which you are destined. Still you are nothing, you belong to Christ.

In this is involved, 1. The denial that we are our own. We do not belong to ourselves, in the sense that our own advantage can be the legitimate end of our pursuit, or that our own will can be the legitimate rule of our conduct.

2. The denial that we belong to the world, to parents, friends, country, mankind, in either of the above senses; that the good of parents, friends, &c., can be the legitimate end, or their will the legitimate rule.

3. Nor do we thus belong to the Church. This could not have entered the apostle's mind. But in after years it became a common form of apostasy from Christ, and still is. Men feel that they belong to the Church, live for and are governed by it, and know no higher end, or rule of duty.

4. Positively, the declaration includes, that we are Christ's in such a sense that his glory is the end, and his will the rule of our life. He, and he alone, has the right to us. To him, and to him alone, is this devotion and submission due.

II. *This proprietorship is founded,*

1. Not specially on creation, for as creatures we belong to God, the Triune God, but,

2. It is founded on gift. We were given to him in the counsels of eternity. From the countless orders of creatures, and from the countless millions of the race of man, the people of Christ were given to him as a possession, as a peculium, a specialty, in which he was to have a peculiar and exclusive right. This ground of proprietorship is supreme. God as sovereign of the universe can give what he pleases, and his will is the only real and stable ground of property or possession.

3. It is founded on purchase. This gives, (*a.*) The right of property as founded on justice. (*b.*) The purchase involving redemption from infinite evil gives the higher and tenderer obligation of gratitude, and (*c.*) The price paid being his own precious blood, it gives the highest of all obligations, that of love.

4. It is founded on the right of conquest. We were the captives of Satan. Christ has destroyed his power, and delivered us who were led captive by him at his will.

This general idea of possession is illustrated in various ways in the Scriptures. 1. We are the δοῦλοι (servants) of Christ, which expresses the relation as founded in justice. We are bound as his δοῦλοι to live for him, and to obey him. Any failure in this devotion or obedience is a violation of our relation to him as his servants or slaves.

2. We, *i. e.*, the Church, are his bride. This includes (*a.*) The idea of exclusive possession. (*b.*) Of preference and peculiar love. (*c.*) Of perfect community of interest.

3. We are his φίλοι, (friends) bound to him by the bond of mutual love and confidence.

4. We are his body, the members of his body. Nothing is so intimately a man's own as his body. It has a common life with him. It has a common consciousness with him. The pains and pleasures of the body are our own pains and pleasures. It has a common interest and destiny with him. So if we are Christ's body, we are bound to him in all these ways. This is nearer and higher than δοῦλοι, φίλοι, νύμφη (bride).

III. *The blessedness resulting from this relationship.*

1. Security. If we belong to Christ, as his δοῦλοι, φίλοι, νύμφη and σῶμα (body), we are secure, here and hereafter, for time and eternity.

2. Participation in Christ's excellence, both as to soul and body; in his happiness, in his glory and dominion.

IV. *Duties.*

1. That we should always act worthily of this relation; remember

that we belong neither to ourselves nor to the world, but only to the Lord.

2. Contentment. We may well be satisfied if we are Christ's; for if we are his, all things are ours.

3. Not merely contentment, but joyful anticipation of Christ's coming and glory.

CXXXII. The Lord is my strength.

[*September* 10*th*, 1865.]

All religion is founded upon the personality of God. A person only can be the object of the religious affections, of adoration, love and confidence. A person only can be addressed in prayer; and it is only with a person that we can have fellowship and communion. Who is the person with whom we stand in the relation indicated in the text? The word Lord is an appellative. There are many Lords. The article renders the term definite. It is *the Lord*, the person universally recognized as standing to men in the relation of Lord. It is the substitute of the proper name, Jehovah. He, therefore, is the person intended. But the Lord of the Old Testament is the same person with the Lord, and our Lord of the New Testament. The person, therefore, who is so designated is the Logos, the second person of the Trinity, the incarnate Son of God. The relation, therefore, here indicated, is not merely the relation which a creature bears to the creator, which man bears to God, but more definitely, that which we bear to God manifest in the flesh, who has assumed the work of our redemption.

The senses, then, in which the Lord is our strength are, 1. The general sense in which all power is derived from God. He is the giver of whatever measure of strength is possessed by any of his creatures. All created power is derived, and not inherent.

2. This power of the creature is not self-sustained. It is not an ability to exist, act, and accomplish its purposes out of God, and independently of him; but it is ability which he constantly sustains. It is in him we live and move and have our being.

3. Not only the general ability of the creature is thus derived and sustained, but the ability to act as efficiently as the emergency demands, the physical, intellectual or moral strength required for any special work or occasion, is given by God; and it is given in different measures to different individuals, and to the same individual, on different occasions.

4. All this pertains to the natural man, or to the natural relation in which men stand to God. And all this is included in the relation in which the believer stands to Christ. He is our strength, as its giver,

its sustainer, and as the source whence all the supplies which we need from time to time are derived. But beyond this, especially in relation to the divine life, and to the duties therewith connected, is Christ our strength. He is the source from which that life is derived. It is sustained by him, and from him come the daily supplies needed for our daily duties. The strength to believe, the strength to understand, the strength to obey, the strength to resist temptation, the strength to bear afflictions, come from Christ only. Paul said that of himself he could do nothing, but through Christ strengthening him, he could do all things. No limits can be assigned to this divine strength. History is filled with examples of men, weak in intellect, weak in character, feeble of purpose, who have been transformed into heroes by the power of Christ. They have subdued kingdoms, stopped the mouth of lions, put to flight the armies of the aliens.

There are here three things for us to learn and to lay to heart.

1. That we have no strength in ourselves; so that the man who depends on himself, his understanding, his will, his efficiency, will fail, whether it be in arriving at truth, in living a holy life, or in doing good to others.

2. The second is, that the Lord is our strength, and that in him there is an inexhaustible supply of strength for all these ends; for attaining knowledge, for becoming holy, and for doing good, and for bearing all our trials in the Lord Jesus Christ. We can be strong in the Lord. Through Christ we can do all things.

3. The third thing is, that the conditions on which we are made partakers of this strength are first, the renunciation of our own, and second, the seeking of his strength in the way of his appointment, that is, by faith in him and by looking to him at all times.

CXXXIII. Good Hope through Grace.

[*Date not given.*]

I. *Nature of hope.*

No man since the fall, probably no creature, can be satisfied with the present. Here is always either some evil pressing on us, some capacity of enjoyment unfilled, or some desire for the perpetuity of what we possess, which passes beyond the present into the future. This expectation and desire of future good is hope. Its object is the unseen. This desire and expectation of future good is, 1. The spring of all activity. 2. With regard to sinners under the sentence of the law, and in prospect of eternity, it is indispensable to any rational peace.

II. *Good Hope;* that is, a well founded hope. It is a hope directed towards what is truly good.

1. Some men are insensible and indifferent with regard to their future destiny. This state of mind is (*a.*) Irrational. (*b.*) Unsatisfying. (*c.*) Precarious. (*d.*) Destructive.

2. Others have a hope, but it is not good. It is founded (*a.*) On the general mercy of God. (*b.*) On their relation to the church. (*c.*) On the assumption that all are to be saved. (*d.*) On assumed revelations. (*e.*) On spurious religious experience of. (*f.*) On the assumption of our own goodness. The general basis therefore, of a false hope is error; either error as to the purpose of God in reference to the punishment of sin, or error as to the conditions on which exemption from sin is promised, or as to our having fulfilled or experienced those conditions. A *good* hope is, therefore, (*a.*) A hope which is founded on the truth, on the promise of God, and the work of Christ. (*b.*) One which we have a right to entertain, *i. e.*, which is the genuine fruit of the Spirit; not an unauthorized anticipation on our part, but one which is inseparable from faith. (*c.*) One which has for its object the infinite blessings of redemption, sometimes Christ's coming, sometimes the resurrection, sometimes the glory of God. Towards this the whole creation looks forward with earnest expectation.

III. *Through grace, i. e.*, a hope which God graciously gives, and gives in the exercise of his grace. God gives us this hope, 1. In that he promises to us the blessings which are the object of our hope.

2. Because he produces in our minds the exercise of our hope.

IV. *Evidence that a hope is good.*

1. That it has a scriptural foundation; that is, that it rests on the promise of God clearly revealed in his word.

2. That it has scriptural blessings for its objects; not earthly good or millennial prosperity, but conformity to Christ, and the enjoyment of him forever.

3. That this hope sanctifies the soul, makes us pure even as he is pure.

4. That it is the fruit of faith, which is by appropriate evidence proved to be genuine.

V. *This hope,*

1. Is a helmet. 2. Is an anchor. 3. Is to the soul what wings are to the eagle. It elevates it above the world. It raises us toward heaven, and fills us with its spirit.

CXXXIV. Assurance.

[*October 23d*, 1859.]

I. *Its nature.*

In general it is the full conviction or persuasion that we are the children of God and the heirs of eternal life.

1. This may be Antinomian, when that conviction is founded on a false view of the plan of salvation, supposing that the elect are sure of eternal life irrespective of their character, and that a man may know his election by other evidence than that derived from holiness of heart and life. So Antinomians in the Protestant church hold that the law is abolished, and Christ is their sanctification by imputation. They pervert the doctrine of salvation by grace; so the Romanist, so the Pharisee, both of whom are Antinomians.

2. There is a form of assurance which assumes that saving faith can exist in no other form. It is held (1) That the object of faith is that God is reconciled to us. (2) That this, if believed at all, is believed without wavering; or that the only faith required is simple assent, of which there can be no doubt.

3. There is another view, which almost discards assurance, or which makes it a rare and almost unattainable gift. This makes hope an inference, drawn from promises in a rational way. God promises eternal life to the renewed. I find in myself the evidences of regeneration; therefore I have a title to eternal life. Here all depends on the clearness of the evidences of regeneration; and as these can seldom or never be so clear as to preclude all doubt, so there can seldom be any scriptural assurance of salvation.

4. The common form of this doctrine is, (a.) That Christ has fully satisfied the law for us. We are not required to do anything to merit salvation. (b.) Christ is freely offered to all who hear the gospel, not only without merit, but just as they are, without preparation, without holiness. (c.) That all who receive him and rest on him shall be saved. In other words, all who believe that he is the Son of God, that he loved us and died for us, shall inherit eternal life. (d.) That the warrant for our having Christ is not our inward state or experience, but the promise of God; and therefore we may believe without waiting for the evidence of sanctification.

II. *The ground of assurance, therefore, is,*

1. The promise of God as perfectly free and unconditional.

2. The consciousness that we do believe; not that we are regenerated, but that we do believe.

3. The witness of the Spirit; or the love of God shed abroad in the heart.

III. *The effects of assurance when genuine.*

1. Peace.

2. Joy and gratitude.

3. Love and zeal for the glory of God.

When spurious, the effects are, 1. Self-righteousness. 2. Neglect of duty, and indulgence in sin. 3. False security.

CXXXV. Hope maketh not ashamed, because the Love of God is shed abroad in our hearts by the Holy Ghost which is given unto us.—Rom. 5: 5.

[*April 26th*, 1857.]

The effects or fruits of justification are,

1. Peace with God.
2. The enjoyment of his favor.
3. Hope of glory.

Man as a sinner is the object of the divine wrath, under condemnation, unable to secure either justification, sanctification or eternal life. These are the necessities of his nature. They cannot be obtained by works. It is only when we are so united to Christ by faith that we become interested in his righteousness and partakers of his life, that we are justified, and being justified, have peace and hope. This hope is sure; it does not disappoint, for the love of God is shed abroad in our hearts.

I. *The love of God, is his love to us.* The fact that we are the objects of a love which embraces all the creatures of God, would not be a ground of hope. But it is, 1. A special love, a love which stands opposed to wrath. It includes reconciliation, or divine favor. To be assured of God's love, is to be assured that he is propitious toward us; that his wrath is turned away from us; that his justice no longer demands our condemnation. It is the love which secures all the benefits of redemption. 2. It is infinitely great. It led to the gift of the Son of God. 3. It is gratuitous. It is not founded on our character. It was exercised towards us when we were sinners. 4. It is therefore immutable. If founded on anything in us, it would continue no longer than our attractiveness continued. But if perfectly gratuitous, flowing from the mysterious fulness of the divine nature, it cannot change.

II. *This love is shed abroad in our hearts:* that is, we have a full conviction and assurance that we are its objects. There might be a conviction that God is love, that his love towards some men is infinitely great, that it is gratuitous and unchangeable, and yet we might remain in the blackness of despair. It is only when we are assured that we are its objects, that we have a hope which sustains and renders blessed.

III. *But how do we know that we are the objects of this love?*

1. It cannot be because God has this love for all men, and, therefore, for us; because this is not true.

2. It is not because we see in ourselves the effects of regeneration or the evidences of holiness, because (*a*.) This love was prior to regeneration, and (*b*.) Because holiness is the fruit of the assurance of God's love.

3. The knowledge is produced by the Holy Ghost. The Holy Ghost produces in our mind the conviction that we are the objects of that love of God which induced him to give his Son for our salvation, which is gratuitous and unchangeable, and which secures all other gifts. But how does the Holy Ghost produce this conviction? We cannot tell, and it is unreasonable to ask. We might as well ask how he produces faith, peace, joy, or any other grace. It is enough to answer negatively, that it is not (*a.*) By exciting our love to God, whence we infer his love to us. The true order is the reverse. Nor (*b.*) By simply opening our eyes to see what a wonderful display of love is made in redemption; for that we might see, and yet suppose ourselves excluded.

IV. *The proof that we are not deluded in this matter, is to be found in the effects of this conviction.* The effects of a conviction of our being the favorites of God, or the objects of his special love, when that conviction is unfounded, are seen in the Jews, the Romanists and in Antinomians. These effects are, 1. Pride. 2. Malignity. 3. Immorality; the divorce of morals from religion. On the other hand, when the conviction is produced by the Holy Ghost, then the effects are,—1. Humility. Nothing so bows down the soul as a sense of undeserved love. 2. The tenderest concern for those who are not thus favored, and an earnest desire that they may share our blessedness. 3. Love to God. Love begets love; and our love to God is mingled with wonder, admiration, gratitude, and zeal for his glory. 4. Obedience. When aliens, and under the law, we brought forth fruit unto death, but now we bring forth fruit unto holiness. The sixth and seventh chapters are designed to show that such are the effects of assurance of the divine love.

CXXXVI. Faith as the Source of Love and Joy. 1 Pet. 1: 8.

[*March 25th,* 1854.]

The three great Christian graces are faith, hope and love, or Peter says, faith, love and joy. As to these graces the Scriptures teach us, 1. That they are inseparable. They never appear one without the others. 2. They stand in a certain relation to each other as cause and effect; faith is the cause of love, and love the cause of joy. It is a joy which is first, unspeakable. (*a.*) Because the objects of it are infinite. (*b.*) Because no words can express its value, or blessedness. It is incomparable. Other things can be measured, as riches, learning, honor, but this can be compared with nothing else in value. We would give up everything for this joy. It is, secondly, full of glory because it elevates, purifies, and renders glorious; and because it is attended with the anticipation of glory.

I. *Why joy is the fruit of love,* is plain. 1. From the fact that love itself is a joyous affection. It is in its nature happy. Though it may incidentally be the cause of anxiety and sorrow, yet in itself it is a source of blessedness. God is love. All the blessed love, and are blessed because they love. 2. From the nature of its object. The exalting feeling of love, to a beautiful child, to anything of special value and excellence, is a matter of experience. And as Christ is the object of the Christian's love, and there is no end to his glory or his worth, the joy connected with love to him is unspeakable and full of glory.

II. *Why faith produces love.* It may be admitted that there is something mysterious in love; that is, that we cannot explain its origin, or tell always why we love. The love of God to his people is thus mysterious. No one can tell why he loved us. Still love in man, so far as it is not instinctive, has a rational ground; and this is, 1. The beauty and excellence of its object. 2. Congeniality, or sympathy; a feeling of mutual interest and delight; a reciprocation of benefits, or at least of benefits and gratitude. 3. Propriety; a consciousness that the object is ours. This is by no means exclusive, and is of course, different in different cases.

Now faith is the source of love to Christ, 1. Because it discerns his beauty and excellence. Christ is supremely glorious and beautiful, (*a.*) As possessed of all divine perfections. (*b.*) As possessed of all human excellence and loveliness. (*c.*) As uniting these in his own person, so that he is the centre, the light, the glory of the universe. He is to all intelligences what the sun is to our system. Faith discerns all this.

1. It is to the soul, what the eye is to the body.

2. It is a cognition or spiritual apprehension. It is not merely light, but discernment. It does not see the object merely, but its excellence also. 3. It produces congeniality. 4. It appropriates.

CXXXVII. Love of God.

I. *The nature of this love.*

Love is used for any form of complacency or delight in an object. Its nature, therefore, depends upon the nature of this object. Men love not only persons but things, and not only things but ideal and abstract conceptions. Properly, however, it expresses an affection of which only a person can be the object.

It includes 1. Desire of union and fellowship. 2. Complacency. 3. Benevolence. This is true of all the forms of love directed towards persons. It presupposes therefore, 1. Community or similarity of nature. 2. Excellence, or what is regarded as such in its object. 3. The possibility of service in some form.

God is a Spirit, infinite, eternal, and immutable in his being, wisdom power, holiness, justice, goodness and truth. Hence a proper object of love. 1. Because he is a person. He is a Spirit, a being with whom intercourse, fellowship, communion is possible. We can say to him, My Father! and he can say to us My Child! It is impossible to love a law, such as the law of gravitation or of attraction. He is the Father of our spirits. He loves us. 2. His excellence is infinite, in his power, wisdom, holiness, justice, goodness and truth. These are objects of complacency. They excite,

(a.) Admiration, reverence, adoration.

(b.) Approbation. They command the fullest consent of the reason and conscience.

(c.) Confidence. Men trust in the Lord because he is thus holy, just and good.

3. Because as a Spirit he is a proper object of benevolence, i. e., of a desire to please, which it expresses (a.) In submission to his instructions, i. e., in docility. (b.) In submission to his dispensations, i. e., in resignation. (c.) In submission to his law, i. e., in obedience. Such is the nature of his love.

II. *The evidences of the love of God.* They are twofold. 1. Our own consciousness.

2. Its effects. (a.) Acquiescence in his truth. (b.) In what he does. (c.) Devotion to the service. (d.) Zeal for his glory.

Men are apt to distress themselves and puzzle others by a too strict analysis of their feelings. They endeavor to determine whether their love is disinterested. They do not act thus in other cases. No son asks these questions of his heart in reference to his parents, nor any parent in reference to his child. For metaphysical theology is apt to produce metaphysical religion. It is enough that we fear, delight in, desire to obey and to honor God.

III. *The excellence of this love.*

1. It is excellent because it includes all other excellence. The love of God comprehends in it the love of all that is good and the hatred of all that is evil.

2. It of necessity leads to all that is good or right—to obedience towards God—to the faithful discharge of all our duties towards our fellow-men—to all right efforts to promote God's glory and the good of his creatures.

3. Because it exalts our nature by bringing us into communion with the infinite God. It raises us up to our original status in the order of created beings.

4. Because it renders us supremely blessed. It fills all our capacity of enjoyments. Men embark their all on the objects of their affec-

tions. If they love the world, they can secure only the happiness which the world gives. If they love God, they have all the happiness which that love can give. "Whom have I in heaven but thee, and there is none upon earth that I desire besides thee." This, therefore, is the great command.

IV. *The means of promoting this love.*

It cannot be forced. It cannot be procured by any effort of the will. It is the gift of God's Spirit. We must do as we would to cultivate love to a parent.

1. We must abstain from offending him. 2. Endeavor in all things to do his will. 3. Cultivate fellowship with him by meditation, reading, prayer, public and private worship, and by all other means.

CXXXVIII. Whom having not seen, ye love; in whom, though now ye see him not, yet believing, ye rejoice with joy unspeakable and full of glory. 1 Pet. 1: 8.

[*May 24th,* 1863.]

The Scriptures divide men into two classes, the good and the bad; the righteous and the unrighteous; men of the world and children of God; carnal and spiritual. Of course there is great difference of character among those included under each general division. Not all men of the world are of the same moral character. But as to the great point, there is no difference. All not the children of God are the children of the evil one. All who do not belong to the kingdom of light belong to the kingdom of darkness. Under the gospel, the distinction which supersedes all others, and determines the status of every man in the sight of God, and decides his destiny forever, is whether he loves the Lord Jesus Christ or not, whether he lives for Christ or for the world. Blessings are pronounced upon all who love our Lord Jesus Christ—in sincerity; and "If any man love not the Lord Jesus Christ, let him be Anathema, Maranatha." 1 Cor. xvi: 22. There must be a reason for this. There must be some adequate ground for pronouncing a blessing upon those who love Christ, and the curse of God upon all who do not love him. That reason is that not to love Christ is the greatest of all crimes, and love to him includes all the excellence of which we are susceptible.

I. *What is love?* II. *What are the grounds of love for Christ?* III. *What are the fruits of that love?*

I. *What is love?*

No word in our language is more comprehensive and difficult of explanation. It is here, as in most cases, all true knowledge comes from experience. We can not know until we have felt. Setting aside the improper application of the word when used in reference to inanimate or irrational objects, it is to be remarked, 1. That love in the Scripture sense of the word, is an emotion, such as joy, fear, anger, an ebullition of feeling. 2. It is not simply an affection in the sense of a conscious state of the mind. Love may exist where there is no present or conscious exercise. A child loves its parent, a parent a child, a sister a brother, when their minds are engaged with other objects, and their feelings are called forth in other directions.

3. Love can no more be defined, than can matter, or spirit. You can only say what it is not, and what are its manifestations. Can any one say what maternal love is? It is not an emotion; it is not a feeling; it is not an affection. It is something which lies back of all these, an instinct, a law. It is that which makes a mother delight in her child; which leads her to seek its good; which makes her live for it, labor for it, and suffer for it, and do all this gladly without any thought of a return.

So also love to Christ is not an emotion, or a feeling. It is that in the soul which makes it delight in Christ; which leads it to prefer the honor and interests of Christ to all other objects; and which leads us to live, labor, suffer and die for him gladly.

II. *The grounds of love.*

1 Excellence of the object. 2. Suitableness to our necessities. 3. Relation to us.

III. *Fruits of love.*

1. Joy unspeakable. 2. Superiority to the World. 3. Holiness.

CXXXIX. Religious Joy and Despondency.

[*March 19th*, 1854.]

I. *The general nature of joy.*

Joy is either a transient emotion, or a permanent, cheerful, and happy frame of mind. It enters into the nature of hope, insomuch as hope is always attended with joy; but it differs from hope inasmuch as the object of the one is future, and of the other present. Worldly joy is that which arises from the possession and expectation of worldly good. Religious joy is that which comes from the expectation or possession of spiritual good. Sorrow and despondency bear the same relation to each other that joy and hope do. The one arises from the experience of present evil, the other from the expectation of future evil. Sorrow enters into the nature of despondency, as joy does into the nature of hope.

II. *Sources or causes of joy and despondency.*

1. Natural temperament.

(*a.*) The fact is undeniable that there is a constitutional difference among men in this respect. Some dispositions are cheerful; others are sad or desponding. Some are inclined to be hopeful; others are always anticipating evil. So some men are contemplative; others active. Some amiable; others morose.

(*b.*) The natural temperament is not changed by regeneration. The same disposition, when natural, which characterized the man before conversion, or as a natural man, more or less characterizes his religious exercises. This is the case unless the measure of divine grace be so great as to infuse, as it were, a new nature as well as a new heart into the soul of the convert.

2. Another source is the state of the body.

(*a.*) The fact is undeniable that the state of the soul, as to its emotions, is intimately connected with that of the body. Exhilarating drinks, gas, atmosphere, the depressing influence of disease.

(*b.*) Besides this general fact, experience teaches that in reference to religious joy and despondency, the connection between the soul and body is not less intimate. This is proved by the fact that physical remedies often produce religious joy or remove despondency; by the fact that men pass from the one state to the other without any rational, as distinguished from physical, cause; and from the periodical nature of these changes.

3. Another source of these emotional frames is that which is suited to their nature; *i. e.*, the possession of good or the experience or dread of evil.

With regard to joy, (*a.*) It is the fruit of the Spirit. (*b.*) It is the effect of faith. (*c.*) It has the blessings of providence and redemption for its sources and objects. (*d.*) The assurance of God's favor, presence and protection. (*e.*) The person and glory of Christ. (*f.*) The glories and blessedness of heaven.

With regard to sorrow and despondency. Sorrow is natural and proper under a sense of our sins. But despondency is a form of unbelief, and is always sinful, so far as it is not the effect of natural temperament or physical condition.

Observe 1. That joy is one of the essential conditions of spiritual health. Happiness is necessary to mental and bodily development. That joy is thus necessary, is proved (*a.*) Because it results from holiness, and is perfect in the perfect. (*b.*) Because it is commanded. (*c.*) Because it characterizes all the exercises of the pious. (*d.*) Because it is the atmosphere of heaven.

2. Hence joy should be cultivated and despondency striven against. The method of action is determined by the causes. The natural and

physical causes must be dealt with according to their nature, the spiritual causes according to their nature.

CXL. Singleness of heart. Acts 2: 46.
[Feb. 28th, 1864.]

There is an analogy between the youth of man, the youth of the Christian, and the youth of the Church.

The state of youth is characterized by, 1. The predominance of animal spirit and of emotional life. 2. A tendency to be governed by the feelings rather than by the dictates of the judgment and of an enlightened conscience. 3. Hence by imprudence and extravagance, *i. e.*, pushing things to extremes. 4. By joyousness and singleness of mind, *i. e.*, having the attention and feelings engrossed with one object. These are the characteristics also of the young Christian. We see in every revival of religion, where these characteristics are brought into full play, this predominance of feeling, this disposition to be governed by emotion, this tendency to extremes, and this joyousness and absorption in the one great object which fills the hearts of young converts.

We see all these traits in the description of the early Church in the Acts. How are the Scriptures to be understood when they describe the experience and conduct of the early Christians? 1. It is a description of genuine religious experience. 2. It is a description founded on facts. The early Christians did feel and act as they are described in the Acts of the Apostles. 3. This experience being actual is not ideal or normal. It was of course modified by their peculiar circumstances, and by their imperfections of knowledge, experience and feeling. Consequently it is not an authoritative example to us. That they continued to attend ·the temple, that they celebrated the eucharist daily in connection with an ordinary meal, that they had all things in common, may have been actual, and the effect of genuine religious feeling; but it does not follow that these things were right then, or obligatory now. They were youthful excesses, which experience and the teaching of the Spirit led them to modify. The life of the early Church was a youthful life, very different from the life of Paul, Peter and John. 1. As devoted so exclusively to devotional exercises. 2. As pressing religious duties, as the celebration of the eucharist, etc., into ordinary life, and thus inevitably leading to its becoming ultimately a formal service, and destroying its solemn religious character. 3. In continuing to attend the temple service. 4. In community of goods. This would have been right if other things had been in due proportion. But the benevolent feeling was far stronger than the disposition to moderation and diligence in business. So that it became ruinous, and would be ruinous now unless among perfect men. 5. In their joyful exultation and singleness of heart. What that means is perhaps something different from what the same English word means elsewhere. Here the Greek word is ἀφελότης, in Eph. vi : 5, Col. iii : 22, the word ἁπλότης. These words differ in signification, although they often agree in usage.

The trait of mind, or the feature in the religious life of these early Christians, which the word here used expresses, is probably that characteristic of youth above referred to, the smooth, uniform flow of life in one current, undisturbed by attention to any other object. These Christians were engrossed in one thing. They thought and cared nothing about anything but their own happiness and blessedness. While there is something beautiful in this, it is not what is meant elsewhere by singleness of heart, which is not a transient state of feeling, but a permanent trait of character. Singleness is opposed both to duplicity, seeming one thing and being another, pretending to be what we are not, and also to diversion or distraction of mind arising from the conflict of different objects of desire, or different principles of action. Singleness of heart consists in having one object of pursuit and one principle of action. To servants it was commanded that they should look to Christ. To do his will should be their sole object, and desire to please him their controlling motive. It should not be partly the fear of punishment, partly the hope of reward, or partly a desire for their own advancement, but simply and solely to do the will of Christ. This is a very high attainment. It is a possible attainment. It gives consistency, strength and peace.

CXLI. Beauty of Holiness.

[*October 31st,* 1858.]

The words with which we are most familiar we find it most difficult to define. We all know what beauty is, or, rather, we are all familiar with that state of mind which the perception of beauty produces; but no one has yet succeeded in defining beauty itself. The theories of philosophers are numerous and unsatisfactory. The τὸ χάλον remains a mystery. It is enough to know, 1. That beauty is that attribute of an object which awakens a peculiar pleasure in the mind, which pleasure we are conscious is not a sensation, and not moral, *i. e.*, not an approbation of the conscience, but æsthetical. This pleasure is a complacent delight in the object itself apart from its relation to us.

2. Therefore it is entirely unselfish. Beauty cannot be appropriated. It is a common good. The beauties of nature no one can

monopolize, and no one would if he could.   It is not the less to one man because enjoyed by millions.

3. Beauty is of different kinds. Of natural objects, as flowers, an animal, a landscape, the ocean when calm, the moon in a cloudless sky ; of works of art, a building, a statue, a picture. In all these cases the pleasure is entirely independent of the perception of utility. Of the human countenance, a beautiful face of a child, of a youth, of a man, of a woman, and that woman a sister or mother, excites a pleasure altogether peculiar to itself. It is the beauty of an intelligent being, and therefore partakes of the nature of intellectual beauty. 4. There is a beauty which addresses itself to the understanding. That is, the objects of the intellect when perceived, excite a pleasure analogous to that produced by a beautiful sensible object ; e. g., beauty of style, which is not mere rythm, but fitness, perspicuity, attributes which address themselves to the intelligence. So there is a beauty in a demonstration, in a logical argument ; there is the eloquence of logic. 5. Moral beauty. This is distinct from moral approbation. The contemplation of a good deed, or of a moral character, of a high order, excites not only approbation, but also a peculiar kind of pleasure, a complacent delight. 6. So there is a higher beauty still, the beauty of Holiness. As there is a beauty which addresses itself to the eye and to the ear, another which addresses itself to the intellect, another to the moral nature, so there is another which addresses itself to the higher life implanted in regeneration. There is a beauty in Holiness; or Holiness is beautiful.

By holiness is meant, 1. Purity. 2. Opposition to all evil. 3. All positive moral excellence. This exists imperfectly in man, perfectly though limited in angels, perfectly and without limit in God. When it is said that holiness is beautiful, it is meant not merely that it is an object of approbation, or of respect, or of fear or veneration, but of complacent delight ; that it gives a peculiar pleasure, and that of the highest kind, which from analogy is called beauty. This beauty is revealed most clearly in the Lord Jesus Christ. He is represented as most beautiful. The Scriptures are filled with descriptions of the beauty of holiness as manifested in Jesus Christ. The Church is represented as ravished with his beauty.

How is this beauty to be obtained?

1. All beauty is a gift. It never can be bought. It is a peculiar form of the manifestation of God. The beauty of holiness in us is the manifestation of God in us. The Spirit of God in us is the Spirit of glory. Therefore, 1. We must have our sins washed away in the blood of Christ. 2. We must have the Spirit of Christ dwell in us. 3. We must converse with the refined and beautiful through the word, sacraments and prayer.

CXLII. The Nature and Evidences of Union with Christ.

[*Oct.* 22d, 1854.]

The scriptural expression to be in Christ, is one of frequent occurrence. It of course indicates a union with him, to which our salvation is attributed. The lowest interpretation of the phrase makes it express nothing more than a union in sentiment and feeling. The Scriptures teach,

I. *As to the nature of this union.*

1. That it is a federal or a covenant union, analogous to that between Adam and his posterity in the covenant of works. It constitutes Christ the head and representative of his people. (*a.*) So that he acts as their substitute in obedience and suffering. (*b.*) Hence his righteousness becomes theirs and constitutes the ground of their justification. (*c.*) This union is from eternity. We were chosen in him before the foundation of the world, and the union secures to those for whom Christ acts, the benefits of redemption. (*d.*) Though existing from eternity in the council of God, and securing the benefits of redemption, it is consummated in time by faith. So that the application of the ulterior benefits of redemption is not made until we believe.

Observe. This teaches us the nature and office of faith as connected with our purification.

2. The union with Christ is not only a federal one, but also spiritual, arising from the indwelling of the Holy Spirit, by which we become partakers of the life of Christ. Hence, he is said to dwell in us, to live in us, and his life is said to secure our life. It is said to be analogous to that between the vine and its branches, the head and members of the same body. As the federal union is the ground of our justification and exaltation, so this vital union is the ground of sanctification.

II. *The effects and evidences of union with Christ are, first, as to this life.* 1. Peace of conscience. 2. Assurance of God's love. 3. Increase of grace. 4. Perseverance therein. These are all the fruits of our covenant relation to Christ.

The immediate effects and evidences of the participation of his life are, 1. Conformity to his image. 2. Love for his person. 3. Devotion to his service.

Secondly, as to the life which is to come, the fruits of union with Christ are, 1. Participation of his glory. 2. Participation of his dominion.

INFERENCES.

1. To be in Christ is the only thing we need desire. We may well

count all things but loss in comparison with this. 2. The sense of obligation which should always attend the belief that we are in Christ. 3. The desire to act in accordance with the dignity and blessedness of our relationship to Christ.

CXLIII. The Excellency of the knowledge of Christ Jesus our Lord. Phil. 3: 8.

[*October 11th*, 1843.]

The analysis of our faculties into our cognitive powers, into our susceptibilities and will, thought, feeling and volition, may be important to the understanding and classification of the phenomena of our nature; but these faculties are neither independent nor distinct. The exercise of the one includes the exercise of the other. There is always an exercise of will in thought, and an exercise of feeling in cognition. The Bible uses language founded on the common consciousness of men, and not on the speculations of philosophy. In the Scriptures, knowledge is not mere intellectual apprehension. It includes that but more. It includes also the proper apprehension not only of the object, but of its qualities; and if those qualities be either esthetic or moral, it includes the due apprehension of them and the state of feeling which answers to them.

The knowledge of Christ, therefore, is not the apprehension of what he is, simply by the intellect, but also a due apprehension of his glory as a divine person arrayed in our nature, and involves not as its consequence merely, but as one of its elements, the corresponding feeling of adoration, delight, desire and complacency. It includes, therefore,

1. A knowledge of his person as God and man.

2. The knowledge of his work in the redemption of man.

3. The knowledge of his relation to us, and of the benefits which we derive from him, justification, sanctification, adoption and eternal life.

This knowledge is superlatively excellent, 1. Because he is himself the perfect object of knowledge. 2. Because eternal life, the hope of the soul, consists in that knowledge. Because the possession of it enlarges and enlightens the intellect, purifies the heart, and renders perfectly blessed. 3. Because without this knowledge we are not only ignorant of God, but ignorant of the way of salvation. We know not how to be justified or sanctified. We of necessity, therefore, are left to seek and trust in other ineffectual methods of obtaining these blessings.

1. All religion is concluded or confined to one thing, to know Christ. To this we should concentrate all our attention and efforts. It is vain to seek the knowledge of God or his favor, to strive after either holiness or peace in any other way. 2. The only test of Christian

character is to be found here. Men may be benevolent, in a certain sense pious, but they cannot be Christians unless they know Christ and find in that knowledge their spiritual life. Our experience must correspond with that of the Apostles and other believers recorded in the New Testament.

3. The only way to save men is not by preaching the doctrines of natural religion, nor by holding up law, nor by expounding the anthropological doctrines of the Bible. These things are important in their place, but they are subordinate to preaching Christ, that is, holding him up in his person, his work, and his relation to us as the great object of knowledge, and as such, the great object of love, the only ground of confidence and our only and all-sufficient portion. It is by being brought to the knowledge of Christ that men are to be converted and the world saved.

CXLIV. Ye are not your own: for ye are bought with a price.—1 Cor. 6: 19, 20.

[*Sept. 9th*, 1855. *Communion Sabbath.*]

The Lord's Supper is a commemoration of redemption. Redemption is deliverance by purchase. The redeemed become the property of the Redeemer. "Ye are not your own: for ye are bought with a price."

I. *The sense in which believers are not their own.*

1. The right of property in us is not in ourselves, but in Christ. There is a sense in which a man may have a right of property in himself, so far as his fellow-men are concerned. His body is his own. His time, his talents are his and not others. He can employ them at his own discretion, and for his own advantage. This is precisely what the apostle denies of believers. They are not their own. They have no right to use their bodies, their time or talents for themselves, at their own discretion, and for their own advantage. They belong to Christ, in the sense in which a slave belongs to his master.

2. This right of property and the consequent right of control extends not merely to the body, but to the soul. It is the soul that has been bought. Therefore our souls are not our own. Our reason, our conscience, our hearts, our whole rational and immortal nature, belong to Christ. He determines what we are to think, what believe, what approve, what condemn, what love, and what hate. The πνεῦμα which is in us is not the πνεῦμα τῶν 'ανθρωπῶν, but the πνεῦμα τοῦ θεοῦ. This is what the apostle says in the connection.

3. This right of property, extending to both soul and body, brings with it the obligation to glorify God in our body and spirit which are his. We are God's in such a sense that the only legitimate end of our being is his glory. If our own we would live for ourselves, but life be-

longs to Christ. We must live for Christ. What the apostle teaches, is, 1. That the right of property in us is not in ourselves but in God. 2. That this right of property and of control extends to the soul as well as to the body. 3. That it involves the obligation of living for his glory.

II. *The foundation of this peculiar relation is not creation, it is not preservation, but redemption.* This redemption gives a rightful possession, because the price given was adequate. It was the blood of the Lamb, the blood of the eternal Son of God.

III. *This right vests in Christ;* not in God as God, but in God in Christ. He is the Redeemer, therefore he is the possessor. As God and Christ are one there is no collision here, nothing inconsistent with our allegiance to God, in our subjection to Christ. This representation, however, pervades the Scriptures, and is essential to the healthful ex-ercise of piety. Many Christians endeavor to live in their natural re-lation to God. Others regard Christ not as the direct object of the re-ligious affections and allegiance, but only as opening the way for our returning to the service of God. This is to degrade Christ and to sub-stitute nature for grace, reason for the gospel. The true doctrine of the Scriptures is that we belong to Christ, and therefore that the speci-fic motive of obedience is love to Christ, and the specific object of pur-suit is the glory of Christ, and the rule of action is the will of Christ. It is only in loving Christ that we love God, in glorifying Christ that we can glorify God, and in serving Christ that we can serve God.

IV. *Are* WE *then redeemed?*

Not if we regard ourselves as our own. Not if we use our bodies, our time and talents as belonging to ourselves. Not if we seek our own glory. Not if we act in obedience to our own will. We are re-deemed from the devil and from hell, only if we recognize Christ as our owner; only if love to him constrains us to live to his glory, and make his will the rule of our conduct.

CXLV. Do all to the glory of God. 1 Cor. 10: 31.

[*November 23d,* 1856.]

I. *The idea of God as set forth in the Westminster Catechism is unpa-ralleled.*

1. He is *a* Spirit, not *the* Spirit; not the universal Spirit of which we are the manifestations, not the ocean of which we are the drops, but *a* Spirit; one to whom we can present ourselves, and distinguish from ourselves, and to whom we can say: Our father. 2. In being a spirit he has all the attributes of a spirit, conscience, intelligence, will and agency, a being of our own nature in this generic sense. He is not so

separate from us by diversity as to have no sympathy with us, or so that we can have no congeniality with him. But then he is an infinite, eternal and immutable spirit. We are finite, limited on every hand as to the place we occupy, as to the powers we possess, as to the excellence we can attain, and as to the blessedness we can enjoy. God is infinite. There is no limit to his presence, to his intelligence and knowledge, to his divine goodness or to his power. He is eternal, without beginning, without end, without succession. And he is immutable in all his being and perfections. The sum of all finites is as nothing to the infinite. 1. The sum of finite being is as nothing to infinite being. 2. The sum of finite intelligence is as nothing to the infinite intelligence. 3. The sum of finite powers is as nothing to infinite power. 4. The sum of finite excellence is as nothing to infinite excellence. 5. The sum of finite blessedness is as nothing to the infinite blessedness of God. The whole universe, therefore, is as nothing to God. What then are we? We are so insignificant a part of this universe that were we blotted out of existence, none but an omniscient eye would miss us.

II. *Now what the Scriptures teach, and what common sense teaches, is that the glory of this infinite Being is the only proper end of all things.* For his glory they are and were created. They teach also that this is the only legitimate end to be contemplated in the acts of intelligent creatures. By the glory of God is meant his divine perfection, his essential and infinite excellence, which renders him the proper object of admiration and adoration. To act for the glory of God, is to act so that his glory should be manifested, brought into view, acknowledged and admired. The exhortation to do all things for the glory of God is, therefore, an exhortation,

1. To make that end the highest commanding end of our actions. That we should recognize it as the chief end, and determine to promote it. Some make (*a.*) Their own happiness their end. (*b.*) Others, their friends. (*c.*) Others, their country. (*d.*) Others, their kind, human beings as a whole. (*e.*) Others, all beings. These are all false ends. The selection of either of them vitiates and destroys religion. It makes something besides regard to God the motive, and something besides God the end of action. That is, it substitutes something for religion, which is not religion. 2. The second thing included in this exhortation is, that the rule, and not only the end, of our actions is to be the glory of God. We are to so act that intelligent beings, men and angels, shall be led to glorify God. When anything comes to be decided, whether it should be done or left undone, the rule is not (*a.*) Whether it will be agreeable or disagreeable to ourselves. (*b.*) Whether it will be agreeable or otherwise to others, *i. e.*, popular! (*c.*) Nor whether it

will be expedient or inexpedient. (*d.*) But whether it will be for the glory of God or not, that is, whether it will tend to make men admire and worship God.

This is a rule which applies to everything, great and small. 1. To the choice of a profession. The question should be, how can I accomplish most in bringing men to glorify God? 2. In determining where we are to labor. 3. In deciding on the distribution and occupation of our time. 4. In determining our outward conduct towards others, our conformity to the world. 5. In deciding on the thoughts, feelings and purposes, the tempers and dispositions of mind, which we shall cherish. 6. In the way we bear reproach, inferiority, neglect, sickness, injuries, &c. In short, it is a simple, comprehensive, universal rule.

III. *The reasons why we should adopt this rule are,* 1. That the glory of God is the highest end. 2. That God himself has made it the end of creation, of providence, of redemption. 3. That the Lord Jesus Christ made it his end. 4. That all saints and angels do the same. 5. That it is essential to the order and happiness of the universe. What would result if, instead of making the sun the centre of our system, some little satellite should set up, or be set up as such? How would it preserve order or harmony? 6. The making any other end than God's glory our object, is the sum and essence of idolatry. It incurs all its guilt and all its evils. 7. It brings the whole life into perfect harmony, inward and outward. It promotes holiness, and happiness, and usefulness. 8. It is the end which we *must* promote, either by our salvation, or perdition.

CXLVI. Glorying in the Cross of our Lord Jesus Christ.
Gal. 6: 14.

[*Oct. 17th,* 1852.]

1. What is glorying? 2. What is the cross of Christ? 3. What is the world? 4. What is being crucified to the world? 5. How is this to be effected?

I. *Glorying.*

1. To rejoice in anything as a source of good. 2. Especially as the source of honor. Men are said to glory—καυχάσθαι—in themselves, in the law, in the flesh, in man, in God, in afflictions, in other men's labors. ὑπέρ, ἐν, ἐπί, κατά, simple accusative.

II. *The cross of Christ.*

1. Not afflictions on account of Christ, as Luther says. 2. But Christ crucified, as in 1 Cor. ii: 7, and ii: 2. To glory in the cross is, 1. To rejoice in it, or in Christ crucified, as the only ground of salvation. 2. To make it the sole ground of confidence. 3. To look for honor to no

other source.   4. To make it the sole instrument of success in preach
ing.

III. *The world.*

1. All things seen and temporal.   2. Mankind as distinguished from
the Church.

IV. *To be crucified unto the world.*

1. Luther says: To condemn the world, as the world condemns me.
The world judges me worthy of death, I judge the world worthy of
death.   2. To die to, to renounce, to be indifferent to, and free from
the power of the world.   The world loses its power over me, and its
attractions for me.   It is implied that this separation is effectual and
painful.

V. *How is this done?*   By which? or by whom?   Better the latter.
Christ thus frees me from the world.   1. By delivering me from its
condemnation.   2. By delivering me from its life, and putting his life
in me.   3. By the revelation of love made in the cross, and the sense
of obligation thus awakened.   4. By the connection of the cross with
the revelation of eternal things.

CXLVII. The Love of Christ Constraineth Us.   2 Cor. 5: 14.

[*May 4th*, 1850.]

(LAST CONFERENCE OF THE SESSION.)

Unity belongs to all the works of God.   This is seen in our solar
system, and in the universe.   It is also seen in the constitution of man.
Diversity is reduced to unity.   So in character.   No man becomes
great or successful, who has not one object, and one constraining motive.
So with the Christian.   There is, and must be, something to give unity
to the character as Christian.   This is the love of Christ as the constraining motive, and the glory of Christ as the one object.   It is this
that gives simplicity, strength, and consistency to the Christian.   It is
the want of this that leaves him driven about by every wave and wind.

It is not enough to look forward to doing good, promoting knowledge, religion, and the happiness of men, and being governed by this
and that motive.   This leaves all vague, indefinite, and changing.   We
must have one definite object, and one constraining motive.   Both are
here presented.

I. *The love of Christ is the constraining influence.*   The "love of
Christ" is his love to us.   (*a.*) Because this is the common sense.   (*b.*)
Because it is that love which is illustrated by his dying for us.   (*c.*) Be-
cause he is so often spoken of as loving us.

"Constraineth us."   The word means to restrain, to have in one's
power.   This is the sense here.   The love of Christ takes possession of

us, of all our faculties, of our thoughts, affections and powers. It masters and controls us. How inconceivable the blessedness of those thus possessed. It elevates them; it fills them with courage, patience and power. If we have this we need naught else for our happiness or usefulness.

This love of Christ is 1. The love of Jesus, of God manifested in the flesh. It is of great importance to have God thus brought near to us. 2. It is not general benevolence, nor is it philanthropy. It is the love of a person to particular persons. "He loved *me*," said the apostle. There is as much difference between general benevolence and personal love as between the diffused rays of the sun and those rays concentrated in a focus. 3. This love is sovereign, not founded on our merit. He loved us when enemies, when ungodly, when lying in our blood. 4. It is infinitely great. It led to the eternal Son of God dying for us. 5. This love is unchanging. A woman may forget her infant, but Christ's love never fails. 6. This love is tender, considerate, sympathizing, ἐκτρέφειν (to bring up), και θαλπειν (to foster), its objects. Go out under the conviction that you are the objects of this love. Let it exert its full influence upon you.

Why has it this power? Because, 1. His death is our death. His love constrains us, because we are convinced that when he died we all died. And the effect of this persuasion that we are the objects of his love, makes us conscious that his death is ours. There are two senses in which this is true. His death avails for all the ends which our death could have accomplished. It satisfies justice, frees from the penalty of the law, honors God, and promotes the good of the universe. Let a man feel this, and he will feel the effect of the love of Christ in dying for us. But, secondly, we died with Christ analogically. As he died to sin, so do we. We renounce it, become free from its power. This is the first reason of the power of the love of Christ, as dying for us, it secures our dying to sin.

2. The second is, that we live not for ourselves, but for him who died for us, and rose again. This, then, is the one object for which the Christian lives, (1.) Not for himself, not that he may be happy, not that he may promote the welfare of others, but,

(2.) That he may glorify Christ.

How is this to be done? 1. By making it the definite object of our lives. 2. By entire subjection to his will. 3. By adherence to his truth. 4. By devotion to his service, *i. e.*, by striving to bring men to know, to love, to worship, and to obey Christ. So far as we accomplish this end, we accomplish all other good ends. Two things you should carry with you everywhere, and to the end of life.

1. That the conviction of the love of Christ, the sense of his love,

its greatness and freeness, should fill you and govern you. 2. That the single object of life is thus to cause him to be glorified. Do this and you will be blessed, and a blessing, go where you will, and suffer what you may.

CXLVIII. And this is the victory that overcometh the world, even our faith. 1 John 5: 4.

[*February 15th*, 1857.]

We are subjected to an inevitable conflict. It cannot be avoided by flight, by surrender, or by refusing to resist. It is a conflict, not for house and home, nor for liberty or security, but of life and death; not of the body, but of the soul; not temporal, but eternal. The enemy is sometimes designated as Satan and the powers of darkness, sometimes as the world, and sometimes as our own evil hearts, or ourselves. These all constitute one. They are different powers of the kingdom of darkness. Satan is the god of this world. The world is subject to him, and constitutes one large corps of his army; and the flesh, *i. e.*, our fallen nature, is his ally.

I. *What is meant by the world, and what is it to overcome the world?* 1. The world is often a collective term for the things seen and temporal. 2. It is often a collective term for mankind. The question is, which is to govern the soul, God or the world? And this includes, (*a.*) Which is to govern, or to determine our convictions? We are under the strongest possible temptation to allow our convictions to be determined by the apparent, by nature, by what is visible, or by the authority of men. Our convictions, both as to what is true and as to what is right, are, in a multitude of cases, controlled by what we see, (we cannot believe in the invisible and eternal), or by the opinions of the community to which we belong. Our life is but a particle in the general life of the world. We are controlled by the latter in our judgments. Where is the man that rises superior to his age, or nation, or his Church? Or if he assert his independence, it is only the independence of himself as a creature, and that is only another form of subjection to the devil. (*b.*) The danger is still greater as regards our affections. The world, and God; the visible, and the invisible; the present, and the eternal. The former address our senses, our constitutional principles. They are ever present. They operate upon us without cessation. The consequence is, that with the vast majority of men the visible is everything. They have their hearts, their hopes, their fears, all directed to the present. They have all their sources of happiness here. Their life is absorbed in what is seen and temporal. (*c.*) It is obvious that what determines our convictions, and engrosses our affections, will control our actions. Our energies will be directed to the objects which have this influence, and our whole outward life will have reference to them.

II. *Now, the question is, what will enable us to overcome the world?* What will enable us to emancipate ourselves from its control, and to live under the controlling influence of God and his word? What will enable us to have our intellect, affections, and outward life filled with the thoughts of God, and of divine things? to have our hearts filled with his love, our lives brought under his control, so as to be devoted to his service and regulated by his will?

1. Not any power in ourselves. As well might a single drop in the Niagara run upward, while the mighty stream is sweeping downward. 2. Not by seclusion from the world, and trying to get into a stream which runs in a contrary direction. This is impossible, for we cannot get out of the world. We are part and parcel of it. An eddy often forms in a stream, and sets backward; but it is only to be deflected in a different line, back into the mighty flood. 3. This cannot be done for us. The Church cannot save us. Neither its power nor its directions are of avail in this case. 4. The apostle tells us that faith is the victory. This includes two very different things. *First*, faith as the substance of things hoped for, the evidence of things not seen, is a new principle and power introduced into our nature. It is a divine, supernatural gift. It overcomes the world, (1). Because it brings eternal things to view. It removes the scales from our eyes, and enables us to see God, things unseen, heaven and hell; to see their truth, and their infinite importance. All other things are seen to be trifles in comparison. (2). Truth is not the only object of faith. It discerns the excellence of the things believed, and, therefore, fills the heart with love and longing. It displaces the world from the heart by introducing a new and infinitely higher affection.

Second. All this is true; but it is not the truth which the apostle meant to teach. The faith of which he speaks has Christ for its object. Who is he that overcometh the world but he that believeth that Jesus is the Christ? What is it to believe that Jesus is the Christ? And how does that overcome the world?

To believe that Jesus is the Christ is to believe, (1.) That he is the eternal Son of God. (2.) That he is God manifest in our nature. (3.) That he is the Messiah. (4.) That all that the Scriptures predicted as the work of the Messiah has been, is and shall be accomplished in him. *How does this overcome the world?* (1.) Because it reconciles us to God and delivers us from the kingdom of Satan. It makes us feel that we are not of the world; that this is not our home, nor our inheritance. (2.) Because it secures for us the gift of the Holy Ghost as a new principle of life. 3. Because it supplies us with a new object of affection, which supersedes and absorbs all others. It becomes Christ for us to live. We care for nothing but Christ. He satisfies all our capacities and desires. "Whom have I in heaven but thee? and there is none upon earth that I desire besides thee."

CXLIX. "It pleased God to reveal his Son in me."—Gal. 1: 16.

[*April 19th*, 1857.]

I. *Meaning of the passage.* 1. To reveal is to disclose, to bring into view what before was hidden, to make known. To reveal his Son, therefore, is to cause me to know his Son. This knowledge is not external acquaintance, such as many who persecuted and crucified Jesus possessed. Nor is it familiarity with the facts of history. Nor is it a speculative knowledge of all the truth revealed concerning Christ. But it is spiritual knowledge, such knowledge as implies just appreciation, and is attended with appropriate affections. The object of this knowledge is the Son of God, *i. e.*, Paul was brought to know that Jesus is the Son of God. Jesus was the historical person so called. That person was the Son of God, *i. e.*, the second person of the Trinity, clothed in our nature. He is God manifest in the flesh. This is what Paul was brought to know. Before, he did not believe it. He was blind to the glory of God in the face of Jesus Christ. As soon as he was brought to this knowledge, he was a new man. He was filled with adoring reverence, love and devotion to the Lord Jesus; to the Son of God who was in himself so gracious, and who for our salvation had assumed our nature, and suffered, and died upon the cross. The fact is that such was the nature of Paul's conversion; and such were its effects.

II. *Such also must in all cases be the nature of genuine conversion.* 1. Because the Scriptures expressly assert the fact, that the knowledge of God is essential to true religion. Religion consists in the knowledge of God, and in right affections and acts. Religion includes, therefore, three things. (*a.*) Spiritual cognition. (*b.*) Right feelings. (*c.*) Corresponding acts. From the nature of the case, there can be no religion without knowledge of God, who is its object. 2. Because there can be no knowledge of God, but through Christ. This the Bible teaches, because whosoever denieth the Son, the same hath not the Father, etc. He is the way, and no man cometh unto the Father but by him. Because the glory of God is revealed in the person of Christ. Not to see it, recognize, and acknowledge it, is to refuse to acknowledge God as God. God as revealed in nature, in the Old Testament and in Christ, is the same God. It is absurd to pretend to believe in and admire the sun under a cloud, and refuse to do so when it is clear. And so it is to acknowledge our Father at a distance, and not when at hand. There can be, therefore, no true knowledge of God without the knowledge of the Son. 3. Because true religion includes in its Christian form the worship and love of Christ, and obedience to him. Take the reverse of these statements, and the truth becomes more familiar. The want of love, reverence and obedience towards Christ proves that a man is no Christian. Christian experience, however manifested, from the beginning consists in this worship, love and service of Christ. All the cultus, the prayers, the hymns of Christians are characterized by these things, and without them there is no Christianity. 4. Not only the experience of the Church as a whole proves this, but also the individual experience of every believer. To believe in Christ, to receive him as the Son of God, to say he is Lord, to bow the knee to him, to kiss the Son, to take him to be our portion, are all forms under which conversion is described in the Bible, and under which it is exhibited in the experience of Christians. Satan blinds our minds, prevents our seeing that Jesus is the Son of God, that he loves us, that he died for us, that he is able and willing to save us. When we are brought to see all this, what is the consequence? It is not simply that we trust in Christ. Faith is not simply trust; but it is receiving Christ as our prophet, priest and king. How is this possible without the recognition of his divinity? It cannot be done.

INFERENCES.

This affords us, 1. A rule for deciding whether or not we are Christians. 2. A rule to direct our efforts in effecting the conversion of others. 3. A rule for deciding on doctrine and preaching. 4. A rule for guiding us how to preach.

CL. Humility.

[*Feb. 3d*, 1856.]

I. *Its nature.*

All Christian graces are products of the truth. So humility is the state of mind which the truth concerning our character and relations ought to produce. It includes,

1. A sense of insignificance, because we are both absolutely and relatively insignificant. We are as nothing before God. We are as nothing in the universe. We are as nothing in the hierarchy of intelligences. We are as nothing in the millions of mankind. We are insignificant in capacity, in learning, in influence and power, compared to millions who have been before us, and to thousands who are now on the earth. Humility is not only the consciousness of this insignificance,

but the recognition and acknowledgment of it, and acquiescence in it. Pride is the denial or forgetfulness of this fact, an unwillingness to be thus of no account, the assertion of our own importance, and the claim to have it acknowledged by others.

2. This form of humility is connected with a sense of weakness. It stands opposed to pride as including self-confidence, and especially pride of intellect, either as consisting in Rationalism, or the refusal to submit to the teaching of God; or in a sense of superiority to others. No man can be a Christian without in this sense being humble. He must be converted and become as a little child in order to enter into the kingdom of God. This form of humility is the product of the truth, concerning the imbecility of the human understanding and of our own personal inferiority.

3. The third form of humility is connected with a consciousness of guilt. It stands opposed to self-righteousness. It is the effect of conviction of sin, which produces the consciousness that we are destitute of all merit in the sight of God. How essential this is, the Scriptures everywhere teach. The Pharisee and Publican are presented in contrast, the one offensive and the other acceptable in the sight of God. A moral man puffed up with a sense of his good desert, is more offensive than an immoral man bowed down with a sense of guilt. When we consider the number and aggravations of our sins, we are lost in wonder that we can be so infatuated as to arrogate merit to ourselves.

4. Nearly allied to this, is humility as a sense of pollution, the consciousness that we are vile, distasteful, offensive in the sight of all holy beings. Men are filled with complacency by the possession of qualifications which render them attractive in the sight of their fellow-men; and they are mortified and humbled by having the conviction forced upon them, that they are disagreeable, or even offensive. Now the truth is, that we are exceedingly vile in the sight of God. The Scriptures exhaust the resources of language and of metaphors, to set forth the truth in this matter so as to produce the proper impression on our minds. We are all described as unclean, as full of sores, as deformed, as blind, as naked. The heart is likened to a cage of unclean beasts. The truth on this subject cannot be believed without producing self-loathing, which is a strong expression for humility. Such is this grace, subjectively considered. Men often think they are humble when their whole conduct proves the reverse.

1. They are disposed to assert their superiority.

2. They wish others to acknowledge it.

3. They resent as an injury all want of such acknowledgment.

4. And often they take pleasure in making others painfully conscious of their inferiority. These are very offensive traits of character.

II. *The importance of this grace appears,*

1. From its nature, as the want of it implies ignorance or disbelief of the truth concerning our true character. 2. From the frequent declarations of Scripture; that God resisteth the proud but showeth grace unto the humble; that those who exalt themselves shall be abased, and those who humble themselves shall be exalted; that the first shall be last, and the last first. 3. From its connection with the whole economy of redemption. God's plan of salvation is intended to humble man. We cannot acquiesce in that plan, or enjoy its benefits unless we are humble. Men must stoop to enter heaven. 4. From its influence on our fellow-men. As nothing is so offensive as pride, so nothing is so conciliating as humility. It disarms hostility, conciliates favor, gives facility of access and influence. Men resist even the truth from the proud, but yield to the persuasion of the humble. 5. From its influence on ourselves. Pride is raging as the wind. It is a troubled sea casting up mire and dirt. Humility is a calm and placid lake. The soul is never at rest except when it is in its right place, and acquiesces in its true relations. The humble are peaceful.

III. *The cultivation of this grace.*

1. Bring your mind under the operation of the truth. 2. Especially live in the presence of God. 3. Never act from the impulse of pride. 4. Humble yourself, by not seeking great things. 5. Seek the indwelling of the Spirit, and the aid of Christ.

CLI. Humility. 1 Pet. 5: 5.

[*Oct.* 31*st*, 1852.]

It is said that the heathen have no word for humble in the religious sense. It is not "humilis," nor "modestus," nor σώφρων, nor ταπεινός. In Hebrew, עָנָה means to suffer; עֲנִי, suffering, and hence עָנִי, poor, humble.

I. *The Christian graces are inseparable.* One cannot exist without the other. There cannot be faith without hope, or repentance without love, or love without meekness. This finds its analogy in physical life. Respiration, arterial action, digestion, cannot be conducted independently of one another. Though this is true, yet one grace may be more prominent than others.

II. *The graces are in themselves distinct.* That is, the state of mind which they express is not simple, but complex, various graces entering into its composition. Thus hope includes faith and desire and love; faith includes love, and love includes faith; repentance includes faith and love, etc.

III. *Humility is not a separate grace.* It is that state of mind which arises from a proper appreciation of the truth in regard to ourselves. 1. A due appreciation of our insignificance as creatures. In this sense it is opposed to self-importance, to self-reliance, to pride of intellect. 2. A due appreciation of ourselves as sinners, including a sense of guilt and of pollution. It is opposed, therefore, to self-righteousness and to self-complacency. 3. A due appreciation of our weakness. Hence, a sense of inability for self-conversion, for sanctification, for usefulness.

IV. *Manifestations.*

1. A disposition to appreciate others, or not to despise those around us.

2. Not to seek after honor or praise.

3. Not to be impatient under contempt.

4. Not to refuse to associate with the lowly.

5. Not unwilling to be least, and to obey.

V. *Benefits.*

Without it there is no religion, no communion with God, no inward peace, no outward power.

VI. *Means.*

1. Comparison of ourselves with God and his law.

2. Contemplation of our guilt, of our pollution, and of our uselessness.

CLII. For we are the circumcision, which worship God in the spirit, and rejoice in Christ Jesus, and have no confidence in the flesh.—Phil. 3: 3.

In all ages and under all dispensations, the Mosaic, the Apostolic, and the Christian, there have been two antagonistic principles at work, two classes among the professed people of God; the carnal and the spiritual; those who relied on externals, and those who relied on what is internal; those who make religion to consist in outward observances and relations, and those who make everything to depend on the state of the heart; an Israel according to the flesh ('Ισραήλ κατά σάρκα), and an Israel according to the spirit ('Ισραήλ κατά πνεῦμα). The great question between these two classes has ever been and is now, who are the circumcision? That is, who are the true people of God?

I. *What is meant by saying, "we are the circumcision?"* Circumcision in the Old Testament is presented in two different aspects. First, it was the symbol of regeneration, of inward purity of heart. And, secondly, it was the sign and seal of a covenant. It designated and sealed those who were the people of God. It distinguished them from other men, and assured them of their interest in the blessings of the covenant. The question, therefore, who are the circumcision? is tantamount to the question, who are the people of God in such a sense as to be his spiritual children, and the heirs of his kingdom? The Jews and Judaizers said they were. Paul said that he and his fellow-Christians were.

II. *The characteristics of those who are the true people of God, or the true circumcision*, as here given, are, 1. That they worship God in the spirit, or as the true reading is, οἱ πνεύματι Θεοῦ λατρεύοντες. The sense is the same. Those who serve or worship God under the influence and guidance of the Holy Spirit. This includes two things. First, that the inward principle of worship or service is no mere principle of nature, whether fear, or natural reverence, or sentiment, but that love and devotion of which the Holy Spirit is the author. And, secondly, that the mode of worship or service is that which the Holy Spirit has enjoined. It is not a will-worship, not the assiduous performance of things uncommanded of God, whether in matters of worship or of life. This serving God, in the spirit, therefore, stands opposed—

(1.) To insincere, hypocritical service. (2.) To mere external, ceremonial or ritual service. (3.) To all such service as the unrenewed, those who are not πνευμάτικοι (spiritual), do or can render. Such was the worship of the Jews generally; such also was that of the Judaizers in Paul's day; and such characteristically is the worship of the ritualists of our day, whether Romanists or Anglicans, and also of all mere formalists, whether Papist or Protestant.

2. The second characteristic of the true circumcision, or people of God, is that they rejoice (καυχώμενοι) in Christ Jesus. That is, they *glory in Christ Jesus*. This includes (1) The recognition of him as to us the ground of confidence. (2) As the source of honor. (3) As the object of delight. He is that in whom we glory as all our salvation and all our desire. How opposite is this spirit to that of the Judaizers, who gloried in the law, in the theocracy, in their descent from Abraham. How different from the spirit of those who glory in the church as their refuge, as the source of their salvation; who boast that they are the children of God because the children of the church.

3. They have no confidence, *i. e.*, they do not confide, in the flesh. "Flesh" includes two things. First, what is external, whether it be descent from Abraham, circumcision, external obedience to the law, or religious rites and ceremonies, or baptism and membership in the true Church. This is not an arbitrary extension of the meaning of the word. It is Paul's own interpretation, as given in the immediate context.

Secondly, "flesh stands opposed to the *spirit*." It means nature. To have no confidence in the flesh, therefore, means to have no confidence in ourselves, *i. e.*, in our own righteousness, in anything in our-

selves, not in our own strength. This also is included in Paul's ampli-
fication. Those who do not trust in the flesh, are those who renounce
their own righteousness and embrace the righteousness of God, even
the righteousness which is by the faith of Christ.

It is by these criteria we are to judge ourselves, and to determine the
true form of religion, and of the church.

CLIII. Hope, the Helmet of Salvation.—1 Thess. 5: 8.

[Dec. 2d, 1866.]

Hope, subjectively considered, is the desire and expectation of future
good. Christian hope is the desire and expectation, the joyful anticipation of the blessings promised in the gospel of Christ. These are summed
up in the expression, "the glory of God," i. e., the glory of which God
is the author. That glory includes, 1. The highest exaltation and perfection of our nature, which implies the restoration of the divine image
to the soul. We shall be like God, conformed to the image of his Son.
This likeness includes inward holiness of the soul, and the transforma-
tion of our bodies, so that they shall be like his glorious body. 2. Exaltation in the scale of being, arising from the enlargement of all our
powers to do, and all our capacity to receive. 3. Dominion, or exaltation in dignity as well as in excellence and power. What and how
great this is to be, we know not. Neither do we know in other matters
what God has in reserve for those who love him. 4. The blessedness
promised or hoped for includes not only these personal excellences and
distinctions, but also the presence, vision and fruition of God, and specially of God in Christ.

For feeble and sinful worms of the dust to cherish such expectations
would be the height of presumption and madness were it not for the
foundation which we have for such a hope. That foundation is, 1. The
promise of God. There is nothing in what has been said which God has
not expressly promised in his word. 2. The infinite merit of the Son of
God. These benefits are not bestowed capriciously, or without a just
reason, as a rich man or king might lavish an estate upon a pauper.
But the eternal Son of God has merited for his people this inheritance.
He has purchased it for them. It is secured to them by a covenant
which cannot be broken. 3. The love of God is infinitely great and
entirely gratuitous. Hence we infer, first, that there is no benefit
which that love is not ready to confer; and, secondly, that the possession
of these benefits, their ultimate fruition, does not depend upon us.
If while we were enemies Christ died for us, how much more shall we
be saved by his life. 4. The witness of God's Spirit with our spirit
that we are the children of God.

Hope is the "helmet of salvation." 1. Because it protects the believer's most vital part from the assaults of his enemies. In the hand-to-hand conflicts of old, the head was the worst exposed. Its protection was of the first importance. Hence the helmet was as necessary as the shield. No soldier could venture into battle without it. So with the Christian, the hope of salvation is necessary to prepare him for the battle on which he enters. (1.) It gives security. (2.) Therefore it gives confidence, courage and endurance. Hope gives security. (a.) From the assaults of Satan, against our faith, against our confidence in God; and from our proneness to neglect eternal things. (b.) It secures the soul from the attractions and the allurements of the world. (c.) From the corruptions of our own hearts.

In thus protecting him, it gives courage, cherfulness and constancy.

3. The helmet was not only a protection, but also an ornament. It was the most attractive part of the warrior's equipment. So is hope to the Christian. It adorns him and enables him to carry his head erect.

INFERENCES.

1. The duty of cherishing this hope, and not yielding to unreasonable despondency.

2. The duty of living as becomes those who have such a hope.

CLIV. Grace be with all them that love our Lord Jesus Christ in sincerity. Eph. 6: 24.

If any man love not the Lord Jesus Christ, let him be Anathema Maranatha. 1 Cor. 16: 22.

[*Date not given.*]

Though so dissimilar, these passages teach the same truth, viz.: that love to the Lord Jesus Christ is the indispensable condition of salvation. The conditions of salvation are unalterable. They are the same at all times, and for all men. We can alter them neither for ourselves nor others.

I. *Why is the love of Christ thus necessary?* There must be some real necessity for it. It is not an arbitrary condition which might be altered at pleasure. It is an absolute necessity, and can no more be changed than God can change. Then why is it?

1. Because Christ is God. He is God in the clearest form of manifestation. It is impossible to love God as revealed in nature, or in the Old Testament, without loving Christ. That would be to love a person imperfectly known, and not love him when more clearly known.

Christ, therefore, includes in himself the sum of divine perfections. All there is in God to command love, is in Christ.

2. Christ is God in our nature. He is thus invested with special attractions. (a.) Because possessed of another kind of excellence. (b.) Because brought into new and peculiar relation to us, a relation which he sustains to no other order of beings.

3. Because he has loved us and given himself for us. He has loved us enough to humble himself, to be found in fashion as a man, and to become obedient unto death, even the accursed death of the cross. To be insensible to such love and to such excellence combined, is indicative of the greatest moral degradation and depravity. God's standard of judgment is different from ours. Many who think well of themselves, and are admired by others, will be abhorred and rejected by God.

4. Because by his love and death he has delivered us from inconceivable degradation and misery, and opened the way for access to eternal life and glory.

5. Because we are shut up to the necessity of loving Christ or Satan. There are but two sovereigns, we must choose between them. Not choosing Christ, is choosing Satan. Here stands Christ, and there stands Satan. Which do you choose?

II. *What is it to love Christ, and how can we tell whether we love him or not?* These questions need not be separated. The answer to the one involves the answer to the other. The difficulty which attends this subject arises from the comprehensiveness of the word "love," and from the variety of its manifestations. We are said to love an infant, and to love God. Yet how different the states of mind expressed by the word! Analyze the love which you have for a father, and see how that sentiment manifests itself. 1. There is a feeling of reverence and complacency, which prevents you from ever treating him with neglect or indignity, and which makes his society agreeable to you. Love to Christ includes these sentiments; reverence for his person. He is an object of adoration to all who love him. Adoration is the expression of love. He is also the object of complacency. We delight in his excellence, and in his love, and are grateful for his benefits. And therefore intercourse with him is a pleasure, and not a burden; and in looking forward to heaven, our desire is to be with Christ, and to behold his glory. 2. Love to a father includes zeal for his honor. Any disrespect shown to him is painful to us, and anything which promotes his honor is a source of delight to us. We love those who love and honor him, and we avoid those who treat him with indignity. If we love Christ, we shall have analogous feelings towards him. We shall be zealous for his glory. Any neglect or irreverence shown the Saviour will wound our hearts. Any honor rendered him will give us delight. We will love those who love and honor him, and avoid those who neglect and abuse him. 3. The son who loves his father desires to please him, to do his will, obey his command, observe his counsel, always and in all places. So those who love Christ, keep his commandments. This is the test of love; not emotion, not excited feeling, but obedience.

What say you? Do you love the Lord Jesus Christ? On this question depends eternity. Here, those who love and those who do not love form a distinct class, though intermingled. Hereafter they will be separated. Do you desire to love? That is love, if it only leads to a constant endeavor to do his will, and to associate with his people.

CLV. That Christ may dwell in your hearts by faith, &c.
Eph. 3: 17.

[November 5th, 1865.]

The names and titles of Christ are used, 1. Sometimes for his office. 2. For his whole theanthropic person. 3. For his humanity. 4. For his divinity or the Logos. The sense in which any designation is to be taken depends upon the context and analogy of Scripture.

I. *What is meant by Christ?* It is,

1. Not here an official designation. 2. Not his humanity. 3. Not his theanthropic person, as the realistic mystics teach. 4. But the Logos, the second person of the Trinity. But the Scriptures say that God dwells where the Spirit of God is. So as the Holy Ghost bears the same relation to the Son as to the Father, and is therefore called the Spirit of the Son, or of Christ, to say that the Spirit of Christ dwells in us and that Christ dwells in us, means the same thing. God and the Son come and abide with the people of Christ, and make their abode with them.

II. *What is meant by dwelling in us?*

1. As God is everywhere, he is said to dwell where he specially and permanently manifests his presence. It is thus distinguished from the general manifestation which he makes of himself in all his works and at all times; and from more transient exhibitions as at Sinai, in the plain of Mamre, and elsewhere.

This dwelling includes 1. Such a manifestation as leads to a sense of his presence; a feeling that he is near, which fills the soul with awe, reverence, peace and confidence. 2. A manifestation of his power. As his presence in nature is revealed by his efficiency, so his presence in the soul is evinced by his control over its thoughts, feelings and purposes. 3. Although the presence of the Father assumes the presence of the Son and Spirit, and the Father and Son are present in the Spirit, yet there is a difference between God dwelling in us and Christ dwelling in us. As we are conscious of standing in different relations to the several persons of the Trinity, so the indwelling of the one is distinguishable from that of the others. When Christ is said to dwell in us, it is God in the person of his Son, God in the peculiar relation which the Son bears to us, who is in us. It is the sense of the presence of Christ as our Redeemer, who loved us and gave himself for us, who is near us. And the effects produced in us are not merely those states of mind which have God for their object, but of which Christ, or God in Christ, is the object. 2. The control or efficiency exerted, is that exercised by Christ as our Prophet, Priest and King, not only out of us and in our behalf, but within us.

III. *He dwells in our heart, i. e., the soul;* not in the body as a temple, although that is true; not merely in the understanding, although that is true also; but in the whole soul, and especially in the heart as considered the seat of the affections, and of the life.

IV. *He dwells in us by faith.* This teaches, 1. That where faith is not, Christ is not. 2. That the state of mind expressed by faith is the essential condition of this indwelling of Christ. We must (*a.*) Believe the record which God has given of his Son, both as to his person and his work. (*b.*) We must appropriate, or receive him as our God, our Saviour and Redeemer. (*c.*) We must constantly exercise towards him the love, reverence, confidence and devotion which are the fruits and manifestations of faith. It is to faith as to the eye of the soul, that he reveals himself; and it is through faith that he exerts that constant influence over us, which is intended and expressed by his dwelling in us.

1. We should reverence ourselves. The temple of God was holy. It could not be profaned with impunity. If we are the temple of Christ we should keep our hearts pure from all defilement of error, suspicion, or sin. 2. We should reverence our fellow Christians, from the highest to the lowest, as we reverence the temple of God. We should dread polluting their minds by error or evil. God will destroy those who defile his temple.

CLVI. The Communion of Saints.

[*November 8th*, 1857.]

Men exist as individuals. These are united by common bonds. 1. Of brotherhood as men. 2. By rational relations. 3. By common descent, as in tribes or clans, *e. g.*, the Jews. 4. By common blood as in families. But there is a communion of saints, that is, a community bound together as saints, and because they are saints. Here are two ideas. (1.) Saints. (2.) Communion.

I. *Those who are thus united are saints.*

It is evident from the nature of the union that it cannot arise from anything external. It is not subjection to the same ecclesiastical head, nor to the same governing body, nor to the same constitution, nor to the same creed speculatively adopted. The saints are not those outwardly consecrated, not mere professors, but those truly sanctified. The union which binds them together arises from their being born again, and being made truly the children of God. Hence the communion of saints is the communion of true believers.

II. *Communion, κοινωνία, having things in common, from κοινωνέω, to have things in common.* The communion of saints arises therefore from the fact, or consists in the fact that they have this in common. 1. They sustain a common relation to Christ. They all partake of him. They are members of his body, of his family, of his flock, of his kingdom. They all partake of the benefits of his redemption. They are all the objects of his love. The more intimate the union with Christ, the more intimate the communion of saints. The more conscious we are of our union with Christ, the more conscious we shall be of our communion with his people. As the union between Christ and his people is a vital one, more intimate than any other, so the bond which unites saints is the most intimate of all bonds. 2. They have the Holy Ghost in common. They are all partakers of the Holy Ghost. He dwells in all. They have a common participation of life. Hence (*a.*) They have a common faith. (*b.*) They have a common experience. The religious experience of one Christian is the same as that of all others. Hence sympathy and congeniality exist. (*c.*) They have common objects of affection and allegiance. They all love and serve the same Master, and are devoted to the same cause. (*d.*) They have a common destiny in this life, and in the life to come. 3. This communion expresses or manifests itself, (*a.*) In mutual affection. (*b.*) In the recognition of each other as Christians. (*c.*) In union, in worship and ordinances. (*d.*) In sympathy or fellow-feeling, so that if one member rejoices, all the members rejoice with it. (*e.*) In community of goods, as far as is best in the present state of the world; that is, so far as it does not destroy the motive to individual exertion, and so far as is consistent with that accumulation of capital, and division of labor which are best suited to the present condition of men.

Consider,

1. The importance attached to the communion of saints in the Scriptures.

2. The lamentable defects of Christians in this respect, not only of churches but of individual Christians. They do not love each other as they ought. They do not sympathize with and assist each other as they ought, but feel and act towards their fellow Christians very much as they do towards other men. 3. The Bible makes Christian communion essential. If we do not feel our union with believers, and sympathize with them, we are not united to Christ.

VII.

CHRISTIAN RESPONSIBILITIES AND DUTIES.

CLVII. Pure religion and undefiled before God and the Father is this, To visit the fatherless and widows in their affliction, and to keep himself unspotted from the world.
Jas. 1: 27.

[*January 20th*, 1866.]

Two errors have extensively prevailed in the Church. 1. That all religion consists in the worship of God and fellowship with him. 2. That all religion consists in the discharge of our social duties. The one assumes that all our duties concern our relation to God; the other, that they all arise out of our relations to our fellow-men. The former has prevailed in the Romish Church. For although that church places a high value on alms-giving, and is distinguished for its eleemosynary institutions and orders, yet, *First*, its most distinguished saints have been separated from the world, have neglected all social duties. *Second*, because if a man receives the doctrines, obeys the authorities, and practices the rites of the church, he is safe, no matter what his moral conduct may be. The other extreme has prevailed more among latitudinarians in doctrine; men who make doctrine and the services of piety of little account; who say that a man's creed cannot be wrong, whose life is in the right, and resolve all virtue and religion into benevolence and its exercise.

The Scriptures teach, 1. That we owe special duties to God, as reverence, love, devotion, worship, constant obedience, etc.

2. That we owe duties to our fellow-men, as parents, children, citizens, neighbors, fellow-creatures.

3. That these duties are not only consistent, the one class with the other, but that they are alike indispensable. That he who claims to fulfill the one while he neglects the other is a self-deceiver or a hypocrite.

4. That those which we owe to God are the higher and more important, and the foundation of the other class. No man ever performed his duties to God aright, without being faithful to his social duties.

5. That the attempt to dissociate morality from religion leads to the destruction of morality, first, because of a natural tendency. Deadness to higher duties cannot long co-exist with devotion to lower; or rather, the latter cannot continue without the former. Besides, the great and efficient motives to moral duties are derived from religion. And as God is the source of all good, nothing good can continue in those who live in alienation from him. And, finally, because God judicially abandons the irreligious to immorality.

6. A sixth great truth is, that obedience to God, obeying his commands from a pious spirit, is the most acceptable worship we can render to him. The Apostle James was contending against the practice of formalities. Among the Jews it was a prevailing whim, that if a man kept the ceremonial law and the tradition of the elders, he was eminently religious, a true worshipper of God. Of the Christian converts some fell into the same error. They held to faith without works. They taught that if a man believed aright, and prayed and worshipped in the sanctuary, he was all that he need be. James said, "faith without works is dead;" that outward profession and the observance of the rites and ceremonies of religion, were of no avail, unless we obeyed the commandments and became doers, as well as hearers, of the word; that the most acceptable way of serving God, is discharging our social duties aright. This was a sacrifice with which God was well pleased. Our Lord taught the same doctrine when he said, "I will have mercy and not sacrifice;" *i. e.*, that the moral is more important than the ceremonial. The prophet Isaiah had taught the same when he said in the name of Jehovah, "To what purpose is the multitude of your sacrifices unto me? I am full of the burnt offerings of rams, and the fat of fed beasts." "Bring no more vain oblations; incense is an abomination unto me." "Wash ye, make you clean; put away the evil of your doings from before mine eyes; cease to do evil; learn to do well." The worship or service of God which is acceptable to God, is to visit the fatherless and the widows in their affliction, and to keep ourselves unspotted from the world. Two things are here included.

1. Kindness to the poor and suffering, not merely in giving alms, but in kind ministrations.

2. Separation from the contaminations of the world. The men who would appear as God's true worshippers must not be immersed in the gayeties, schemes and machinations, much less in the vices of the

world. They must be a holy, a peculiar people, and they must be active in the discharge of all the duties of benevolence. But if this is done as a matter of parade, to gain credit with men, it is nothing. If done to work out a righteousness of our own, or to make atonement for sin, it is nothing. If done out of mere kindness, human sympathy, it is good as far as it goes, but it is not θρησκεία, religious worship, or religion. A man may give all his goods to feed the poor, and even his body to be burned, yet if he have not charity, he is nothing. This service must be rendered from Christian motives, (a.) Because we thus honor Christ. (b.) Because the poor are his brethren. "Inasmuch as ye have done it unto one of the least of these my brethren, ye have done it unto ME."

CLVIII. If any man will do his will, he shall know of the doctrine, whether it be of God, or whether I speak of myself. John 7: 17. He that is of God, heareth God's words; ye therefore hear them not, because ye are not of God. John 8: 47.

[January 29th, 1868.]

What our Lord here asserts is: First, that if a man is in a right state of mind, he will know and believe the truth. Secondly, that those who are in a wrong state of mind reject the truth. This is saying that the cause of faith, or the reason why a man believes, is to be found in his right moral state, and that the cause of wrong belief and of infidelity, is a wrong moral state. This, reduced to one proposition, is saying that the faith of a man, so far as religious truth is concerned, depends on his moral state.

Proof that this is true.

1. This declaration of our Lord is of itself a sufficient proof of the truth of the proposition. It is plain that the expressions, "If any man will do his will," and "He that is of God," amount to the same thing. The one means If any one sincerely desires to please God, and the other, If any man is godly, *i. e.*, of the same mind as God, congenial with him. Faith in the truth of God, he says, certainly flows from this congeniality with God, and, on the other hand, unbelief is due to, and therefore is the evidence of a want of this congeniality with God. This is a direct affirmation of the truth of the above proposition.

2. This, however, is proved by many other declarations of our Lord, and of the sacred writers generally. Christ says, "If God were your Father, ye would love me." He uniformly refers the unbelief of the Jews, and their rejection of him, to their wickedness. It was because

they were of their father the devil, that they rejected and hated him. The apostle John asserts that "He that knoweth God heareth us," and that believers have the witness or evidence of the truth in themselves. The Holy Spirit, or an unction from the Holy One is given to all God's people, whereby they know the truth. Paul says that the natural or unrenewed man, and because he is unrenewed, perceives not the things of the Spirit; whereas, the spiritual man, and because he is spiritual, perceives all things. He elsewhere says, "If our gospel be hid, it is hid to them that are lost." This is the constant doctrine of the Scriptures.

3. It is also the doctrine of experience. The good uniformly believe the truth, the wicked disbelieve, or neglect it. You may trace the history of the Church, and you will uniformly find truth and piety united on the one hand, error and irreligion, on the other. The more serious the error, the more clear is the evidence of the sinfulness of those who adopt it. This is true of all the grades of error, from the lowest to the highest, from the denial of unessential doctrines, to atheism. You may travel over the world, and you will everywhere find the same thing to be true. The infidels of England, France and Germany are uniformly irreligious, and generally immoral. On the other hand you never find the evidence of godliness without finding with it the firm belief of all truth connected with religious experience. Experience, therefore, is in accord with the Scriptures. A man's faith, so far as religious truth is concerned, depends upon the state of his heart.

4. A fourth argument on this subject is from analogy. There are different kinds of truth. For the sake of distinction we may call some speculative, as addressed to the intellect, as the truths of mathematics, of science, and of history. Some are æsthetic, as addressed to the taste, or sense of the beautiful. There is a standard of beauty. Some things in nature, in art, and in literature give delight, others excite disgust. This is not arbitrary. Some are moral, and suppose a moral sense for their apprehension. Some are religious or spiritual, and suppose a religious or spiritual state of mind for their due apprehension. The evidence of any one of these classes of truths is suited to its nature. The evidence of speculative truths is addressed only to the understanding, and requires only intellectual ability to comprehend and receive them. They force assent. The evidence of æsthetic truth supposes cultivation and refinement. If a man denies the beauty of what the mass of educated and cultivated men pronounce beautiful, it is proof positive of his want of taste. The standard by which a man's taste is legitimately judged, is that he delights in what is truly beautiful. So of moral truths.

A good man inevitably approves of what is morally right and good.

If a man pronounce the Decalogue evil, or the sermon on the mount immoral, it is proof positive that he himself is immoral. If this is so, why should it not be true that the religious or godly man should receive religious truths, and the ungodly man reject them?

INFERENCES.

1. The folly of the opinion that a man is not responsible for his faith. This is transferring a maxim true in one sphere to another in which it is not true. Our character is determined by our faith, because our faith depends upon our character.

2. Therefore we should be humbled on account of our unbelief; consider it an evidence of a dull and sluggish heart.

3. We see the true way to increase the strength of our faith. We must grow in holiness.

4. The consolation and security of believers. No speculative objections can subvert a faith founded on moral or religious evidence. Science can never disprove the Decalogue.

CLIX. Be not conformed to this world. Rom. 12: 3.

[*April 12th*, 1857.]

I. *What is the world?*

The terms used are κόσμος and αἰών. They are very different in signification, but often the same in sense. In such connections as "Ye are not of the world," "As I am not of the world," "Love not the world," "The world hateth you," and the like, it means the mass of unrenewed men, as distinguished from the Church, or people of God. The world in this sense belongs to Satan; it is his kingdom. It has a reigning spirit. It has its laws and maxims. Its manners and customs are determined by its reigning spirit. It has its objects of desire and pursuit; and it has its consummation, which is perdition.

II. *What is it to be conformed to the world?*

1. It is to be inwardly like men of the world, in the governing principle of our lives; that is, to have a worldly spirit, a spirit occupied with, and interested in worldly things; a mercenary, selfish, earthly spirit.

2. It is to allow ourselves to be governed by the maxims and manners of the world, so that with us the question is not, What is right or wrong? What is agreeable to the will of God? but What do men do? What is the custom of society? or What does public sentiment command? To this the most slavish and ruinous subjection is rendered by the mass of men, and by many who call themselves Christians.

3. It is to allow ourselves to be carried away by the world, so as to

be undistinguishable from men of the world in our manner of living, i. e., (a.) As to the objects which we seek. (b.) As to our amusements. (c.) As to our general conduct.

III. *The consequences of this conformity.*

1. Those who identify themselves with the world, who are not distinguishable from it in their spirit, their pursuits, their principles of action, their mode of living, will undoubtedly perish with the world. If not separated from it here, they will not be separated from it hereafter.

2. It obliterates all distinction between the Church and the world. It destroys the power of the Church for good. It belies the profession of its members. They profess to renounce the world, the flesh, and the devil; and this profession is constantly contradicted, when professing Christians are as eager in the pursuit of wealth, as gay and devoted to frivolous amusements, as unscrupulous in their business habits as other men.

3. It is destructive to spirituality. It is impossible to live near to God, and yet be conformed to the world. It brings the Christian into innumerable dangers and temptations. It grieves the Spirit of God, and leads him to withdraw his influences.

IV. *By what rule are we to determine what is, and what is not, sinful conformity to the world?* This is more a theoretical, than a practical difficulty. 1. The man who is really filled with the Spirit of Christ, and devoted to his service, will not find much difficulty in determining what is, and what is not sinful conformity. 2. There are many things which the world does, which are in themselves sinful, and which, of course, Christians should avoid. 3. With regard to things indifferent, the rule laid down by the Scriptures is, that one man should not judge another, but determine for himself what is, and what is not injurious to his spiritual interests. 4. Another rule is that we are bound to avoid things in themselves indifferent, even though harmless to ourselves, which are injurious to others.

5. Another rule is that we should avoid things innocent in themselves, which by association are connected in fact, or in the minds of men with evil, as cards, dancing, the theater, etc.

6. The same rule as to particulars of dress and modes of living does not apply to all persons and places. It depends on usage, on rank, or on other adventitious circumstances. There is great danger of becoming pharisaical, and making religion consist in externals.

V. *How should ministers act in endeavoring to prevent conformity to the world?*

1. They should set a good example in themselves and in their families.

2. They should labor to promote a spirit of devoted piety, and get their people occupied and interested in good.

3. They should enlighten their consciences, and endeavor to govern them by motives rather than by coercion.

4. They should never resort to Church discipline for anything which is not forbidden in the word of God. The only ground of discipline is an offense.

CLX.   And he that taketh not his cross, and followeth not after me, is not worthy of me. Matt. 10: 38.

[Sept. 25th, 1864.]

There are two modes of presentation, as to the method and conditions of salvation, running through the Bible, the one representing the attainment of eternal life as easy, the other representing it as difficult. At one time we are told that "he that believeth and is baptized shall be saved;" and that whosoever confesses Christ before men, will also be confessed by him before his Father which is in heaven. We are not required to ascend to heaven, or go down to hell, but simply to believe with the heart and confess with the lips, that God has raised up Jesus from the dead. "Whosoever shall call on the name of the Lord, shall be saved." This is illustrated in many cases besides that of the dying thief. It is vastly important. We need a method of salvation, in which, in one sense, we have nothing to do. We cannot atone for our sins; we cannot merit eternal life; we cannot change our own heart. We have a Saviour who has done all things for us. All that is required, in this view of the case, is that we should be willing to be saved. We are the recipients and subjects, and not the agents of salvation. On the other hand, however, we are told that the righteous are scarcely saved. We are commanded to work out our salvation with fear and trembling; to strive to enter in at the strait gate; that many shall seek to enter in, and not be able. We are to crucify the flesh, to overcome the world, to resist the devices of Satan. We are laborers, soldiers, wrestlers, runners in a doubtful race. These two modes of representation are of course consistent. The one regards the work of Christ, and its appropriation by us; the other concerns our acting consistently with the new relation into which we are brought to God. It may be easy to obtain adoption into a family, and difficult to live accordingly. It may be easy to have the eyes opened, the withered arm restored, but difficult to use those renovated members agreeably to the will of God. It is easy, in one sense, to believe; but to live a life of faith, to live so as to prove that our faith is genuine, may be a difficult task.

1. One of the conditions of salvation, that is, one of those things which we must do in order to prove that we truly believe, and belong to Christ, and which all who do believe will strive to do, is to live a holy life. That is, we are to avoid all sin, to exercise all right affections toward God and our fellow-men, and to be devoted to his glory and service.

2. Another thing is, to be willing to suffer for Christ. The cross is the emblem of suffering. To bear the cross is to endure suffering. The context shows that this is the meaning of the Lord in this place.

3. Another thing is, that we must love Christ more than any other object; more than our lives. And, therefore, if the sundering of all earthly ties be necessary to the service of Christ, we must be ready to submit to the sacrifice.

These are difficult conditions to fulfill; but, 1. They are essential. 2. They are reasonable. Nothing is required but what we ought to be gladly willing to perform. The difficulty arises not from the nature of the work so much as from our own state. If we were what we should be, if we were filled with faith and love, we should find all this easy. The early Christians did not find it hard to submit to the spoiling of their goods; they suffered it joyfully. Paul did not find it difficult to preach, to labor, to suffer. He rejoiced in all that he was called upon to do and to suffer in the cause of Christ.

Now this is illustrated and confirmed by the whole history of the Church, in its martyrs, confessors, missionaries, etc. They have been the happiest men on earth. We should bear in mind, then,

1. That we must be willing to suffer for Christ, and to renounce all things for him.

2. That those who do this are sustained in doing it. They receive in this world even a hundred-fold. Christ's heaviest burden is made light.

3. That these light afflictions are not worthy to be compared with the glory which shall be revealed in us.

4. That to refuse to suffer for Christ, to prefer father or mother, brothers or sisters, houses or land to him, involves the forfeiture of this life, and of the life that is to come.

His cross. Each man has his own cross. One has that form of trial referred to in the context; another, sickness, feebleness of body; another, poverty; another, want of success; another, reproach; another, insignificance. In any case we must bear our burden cheerfully, looking unto Christ as our example, our helper and our reward.

CLXI. Let this mind be in you which was also in Christ Jesus.—Phil. 2: 5-11.

[*Oct. 3d*, 1858.]

Sir Isaac Newton said that if he differed from other men, it was in the power of attention. If this is so, what wonders that one power wrought, not only subjectively in the expansion of Newton's own mind, but also in the discoveries to which it led. Whether this is correct of Newton or not, the point of difference between one Christian and another, so far as second or proximate causes are concerned, is mainly in the power or habit of contemplating divine truth long enough to allow it to produce its proper effect. All large subjects require time for the mind to adjust itself to them. So of works of art and of nature, so of Niagara, of the Alps, the heavens. The great doctrines of the Scriptures must in like manner be contemplated with a steady and protracted gaze. And here too, as in the analogous cases, it is passivity that is required. It is not active, discriminating thought, but clear and constant vision that is necessary. The same remark is applicable to particular passages of Scripture. This wonderful passage, Phil. ii. 5-11, is a constellation of truths to which there are few comparable in all Scripture. If God should give us grace, we might sit down before it and gaze on its ever expanding wonders and glories until we were transformed and translated. Such is not now our duty. We are to consider the exhortation of the apostle, and the motive which he presents to enforce it.

I. *The duty to which he exhorts us is entire self-negation, and devotion to the good of others and the glory of God.* This is enforced by the example of Christ, which affords the most stupendous instance of self-renunciation and devotion which the history of the universe furnishes.

Consider, 1. Who Christ was. He existed from eternity in the form of God and equal with God. The form of anything, is the thing itself in any given mode of manifestation. To exist in the form of God, is to exist as God. It involves equality with God. It is, therefore, equivalent to saying that Christ was a divine person. The passage is parallel to Heb. i. 3, and Col. i. 15.

2. Consider what he did. *a.* He made himself of no reputation, and took on him the form of a servant, and was made in the likeness of men. He emptied himself, laid aside his divine majesty. Instead of appearing on earth as a God, he appeared as man, not in the transient semblance of a man, but in reality. He became a man, subject to like infirmities and sorrows with us. He did not thereby cease to be God.

He was God in the fashion of a man. He was God, who was born, lived, suffered and died.

3. Therefore, it is added that he, *i. e.*, who was equal with God, humbled himself, even as a man, to be obedient unto death, *i. e.*, so obedient as not to refuse to die, and even not to refuse to die on the cross, therefore as a malefactor.

It is to be remarked that the subject does not change in this whole connection. He—the same person who was equal with God—emptied himself, was made a man, humbled himself, to die on the cross!

4. Consider why he did this. The immediate object was our redemption, which could be effected in no other way. The motive was love for us.

The inference which the Apostle draws is, that the believing apprehension of the truth here set forth will make us like Christ.

1. Negatively, in not seeking our own.

2. In being willing, for the good of others and the glory of God, to humble ourselves.

3. In fact, that we will, as Christ did, renounce all self-seeking, and consecrate ourselves to the good of others, and to the glory of Christ. If we do not do this, it is evident that we do not believe what Paul has written concerning Christ.

CLXII. Living for Christ.—Col. 3: 24. 2 Cor. 5: 14.

[*May 8th*, 1855.]

I. *Unity of purpose is necessary.*

1. For the development of character. 2. For success in life.
Illustrations as to character.

Glory, duty, self-interest, benevolence, each gives unity and force, whereas a man without any such governing principle becomes weak.

As to success, it is by making one object predominant, and seeking that object, that great results are attained.

II. *That which gives unity to the Christian life is Christ.*

1. He is the unifying principle of Christian theology. 2. Of the inward life of the Christian, or of his religion. 3. Of his outward and active life. We have an illustration of all this in Paul, in his theology, in his religious experience, and in his outward life. Negatively—he did not seek wealth or honor, either as his main, or his subordinate object. He sought simply the glory of Christ. Now this is what we ought to do. This is what we expect you to do, and especially those who are now going away.

1. Because this is your duty. This is the highest thing you can do. Whatever else you do will in the end be regarded as nothing.

2. Because your own inward holiness and happiness will thereby be best advanced.

3. Because thus only can you be really useful. Thus only do you associate yourself with the saints and angels. The extension of Christ's kingdom is the only thing worth living for.

4. Because Christ has died for you. Paul thus judged that if one died for all, all should live for him.

CLXIII. Having therefore these promises, dearly beloved, let us cleanse ourselves from all filthiness of the flesh and spirit, perfecting holiness in the fear of God.
2 Cor. 7: 1.

[*April 27th*, 1856.]

The promises referred to are, 1. "I will dwell in them, and walk in them; and I will be their God, and they shall be my people." 2. "I will be a Father unto you, and ye shall be my sons and daughters, saith the Lord Almighty."

I. *The duty.* II. *The motive.*

I. *The duty is to cleanse ourselves from sin.*

1. These sins are of two kinds, those of the flesh and those of the spirit. 2. This is to be done by perfecting holiness. 3. This is a form of religion, it is to be in the fear of God. Sin is a defilement. It is something which is offensive, debasing, marring the beauty of God's work.

1. This is true of sins of the flesh. In all false religions this class of sins are either denied to be sinful, or extenuated. According to the Scriptures they are debasing. (*a.*) Because the excellence of man consists in the harmony of his complex nature, in the due subordination of the lower to the higher element in our constitution. (*b.*) This harmony and subordination are destroyed by such sins. The sensual element is strengthened. If it gains complete ascendency, the man becomes brutal. (*c.*) The body belongs to Christ, is the subject of redemption, and the temple of the Spirit. It is a profanation, therefore, to make our members the instruments of unrighteousness. (*d.*) These sins grieve the Spirit. They are the evidence and consequence of reprobation. (*e.*) They are peculiarly destructive of our own excellence and of the welfare of society.

2. Sins of the spirit, such as pride, envy, malice, vanity, selfishness, indolence, as well as unbelief, impenitence, ingratitude, &c., are no less defilements. They render us offensive in the sight of holy beings.

We are to cleanse ourselves from these,

1. By washing in the blood of Christ.

2. By the work of the Holy Ghost.

3. By the use of the means of grace.

4. By avoiding evil, and perfecting holiness, *i. e.*, endeavoring to be holy as God is holy.

5. By acting in the fear of God. We can be moral only by being religious. Men propose different theories of morality. (*a.*) Regard to the happiness of the universe. (*b.*) Regard to our own happiness. (*c.*) The nature of things, or the essential distinction of right and wrong. (*d.*) Self-respect, the dignity of our own spirit. All these are irreligious. They leave God out of view. Religion is the only basis of morality.

II. *The motive, viz. the promises.*

1. Great power is in the Scriptures attributed to the promises. By them we are made partakers of the divine nature.

2. They are thus powerful because they enable us to draw near to God, to enter into that fellowship with the divine being, which is the source of life.

3. The special promises here referred to, are the great means and inducements to holiness. They are 1. God's presence, or indwelling. 2. His love. "I will be their God, and they shall be my people;" or "I will be their Father, and they shall be my sons and daughters." This includes everything.

If we are to stand in this intimate relation to God, then we must be holy. 1. Because otherwise he will cast us off. 2. Because otherwise we will be unable to apprehend his presence, or to enjoy his love. We must choose between sin and God. If we cherish or indulge sin, we renounce God. If we take God as our portion we renounce sin.

CLXIV. And have no fellowship with the unfruitful works of darkness, but rather reprove them. Ephesians 5: 11.

[*March 12th*, 1865.]

Light and darkness are familiar figures for knowledge and ignorance. Knowledge is intellectual light, and ignorance is intellectual darkness. And as we know, in the Scriptures, knowledge and holiness, ignorance and sin, are always associated. Those who have the knowledge of God and divine things are holy, and they only ; and those who know not the things of the Spirit are the unregenerated. This is not an arbitrary usage. Knowledge produces holiness, and ignorance produces sin. The works of darkness are works which proceed from ignorance of God, or from the unenlightened, and therefore unrenewed, and therefore the polluted soul of man. It includes, therefore, all evil works such works as the heathen committed, and which unrenewed men everywhere commit. Such works are called "unprofitable" or "unfruitful" because they produce no holy effects, but are pernicious and destructive.

I. *Our first duty with regard to such works is, not to have any fellowship with them,* or rather, as the word is συγκοινωνεῖτε, have no fellowship or companionship with the children of disobedience in works of darkness. The thing forbidden includes, 1. Congeniality with, or complacency in evil. 2. Companionship, or fellowship with those who do evil. We are not to share the state of mind of those who delight in sin, and we are not to take part with them in its commission. The evil here meant includes not merely, 1. Acts of gross immorality. 2. But all acts which, although not esteemed evil in the world, are really such in the sight of God. 3. The whole course of conduct and amusement characteristic of the men of the world.

This fellowship with evil may be, 1. Internal. It may be cherished in the heart, and by our reading and observation. 2. It may be external, either when we actually participate in what is wrong, or when we connive at it or countenance it in any way. This may be done, (*a.*) By our words. (*b.*) By our writings. (*c.*) By our conduct. A large class of professing Christians are, by the opinions which they advocate, and the course of conduct which they pursue, in fellowship with evil. They evince congeniality with it, and do much to promote it.

II. *But we are to reprove them.*

To reprove is, 1. To convince. 2. To rebuke. The duty enjoined is therefore, 1. Not to be silent in the presence of evil; not to pass it over. 2. But to show it to be evil. Convince those who advocate or practice it, of its true character. 3. To rebuke, *i. e.,* to declare that those who do evil offend God, and expose themselves to the consequences of his displeasure.

This duty, 1. Is a difficult one. 2. It should be performed with humility, with wisdom, with gentleness, and with a benevolent spirit, as well as with a zeal for the law and honor of God. 3. It should be done officially, by ministers in the pulpit and out of it; by private Christians, whenever the occasion calls for it; not when it is obvious that it would be useless or worse, for we are not to cast pearls before swine. 4. It is often better done privately than publicly.

The great thing is to be holy; to be illuminated by the Spirit; to shine as lights in the world, so that our spirit, opinions and conduct shall be a continual rebuke to evil. This requires that we should keep ourselves unspotted from the world and in fellowship with God, his truth and his people.

CLXV. Delighting in the Law of God.

[*Feb. 24th*, 1861.]

I. *Different senses of the word Law.*

1. That which binds; hence the law of God as a rule of life, whether revealed in the Scriptures or in the heart.

2. The law as distinguished from the prophets.

3. The law as distinguished from the Gospel.

4. The whole revelation of God as contained in the Scriptures. This is the sense in which the word is often used in the Psalms, and the sense in which we are now to take it.

II. *What is meant by " delighting in ?"*

In general, "to delight in," is to regard with lively satisfaction and pleasure. But what the expression really implies, depends on the nature of the object. When we say we delight in a landscape, we express a very different state of mind from that expressed when we say we delight in a friend; or, when we delight in a poem, the state of mind is very different from that of delighting in the law of God. There is, 1. An æsthetic delight in the Scriptures; such as Bishop Lowth so strongly expresses in his work on Hebrew Poetry. Many greatly admire the historical narratives, the prophetic exhibitions, the portraiture of character, etc., in the Scriptures. 2. An intellectual delight in the wisdom of the laws and institutions of the Scriptures. The principles of its jurisprudence and government have been the admiration of statesmen and legislators, and the model of modern nations and states. 3. A mere delight in the purity of its precepts. This is exhibited by those who deny its divine origin. All this is very different from what the Scriptures mean by delighting in the Law of God.

On this point the Scriptures teach,

1. That the natural or unrenewed man does not delight in the law of God. He does not do it, and he cannot do it, because he cannot know the things of the Spirit.

2. That this delighting in the law of the Lord is peculiar to the spiritual man, and is due to the influence of the Spirit. This influence is two-fold, or produces a two-fold effect. *First*, a subjective change in the state of the mind analogous to opening the eyes of the blind. It is such a change as imparts the power of spiritual vision, *i. e.*, the vision of the spiritual excellence of divine things. This is not enough. A man may have the *power* of vision in a dark room. *Second*, it produces a revelation of the truth, a presentation of it to the mind in its true nature and relations. This is a special work of the Spirit. It is experienced much more abundantly at some times than at others. The

effect of these operations of the Spirit is delighting in the law of God, which includes,

1. An apprehension of its truth and consequent conviction of its divine origin.

2. An apprehension of its excellence, of its purity, of its justice, and its goodness. It is seen to be right, to be morally glorious.

3. An experience of its power to convince, to sanctify, to console, to guide, to render wise unto salvation; an experience of its appropriateness to our necessities. It is seen to suit our nature as rational beings, as moral beings, as sinners.

4. An acquiescence in it, and rejoicing in it, as an exhibition of the character of God, of the rule of duty, of the plan of salvation, of the person and work of Christ, and of the future state. The Scriptures, therefore, are the treasury of truth; the store-house of promises; the granary of spiritual food; the never-failing river of life.

INFERENCES.

1. It is a fact that the people of God in all ages do thus delight in his law.

2. That if we are his people, this must in a measure be true of us.

3. That the more we delight in the law of God, the more we shall be conformed to it, and the better able to teach and preach it.

CLXVI. Fidelity in the service of God.
[April 24th, 1864.]

Fidelity is that disposition of the mind and purpose of the will which secures the punctilious (or scrupulous) discharge of all our obligations. A faithful parent, a faithful magistrate, a faithful servant, a faithful Christian, and a faithful minister, is one who desires and endeavors to discharge all the obligations arising out of his peculiar relations.

I. *Fidelity requires a knowledge of our obligations,* and, therefore, those who wish to be faithful will endeavor to obtain clear and correct views of what they are bound to do.

II. *It requires an enlightened view of the grounds of those obligations.* Without this there can be no rational desire or fixed purpose to discharge them.

III. *It requires superiority over all conflicting tendencies.* A man may have a desire to do his duty, and he may have a general purpose to perform it, but these may be too weak to withstand temptation. A son, a citizen, or a minister may have a desire to be faithful, and a general purpose to discharge his duty, but indolence, the love of pleasure, the desire of gain of some kind, may tempt him to disregard or neglect his most sacred obligations.

Fidelity in the service of God requires, therefore, 1. A knowledge of what he would have us to do, as men, in all our relations of life, as Christians or as ministers.

2. Such views of our relation to Christ and of our obligations to him, as shall awaken in us the desire to do his will, and lead us to form the purpose that we will in all cases endeavor to perform it.

3. Such a strength of this desire, and such firmness of this purpose as render them actually controlling over our whole inward and outward life.

IV. *From this statement of the duty it is plain,*

1. That it is a very simple' one. There is no difficult point of casuistry about it. It is the desire and purpose to do what Christ requires, to carry out his will.

2. It is no less plain that it is a very comprehensive duty. It in fact includes all others. In saying that a servant is faithful, you say that he is diligent, honest, obedient, in short, that he performs all his duties as a servant. To say that a Christian is faithful, is to say that he receives God's truth, that he is assiduous in all his religious and social duties. So of a minister; to say that he is faithful, is to say that he is diligent in study; that he dispenses the truth, and nothing but the truth; that he does this in season and out of season; that he conscientiously discharges his obligations as a minister, to the ignorant, to the wicked, to the sick, to the suffering, to the young and to the old. It is also to say that he is devoted to his work; that he gives himself wholly to it; that he does not serve God and mammon, Christ and Belial, himself and his Master, but that his eye is single and his life undivided.

3. It is also plain, that as this duty is simple and comprehensive, so it is one of constant obligation. It is not a debt to be paid and forgotten. It is not a service to be rendered at a particular time or place, but one which lasts as long as we live. We are to be faithful unto death. If a man could be faithful for years, and become unfaithful, his former fidelity would count for nothing.

4. This duty being thus simple, comprehensive and permanent, is obviously exceedingly difficult. It supposes renunciation of ourselves and of the world. It supposes the mastery over all the evil principles of our nature, over our indolence, our passions, over the love of the world, over the fear of man, over the desire of wealth or applause. It supposes an entire consecration, not as a momentary act, as we might consecrate a votive offering, but as the surrender of our whole being unto Christ.

5. It is very clear that this cannot be done unless we have, (a.) The clearest apprehension of, and the strongest faith in, his divine majesty

and glory. (b.) The firmest conviction of the value and absolute necessity of what he has done for our salvation. (c.) And thirdly, the scriptural hope and assurance that we are objects of his love, and reconciled to God through him.

6. It is, finally, more clear than anything else, that we cannot be faithful, that we cannot discharge this high though simple duty, unless we are at all times filled by the Holy Ghost. It is only as he lives in us that we can live in Christ. "Yet not I," says the faithful Paul, "but the grace of God which was with me."

7. The encouragements to fidelity are abundant.

CLXVII. Therefore, my beloved brethren, be ye steadfast, unmoveable, always abounding in the work of the Lord, forasmuch as ye know that your labor is not in vain in the Lord. 1 Cor. 15: 58.

[April 26th, 1867.]

Here are two duties, and the motive to obedience. The FIRST duty is *steadfastness.* The two words are used only for the sake of the climax.

I. *Steadfast in the truth.* This, Paul has specially in view. The Christians of his time were exposed to great temptations. (a.) From Judaism. (b.) From false philosophy. We also are so exposed, because we too are liable to be led away from the truth. How great this danger is, is shown by the history of the Church. In all ages the Church has been thus perverted, and it is now, in all countries, more or less turned aside.

Means of steadfastness. 1. A sense of danger. 2. Settled principles as to the source of truth. (a.) That it is not from reason, but by revelation. (b.) That it is revealed in the Scriptures. (c.) That the Scriptures are to be interpreted by ordinary rules. (d.) That the office of the theologian is simply to ascertain, arrange and vindicate the truth as taught in the word of God.

3. Diligence in reaching clear and firm convictions.

4. Dependence on the grace of God, and constant prayer to be preserved from error.

II. *Steadfastness of purpose, as well as of faith.*

(a.) Steadfast purpose to be a Christian. (b.) To be devoted to the work of the ministry, not to give it up for anything else. (c.) To be steadfast in that department of labor to which God may call us.

The SECOND duty is to abound in the work of the Lord. To abound is to be abundant in labors, opposed to negligence and selfishness. It is to be active and diligent, improving our time, talents and opportunities constantly.

The work of the Lord is the work in which the Lord is engaged, the work of instructing, correcting and saving men. It is not any secular or worldly work, in which we are engaged, but the work which the Lord came down from heaven to accomplish; which he is now carrying on by his providence, by the ministry of angels, by the Church, and which is to be consummated in the kingdom of heaven. We are co-workers with God, with Christ, and with the Spirit. It is a great and glorious work in comparison with which everything else is insignificant.

The *motive* is that our labor is not in vain in the Lord. This is the negative statement implying the positive.

1. Our labor is not ineffectual. The work, though difficult, is not hopeless, but sure to succeed.

2. The labor is not in vain as to ourselves. God giveth us the victory.

CLXVIII. Walking with God.

[*February 18th,* 1866.]

Walk is a word frequently used in the Scriptures in a figurative sense to denote the characteristic mode of life, as walking in the flesh, in the Spirit, walking after the manner of the world, &c. Walking with any one expresses a uniform and intimate fellowship or communion with him. It has this sense when the Bible speaks of our walking with God. This presupposes, first, that God is a person. Without that, personal communion with him would be impossible. It is therefore important that we should habitually think of him under this aspect. This is not inconsistent with his being infinite, immutable and eternal.

Secondly, it presupposes that this person is accessible to us, can hear and communicate with us. We may believe in the personality of Gabriel, but we cannot walk with him. We may believe in the continued personal existence of departed saints, and of our own friends, but we cannot walk with them. We may cherish their memory. Our hearts may frequently go out after them. But this is a matter of feeling. There is no real intercourse.

Thirdly, it presupposes reconciliation. How "can two walk together except they be agreed?" This reconciliation with God, which is the necessary condition of our walking with him, includes justification and sanctification. He must cease to regard us as under the sentence of his law, and we must have congeniality of mind with him. All these preliminaries, or antecedent conditions may be admitted, and may be present, and yet God and we be comparative strangers. This walking with

God is a rare and high attainment, as it implies more than casual or occasional intercourse. There is all the difference between the intercourse of ordinary Christians with God and habitual walking with him, that there is between an occasional intercourse, however agreeable, with a man whom we meet occasionally, and our daily communion with an intimate friend, or member of our own family. Walking with God, therefore, means uniform, habitual communion with him. This includes, 1. An abiding sense of his presence. 2. An abiding sense of his favor. 3. A constant outgoing of our thoughts and feelings towards him. 4. A constant address, or direction of our desires to him for guidance, for assistance, for consolation. 5. An expectation and experience of his response. Communion cannot be one-sided. There must be conversation, address and answer. God does thus commune with us. He reveals himself to his people as he does not unto the world. He assures them of his love. He awakens in them confidence in his promises. He brings those promises to their minds, and gives them the power of response. These promises become his answers to their requests. And they experience a renewal of faith, love, zeal, etc., which is the manifestation of his presence with the soul. This is not imaginary. It is real. It is not enthusiasm. It does not suppose anything miraculous, no responses by voice, no unintelligent impulses; but the consciousness of the presence of the Infinite Spirit with our spirits; the conviction that he hears and answers us. We have probably all seen examples of this walking with God, men (as John S. Newbold) who lived in habitual communion with God through Christ.

The effects of this walking with God are,

1. Raising the soul into a higher sphere, above the passions and sins which disturb the mind, above the cares and anxieties of the world.

2. The rapid growth of the soul in grace.

3. A peace of mind which passes all understanding.

4. It invests the man with a halo of holiness, which is unmistakable and potent.

5. It renders him fit for all service and all trials.

The means.

1. We must, as already said, be justified and reconciled.

2. We must avoid all known sin.

3. We must not only seek fellowship with God in the closet, but also keep him constantly before us all the day.

4. We must constantly address him, asking his guidance and support, and referring everything to him.

CLXIX. Walk in wisdom toward them that are without, redeeming the time.—Col. 4: 5.

[*Sep. 30th*, 1855.]

Wisdom is a comprehensive word in the Scriptures. It is often used by Paul for the philosophy of the schools, or for human reason and its teachings; often for prudence and discretion; often for knowledge and understanding of the things of God, and hence for religion in a subjective sense, and for the gospel, the sum of truth, the highest form of truth. Frequently the same word is used both in an objective and subjective sense. It is so with "knowledge;" it is so with "righteousness," "hope," etc. So it is also with wisdom. This is either the system of divine truth, or the state of mind which the sincere reception of that truth produces. The latter is the sense here, as in Jas. iii. 17. This is the wisdom by which our conduct is to be characterized.

1. *It is from above.* It is the gift of God, not a self-induced virtue. It is something supernatural and divine.

2. *Pure.* ἁγνή, as a dress or person newly washed; without spot, or defilement of any kind; as the garments of the saints who are clad in white. Thus pure should we be in all holy conversation and godliness.

3. *Peaceable.* Negatively, it does not promote dissension, conflicts, or wranglings. Therefore it is not censorious, or disputatious. Affirmatively, it promotes peace, it heals divisions, allays animosities, assuages anger.

4. *Gentle.* ἐπιειχής, courteous, decorous, proper or beseeming, suitable to the circumstances of each particular occasion.

5. *Easy to be entreated;* εὐπειθής, obsequious, open to conviction, ready to listen to admonition or reproof.

6. *Full of mercy and of good fruits;* full of kind feeling, and abounding in acts of piety and beneficence.

7. *Without partiality;* ἀδιάκριτος, unambiguous, unmistakable, that which is manifestly what it appears or pretends to be, and therefore connected with the next term.

8. *Without hypocrisy.* It is always what it pretends to be.

Such is the deportment we are to maintain in the world.

Those without, are those without the Church.

Redeeming the time. Availing ourselves of every opportunity to do good, so as to make the most of it, and so as to redeem it from evil.

1. The excellency of such a life.

2. It is honorable to religion and to our Saviour.

3. It is blessed in itself; it is a heavenly life.

4. It is beneficent. If all Christians were thus to live, the world would soon be as God's holy mountain, where there is nothing to hurt

or to destroy. And if this community should thus walk, this house would be the ante-chamber of heaven.

CLXX. Earnestness in the service of God.

[*March 24th*, 1861.]

I. *God is defined to be a Spirit infinite, eternal and immutable in his being, wisdom, power, holiness, justice, goodness, and truth.* In the presence of his immensity all creatures sink into insignificance. In the presence of his excellence, all sink into worthlessness. In the presence of his power, all else is weakness; and in the presence of his wisdom, all else is ignorance. He is so infinitely exalted above all things that all things are as nothing in comparison with him. His honor, his will, his blessedness is therefore the highest conceivable end of all things. To put anything in comparison or competition with this is supreme folly and wickedness.

But thus God in infinite condescension to the necessities of our race, and for man's redemption, has assumed our nature. He was found in fashion as a man. He was made under the law. He bore its curse. He died for our sins, and rose for our justification. He, in the person of the Son, is head over all things to the Church. To him, to God incarnate, our allegiance and devotion are due, not only as to God the Creator, but as to God the Redeemer, and as united to us by the bond of a common nature, and the indwelling of his Spirit. This is the God whom we are called upon to serve. The service of Christ is the service of God. There can be no service of God other than the service of Christ.

II. *What is this service?*

First, it is the inward subjection of our mind and heart to the revelation of his will. It is the acquiescence of our views of truth with the declarations of his word. It is the accordance of all our affections with his will. We love what he would have us love: himself, his people, all mankind. We hate and avoid all that he hates; sin, evil passions, inordinate desires, a worldly or selfish spirit. Much of the service of Christ consists in bringing down every imagination, and every thought into subjection to his teaching, and in the inward life of the soul, as he is Lord, not of the body only, or of the outward life, but of the soul and all its states and exercises.

Second, the service of Christ includes the regulation of our outward life in obedience to his will. It is avoiding everything in our conduct which is unholy, unjust, unkind, impure, or unbecoming our character as his servants and children. It is the faithful performance of all our duties, private and social; our duties to our family, friends, neighbors, to the Church, and to the state. All this is properly his service, or obedience to him, because it is done according to his commands, out of regard to his authority, to please him and promote his glory.

Third, it includes the consecration of ourselves to the accomplishing of the work in which Christ is engaged. He came to save men, to redeem the world, to bring men to the knowledge and obedience of the truth, to cause all nations to love, worship and obey the Son of God. This is the end to which all things are directed, to which the Church is set apart. It is the highest end. It includes the highest happiness and excellence of our race, the highest good of the intelligent universe, and the highest glory of the Redeemer.

III. *We are called upon to be earnest in this service.*

Earnestness includes two things; *first*, fixedness of purpose, and, *second*, energy in exertion. It is not so much a matter of feeling. A man may be very calm, who is very much in earnest. Indeed those most excited and commonly in a flurry, accomplish little good. What we want is,

1. Fixedness of purpose; that is, such a sense of the greatness, sacredness and importance of the end in view, and of the obligations which rest upon us, that we shall deliberately and of settled purpose, determine, *negatively*, that we will not serve ourselves, or the world, or Satan; but *positively*, that we will serve God in Christ; that the regulation of our inward and outward life according to his will, and the consecration of our time, efforts and talents to the promotion of his kingdom, shall be the end of our being.

2. Energy in the prosecution of this end, or execution of this purpose. What we suffer from is the distraction arising from the multiplicity of objects. We purpose to seek Christ as the main end, but there are so many subordinate ends, so many other things which we seek, that we lose all unity and force in our life. A stream divided into many channels, flows shallow and feebly in them all. It is only by collecting all the water into one channel that the current becomes deep and strong. So it is with life. If you would serve Christ with earnestness, you must serve him alone.

CLXXI. Self-knowledge.

[*February 6th*, 1853.]

I. *Its nature.* II. *Its difficulties.* III. *The means of its attainments.*
I. *Its nature.*

All the objects of knowledge are included under the two heads of ourselves and what is not ourselves, the me and the not me. The two divisions are not equal, though both are vast. Self-knowledge philosophically considered, is the science of anthropology, including our nature, as to the elements of its constitution, and its relations to God and the world ; physiology, or the science of the φύσις, the sentient, living organism; the science of mind, or mental philosophy; the science of morals, or moral philosophy.   Here are four of the widest and most difficult fields of human knowledge, all embraced under the head of knowledge of ourselves.

Practically considered, self-knowledge includes 1. A correct apprehension of ourselves as intellectual beings.   2. A correct view of our peculiar dispositions and traits of character.   3. A correct knowledge of our religious or spiritual state.

A. KNOWLEDGE OF OURSELVES INTELLECTUALLY.

1. Correct view of our peculiar intellectual gifts.   Men differ ; some men have a talent for one thing, some for another, some for one pursuit in life, some for another.   It is not true that this is acquired.   It is of great importance to know ourselves in this respect, (a.) In order to decide our profession, (b.) In order to determine our field of labor. Great mistakes are often committed, in choosing a wrong profession or a wrong field of labor.

2. A correct view of our relative ability.   (a.) Some men underrate themselves.   (b.) Some, and most, overestimate their talents.   The one produces despondency, and the other, pride and vanity, and often egregious mistakes.

B. KNOWLEDGE OF CHARACTER.

1. Of our natural dispositions.   2. Of our characteristic traits, as pride, vanity, irritability, selfishness, censoriousness, moroseness, obstinacy.

C. KNOWLEDGE OF OUR SPIRITUAL STATE.

1. As to the reality of our conversion. 2. Our religious state, absolutely and relatively.   Self-ignorance on these subjects is very common, as for example in the case of the Pharisees, the Papists and persecutors generally, fanatics of all classes.   Real Christians are often under delusion.

II. *Its difficulties.*

They arise, 1. From the nature of the subject, the soul.

2. From the perverting medium of self-love and sin.

3. From the want of due attention.

4. From a wrong standard of judgment, as to knowledge, character and religion.

III. *Means of obtaining self-knowledge.*

1. Self-examination and constant watchfulness.
2. The word of God as a light and a rule.
3. The illumination of the Holy Spirit.
4. Collision with our fellow-men.
5. Providential trials revealing to us what we are.

CLXXII. Self-examination. (No. 1.)

[*Dec. 13th*, 1868.]

Nothing to us is so important, and nothing so mysterious as self. What is the self? Wherein does the selfhood consist? Is it something real, or merely phenomenal? According to some the self is only a transient form of the infinite, as a wave is a form of the sea. Thus the self is of little value. According to others, what we call self is merely an affection of the body, and ceases when the body is dissolved. According to the Scriptures, and the common judgment of men, self is an individual substance and subsistence, having certain essential properties or attributes, intelligence, feeling and will; having a moral nature as well, and moral because a rational nature. If any of these essential attributes be wanting, self, a human personality, does not exist. This self is immortal, hence its infinite value. Its future destiny depends on its character, hence the unspeakable importance of knowing its true character, and hence the importance of self-examination.

In this work self is the subject, self the judge, and self the witness. But it is not the rule or standard. This is fixed and immutable, and it is fixed by an authority out of, and higher than ourselves. That standard is the word, which teaches what men are and should be, what a Christian is, and what is or is not consistent with Christian character.

Three great ends are to be answered by self-examination.

First, conviction of sin, as necessary to repentance and faith in Christ. It is by examining himself and comparing himself with the law that the sinner becomes convinced of his guilt and just exposure to wrath; of his pollution, and is thus led to abhor himself; of his helplessness, so that he is prepared to believe in Christ, and look to him for salvation.

Second, the Bible teaches us what a Christian is, and thus enables us to determine whether or not we are Christians.

A Christian is, 1. One who believes that Jesus is the Son of God. 2. That he is the Prophet, or infallible teacher. 3. That he is the High Priest, who by offering himself a sacrifice for sins, has reconciled us to God. 4. That he is our faithful and absolute sovereign, whose will we are bound to obey, in whom we must trust for protection, and to whose service we must be devoted. A Christian then, is one over whom these truths exert a controlling influence, both as to his inward and outward life. Is then, Jesus our God? Do we love and worship him as such? Do we receive his doctrines? Do we trust in his sacrifice and intercession? Do we obey, trust in, and serve him as our king? If so, we are Christians. It is not so much by the analysis of our experiences as by determining our principles, purposes, and course of life, that these questions are to be decided.

The *third* object of self-examination is a knowledge of ourselves, as Christians, *i. e.*, whether our conduct be consistent, our motives pure, and our progress in the divine life what it ought to be. This should be a daily exercise. We should call ourselves to account every day, to see where we have failed.

CLXXIII. Self-examination. (No. 2.)

[February 11th, 1855.]

I. *The object of self-examination and self-knowledge.* It is to determine, 1. In general, what we are; whether or not we are the children of God. 2. Whether we are making progress in the divine life or not; whether our general deportment is consistent. 3. Whether in any given case we have acted agreeably to the gospel.

II. *Self-examination requires*, 1. A right standard of judgment. This is the word of God. (*a.*) It is not the experience or conduct of others, which in reference to our state or conduct is so often made the rule. (*b.*) It is not public opinion, or the standard of the class to which we belong. Merchants, lawyers, ministers, professors of religion in different churches, commonly adopt this standard. The only standard by which we should judge ourselves is that by which God will judge us in the last day. It is, therefore, of the first importance that we be well acquainted with the Scriptures as a rule of character and of conduct, to determine what we are, and what in any given case is right.

2. Self-examination requires an impartial, faithful and attentive judge. No matter how accurate the rule, if we are partial, unfaithful, and indifferent in applying it, we shall err.

3. It requires time. There must be a day of judgment. There are set times which are especially appropriate; for example, the close of the day, sacramental occasions, any period of emergency. The great evil is, that the work is neglected because of the want of a set time for it.

III. *The difficulties of the work.*

1. It is irksome, as an act of introspection. It is hard to determine

the character of our feelings. The heart is deep, it is unsteady, it is deceitful.

2. It is not only irksome, but we are liable to many perverting influences, (*a.*) From self-love. (*b.*) From public sentiment. (*c.*) From the opinions of others regarding us.

3. Another difficulty arises from slothfulness, which leads to the slight performance of other religious duties.

IV. *The advantages and obligations of self-examination.*

1. It is a commanded work.

2. It is an indispensable work. It must and will be performed. We cannot fail to pass judgment on ourselves. The only question is, whether this judgment shall be hasty, biased and erroneous, or deliberate, formal, on a right standard and worthy of reliance.

3. It is necessary as a preservative against false hopes.

4. It is necessary to give us rational and Scriptural grounds of rejoicing in hope of the glory of God.

5. As a means of correcting our errors and avoiding sin.

CLXXIV. Gravity.

[*October 1st*, 1856.]

I. *It is a law of our nature that the outward expresses the inward.* What a man is, will by necessity of nature, be revealed by his conduct.

Illustrations, are the proud, the selfish, the frivolous, the sedate, the generous, the devout, etc.

Exceptions. A man may profess what he does not believe. He may practice secret sins. He may pass for a Christian when he is not, because the reputation for religion may be secured by outward correctness joined with profession. Still the general truth remains.

II. *Hence the only way for a man to appear good is to be good, to appear grave is to be grave.* In other words, the only way to secure an outward deportment which is desired is to cultivate the inward disposition of which such deportment is the natural expression.

III. *Gravity.* The words by which this virtue is expressed as a quality are σεμνός and σώφρων, the former expressing the inward quality, the latter its outward manifestation. It is, in one view, that state of mind which secures respect, in opposition to those states which excite disapprobation or contempt. This is σεμνότης (gravity, dignity). In another view, it is that state of mind and outward deportment which is in accordance with our true character, circumstances and destiny.

We are to feel and act as immortal men, as sinners, as redeemed sinners, as ministers. That is, we are to cherish a state of mind, and exhibit a deportment, which corresponds to these various relations. This is not opposed, 1. To cheerfulness. 2. To a natural and unrestrained deportment. But it is opposed, 1. To frivolity. 2. To moroseness. 3. To sanctimoniousness.

IV. *Benefits or advantages.*

These are of two kinds. 1. The advantage to ourselves. It is the state of mind congruous to our circumstances, and, therefore, the best adapted to secure the right impression of truth upon the heart. 2. The effect it has on others. A large part of the power of one man over others lies in his character or excellence. Everything which increases our excellence increases our power, and everything which increases the respect and confidence which others entertain toward us, increases our influence over them for good. This is eminently a clerical virtue, necessary to the successful discharge of the duties of the ministerial office.

V. *Means of cultivating this grace.*

1. Cultivating intercourse with the great truths of the Scriptures. Let them have their appropriate influence.

2. Employ yourselves in important and serious work.

CLXXV. Fasting.
[*Feb. 4th*, 1855.]

I. *Its nature.* II. *Its obligations.* III. *Its benefits.*

I. *Fasting in a religious sense is a voluntary abstinence from food for a religious purpose.* It is a natural expression of sorrow, because sorrow destroys the desire for food and the power to digest it. In all ages, therefore, fasting has been connected with religious services in times of humiliation and distress. It was prescribed on certain occasions under the law, voluntarily practiced by good men, and recognized in the New Testament. This abstinence is either total or partial, either for a day or for protracted periods.

II. *Its obligations.*

1. It is nowhere enjoined in Scripture, and therefore cannot be made obligatory. When recommended by civil or ecclesiastical authority, it should be observed, unless for due reasons to the contrary. Stated fasts are not desirable, because they are apt to be regarded as binding.

III. *Benefits of fasting.*

1. The fact that fasting was enjoined under the Old Testament, and that it has entered so largely into the religious observances of men, render it probable that there is a real ground for it.

2. The psychological, or physiological ground for it is the relation between the soul and the body, which as far as this matter is concerned,

shows, (a.) That fasting is a natural effect of sorrow. (b.) That the mind is indisposed to act when the body is replete with food. (c.) That as the body sympathizes with the soul, so the soul does with the body.

3. The moral or religious ground. (a.) All acts of self-denial, the refusal to gratify the lusts of the flesh, even when natural and proper, is an assertion of the supremacy of the soul over the body, and tends to strengthen its authority. (b.) It is a general law of our nature that the outward should correspond with the inward. No man can maintain any desired state of mind while his bodily condition and acts are not in accordance. He cannot be sorrowful in the midst of laughter. This is the ground for reverential postures, and for decorum in dress and manner in public worship. This is a widely operating principle. There is, therefore, a scriptural, a psychological, and a moral and religious ground for fasting.

4. There is also the further ground of experience and the example of God's people. All eminently pious persons have been more or less addicted to this mode of spiritual culture. (1.) It must, however, be sincere. The hypocritical fasting of the Pharisees and Papists is at once hateful and destructive. (2.) It must be regarded as simply a means and not an end. (3.) It must be left free.

CLXXVI. The responsibility arising from the possession of special privileges.

[*April 29th*, 1855.]

The Scriptures teach that there is such a responsibility. Our Saviour said, "Unto whomsoever much is given of him shall much be required." The parable of the ten talents teaches the same: so his denunciations of Capernaum and Bethsaida. Paul says God will render to every one according to his works, to the Jews *first* and also to the Gentiles. The principle is one of natural justice. It is not with its correctness, but with its practical application that we have to do.

I. *Our peculiar privilege as to personal religion.*

1. As compared with the heathen. 2. With the ancient people of God. 3. With most other Christian nations. 4. With the great mass of men in our own country. We should, therefore, be among the best men in religion. Have we in any good measure made a proper improvement of these advantages? We shall assuredly be judged according to them. What can prevent our being rejected as slothful and unprofitable? Not our saying, "Lord, Lord, hast thou not prophesied in our streets?" Not our saying "God be merciful." Even if saved, it will be so as by fire.

II. *Our privileges as to attainment of knowledge and other qualifications for usefulness.* Compare these again with those possessed by others in other lands and in our own country. Who can look back over life without the deepest humiliation and sorrow, seeing we have attained so little in our school-days, in our college terms, in the seminary, and since. No one has done his best; scarcely any one has done what his conscience can at any moment be satisfied with. Is not God greater than our conscience? Again have we not reason to fear that we shall be rejected as slothful servants?

III. *As to our opportunities for doing good.*

1. In relieving the wants of our fellow-men.

2. In alleviating their sufferings.

3. In promoting their salvation. What time and effort, what anxiety and prayer, have we devoted to these objects? Remember, the rule is not the effects, but the desire and the labor. Many labor much and accomplish little. Many labor little and accomplish much. The former are the most blessed. A man may write a book which costs him little trouble, and yet it may be the means of great good. This is no thanks to him. He is rewarded according to the labor and self-denial which it cost him, and not according to the good accomplished. The value of the widow's mite did not depend on the amount of food it would purchase for the hungry. Here again few have had our advantages. What have we done? How much have we labored, or denied ourselves for the good of others? How much reason have we to hide our heads in shame? How will many rise up in the day of judgment and condemn us?

II. *What is to be done? What effect should the consideration of this subject have on us?*

1. It should lead us to deep humiliation and repentance before God.

2. It should destroy all disposition to think ourselves better than others, especially to value ourselves on account of our advantages.

3. It should lead us to seek forgiveness for the past through the blood of Christ.

4. To the determination to redeem the time, to make the best use of the short, uncertain future, knowing that the day is far spent, and that the night is at hand in which no man can work.

CLXXVII. Take heed what ye hear.—Mark 4: 24.
Take heed therefore how ye hear.—Luke 8: 18.

[December 9th, 1855.]

To hear is either, 1. To perceive by the ear. 2. To understand. 3. To answer, or respond to, or obey.

I. *Faith cometh by hearing.*

This means 1. Faith comes from knowledge, *i. e.,* there can be no faith without knowledge. How shall they believe in him of whom they have not heard?" About this there can be no dispute.

2. But secondly, it means that the living preacher, as opposed to mere instruction out of books, is the great means of producing faith. This does not mean, 1st. That God does not employ his written word, and written expositions of his truth in producing faith and holiness. 2d. Nor does it mean that the proclamation of the gospel, or what is commonly called preaching, is the only method of making the gospel heard, and thus of producing faith. But 3d, it means that the instruction by the ear, as coming from a living preacher, is the ordinary method of salvation.

Proof from Scripture and experience.

1. From Scripture. The command to preach and to teach indicates this. "It pleased God by the foolishness of preaching to save them that believe." "How shall they hear without a preacher?" (*Χωρὶς κηρύσσοντος,* without one preaching.) Christ gave some apostles, some pastors and teachers, &c. Eph. iv. 11.

2. From experience. No nation is ever converted, no church ever gathered, no church ever sustained, without the living preacher. Few comparatively are ever converted without his intervention.

II. *Why is hearing, or the living preacher, necessary? Why may not books and Bibles answer for the conversion of men?*

1. The sufficient answer to the question is the divine appointment. If God has determined, for wise reasons, to advance his kingdom in a certain way, no other can succeed.

2. Because from the constitution of our nature, what is addressed to the ear has more power in arousing attention, in producing conviction and exciting feeling, than what is addressed to the eye. This is universally acknowledged. Hence a sermon heard has ten-fold more power, in most cases, than a sermon read; the sermons of Whitefield, for example.

3. There may be, and probably is, a deeper reason than the preceding one. There is a law of propagation of divine life analogous to the propagation of vegetable and animal life. The various productions of the vegetable kingdom are not new and independent products. The life of the parent plant is in the seed which it produces. The life of the parent animal passes over to its offspring. So in the Church it is the general law that the spiritual life is communicated through and by living members of the Church. This is not always the case with either plants or animals; there have been many creations. Nor is it always the case with the communication of spiritual life. We might as well

ask why the Spirit does not operate without the written word, as why he so seldom operates without the living preacher. In both cases we can only say: "Even so Father, for so it seemed good in thy sight."

Two inferences flow from this truth. *First,* that we should hear for ourselves, and cause others to hear the gospel, not being content in either case with books, to the neglect of the living teacher. *Second,* that we should be careful *what* we hear, and *how* we hear.

If salvation is connected with hearing, there is abundant ground for both these exhortations, "Take heed what," and "Take heed how ye hear." The exhortation in Mark iv: 24, may indeed mean nothing more than "attend to what you hear." It is then of vast importance. But it may be also understood as including an exhortation to be careful as to what we hear. Salvation does not come from hearing error. It is of the last importance, therefore, that we take heed what we hear. Never go where error is taught. This is as foolish as going into places of dissipation and debauch, or profanity; or as foolish as going into pestiferous regions, unless in either case on errands of mercy. If from curiosity or for amusement, the result will be evil in the one case as certainly as in the other. Secondly, "Take heed how ye hear."

1. The object of hearing, viz.: salvation, spiritual edification, must be kept in view, and be our governing motive; not pleasure, not criticism.

2. The mind must be prepared for the reception of the truth. The Scriptures tell us how. The apostle says, (1 Pet. ii: 1), "Wherefore, laying aside all malice and all guile, and hypocrisies, and envies, and all evil speakings, as new born-babes, desire the sincere milk of the word that ye may grow thereby." And St. James says, (i: 21), "Wherefore lay apart all filthiness and superfluity of naughtiness, and receive with meekness the engrafted word, which is able to save your souls." These passages teach, 1st. That everything hostile to the truth must be removed from the mind and from the heart. All cares, thoughts of other things, doubts, unbelief, should be banished from the mind, and all evil feelings from the heart, and all indulgence of those feelings from the life. Secondly, they teach that we should be as new-born babes, *i. e.,* desirous, submissive, confiding.

This with prayer includes our duty as to hearing. With this will be connected laying the truth up in our hearts, and practicing it in our lives.

CLXXVIII. Brotherly Love.

[*March 27th,* 1864.]

Few words have a wider sense than love. The general sentiment may exist and does exist under the most diverse modifications. Its object may be some inanimate object, a house, a tree, our home, the land in which we were born. It may be some irrational animal. A man's love for his horse, his faithful dog, or the shepherd's love of his sheep is a strong and abiding sentiment. It may be a rational being, where the love of sympathy is only a natural relation, independent of the character of the object. It may be a companion or friend where the ground is congeniality of character and natural good offices. Or it may be a superior where the sentiment is founded on reverence for his character and benefits conferred. Or it may be God himself. In all cases the sentiment is love, although the word stands for very different states of mind. In its modifications love includes, 1. Delight in its object. 2. Desire for its well-being. 3. A desire for its possession and enjoyment.

Brotherly love is the love which arises out of the fraternal relations of men. There is a common brotherhood among all mankind, founded, 1. On their having God as a common Father. 2. Community of nature, being all descendants of the common parents of the race. 3. Common necessities, sympathies, affections and destiny. A man, therefore, who does not love his fellow-men, who does not estimate their value as men, recognize the bond of relationship between himself and them, desire their well-being, and seek appropriate intercourse with them, violates the first of all duties next to that of honoring God. The first command is, Thou shalt love the Lord thy God; the second is, Thou shalt love thy neighbor, thy fellow-man. Within this vast brotherhood of man there are more intimate bonds of relations. The people of one race, one nation, of the same tribe, of the same household, are bound by peculiar ties and have the general obligation of love modified and strengthened by these special relations.

In the Christian sense of the terms, brotherly love is the love which should exist among Christians as brethren in Christ. This is founded, 1. On their common relation to Christ. They are all united to him, and therefore are united to each other. They constitute his kingdom, his fold, his household, his body. He is their common Lord, common Saviour, their common portion, the object of supreme love to each, and therefore the bond of union between them.

2. Upon the indwelling of the Holy Spirit; so that they have a common spiritual life, involving, (*a.*) one faith, (*b.*) one hope, (*c.*) one experience.

3. Upon the congeniality of nature or feeling. They sympathize in all their likes and dislikes, in their aims, in their characteristic pursuits.

II. *This love is not merely an obligation.* It is a necessary result of the relation in which believers stand to each other ; so that if this love does not exist, that relation does not exist. If a man does not love his Christian brethren, he does not love Christ; is none of his.

This love manifests itself, 1. In a disposition to recognize Christians. 2. In delight in their society. 3. In a desire to promote their welfare. 4. In a sympathy with them in all their joys and sorrows, in their trials and conflicts; in espousing their cause, standing by them and defending their character. 5. In forbearance. 6. In charitable judgment.

It stands opposed, 1. To hatred. 2. To a desire to degrade, or injure, or wound the feelings. 3. To envy or jealousy, regretting that they are honored or advanced. 4. To evil speaking and censoriousness. 5. To contemptuousness, or harshness of spirit or demeanor.

Love reduces men to a level. A man who is actuated by Christian love is a Christian gentleman. No matter what his birth, his culture or social position, he will be a gentleman in character and conduct; and on the other hand, a man not under the control of love will not be, and cannot be a gentleman, no matter what his birth or position may be. This love is the cement, the life, the blessedness of the Church, and of any society on earth. Its perfection is heaven. In proportion as it is wanting in a man, or a community, or a church, in that proportion do they approach the character and condition of the lost.

CLXXIX. It is good neither to eat flesh, nor to drink wine, nor anything whereby thy brother stumbleth, or is offended, or is made weak.—Rom. 14: 21.

[Oct. 24th, 1867.]

Some things are unlawful in their own nature, and can never be right. Others are wrong because positively forbidden; are wrong only so long as the prohibition continues, and only to those upon whom the prohibition is laid. Others are wrong on the grounds of expediency, and therefore are sometimes wrong, and sometimes right. It is not always easy to discriminate these classes. There are, however, certain criteria by which we can distinguish what things are wrong in their own nature, and what are in their nature indifferent.

1. One of these criteria is to be found in our own moral constitution. We can see intuitively that malice, envy, pride, etc., are in their nature wrong. They are evil, not because they are forbidden, not because of their injurious tendency, but they are essentially evil.

2. The Scriptures condemn such things as are in their nature evil, not for one people, nor for a limited period, but for all men in all times.

With regard to things indifferent in their own nature, the Scriptures lay down the following rules:

1. If prohibited for any special reason, they are unlawful while that prohibition lasts.

2. When the prohibition is removed, they are right or wrong according to circumstances ; wrong at one time and place, and not at another. 1st. They are wrong when their use or enjoyment would do harm to others. 2d. They are right when no such evil is to be apprehended. 3d. That principle is never to be sacrificed to expediency ; that is, when doing or not doing anything would imply the denial of an important truth. All these principles are illustrated by the apostle's conduct and teaching in relation to the three matters, in themselves indifferent, which troubled the early Church. These were circumcision, the observance of the holy days of the Jews, and eating meat forbidden by the Mosaic law, or which had been offered to idols. With regard to these Paul taught,

1. That there was no harm in doing or neglecting them. Circumcision was nothing. If any man chose to circumcise his son, he was free to do so. If he chose to observe a holy day, he might do so. If he chose to abstain from meats sacrificed to idols, he might do so.

2. That he must not make his judgment a rule of duty to others. He must not condemn those who thought and acted differently. "To his own master he standeth or falleth." "Let no man therefore judge you in meat, or in drink, or in respect of a holy day, or of a new moon, or of the Sabbath days."

3. But if any of these became a source of evil, caused the weak to offend, then the law of love forbids our indulging in them, or availing ourselves of our Christian liberty.

4. But if any of these things were urged as a matter of duty, or a condition of salvation, then it became a sin to make things indifferent necessary. Paul, therefore, although he circumcised Timothy, refused to allow Titus to be circumcised. It is difficult to determine whether compliance with the prejudices of others is right or wrong. Our Lord disregarded the prejudices of the Jews in regard to the Sabbath. In other cases he complied in order to avoid giving offense.

There are certain principles important to have fixed, as guides of conduct.

1. Nothing is right or wrong which is not commanded or forbidden in Scripture.

2. We must stand fast in the liberty wherewith Christ has made us free, and not allow any rule of duty to be imposed upon us.

3. In the use of this liberty, and while asserting and maintaining it, we should not so use it as to do harm to our neighbors.

4. Nothing indifferent can be a proper ground of church discipline. or a condition of church fellowship.

These principles are often violated, as in the course pursued by many on slavery, temperance, tobacco, dress, church ceremonies, &c., &c.

CLXXX. Christian Forbearance.

[*Jan.* 11*th*, 1857.]

Every particular is a manifestation of something general. Every grace is a form of the same general principle of piety. The divine life manifests itself, 1. In the intellectual apprehension and belief of the truth ; not of this truth to the exclusion or neglect of others, but of all revealed truth. It is not by urging the claims of any doctrine admitted to be revealed that it becomes a matter of faith, or that our experience of its power is increased, but by strengthening the principle of faith.

2. It manifests itself in the affections, in love to God, to Christ, and to our fellow Christians.

3. In the exercise of the social virtues. In all these cases the degree in which the effects are manifested depends on the vigor of the principle of life. It is analogous to the case of a tree. It is not so much by attention to the fruit, as by attending to the health of the tree which produces the fruit, that success is secured. This is a general remark, applicable to all questions of this kind.

By forbearance is meant abstaining from action. In a moral sense, it is abstaining from cherishing or exercising those feelings which insult or injury is adapted to produce. Such conduct, (*i. e.*, insult and injury) is adapted to produce resentment and retaliation. Forbearance is abstaining from exercising such resentment, and from endeavoring to retaliate. Christian forbearance is forbearance exercised from Christian motives. A man, when insulted, or injured, may forbear from mere interested or prudential considerations, or from self-respect, or from the desire of approbation ; but in such cases there is no religion in the act. It is only when the forbearance is determined by Christian motives that it is a Christian grace. What then are the Christian motives which give a gracious character to our forbearance?

1. A sense of our own ill desert, *i. e.*, vileness and unworthiness. The quickness to resent an injury or insult is in proportion to the value we set upon ourselves. If, therefore, we are truly humble, if we are really conscious of our vileness and unworthiness in the sight of God, we shall be little disposed to be offended when others manifest towards us a want of respect or of kind feelings. We shall know in our hearts that we little deserve the respect or affection of any human being. We often deceive ourselves in this matter, and call ourselves the chief of sinners, when, if men seem to think us so, we feel greatly injured.

2. A sense of guilt; a consciousness that we are even greater sinners against God than any human being can be against us. Such is our moral hebetude that we are obliged to take extreme cases to awaken in us the feeling which we wish to describe. Suppose, then, a man guilty of patricide, or still worse, of matricide; suppose such an one brought to a sense of his guilt; would it be possible to awaken in his mind a feeling of resentment by any amount of insult or injury that could be heaped upon him? Would he not feel that he deserved it all? And what are we? I will not say that we are as wicked as a murderer of his father, but this I will say, that no patricide ever abhorred himself half so much as it would be just for us to loathe ourselves. Can we look at the cross and ask why Jesus died, without feeling ourselves guilty of his blood? Put it to yourselves. If the conduct of a people had been so rebellious that it was impossible to pardon them unless their prince should die for them, would they not feel that they were the guilty authors of his death? And suppose further, that they, instead of being penitent and won to obedience by the exhibition of his love, treated him with neglect and continued in their rebellion, what would they think of themselves if they were brought to a right state of mind? It is impossible for us to exaggerate our guilt in the sight of God. We are more guilty than we ever have conceived, or ever can conceive ourselves to be; and depend upon it, the more honestly and truly we feel this, the more forbearing will we be towards those who neglect or injure us.

3. The fact that Christ is so forbearing towards us, will render his true disciples forbearing towards others. Christ, notwithstanding our vileness, and notwithstanding our guilt, treats us as though we were pure and innocent. That is, he loves us and receives us into his favor. He not only forgives us offenses infinitely greater and more numerous than any we ever can experience from our fellow-men, but he continues to heap his favors upon us while we are trying his patience to the uttermost. If he forgives us ten thousand talents, should we not forgive our fellow-servant an hundred pence? He who feels that he has been forgiven much, will be disposed to forgive much.

4. Another Christian motive is the peculiar relation in which believers stand to each other. They are children of the same Father, members of the same family, united to the same Saviour, heirs of the same inheritance, partakers of the same Spirit. Paul exhorts believers not to lie; not because of the obligation of truth, or the evils of falsehood, but because believers are members one of another. When the hand resents the imperfections of the eye, or the head execrates the stumbling of the feet, then may one believer be resentful against another.

5. "Brethren, if a man be overtaken in a fault, ye which are spiritual, restore such a one in the spirit of meekness; considering thyself, lest thou also be tempted. Bear ye one another's burdens, and so fulfil the law of Christ."

CLXXXI. Judge not that ye be not judged. Matt 7: 1.

[*Feb. 12th,* 1854.]

Moses on Mt. Sinai ; Christ on the mountain of Palestine.

1. The one was terrible, the other attractive.

2. The one was legal and ceremonial, the other spiritual and evangelical.

3. The one was ministerial, the other authoritative

4. The one was in form earthly, the other heavenly.

This discourse is distinguished, 1. By its heavenly character. 2. By the comprehensiveness and spirituality of its precepts. 3 By its catholicity.

The peculiar command, Judge not.

1. The word $\varkappa\rho\iota\nu\varepsilon\iota\nu$ means simply to pronounce on the conformity, or want of conformity of an act or person to the law. This may be done, 1st, Officially and with authority. 2d, It may be done unofficially, as when we express a conviction regarding a person or act, that he or it is worthy of praise or blame. 3d, As intermediate between official judgment and the mere expression of approbation or disapprobation, is the decided condemnation of our brethren, or a pronouncing them guilty before God. The former is the expression of our own judgment, the latter is a declaration of what is the judgment of God. In the first sense there is of course no sin in judging. As to the third sense, it does not belong to us.

1. We have the right and duty to declare what God's judgment is, so far as it is revealed, *e. g.*, that no one who denies Christ, or says that Jesus is accursed, is of God; that no unclean person, or unjust, or murderer, or drunkard hath any part in the kingdom of God.

2. But beyond this we have no right to go. 1st. We have no right to pronounce that sin which God has not so declared—meats, days, etc. 2d. We have no right to judge the heart, or to pass sentence upon motives. Paul refused to be thus judged by the Corinthians.

(*a.*) We are utterly incompetent for this office.

(*b.*) This is not the time for judging.

(*c.*) We have no authority. It is an office which belongs to Christ. It is a usurpation on our part.

The second kind of judging, viz., the expression of approbation or disapprobation.

This is right, 1. When done with competent knowledge. 2. On suitable occasions. 3. From proper motives and design. 4. With proper mildness.

It is wrong on the other hand—and what is here condemned—when it is accompanied with,

1. Undue severity of judgment.

2. A disposition to condemn, to put the worst construction on acts, or to censure when we are not called upon to do it.

3. It is wrong to condemn where we are not competent to form a right judgment.

4. Where the motive is bad, to gratify malice, to wound the feelings, or to amuse others.

Reasons against judging :

1. We shall be judged, here and hereafter.

2. We are guilty of folly.

3. We cherish evil feelings ourselves.

4. We promote them in others.

CLXXXII. Christian Rebuke.

[*Jan.* 31*st*, 1864.]

In the Scriptures we have a two-fold description of the Church; as a whole, of individual churches, and of believers as individual men. The one description sets forth the ideal of the Church catholic, of a congregation, and of a believer; the other sets them before us as they actually are. The Church as a whole is described as the body of Christ, as his fold, as his kingdom, his family, his temple; all of which is intended to express its relation to him as his dwelling, as his possession, as the object of his delight, and as filled with his Spirit and presence.

I. *In virtue of this relation to Christ, the Church is,* 1. One in faith, in experience, in communion, and fellowship; so that if one member suffers, every member suffers with it. They are also in mutual subjection, and united in discipline and worship. 2. It is holy, sacred, set apart from the world, undefiled, conformed to the will of Christ, devoted to his service, and pure from the corruption of heresy and sin.

II. *As the Church is what it is just described to be, a body filled by Christ's Spirit, taught and controlled by him, it has the prerogative,* 1. To teach others. 2. To bind and loose, to receive into, and reject from her communion. 3. To reprove and rebuke, as well as to exhort.

III. *Now, as every man is a microcosm, so every believer is an epitome of the Church.* What is true of the Church as a whole, is true of every believer in his measure. 1. The relation in which every believer stands to Christ is that which the Church as a whole bears to him. If he is the king, the head, the shepherd, the prophet, the priest, the husband of the Church, so he is of each and every believing soul. If the Church is filled by his Spirit, enlightened, sanctified and guided by him, so is each believer. 2. Therefore the attributes of the believer are essentially the attributes of the Church. He is holy, separate from the world, purified from sin. He is free from heresy and defilement. 3. Consequently the prerogatives of the believer are the same in his sphere and measure with the prerogatives of the Church. 1st. He has the right to teach. 2d. To bind and loose. 3d. To exhort and rebuke with all long-suffering.

The *first* remark which this view of the matter suggests is, that the relation both of the Church and of the believer to Christ is not an external one, but an internal and vital one. It is not by outward profession, nor by external rites that this relation is consummated or preserved, but by a living faith and the indwelling of the Spirit; and consequently no individual man, and no body of men have a right to be regarded, treated or obeyed as a part of the Church catholic, except so far as he or they give evidence of this real union with Christ.

The *second* remark is, that the prerogative of the Church and of believers severally, to teach, to give or withhold Christian fellowship, to exhort or rebuke, is founded on this relation to Christ, and conditioned on the possession of the attributes or character which flow from that relation: holiness, faith, love, meekness, etc. We are not bound to obey in the Lord those who are not in the Lord. Protestants were right in resisting the authority of Rome; so were the Presbyterians in Scotland, and the Puritans in England right in resisting those who claimed the power of the Church over them. So the right to teach, to exhort and reprove belongs to those who are members of Christ's body, and are governed by his Spirit; and it belongs to them only so far as this is actually true concerning them.

Third. It follows from what has been said, viz.: that it is the prerogative of the Church and of the believer thus to teach and to rebuke, that it is also his duty. He cannot see ignorance or sin without doing what he can to remove them.

Fourth. If this be the prerogative and duty of the believer and of the Church, then it is the duty of others to receive instruction and rebuke with a humble and submissive spirit. Here, as elsewhere, we do service not to men, but to God; we bow to the authority of God, or of the Holy Spirit in the humblest of his organs which he sees fit to employ.

As the actual Church is far from corresponding to the ideal, or the actual Christian to the ideal believer; as neither the Church as a whole, nor any of its members are really conformed to the standard of the Scriptures; as neither live worthily of the relations which both sustain to Christ, and neither possess in their fulness the internal character or attributes which flow from that relation, it follows,

First, that neither should be forward in claiming the prerogatives which are founded on that relation to Christ, and on the possession of its consequents. It has ever been the case that those bodies who possess the least of the attributes of the Church, have been most strenuous in the assertion of its prerogatives. Romanists proceed on the principle that the Church actual is the Church ideal, that the visible body is all that the Scriptures say the real and perfectly redeemed body is, or is to be. And it often happens that those individual Christians who have least of the spirit of Christ, are most disposed to exercise his power. Hence censoriousness results.

Second, as the rebuke comes from the indwelling of the Spirit, as the Christian does not act in his own name, it follows (*a.*) That the rule of his judgment must be the revealed will of the Spirit. (*b.*) That the motive must be the good of the offender. (*c.*) That the manner and tone must be such as the Spirit dictates.

Third, as concerns those who receive rebuke, it follows from what has been said, (*a.*) That they should recognize the right and duty of their brethren to administer it. (*b.*) That they should receive it as coming from the Lord. (*c.*) That as neither the Church nor the believer, whether the rebuker or the rebuked, is perfect, imperfection in the character of the reprover, or in his manner or spirit, would not justify us in resenting or resisting it. The Church is one. We should bear each other's burdens, sympathize in each other's sorrows, and endeavor to correct each other's faults.

CLXXXIII. Forgiveness of Offenses.

[*Dec.* 17*th*, 1854.]

I. *A personal offense is anything whereby we are personally injured in our feelings, our reputation, our person or estate.*

A public offense is one by which the Church or the community is injured in any of its interests.

II. *The question is, what is our duty in reference to personal offenses?*

1. We should not cherish any malignant or revengeful feelings towards those who injure us.

2. We should not retaliate, or avenge ourselves on our offenders. If the offense is of such a nature that the interests of society or of the Church require it to be punished, it is right in us to desire such punishment.

3. We should cherish towards those who offend us, the feelings of kindness, regarding them with that benevolence which forbids our wishing them any harm.

4. We should treat them in our outward conduct with kindness, returning good for evil, and acting towards them as though they had not injured us.

III. *When are we to forgive?*

There are two classes of passages which bear upon this subject. 1. Those which prescribe the condition of repentance. "If thy brother trespass against thee, rebuke him; and if he repent, forgive him." 2. Those in which no such condition is prescribed. "For if ye forgive men their trespasses, your heavenly Father will also forgive you." (Matt. vi: 14.) "How oft shall my brother sin against me and I forgive him?" (xviii: 21.) "Love your enemies, bless them that curse you, do good to them that hate you, and pray for them which despitefully use you and persecute you." (Matt. v: 44). So God does. "He maketh his sun to rise on the evil and on the good, and sendeth rain on the just and the unjust." (Matt. v: 45). So Christ prayed for his crucifiers. So Stephen prayed. So is God in his dealings with us.

These passages are not inconsistent. The word forgiveness is used in a wider or a stricter sense. In the wider sense, it includes negatively, not having a spirit of revenge, and positively, exercising a spirit of kindness and love, and manifesting that spirit by all appropriate outward acts. This is forgiveness as a Christian's duty in all cases. In a more restricted sense it is the remission of the penalty due to an offense. This is illustrated in the case of an offense against the Church. Repentance is the condition only of the remission of the penalty, not of forgiveness in the wider sense. There are penalties proper to private as well as to public offenses.

IV. *Grounds of the duty.*

1. God's command.

2. God's example.

3. Our own need of forgiveness. Our sins against God are innumerable and unspeakably great.

4. The threatening that we shall not be forgiven unless we forgive others.

5. It is a dictate of Christian love.

CLXXXIV. Let not then your good be evil spoken of.
Rom. 14: 16.

[*January 13th*, 1855.]

1. The Scriptures speak much of the beauty of holiness. They represent the Lord Jesus as the chief among ten thousand, and the one altogether lovely; as fairer than the children of men. He is divinely beautiful. His beauty consists in his perfect excellence, in the absolute wisdom and symmetry of his whole character.

2. Believers are the epistles of Christ. They are his witnesses. They represent him among men. It is their solemn duty to make a fair representation of what he is, and of what his religion is, before the world. This idea is often presented in the Old Testament, and the people were often upbraided because the name of God was blasphemed among the gentiles for their sake.

3. There are two ways in which believers dishonor Christ, and make a false representation of him and of his religion: *First,* when by breaking the law, they give men to understand that Christ either allows or approves of such transgressions, and *secondly,* when they cause even their good to be evil spoken of; that is, when they either so act on right principles as to give those principles a bad character, or so conduct themselves as to mislead others as to the true nature of the gospel. This is done (1.) When men so use their Christian liberty as to injure their brethren. The distinction between months and days, between clean and unclean meats, had been abolished. It was right that this fact should be asserted and taught. It was right that Christians should act upon this liberty; but if they so used it as to destroy their brethren, without any regard to their interest, they sinned against Christ; they caused what was good to be evil spoken of. So now in regard to temperance, men may make such a use of truth, and so act on true principles, as to do great harm. (2.) This is done when undue stress is laid on trifles. Paul says that religion does not consist in meat and drink; and to act as though it did, is to slander the gospel. All who make that essential which is not essential are guilty in this matter. They cause the gospel to be misunderstood. This is true of the Papists; it is true of High Churchmen; it is true of the seceders; of fanatics of all classes, and of all bigots. They belie religion, as the tattooed New Zealander, or the painted Indian, or the Hindoo with his smeared countenance, all misrepresent the human face divine. (3.) This is done also by the sanctimonious, who make a false representation of religion, and cause it to be evil spoken of when they hold it up thus caricatured before men. (4.) It is done also by the censorious, not

only in making non-essentials of too much importance, but also in misrepresenting the spirit of their Master. His religion does not justify their harsh judgments. (5.) It is done by those who carry any right principle to excess. (a.) By the Puritans in regard to the Sabbath, to things indifferent in worship, to days of religious observance. (b.) By the Quakers in regard to dress and conformity to the world. (c.) By those who deny the Church any liberty in her organization.

In every case of this kind, the human degrades the divine. What is indifferent is made essential, and what is essential is made indifferent. Let not then your good be evil spoken of.

1. By making a wrong use of Christian liberty.

2. By teaching trifles as matters of vital importance.

3. By sanctimoniousness.

4. By censoriousness.

5. By pressing right principles to an extreme, as the Puritans did, and the Seceders and Quakers do. Make a fair exhibition of the gospel, and to this end, 1. Study Christ and his work. 2. Be filled with his Spirit.

CLXXXV. Waiting on God.

[*November 21st*, 1852.]

I. *Two conditions are necessary to physical life*, viz. : *repose and activity.* So also in the spiritual life there are two conditions of health, viz. : passivity and exercise. The former is expressed by WAITING, which implies,

1. Passivity; a state in which we are the recipients, in which we do nothing, but quietly expect something to be done. Thus men wait for the morning; they wait for the salvation of God; for the fulfillment of his promises; they wait for the coming of the Lord.

2. It implies confidence in God, an assurance that he will reveal himself, that he will accomplish his word.

3. It implies desire and expectation. Men who wait for the morning both expect it and long for it. So those who wait for God, for his salvation, for his coming, expect it and long for it.

4. It implies patience and submission; patience, because we know that the good waited for will not be granted before God's time; submission, because we know that it is in God's power to grant or to withhold, and that our only hope is in him.

Waiting, therefore, though it implies passivity, is the opposite; (1.) of indifference; (2.) of despair; (3.) of rebellious discontent.

II. *Those who wait on the Lord renew their strength.*

1. Because God flows in upon the soul, imparts larger measures of

life. As occurs in sleep. As touching the ground according to the fable.

2. Because God approves and blesses those who thus confide in him and long for him.

III. *Times in which we should wait.*

1. In seasons of devotion, private and public.

2. In times of sickness and sorrow.

3. In times of spiritual dearth.

4. All the time of our continuance in this world, is a time of wait-ing for the salvation of God.

CLXXXVI. Fight the good fight of faith.—1 Tim. 6:12.

[*April* 10*th*, 1853.]

The attainment of eternal life is a great and difficult work. It is not to be attained without great effort.

1. Because it implies victory over sin, bringing ourselves into sub-jection to God, and into conformity to his image.

2. Because the enemies which stand in our way are so numerous.

This truth is variously presented in the Scriptures. It is presented by our Saviour's exhortation to strive to enter in at the strait gate; by the command to work out our own salvation with fear and trembling; by comparing the Christian life to a race, to a conflict, etc. The latter is the figure here used.

I. *What is meant by the fight of faith?* II. *Why is it called a good fight?* III. *What is the nature of this conflict?* IV. *What are the means, or weapons of this warfare?*

I. *What is the fight of faith?*

1. The Christian life, considered as a fight.

2. It is called the fight of faith, not because it is a conflict in behalf of a creed, but because faith is the contending principle; it is a fight in which faith is the combatant. Such is the life of faith, the walk, the triumph of faith. It is explained by 2 Tim. iv. 7: "I have fought a good fight,—I have kept the faith;" that is, faith in the subjective sense. He had not lost his faith, he had kept it unto the end. On this salvation is suspended. "If we hold the beginning of our confi-dence steadfast unto the end," we are made partakers of Christ. The fight, therefore, which we have to endure, is a conflict to preserve the inward life of the soul, which consists in faith.

II. *Why is it called a good fight?*

1. Because it is the conflict in behalf of what is good; not for riches,

honor, or dominion, but for holiness.   2. Because it is a conflict which
ends in triumph.

III. *Nature of the conflict.*

The faith here spoken of is, 1. Not merely faith in the being, perfections and government of God.   To maintain such a faith is a great
thing, considering all the sources of doubt and difficulty which surround us.

2. But it is also faith in the gospel, *i. e.*, faith in Christ; in his
divinity, incarnation, atonement, intercession, etc.

3. Faith in our interest in his redemption, or rather, faith considered
as the appropriation to ourselves of the promises of the gospel, and the
consequent union of the soul with God.

The enemies of faith are,

1st. A spirit of skepticism.   (*a.*) The sources of this evil.   (*b.*) The
cure of it.

2d. A spirit of despondency.   (*a.*) On account of sin, *i. e.*, its power.
(*b.*) On account of guilt.

3d. A distrustful, gloomy spirit.   (*a.*) As to our destiny in this life,
and hereafter.   (*b.*) As to our usefulness.

4th. A worldly spirit; a disposition to seek, to fear, to obey the
world.

IV. *Means of maintaining faith.*

1. Nearness to God, and sense of dependence.

2. Use of the means of grace.

3. Exercise of our faith.

CLXXXVII.   Rejoice in the Lord.

[*January 24th*, 1864.]

Joy is either a transient emotion produced by the expectation or enjoyment of good, or it is a permanent state of the mind, an habitual,
cheerful and happy frame of the spirit, arising from the sense of
security and blessedness.   The command is,—

I. *To be happy.*   II. *To be happy in and through the enjoyment of*
spiritual good.

I. *The command is to be happy.*   This is not inconsistent with the
duty of mourning for our sins, nor with the duty of sympathy with the
sorrows of others, weeping with those who weep, nor with being duly
and naturally affected by the trials and afflictions of life, nor with the
declaration that God looks with special favor upon such as are of an
humble and contrite spirit, and tremble at his word.   There may be
joy in sorrow.

But the command to rejoice is, 1. A condemnation of a sad, desponding, discontented state of mind. It is a condemnation, 1st. On the one hand, of the doctrine that such sadness or despondency is in itself a desirable or profitable state; that it tends to holiness, or is the appropriate condition of the Christian. 2d. On the other hand, of the doctrine that these feelings should be cherished and rendered habitual. This is a common opinion. There is much to make it plausible. The awful interests of eternity which must be more or less in doubt until our destiny is decided, the amount of evil in our own hearts, the prevalence of evil in the world, the state of those dear to us, the low condition of the Church, the certainty of the perdition of so large a portion of the human race; these as well as our own personal sorrows and difficulties, would seem enough to banish all happiness from the heart of those who take a believing and enlarged view of the realities by which they are surrounded. Nevertheless joy, and not sadness, is the normal state of the Christian; and this state of depression of spirits is not itself good, nor a state of mind to be cherished as desirable and productive of holiness. 2. It is not only, however, a condemnation of habitual sadness, but it teaches, 1st. That the opposite state is the one which we ought habitually to enjoy; and 2d. That it is the one which we ought habitually to cherish. And this for two reasons. *First*, the Christian has abundant cause to be habitually joyful; reasons which cannot be duly and believingly apprehended without producing joy. Sadness, therefore, is the fruit and evidence of unbelief, as spiritual joy is the fruit and evidence of faith. The fact, (1.) That the Christian is forgiven. (2.) That he is reconciled to God and is the object of the divine love. (3.) That he is united to Christ. (4.) That all the exceeding great and precious promises of the Word of God are his. (5.) That Christ is set before him as the object of love, adoration and delight. (6.) That heaven is his everlasting inheritance. (7.) That all power is in the hands of Christ, that all things must work together for good, and that the final consummation will result in bringing infinite good out of the infinite evil that is in the world; these are rational sources of joy. It is unnatural and wrong, unbelieving and ungrateful for those who have all these sources of joy to be habitually sad and desponding. Nothing is more difficult to bear than for a father to see a child, surrounded by everything necessary to render him happy, habitually and causelessly miserable.

The *second* reason why we are commanded to be happy is that this state of mind is healthful. It tends to holiness. It is to the graces of the Spirit what the light of the sun is to nature. It renders them more healthful, vigorous and beautiful. Happiness belongs to heaven; misery, to hell.

II. *This command to be happy is, however, not a command to be happy simply, but to be happy in the Lord.* This is, 1. A prohibition against seeking happiness in the world. It is not a prohibition against opening our hearts to the sources of pleasurable emotion which surround us in the world. But it is a prohibition against seeking our happiness from that source, or even enjoying them as merely worldly. They should be received and enjoyed religiously. This moderates, modifies and regulates all worldly joy.

2. It is a command to seek our happiness in God, and in the things of God. We must choose. If we come to the fountain of living water we shall not only be refreshed, but also enabled to enjoy worldly good more, and be safer than if we had made that good our portion.

III. *In what sense is this joy a fruit of the Spirit?*

1. The Spirit is the author of that gracious state of mind out of which joy springs.

2. He bears witness with our spirits that we are the children of God, and he is the earnest of our inheritance.

3. He sheds abroad the love of God in our hearts, and directly infuses the special grace of joy.

IV. *The reasons for this command.*

1. Joy is healthful in all its natural influence and tendencies. Pain and sorrow are the reverse. The one is the inseparable companion or consequence of holiness; the others are inseparable from sin. The one tends, therefore, to produce holiness, and the others, sin. Pain and sorrow may be useful as medicine, not as food. Joy, however, is the natural atmosphere of the soul, out of which it cannot live. Or, it is as oxygen in the air; it is its vital principle. Take joy out of heaven, and what would it be? It would be as though the oxygen of our air were removed; all that lives would die. For our own good, therefore, we should rejoice.

2. This joy is a holy exercise. 1st. Because its objects are holy, pure, spiritual. 2d. Because it is in its nature the exercise of holy feeling.

3. It is a gift of God and the fruit of the Spirit. "These things have I spoken unto you, that *my* joy might remain in you, and that your joy might be full." (John xv: 11.) "And now I come to thee; and these things I speak in the world, that they might have my joy fulfilled in themselves." (John xvii: 13.) "For the kingdom of God is not meat and drink; but righteousness, and peace, and joy in the Holy Ghost." (Rom. xiv: 17.) "But the fruit of the Spirit is love, joy, peace," etc. (Gal. v: 22.) "Now unto him that is able to keep you from falling, and to present you faultless before the presence of his glory, with exceeding joy, to the only wise God our Saviour, be glory and majesty,

dominion and power, both now and ever. Amen." (Jude 24, 25.) Surely, that which is the gift of Christ, the fruit of the Spirit, and the atmosphere of heaven, must be holy, and worthy of being assiduously cherished.

4. It beautifies, adorns, and renders attractive the Christian character. A gloomy Christian is not only a burden to himself, but also a source both of unhappiness and of evil to those around him. We are bound, therefore, to be joyful as a means of honoring God, and being useful to our fellow-men.

5. Surely we of all men have abundant cause for joy. The absence of joy is a proof of unbelief. How can a man who believes that he is united to Christ, and therefore partaker of his righteousness, the temple of his Spirit, a child of God and an heir of heaven, fail to rejoice? If assured of great earthly good, we should not fail to overflow with joy. How then can we believe that we are partakers of Christ's glory, and not rejoice?

CLXXXVIII. Zeal.

[*December* 18*th*, 1853.]

I. *Its general nature.* II. *Criteria by which to distinguish between true and false zeal.* III. *The duty and importance of being zealous.*

I. *The general nature of zeal.*

Zeal is fervor. $Z\tilde{\eta}\lambda o\varsigma$ is from $\zeta\acute{\epsilon}\omega$, to boil. It stands opposed (*a.*) To opposition. (*b.*) To indifference or lukewarmness. Its object may be good or bad, a person or thing, truth or error. The Jews and Paul were zealous for the law, and for the tradition of their fathers. Paul through zeal persecuted the Church.

II. *Criteria of true and false zeal.*

1. They are not determined by their object. There can indeed be no holy zeal for sin or error; but there may be an unholy zeal for God and truth. Of this the Jews were an example.

2. True or false zeal is not determined either by its energy, or by the self-denial and exertions to which it leads. Many unholy men are exceedingly fervid in their zeal, and many such make the greatest sacrifices for their ends.

3. It is determined, first, by its source. The source of false zeal is either, 1st. Some selfish interest, as in the case of the Jews, the high churchman, the Romanist; or, 2d. Party spirit, national feeling, *esprit de corps;* or, 3d. False doctrine, hatred of the truth. The source of true zeal, *i. e.*, of zeal as a Christian grace, is, 1st. The Holy Spirit, as the author of all good. 2d. Spiritual apprehension of the dignity and excellence of its object, whether it be God, the truth, or the Church.

Second, it is determined by its concomitants and effects. 1st. False zeal is malignant; true is benevolent. The one is the fervor of an unrenewed mind; the other of a renewed mind. Illustrations of this are, Jesus, and the Jews. 2d. False zeal is proud; true zeal is humble. The former arises often from a sense of superiority which it seeks to vindicate and assert; the latter, from such views of God and things divine as tend to produce humility. 3d. The one is reverent and the other irreverent. The fear of the Lord is the beginning of wisdom. The want of this attribute vitiates, or proves to be spurious, much that passes for religion. 4th. True zeal is connected with a holy life. It is remarkable how often the greatest zealots for God, the Church, and sound doctrine (as they regard it), have been unholy and even immoral in their lives.

III. *The duty of zeal.*

1. This state of mind is demanded by the infinite importance of the interests at stake : the glory of God, the Redeemer's kingdom, the progress of truth, the salvation of men. To be unconcerned about these things is the greatest sin and evil.

2. God, therefore, declares his special abhorrence of the cold and lukewarm.

3. Our relation and obligations to God and Christ call for zeal. A child is zealous for its father, a subject for his sovereign, a soldier for his commander, a captive for his redeemer. Our zeal should be proportioned to our obligations.

4. Zeal is the chief source, or one of the chief sources of spiritual power. God employs living souls to communicate life. In all ages, men of zeal have produced great results. This qualification, in the absence of others, can accomplish wonders.

IV. *Means of cultivating zeal.*

1. Avoid all pretence or affectation, all expression of more interest than you feel.

2. Gather warmth by continual intercourse with God, and cherish the influence of his Spirit.

3. Keep your minds filled with the subjects about which you should be zealous, and your attention devoted to them.

4. Remember that zeal is a gift of the Holy Spirit; that whatever grieves the Spirit quenches our zeal, and that the more we are filled with the Holy Ghost, the more shall we be filled with godly zeal.

VIII.

THE MEANS OF GRACE.

THE SCRIPTURES, MINISTRY, SACRAMENTS, &c.

CLXXXIX. The Means of Grace.

[*March 6th*, 1853.]

I. *Meaning of the terms.*

1. Grace signifies goodness, love, divine influence.

2. The means of grace are the means appointed and employed in applying to men the benefits of redemption. These are the word, the sacraments and prayer; or more properly, the word and sacraments.

II. *Wrong views on this subject.*

First, that which depreciates their importance, their necessity. This is done, 1. By those who teach that reason and nature contain, or may discover truth enough to sanctify and save the soul. This is disproved, (*a.*) By Scripture. (*b.*) By experience. 2. By those who teach that the Holy Spirit is given to all men as a revealer of truth. This is disproved, (*a.*) By the Scriptures, which everywhere teach the necessity of the written or preached word. (*b.*) By experience, which shows that wherever the written word is forsaken, and inward illumination relied on, the result is folly and heresy.

Second, the doctrine which attributes an inherent efficacy to these means, and teaches, 1. That they are the only channels of divine influence and of saving benefits. 2. That they are always efficacious. 3. That their efficacy is independent of the state of the recipient (if non-resisting), and of the ab-extra power of the Spirit.

III. *The true doctrine on the subject, is,*

1. That they are absolutely necessary, except in the case of infants.

2. That their efficacy is due to the attending power of the Spirit.

3. That this power is given when and to whom God sees fit. That

this divine influence, not being given independently of these means, our growth in grace depends on the proper use of them.

IV. *The proper use of the means includes,*

1. A proper understanding of their nature and importance. If we approach the Scriptures or the sacraments with wrong views of their nature, either too low, as though they were merely human, or with superstitious views, as though they had magical power, we shall fail.

2. A deep conviction of the necessity of divine influence, in order to render them efficacious.

3. A due preparation of mind, preparatory to their use. This is secured, (*a.*) By discarding other things, and especially by forsaking sin. (*b.*) By awaking a desire for spiritual nourishment.

4. The exercise, in the actual use of them, (*a.*) Of faith, as well as attention. (*b.*) Of self-application. (*c.*) Of the purpose to believe and act in accordance with the truth communicated.

5. Prayer and converse with God.

CXC. The Word of God as a Means of Grace.

[*November* 30*th*, 1856.]

I. *What is the meaning of the phrase "means of grace?"*

1. They are not means in the Romish sense, *i. e.*, rites which have the power to confer grace. 2. Nor any service or thing which may be the means of good, such as dispensations of Providence, afflictive or otherwise, nor forms or ceremonies of man's arranging, though ever so useful. But, 3. Those which are appointed by God for the purpose of conveying grace, and which he has promised to attend by his divine influence. This supposes that God works by means. This he does, 1st. In the material world, which is governed, not by the blind laws of matter, but by the continual operation of God in sustaining and guiding those laws to intelligent ends. 2d. In the intellectual world, in the development and exercise of the minds and character of men; in sustaining, controlling, restraining and guiding their exercises, so that they with perfect freedom work out their own pleasure, and yet the purposes of God. 3d. In the world of grace, where also there is a continual agency of God in combination with the agency of man, in the development of the graces of the Spirit, and in attaining eternal life.

From this it follows (1.) That the means are adapted to the end. The laws of matter are to be employed and followed in attaining physical results; the laws of mind, or rather of human nature, are to be employed in attaining intellectual and moral results. (2.) That in all cases these means are appointed and determined by God. We can not substitute others in their stead. We must use those which God has appointed, or none at all. (3.) These means are absolutely essential, and not more so in one department than in another. (4.) In all cases the means are inefficacious without God's presence. God gives life and power to natural causes; and he gives efficacy to the means of grace, according to the laws of the kingdom of grace.

II. *What are the means of grace?* The word, sacraments and prayer. There are no others. Our subject is the Word as a means.

1. By the Word we mean the Bible and its contents; the whole system of facts, doctrines, promises and principles therein revealed. 2. This is a means of grace, the means which God has appointed, and which we are commanded to use for the promotion of a work of grace in ourselves and others.

First, as to ourselves. 1st. It must be understood. It must become an object of knowledge. It is only as known that it exerts for us, or exerts over us any power. This knowledge supposes (*a.*) Familiarity with what the Bible says. (*b.*) An understanding of the meaning of what it says. If we attach a wrong sense to the language of the Bible, it is not the truth which it contains which is before our minds, but some form of human thought to which no promise is made.

2d. It must be spiritually discerned. That is, it must be apprehended in its spiritual excellence, as it is addressed to the heart as well as, in its logical relations, to the understanding. These may be so far separated that the intellectual may exist without the spiritual; but the spiritual cannot exist without the intellectual. A man may see a thing without seeing its beauty, but he cannot see its beauty without seeing the thing itself.

3d. The word of God must be studied with both these objects, that is, to know what it teaches, and to apprehend its spiritual power. With regard to this point, I would remark, (*a.*) That the two things are perfectly distinct. The ends aimed at are different, the means employed are different, and the posture of mind is different. (*b.*) Being thus different, the one can not be substituted for the other, the critical for the devotional, or the devotional for the critical reading. (*c.*) They may, however, be combined. The mind may pass instantaneously from the one posture to the other, or turn its eye from one aspect to another, of the truth contemplated; as does the astronomer in the study of the heavens, or the man of science in the study of the laws of matter, or the physician in studying the structure of the human frame, or the lawyer in studying the principles of human justice.

4th. As the word is the great means of grace, it must be dilligently used for this end. (*a.*) It must be brought frequently and for protracted periods before the mind, and contemplated in its spiritual character, as designed and adapted to excite the proper emotions.

That is, time must be devoted to the devotional reading and meditation of the truth. (*b.*) It must be read with constant self-application. As a means of communion with God we must read the word as if God were speaking to us; and we must answer in the words of gratitude, reverence, faith, joy or fear, as the thing said may require. (*c.*) The mind should be stored with the truth and with the words of Scripture. (*d.*) We should cultivate the habit of casual meditation, or of recurring to the word of God continually [*a.*] as matter or subject of thought, [*b.*] for direction, [*c.*] for support, and [*d.*] for consolation.

5. As the means, though divinely appointed and divinely efficacious, is powerless in itself, we should always pray for the Spirit, and depend on his promised aid, without which the word will be to us only a savor of death.

Second, as to others.

1. The truth is the only, and the absolutely indispensable means. 2. We must endeavor, therefore, to bring men to the knowledge of the truth. 3. We must try to make them employ it in the way of God's appointment.

CXCI. Search the Scriptures.

[*February 18th*, 1854.]

I. *What are the Scriptures?* II. *For what are they to be searched?* III. *How are they to be searched?*

I. *What are the Scriptures?*

The sacred writings contained in the Old and New Testaments are,

1. The Word of God. In the sense in which the works of a man are his words, revealing his thoughts, will, purposes, the Scriptures are the word of God. He is their author. Their contents rest on his authority. They are not merely his as written by pious men, not a human form of divine truth, but God's own exhibition of truth. This is opposed, first, to the Deistical, secondly, to the Rationalistic, and thirdly, to the Quaker views.

2. From this it follows, (*a.*) That they are infallible. (*b.*) That they are holy. (*c.*) That they are powerful. (*d.*) That they are consistent. (*e.*) That they are the appointed means of salvation. We are begotten, enlightened, sanctified, and saved by the truth.

3. They are complete, as containing all the extant revelation of God.

4. They are plain, so that every one can learn for himself what God says. They are the light of the world. They are the fountain of life. They are the treasury of divine things.

II. *We should know what we seek when we search.*

We should search the Scriptures, 1. For knowledge of God, of Christ, of truth, of duty. This knowledge is speculative, and spiritual.

2. For consolation.

3. For holiness.

III. *How are we to search the Scriptures?*

1. Reverently and submissively, with the fixed determination to believe every truth which they affirm. Everything is right which they command, and everything is wrong which they condemn. We are not to sit in judgment on the Scriptures.

2. With diligence, (*a.*) Studying them much. (*b.*) Studying them consecutively. (*c.*) Investigating what they teach on particular subjects. (*d.*) Availing ourselves of all aid; fixing right principles, and availing ourselves of all subsidiary means.

3. With dependence; convinced that without divine guidance we shall obtain neither right speculative knowledge, nor right spiritual views.

4. Therefore with prayer, previous and continued.

5. With self-application.

CXCII. Mighty in the Scriptures.—Acts 18: 24.

[March 15th, 1863.]

I. *The Scriptures are like the ocean, boundless and unfathomable.* No man can ever exhaust the stores of knowledge treasured in the ocean. It may be studied for a life-time under different aspects. 1. It may be viewed in reference to its distribution and topography; its great expanse, as it spreads between Asia and America, between America and Europe and Africa, between Africa and India; its indentations, gulfs, bays, etc., and the effects which this distribution has on climate, winds, rain, fertility, and hence on commerce, and the destiny of the human race. 2. It may be studied as to its basin, its mountains and valleys, the configuration of the crust of the earth on which it rests, and the nature of its bottom in different places. 3. It may be investigated as to its animals, the innumerable genera and species of living organisms with which it abounds, from the whale to the animalcule, and the changes produced by the presence and labors of the millions of insects, rendering luminous miles of its surface, or building up reefs and islands and continents from its deeps. 4. It may be studied as to its tides, its currents, its prevailing winds. 5. As to its chemistry. 6. Besides all these kinds of knowledge, there is another kind, which can be obtained only by living on it; the knowledge of how to use it, how to avail our-

selves of its power and resources. It is plain that a man may have
much of the other kinds of this oceanic knowledge, and very little of
the last kind. We should not like to go to sea in a ship commanded
by Dr. Guyot or Prof. Agassiz.

All this may be applied to Scripture. It may be studied under different aspects, and in each, furnish inexhaustible stores of knowledge.
1. It may be viewed as a history extending from the creation to the
present time, including its genealogical periods, its antediluvian period,
its patriarchal period, its Jewish period, its life of Christ, its apostolic
period. A man might spend his life in getting a clear knowledge of its
facts, then of the bearing of those facts on ethnography, on the civilization of the world, on the destiny of the nations generally, and on the religions of men. 2. Scripture may be studied in its organic relations; the
relation of the Adamic period to the Abrahamic, of the Abrahamic to
the Mosaic, of the Mosaic to the prophetic, and of all to the culmina-
tion of all in the Christian period. 3. It may be studied as to its doctrines; what it teaches of the nature and perfections of God, of his relation to the material and spiritual world, of the distinction of persons in
the Godhead, of the person and work of Christ, and of the Holy Spirit;
what it teaches of man, his original state, his fall, his moral condition
since the fall, of his ability and responsibility; what it teaches of the
plan of salvation, of the application of the redemption purchased by
Christ, and of man's destiny hereafter. 4. The moral code of the
Bible is another wide field, including our religious, social and political duties, and the limits of human authority in church and
state. 5. There is a knowledge given in special and general introduction. 6. In the study of the Church as the body of Christ, and as a
visible society, from Adam to the present time; its organization, officers, prerogatives, attributes and discipline. 7. There is a knowledge
which is due to the illumination of the Spirit, including spiritual apprehension, deeper insight into the meaning of the word of God, and a
firmer conviction of its truth than can be derived from any other
source. 8. Besides all these kinds of knowledge, there is a familiarity
with its language, a knowledge lodged in the memory, so that it can be
readily quoted and applied. This is a great gift or attainment.

But as scientific knowledge of the ocean may be possessed without
practical skill in navigation, so a man may possess a knowledge of
Scripture history, of the relation of the parts of Scripture to one
another, of its doctrines, of its moral code, of its literature and
analysis, of the theory of the Church therein revealed; he may have
spiritual knowledge, and have his memory stored with scriptural
language, and yet not be *mighty in the Scriptures*. These are the
requisite conditions of power, the materials rather, which power uses,

and without which he can accomplish nothing; but the power itself, is the ability to use this knowledge effectively. This includes three things. 1. A mental ability; a clearness and power of the intelligence, to bring to bear the truths and facts of Scripture so as to produce the desired effect, whether that be conviction of the truth, or submission of the conscience, or the obedience of the will. 2. There is a might or power in feeling, strong conviction of the truth and importance of what the Bible teaches, and fervent desire that it should be recognized and obeyed. 3. There is a power of utterance, eloquence, the ability to convince, to persuade, and to excite.

II. *After the nature of this gift of being mighty in the Scriptures, comes its importance.* On this it may be remarked that the whole power of a minister as such, not as a man, or a Christian, but as a minister, is a power in the Scriptures. This exists in different degrees, but it is all any minister has, be it much or little. It is therefore the one object to be sought in preparing for the ministry, without which a minister, no matter what else he may have of knowledge or talent, will accomplish no good and may do immense harm.

III. *The duty of becoming mighty in the Scriptures.*

1. It is our duty to obtain all the kinds of knowledge of Scripture above mentioned, especially committing it to memory, so as to be able to quote it abundantly, correctly and appropriately.

2. To acquire the ability to use that knowledge. This is partly a mental discipline, partly a spiritual exercise, and partly an art—the art of effective public speaking.

CXCIII. Prayer as a means of Grace.

[*September 18th*, 1859.]

I. *What is prayer?*

It is not simply petition, but converse with God, including, therefore, 1. The expression of our feelings in view of his greatness and glory, *i. e.*, adoration. 2. The expression of our feelings in view of his goodness, *i. e.*, thanksgiving. 3. The expression of our feelings in view of our sins and sinfulness, *i. e.*, confession. 4. The expression of our feelings in view of our wants, *i. e.*, supplication. Of course this converse with God may be,

1st. Solemn and formal, in the use of articulate words and on set occasions, in the closet, family, or sanctuary.

2d. Occasional and ejaculatory, and thus constant, as the bubbling of a spring of living water.

3d. Or in the unuttered aspirations and longings of the soul after God, like the constant ascent of the flame towards heaven.

II. *Prayer, or this converse with God, is a means of grace.*

1. It is not merely a means of spiritual improvement, nor a means of securing divine blessings, but one of the appointed means of supernatural, divine communications to the soul from God.

2. This, therefore, is not due to a law of nature, according to which we are assimilated to those with whom we converse, but to the fact that in prayer God communicates himself, reveals his glory and his love to the soul.

3. The Holy Ghost is the Spirit of prayer, in the sense, (*a.*) That he reveals those objects which call forth spiritual affections, viz., the glory of God, his love, the glory and love of Christ, the inexhaustible riches of the divine promises, our own sinfulness and necessities. (*b.*) That he not only presents these objects, but also awakens the appropriate feelings. (*c.*) That he leads us to clothe those feelings, those adoring, penitential, grateful or craving feelings, in appropriate language, or in groanings which cannot be uttered. Thus he maketh intercession for us. Thus he is our παράκλητος, (advocate). Prayer thus inspired is not only always answered in some way, and that the best, but it is also a means of grace. It is the occasion and the channel of infusing new measures of divine life into the soul. It is not therefore prayer as the mere uttering of words, nor prayer as the uttering of natural desires of affection, as when one prays for his own life or the life of those dear to him; but it is prayer as the real intercourse of the soul with God, by the Holy Ghost, that is, the Holy Ghost revealing truth, exciting feeling, and giving appropriate utterance.

III. *Our duty in the premises is,*

1. To remember that this intercourse with God is optional. We can gain access to him only when he pleases to admit us.

2. That as it is the life of the soul, we should most earnestly desire and diligently seek it.

3. That we must seek it in his appointed way, that is, through Christ and the Spirit.

4. That we must seek it on the occasions on which he is wont to grant it, in the closet, the family, and the sanctuary.

5. That we must not wait for it, so as to pray only when we feel the spirit of prayer. We must go to his courts, knock at his door, bow before the oracle, and expect him in the use of his appointed means.

CXCIV. Prayer.
[*Jan.* 27*th,* 1856.]

I. *General idea.*

1. Prayer is converse with and to God. It is not merely petition, nor confession, nor thanksgiving, nor adoration, but all the intercourse

of the soul by address to God. It is distinguished, by being address, from contemplation and meditation. This address may be, (1.) Oral or mental. (2.) Occasional or constant. (3.) Formal, in the good sense of the word, and ejaculatory.

2. It is therefore a form of spiritual activity, as essential to spiritual life as the pulsation of the heart is to natural life. (1.) Because it is the evidence and exercise of life. (2.) Because it is necessary to its continuance. A prayerless Christian and a pulseless man are alike impossible. The pulse is the great criterion or index of the health of the body ; so prayer is of the health of the soul.

II. *The attributes of acceptable prayer.*

They are such as flow from the state of mind produced by the Spirit. For the Spirit is the author of all genuine prayer, as it is by the Spirit that we have access unto God. Those feelings and graces which the Spirit calls into exercise, and which find their expression in prayer, are, 1. Those of admiration and reverence, giving rise to praise and adoration. 2. Those of penitence, giving rise to confession. 3. Those of faith, (1.) In God as the hearer of prayer. (2.) In Christ as our mediator and intercessor. (3.) In God's ability and willingness to answer. (4.) In his actual promise to answer our prayer. 4. Those of gratitude, giving rise to thanksgiving. 5. Those of longing desire after spiritual blessings, and for other things needful for ourselves and others. 6. Those of patience and submission, manifested in perseverance and humble importunity.

III. *The efficacy of prayer.*

1. As it regards ourselves. It calls into exercise and strengthens all the graces of the Spirit. 2. It is an appointed means to an end, and has the same relation in the moral government of God that other second causes have to their effects. It is an antecedent *sine qua non.* The objection that God has determined either to give or not give those blessings for which we pray, and that his purpose cannot be changed by our prayers, has no more force than in any other case where means are connected with an end. The objection that it is derogatory to God to be pleased with our praises and thanks has no force, if it is right to praise and thank him. God is pleased with what is right. The objection confounds God with man. Because it is unseemly to praise a creature, it is assumed to be unseemly to adore God.

IV. *The importance of cultivating the gift and habit of prayer.* To improve in this gift, 1. It is necessary to cherish the right feelings, otherwise all prayer is offense. 2. To cultivate the mind for public prayer, an intellectual exercise. This is as much incumbent on us in prayer as in preaching, especially as others join with us. We lead them ; they say what we say. We should not, therefore, make them

say what is revolting or unsuitable. 3. The careful, devout reading of
the Scriptures, and storing the mind with Scriptural expressions, is
necessary. These are the forms in which the Holy Ghost has given
utterance to the thoughts and feelings which we desire to express. 4.
Premeditation is as necessary here as in preaching. The design is, (1.)
To collect and arrange our thoughts. (2). To call into exercise the
proper feelings. (3.) To adapt our prayer to the occasion. The want
of this adaptation is a serious evil. 5. Devotional composition is another means much practiced by many devout men, who have attained
excellence in this part of social and public service.

This is a very important object, both as regards our own improvement and the edification and honor of the Church.

CXCV. The Prayer of Faith.

[*April 9th*, 1854.]

The passages relating to this subject are Mark xi. 23; Matt. vi. 7;
John xiv. 13, 14; xv. 7; xvi. 23; James i. 5, 6.

Such passages may be divided into three classes. 1. Those relating
to the faith of miracles, and to those only who have the gift of miracles
2. Those which relate to the officers of the church in the discharge of
their duties. 3. Those which relate to believers generally.

I. *A false doctrine has been deduced from these passages,* viz.: that
every specific request made with the assurance of its being granted,
shall be granted. This cannot be true.

1. Because it would be to submit the divine government to the
erring wisdom of men.

2. Because it would lead to undesirable or disastrous consequences.
Men might pray for things which would be their own ruin and the
ruin of others.

3. It is contrary to all experience.

4. It is contrary to the desire of every pious heart, as every Christian
would rather that God's will than his own should be done.

5. The doctrine rests on a false principle of interpretation of the divine promises. The principles which should determine the interpretation
of such promises are, (1). The analogy of Scripture, of other promises,
(*a.*) As to parents in regard to their children. (*b.*) To the Jews. (*c.*)
To the Church. (2.) The nature of the case, or the nature of the thing
promised. (3.) The actual dispensations of God. We find that he does
not answer always. All these prove that these promises cannot be understood absolutely. Those that are general declare a general principle of God's administration; as "The hand of the diligent maketh

rich ; " "Train up a child in the way he should go, and when he is old he will not depart from it ; " the seed of the righteous shall not beg their bread, etc. These do not apply to every case, but assert the general course of providence. And this is enough for encouragement and direction.

Again, all promises of this kind are conditional. The promise of grace to the children of the pious is conditioned on the fidelity of the latter, etc. These promises are conditioned, of course, on the assumption, (1.) That the thing asked for is right. (2.) That it would be for the glory of God, and the good of those who make the request. All true prayer is the fruit of the Spirit, and he can ask for those things only which are according to the mind of God.

II. *The true doctrine concerning the prayer of faith is, that the only kind of prayer to which the promise of any favorable answer is given, is such as is offered in faith. This faith includes,*

1. Belief that God is.

2. That he is the hearer of prayer ; that prayer is not superstitious, fanatical, or inefficacious, but a divine appointment, a means connected with the attainment of the end desired.

3. Faith in Christ, or praying in his name. This includes, (*a*). Trust in Christ as the medium of access to God, and (*b*). Reliance on his merit and intercession, as the ground on which we hope to be heard.

4. Faith that we shall receive what we ask, provided it be for the best. It implies that filial confidence manifested by a child in coming to a father in whose ability, affection and wisdom he has full confidence. Every such child knows that his request will be granted provided it meets with the approbation of his father.

Faith stands opposed to distrust ; distrust of God's power, of his love, of the sufficiency of Christ, or of his actually interceding for us ; distrust of God's disposition to grant what we ask, even though it would be for the best. This is is illustrated often by the disposition of children who lack confidence in their parents.

The relation of prayer, therefore, to the end is not, (1.) that of an efficacious, nor (2.) of a meritorious, nor (3.) of an instrumental, nor (4.) of an occasional cause ; but (5.) of a condition antecedent, *e. g.*, the case of Hannah, (1 Sam. i. 10, etc.), or of the blind and deaf in the time of Christ.

III. *The importance of this doctrine concerning the prayer of faith.*

1. As a preservative against the false presumptuous spirit before referred to.

2. As a ground of consolation and assurance. That we have access to the ear of our heavenly Father, who has promised to hear all our

prayers when they are according to his will, is the greatest possible ground of comfort.

3. It should lead us to cultivate faith, as an element of Christian life, and as the source of our power with God.

CXCVI. Intercessory Prayer.

[*Nov. 26th*, 1865.]

I. *To intercede, in the Scriptures, is to approach a person for another.* In this sense Christ intercedes for his people, and we intercede for each other. Our intercession is simply approaching God in prayer in behalf of others.

1. This is a commanded duty. "I exhort therefore, that, first of all, supplications, prayers, intercessions, and giving of thanks be made for all men." (1 Tim. ii: 1.) James says, "Pray one for another." Our Lord commands us to pray for our enemies, to bless those who curse us.

2. It is often exemplified in the Scriptures. Abraham intercedes for the people of Sodom and Gomorrah, Moses often for the people, Elijah for the Israelites of his day, and Daniel and Nehemiah for those of their time.

3. Such prayers being authorized and commanded, are peculiarly effectual, as in the cases above mentioned. In Jeremiah xv: 1, God says, "Though Moses and Samuel stood before me, yet my mind could not be toward this people." Paul expected the prayers of believers to be heard on his behalf. James says of intercessory prayer, that the prayer of faith avails much, and illustrates its efficacy by a reference to the case of Elijah.

II. *It is the exercise of a priestly function.*

1. Such is the union of believers with Christ that they share his offices.

2. Hence they are prophets. The Spirit of Christ is the Spirit of prophecy; that is, those in whom the Spirit dwells become prophets or spokesmen. Hence they are called Christ's witnesses, and those who hear them hear Christ. The Church is Christ's messenger to teach all nations, to act the part of prophets to them. As Christ executes the office of a prophet by revealing to us the will of God, so we execute that office by making known that revelation in his name and by his authority, to our fellow-men.

3. They are kings. They share his authority. (*a*). To them are committed the keys of the kingdom of heaven. They are invested with authority from him to rule in the Church. (*b.*) They are to rule over all the earth. The kingdom and dominion, and the greatness of the kingdom under the whole heaven, shall be given to the people of the

saints of the Most High." (Dan. vii: 27.) The saints shall judge the world. (*c.*) Hereafter they are to sit with Christ on his throne.

4. They are priests. A priest is one authorized to approach God for others. This is confined by the Romanists to the clergy, or to those who in heaven (angels and the canonized) have liberty of access. The priesthood of believers consists, 1st. In their being permitted to draw near to God. 2d. In their offering to him prayers and praises. 3d. In interceding for others. This is especially a priestly function. The High Priest interceded for the Jews. Christ intercedes for his people. We intercede for one another. Hence intercessory prayer is (*a.*) Commanded. (*b.*) Often exemplified. (*c.*) Available or efficacious.

This then is a great duty, a great privilege, and a great source of consolation; one too often neglected and undervalued.

CXCVII. Prayer for Colleges.

[*February* 26*th*, 1857.]

I. *The observance of a day of this kind has the sanction of the word of God.* Numerous examples of the people meeting for prayer are recorded, as among the exiles in Babylon, on their return to the holy city, among the apostles. Numerous exhortations and commands to observe such meetings are found in the Law and in the Prophets. What the word of God sanctions, our nature dictates. When a common necessity presses, or a common desire impels, men will unite; parents for children, children for parents; the family, the college, the Church, the whole body of the faithful. The law of our social nature demands communion in religion as in other things. The sanction of God's dispensations, as well as of his word and of our nature, shows the value of such seasons of special prayer.

II. *But these days may be abused.* If they do not do good, they do harm. We know how it is when we draw near to God only with our lips; and we know, I trust, what it is when we are really admitted to his presence. When we behold his glory, are assured of his love, and receive the communications of his Spirit, then our strength is renewed, the intellect is enlightened, the heart enlarged, faith and every grace enthroned, and a holy peace and elevation above the world fill the mind. These are the subjective effects; but they never come alone. If God revives his people, it is that he may communicate life through them to others. It is of vast importance, therefore, to ourselves and others, that we should really draw near to God in an effectual manner.

III. *How is this to be done? What are the requisites?*

1. *Humility.* We cannot be filled with God, unless emptied of our-

selves. We must come with the conviction of sin and unworthiness, with the conviction also of our helplessness, our complete and absolute dependence on God; and, still further, with the conviction that it would be perfectly just in him to refuse us access to himself or to grant our requests.

2. *Faith.* This includes a great deal.

1*st.* Faith in the efficacy of prayer. The reasons why men doubt it are various. But we have proof of its efficacy from Scripture, from the constitution of our nature, and from experience. 2d. Faith in God as reconciled and willing to hear prayer. 3d. Faith in his promise to give what we ask in accordance with his will, that is, what is right, is for his glory and our good. 4th. Faith in Christ as the Son of God, as High Priest, as having passed into heaven, and as effectually interceding for us.

3. *Desire for the blessings sought.* This includes, 1st. A sense of their importance. 2d. A longing for them which leads to importunity and constancy, which takes no denial.

In the present case these blessings are the conversion of our youth, and their preparation for usefulness. On this depends under God, (*a.*) Their salvation as individuals. (*b.*) The interests of the institutions with which they are connected. (*c.*) The interests of the Church. (*d.*) The interests of the world; the accomplishment, in short, of the work of redemption.

4. The purpose to live in accordance with our prayers; that is, to live as if we felt the importance of the blessings sought, so that we shall continue to pray for them, and also to labor for them.

CXCVIII. Meditation as a Means of Grace.

[*Oct.* 28*th*, 1855.]

I. *What is meditation?*

It is the serious, prolonged, devout contemplation of divine things. 1. This is distinguished from mere intellectual examination or consideration. It has a different object. The object of the one is to understand, of the other to experience the power. 2. It is distinguished from casual devout thought and aspiration.

II. *It is a means of grace.* By means of grace is meant a divinely appointed instrumentality for promoting holiness in the soul. That meditation is such a means is proved, 1. From its being frequently enjoined in Scripture for this end. 2. From the example of the saints as recorded in Scripture. 3. From the experience of the people of God in all ages.

III. *Why is it thus salutary?*

1. Because God has appointed his truth as the great means of sanctification.

2. Because the truth, to produce its effect, must be present to the mind. "God is not in all his thoughts," it is said of the wicked. "Estranged from God," is the description of the ungodly.

3. The intimate relation between knowledge and feeling, between the cognition and recognition, the γνῶσις (knowing), and the ἐπίγνωσις (acknowledgment) of divine truth.

4. Because all unholy feelings are subdued in the presence of God, unsound principles are corrected in the light of divine truth. We become conformed to the things with which we are familiar.

IV. *Subjects on which we should meditate, are, God,—his law,—his Son,—the plan of salvation,—our own state as sinners,—heaven, etc.*

V. *Difficulties in the way of this duty.*

1. The difficulty of continuous thought. 2. Preoccupation with other things. 3. Indisposition to holding communion with God. 4. Want of method and purpose.

VI. *Directions for the performance of the duty.*

1. Form the purpose to be faithful in its discharge, from a sense of duty and conviction of its importance.

2. Have a time and place sacred to the duty.

3. Connect it with prayer, not only in the formal sense of the word, but also as meaning converse with God. 4. Connect it with the reading of the Scriptures. Meditate on the word. Read it slowly, with self-application, and pondering its import. 5. Cultivate the habit of controlling your thoughts. Do not let them be governed by accident or fortuitous association. Keep the rudder always in your hand. 6. Do not be discouraged by frequent failure; and do not suppose that the excitement of feeling is the measure of advantage. There may be much learned, and much strength gained when there is little emotion. 7. Consecrate the hours especially of social and public worship to this work. Let the mind be filled with God while in his house.

CXCIX. Meditation.

[*Jan. 3d, 1859.*]

I. *There is a relation of truth to the human mind, analogous to that of light to vision, or of sensible objects to the senses.* This applies to truth in general, and to religious truth, or things of the Spirit; to the spiritual understanding, *i. e.*, to the understanding when illuminated by the Spirit.

1. There is the power of perception. Light is powerless for the purpose of vision when there is no organ of vision. The same is true

of sound. So without reason there is no apprehension of truth, and without spiritual understanding, no perception of the things of the Spirit.

2. But where there are the organs, there is no sight or hearing, unless there is light or sound. So there is no exercise of the understanding and none of the religious life without truth. Nothing can be substituted for light or sound, and nothing can be substituted for truth.

3. The same visible object, or the same sound affects different persons differently. So the same truth affects different minds differently. The cause in both cases is subjective.

4. Where the percipient is the same the effect depends on the character of the light or sound; so the effect of error, on any given man, is different from the effect of truth.

5. The same object of sense may be the object of attention under different aspects and for different purposes. If we look on a picture to criticise it, to decide on the accuracy of the drawing, or the style of the coloring, or the disposition of the lights and shades, then we experience no æsthetic effect. So if truth is contemplated with the eye of a critic or philosopher, it produces no religious impression. Meditation is not, therefore, simply continuous attention.

6. The senses can be indefinitely improved by cultivation. So the faculty of spiritual discernment and the consequent spirituality of mind is increased by meditation.

7. The effect produced by sensible objects is either from often-repeated acts of perception, or by long-continued contemplation. So in spiritual things, the thoughts of God, of Christ, of eternity, which are constantly floating through the mind produce a constant effect, but this is no adequate substitute for long-continued meditation.

8. Although the cases are thus analogous, yet the one is natural and the other is supernatural. For the knowledge which we seek and need is of the nature of a revelation. Paul prays that the Father of glory would give the Ephesians the spirit of wisdom and of revelation in the knowledge of himself. (i: 17.) From this two important inferences follow. First, that meditation is a waiting for the manifestation of the truth. We cannot force ourselves by any act of attention into the discovery of its divine glory. We must humbly, prayerfully wait for the revelation. Second, this revelation being to the spiritual sense, through the understanding, it never takes place except when the truth is before the mind. That is, the supernatural supervenes on the natural, and in the use of the natural means. Hence it is vain to expect these spiritual disclosures unless we meditate.

II. *The importance of this subject is manifest,* 1. From the nature of the case, as presented above. 2. From the example of the people of God in all ages.

III. *The difficulties in the way are,* 1. Natural. 1st. The difficulty of fixing the mind on any subject. 2d. The difficulty of discarding other objects from the mind. These difficulties are to be counteracted by natural means, *i. e.,* by practice and by the aids to continued thought, such as articulate utterances, reading, prayer. 2. Spiritual. 1st. Disinclination arising from worldliness and sin. 2d. The weakness of our faith or principle of spiritual life. There is a great difference between meditative, recluse Christians, and active Christians. There should be a combination of the two elements as in Paul.

CC. The Sabbath.

[*March* 11*th*, 1866.]

I. *All the institutions of the Old Testament had a special foundation.* They were divided into three classes.

1. Those which have a foundation in the common necessities of men, and the common relation of men to God. These were not peculiar to the Jews, but were incorporated into their system because they were men. To this class belong all moral precepts, and the institution of the Sabbath.

2. To the second class belong those institutions and ordinances which had respect to the peculiar circumstances of the Jews; such as the distinction between clean and unclean meats, circumcision, and many of their judicial and political exactments. These bound the Jews as Jews, and only as Jews.

3. The third class includes all that was designed to be typical of the Messiah, his work, and kingdom. These were mostly incorporations of prior institutions with the Mosaic Law.

II. *That the Sabbath belongs to the class of universal laws, binding all men and all ages, is evident,* 1. Because it was instituted before the giving of the Law. 2. Because the ground of its observance was a general ground, one in which all nations were concerned. 3. Because it was predicted that it would be observed under the reign of the Messiah. 4. Because its observance has been in fact continued, by divine injunction, by the whole Christian Church. 5. It is incorporated in the decalogue.

III. *The reasons for the institution of the Sabbath are either specific or general.* The first class includes the reasons why the seventh day was first selected, and then why the first day was appointed. The other class relates to the reasons why one day in seven should be devoted to God.

IV. *Special reasons.*

1. The reason why the seventh day was originally appointed was

that it was to commemorate the work of creation. This is the foundation of all religion, and it is therefore of fundamental and universal importance that it should be remembered. 2. The special reason for the observance of the first day was the commemoration of the resurrection of Christ, on which rested the truth of the gospel. If Christ rose, then the gospel is true. If the world was created, then there is a personal God, the maker, preserver and ruler of the universe. No one, therefore, can overestimate the importance of the observance of the Sabbath. It is analogous to that of the observance of the Lord's Supper.

V. *Reasons why one day in seven should be observed, are*—

1. The physiological reason ; the necessity of rest for man and beast ; rest for the mind, and for the body. Whether one day in eight, nine, or ten would have answered as well, it is idle to inquire. Probably it would not. As the daily rest is needed, and cannot be less than daily, so the weekly rest is needed, and cannot safely be made more or less. All history and experience show this. Excess either way is injurious. 2. To afford time for public worship. 1st. This is essential for the preservation of truth and for its diffusion. It is a day of instruction for the people, without which they would sink into ignorance. 2d. It is necessary as a means of conversion, as it is by the preaching of the gospel that men are saved. 3d. As a means of edification, as public and social worship are essential to keeping alive the piety of the heart, when attendance is not impossible. Hence a Sabbath-breaking or Sabbath-neglecting people are notoriously irreligious. 4th. It is necessary as giving the only opportunity of rendering that public worship, thanksgiving and prayer to God, which is the duty of every community as such, as much as of every individual. 3. To arrest the tide of worldliness ; to cause men to stop and remember that this world is not all, and is not the greatest. Without this we should not be aware of our progress toward eternity.

VI. *The mode of observance is determined by the object of the day.* First, it includes rest from all worldly avocations and amusements. Second, the cultivation of a religious spirit, and the discharge of religious duties. The Pharisaical way of observing it is one extreme, the latitudinarian is another. The latter is the tendency now. The European way is worse still. The lessons of experience on the subject confirm the principles before stated, and are very conclusive.

CCI. The Sabbath was made for man, and not man for the Sabbath.—Mark 2: 27.

[*Sept. 23d*, 1866.]

The principle which underlies this passage is, that the end is more important than the means, and should not be sacrificed to it. The application of this principle to the Sabbath is plain. The Sabbath was designed to promote the best interests of man and beast. When an enlightened regard to those interests required a violation of the Sabbath, such violation was proper and obligatory. The Pharisees acted on that principle in relation to their animals. They led them away to watering; they extricated them from a pit into which they had fallen. Christ only acted on the same principle when he healed the sick on the Sabbath; when he allowed the disciples to pluck the ears of corn. We, therefore, may act on the same principle. It is the foundation of the exposition given as to the rule of observing the Sabbath, viz., that works of necessity and mercy are lawful on that day. The same principle is recognized in the Old Testament. Hosea says, "I will have mercy and not sacrifice;" that is, moral duties are of higher obligation than positive commands. God had commanded sacrifices, but he had also commanded the exercise of mercy. When the two came into conflict, so that the one must yield to the other, it was the positive that was to give way.

The soundness of the principle and its incalculable importance are plain from the innumerable evils which have resulted from its violation. 1. The whole apostacy of Judaism into formality and ritualism was simply the result of carrying out the idea that the outward was more important than the inward; that rites and ceremonies, observance of fasts and festivals, tithing mint, anise, &c., were more important than the weightier matters of the law. The Pharisees considered themselves holy, because they observed all these external prescriptions, although they were morally depraved in heart and life. 2. In like manner the Papal apostacy is the same subordination of the end to the means; what is positive, to what is moral. If a man conforms to the Church, he is saved; if he neglects these externals, he is lost. No matter how holy a man may be, he is rejected if he fails in these externals. Hence the utter perversion of religion in Papal countries. 3. The same is true of High-Churchmen of every class. If a man conforms to ecclesiastical rites and observances, he is allowed great latitude in more important matters. Thus a ceremonial and ritual religion takes the place of true godliness. 4. The same evil often manifests itself even among true Protestants. Some exalt baptism above religion; some, the use of a particular form of hymnology; some, the strict observance of the Sabbath, &c. It is of great importance, therefore, that we adhere to the principle which our Lord inculcated. This is the principle which governs the interpretation of the moral law. The opposite extreme, however, is to be guarded against. Because the end is more important than the means, we are not to infer, 1. That the means are not obligatory. Christ did not teach that the obligation to observe the Sabbath had ceased. Nor are we to infer from what he says that any divinely appointed means is not binding. "These ought ye to have done, and not to have left the others undone." 2. The means are not to be neglected. They are not only obligatory as matters of duty, but they are important, and as a general rule greatly subservient of the end. It was well to keep the Sabbath, to offer sacrifices, to tithe mint and anise, and the wilful and uncalled-for neglect of these divine appointments was followed by the loss of the end proposed. So we are bound to use the word, the Sabbath, the ordinances of God's house, and their neglect is fatal. This passage suggests that the rule for the observance of the Christian Sabbath is not the Jewish law, especially not that law as perverted by the Pharisees ; but the design of its institution, whatever it may be, is to furnish the rule. "THEREFORE the Son of man is Lord also of the Sabbath;" *i. e.*, because the Sabbath is subservient to his cause and subject to his will. The Son of man is Christ. He is the Lord of the Sabbath, that is, has supreme control over it; can abrogate it, or lay down the rule for its observance.

CCII. Praise.

[*Sept. 30th*, 1866.]

I. *Praise is the ascription of anything commendable to its object.*

Since it includes, 1. The ascription of commendable attributes. 2. Of praiseworthy acts, that is, of acts which evince excellence. 3. Of benefits, which reveal the power and the disposition to do good. Hence in Scripture men and all rational creatures are called upon and required to praise God.

1. For all his divine perfections, natural and moral, his infinite greatness; for his wisdom, power, holiness, justice, goodness and truth.

2. For his wonderful works, of creation, of providence, of redemption.

3. For all his blessings, of creation, providence and redemption. These are inexhaustible topics of praise, for all creatures and for all eternity.

II. *Praise is a natural and proper exercise.*

1. Because it is due to God. It is objected that God does not delight

in hearing his goodness and greatness recounted. This is one of the mistakes arising from reasoning from man to God. Because adulation and laudation may be inappropriate or offensive to men, it is argued that it must be to God. But it is inappropriate and offensive when addressed to men. 1st. Because creatures are not in themselves worthy ; and 2d. Because the exercise of such feelings and their expression are not healthful. But in the case of God, these reasons do not apply. God is infinitely worthy, and the expression of the sentiments and feelings in view of his perfections, is in the highest measure beneficial.

2. Therefore the second reason is, that praise is as it were involuntary. It is forced from us by the exhibition of beauty, excellence and goodness, and especially of that goodness as exercised toward ourselves.

3. It is not only thus natural; it is also healthful. It raises the soul measurably into sympathy and fellowship with the excellence commended. It is therefore an indispensable part of worship.

4. Because the Scriptures command us to praise God; they are filled with examples of that part of worship.

5. Heaven is represented as a state and place in which this vocation is uninterrupted. It is therefore the expression of blessedness, and productive of it.

III. *The mode of praising God.*

1. It must be in the heart and with the understanding. If these do not concur, it is an offensive and injurious mockery.

2. In silent contemplation, when the soul is filled with admiring views of God, Christ, the glory of God in himself, in his works, and in his benefits to us. This may be special and occasional, or it may be habitual and constant, as the incense never ceased and the lights were never extinguished.

3. In our prayers, and in every other form of utterance, in our intercourse, or address to our fellow-men.

4. In singing. That it is proper is plain, 1st. Because it is natural. 2d. Because it tends to exalt the feelings of admiration and gratitude. 3d. Because it is commanded in Scripture, and practiced by divine appointment in the Church.

5. The singing or music of the Church should be conducted on the following principles. 1st. On the principle that it is a means and not an end. Whenever the singing or music is so elaborate as to distract attention from God to itself, it is subversive of the end designed, and productive of evil. This is a common evil in the Greek, Latin, and often in Protestant churches. 2d. It should be as excellent, with the limitations specified, as possible, because it answers its end in proportion to its excellence, and exalts and refines the people. 3d. It should be appropriate, *i. e.*, not martial nor festive, but devotional music. 4th.

It should be so conducted as to secure the co-operation of the people. This is their right, and it is a great good to them. In prayer there must be one to lead, and others join in silence, because a multitude praying together would produce confusion even when having the same form of prayer; but in praise, no such confusion is occasioned, but the highest end of singing is thus secured.

The happiest, holiest, and most useful Christians, those most heavenly in their disposition and state, are those who praise God most and best.

CCIII. The Unity of the Church.

[*Jan. 13th*, 1866.]

The Church is one, not in the monarchical sense, as Romanists believe; not in the sense of historical descent of an external organization, as Prelatists teach, but in the sense of a mystical body united to Christ their common head. The consequences of the union with Christ are,

I. *Our Justification.* We become partakers of his righteousness because that righteousness was vicarious, wrought out not for himself, but in the name and behalf of his people. It becomes theirs not in virtue of its being wrought for them, nor in virtue of the spiritual union between them and him, but because it is imputed to them. And it is imputed to them, if adults, as soon as they believe, and to infants as soon as they are united to Christ by the renewing of the Holy Ghost.

1. This righteousness is by covenant truly and properly ours. It avails for us as completely as though it had been wrought out by ourselves. 2. This righteousness is infinitely meritorious, because it is the righteousness of God. There is no more probability of a sinner's being condemned, if this righteousness is imputed to him, than that Christ himself should be condemned. It renders the believer, therefore, absolutely and forever secure. 3. It secures not merely exemption from the penalty of transgression, but title to all the blessings of redemption. That God shall bestow on those who are justified eternal life and all that it implies, is as certain as that Adam would have lived had he not sinned. This is certain because demanded by the justice and fidelity of God.

II. *The second effect of this union to Christ, which is common to all believers and tends to make them one body, is their sanctification.* They become partakers of the divine life. They are raised from spiritual death, and the principle of life communicated to them is sustained and developed, 1. By the nourishment derived from the word and ordinances. 2. By fellowship with Christ; intercourse with him in acts of adoration, praise, prayer, confession and intercession. 3. By the inter-communion of the saints. As one member of the body is sustained and grows in virtue of the ministration of all the other members, so it is with the mystical body of Christ. 4. This supposes organic unity, and diversity of gifts; some apostles, some teachers; some have one gift, and some another. With regard to these Paul teaches, 1st. That this diversity is essential. 2d. That the position of each member is assigned by God, and not by himself or by the body. Hence, we infer, (*a.*) That each should be content. (*b.*) That all should sympathize, one with the others, and, (*c.*) That all should cordially co-operate. It is thus that the work of sanctification is carried on, not in the iso-lated individual, but in the soul as partaker of a common life, and a member of an organic whole. So in regard to the state, what would individual gifts and attainments be to a man isolated in an uninhabited land.

III. *The third effect of this union to Christ, which pertains to the indi-vidual believer and to the Church as a whole, is security.* No man can pluck them out of the hand of Christ. All given to him shall come to him, and he will raise them up at the last day. The gates of hell can never prevail against the Church. This security rests, 1. On the pro-mise and covenant of God. 2. On the fact that Christ lives, and his life secures the life of the believer and of the Church. 3. On the fact that he has power in heaven and earth. 4. On the fact that he has a covenant right to the co-operation of the Holy Spirit, and because he has conquered sin and Satan.

IV. *The fourth effect is the glorification of the believer and of the Church.* This includes, 1. The resurrection of the body. 2. The full perfection of nature granted to all. 3. Exaltation to great dignity and power. 4. The external circumstances of their being. 5. Participa-tion in the glory of Christ.

V. *Evidences of union with Christ.* These are the fruits of the Spirit.

VI. *Duties to our fellow-believers as flowing from this union with Christ.* 1. Love. 2. Sympathy. 3. Assistance. 4. Joy in their success. 5. Abstaining from envy or depreciation.

CCIV. Aggressive Character of Christianity.

[*April 19th*, 1863.]

There is a great difference between the knowledge given in con-sciousness and that attained by the logical understanding. For example, all men know from consciousness what beauty is; but if the question be asked, What is beauty? and the answer be sought from the logical understanding, there is the greatest perplexity and diversity. Dissertation after dissertation, and volume after volume have been written in answer to that question. So we all know what Christianity is; but when the question is asked, What is Christianity? the answers become uncertain and divergent. It might seem useless to ask the question if we know without asking, and cease to know when asked. But the difficulty is men will ask, and will give wrong answers; answers not merely incorrect, but fatally injurious. Of all the theological questions of our day, especially in Germany and among English and American theologians addicted to German modes of thinking, none has been more debated, and none is more vitally important than the question, What is Christianity? If we are to think or speak intelligently of the aggressive character of Christianity, we must know what Christianity is. It has been defined, 1. As a form of knowledge, *i. e.*, the system of divine truth revealed in the Scriptures. 2. As that *modus Deum cognoscendi et colendi* introduced by Christ. 3. As simply and exclusively a life. By this some mean a form or state of the religious consciousness, while others intend by that expression the theanthropic life of Christ as communicated to his people, humanity restored in him, as it was corrupted in Adam. The objection to these answers is that they are too limited. (The last, as explained by mysticism, is false). Christianity is a form of knowledge; it is a religion; it is a life. It is not exclusively the one or the other, but it is all. The best way to determine what Christianity is, is to ask what makes a man a Christian in the true and proper sense of the term. A Christian is one who knows and receives as true what Christ has revealed in his word, whose inward state (religious consciousness) is determined by that knowledge, and whose life is devoted to the obedience and service of Christ. Christianity is therefore a system of doctrine, it is an inward life, and it is a rule of action. When, therefore, we speak of the aggressive character of Christianity, we may mean the antagonism of truth to error, the expansive power of the principles of spiritual life, or, the opposition of good to evil, of holiness to sin, in the outward life; or we may include all these, as they are all included in the religion of Christ. Or, as the Scriptures call it, the kingdom of God; we may mean by the aggressive character of Christianity, its inherent force, by which it tends to gain more and more the complete control of the individual man and of human society, by controlling all the forms of human thought, the inward character of men and their outward conduct.

I. *Christianity is thus aggressive.* It does tend and strive to subdue. 1. This is variously taught in the Scriptures. It is compared to a stone cut out of a mountain, which gradually fills the whole earth; to a tree whose branches extend over all lands; to leaven hid in a measure of meal; to a great temple in the process of erection; to the sun in its course through the heavens, and from tropic to tropic.

2. It is deducible from its nature. Truth is necessarily antagonistic to error, and holiness to sin. The one must strive to overcome the other both in the individual and in the world. Besides, being a religion suited to the necessities of all men, and absolutely essential to their well-being here and hereafter, it cannot be embraced by the individual man without the consciousness on his part of the obligation to uphold and extend it. A Christian, from the nature of the case, is fired with zeal for the glory of Christ, and with love for his fellowmen. His Christianity makes him an advocate of the truth and a proselyter.

3. It is further proved and illustrated by the history of the Church. The original promise that the seed of the woman should bruise the serpent's head has expanded into the full system of Christian doctrine. The one hundred and twenty disciples in Jerusalem in the age of the apostles occupied Syria, Egypt, Greece, Italy; and since then Christianity has gained the civilized world. It has banished polytheism and idolatry, it has elevated woman, exalted man, and moulded human society.

4. It is proved in the experience of every Christian. His inward life is a progress. He passes from infancy to maturity; from a νήπιος (infant) to a τέλειος (grown), and from a τέλειος to the full measure of the stature of Christ. The truth becomes better known and more firmly believed. Indwelling sin becomes weaker, and grace stronger; and the outward life is made more and more consistent with the gospel. When this is not true, there is no true life.

II. *To what is the aggressive power of Christianity due?*

1. It is not due to anything in itself as a system of truth. If revealed to the lost in the other world, it would be powerless. If revealed to fallen man, sent in books or by living teachers to the heathen, it would, if left to itself, be universally rejected. The opposition of Satan and of the evil heart would be too much for it.

2. It is not due to the subjective effect on the hearts of those who are led to embrace it. If nothing were done *ab extra* but to induce the reception of the gospel, the inward effect and the outward efficiency would fade away.

3. But it is supernatural in its character. It is due to the purpose of God and the co-operation of the Spirit. When a woman puts leaven into a measure of meal, she is sure that the whole will be leavened, because the effect is due to the operation of invariable physical laws. But when the gospel is introduced into a community or a nation, whe-

ther it will take root and extend or not, depends on an *ab extra* sovereign working of divine power. Hence a sense of dependence is to be acknowledged and cultivated. It is because Christianity is the life of God (*i. e.*, of a present Christ), that it must prevail.

4. Although the gospel is thus dependent upon supernatural agency for its preservation and extension, yet human co-operation is ordained as the means. Faith and love are the powers which we are to wield, depending on the Spirit of God.

CCV. Call to the Ministry.

[*September 28th*, 1856.]

I. *The doctrine of the Church, its officers, as well as its attributes and prerogatives, is evolved from the radical idea that it is the Body of Christ.* Hence,

1. It consists of those in whom his Spirit dwells.

2. Hence the community thus animated has the unity and holiness, the perpetuity and universality which belong to the mystical body of Christ.

3. Hence it has the authority to teach, and to bind and loose.

4. Hence the diversity of gifts and offices of its members. To each is given a manifestation of the Spirit.

The illustration of the human body is used by the apostle: to one organ the Spirit gives the power of vision, to another the power of hearing, etc. So it is in the spiritual body; one has one gift, and one another.

II. *From this it follows*, 1. That no one can be called to any office in the Church but he who is in the Church. This excludes not only magistrates, as such, but also the unconverted. 2. It follows that no one in the Church can assume any office of his own will any more than any part of the body can make itself an eye or hand. 3. It follows that the body itself cannot confer office, any more than the hands and feet can vote some other portion to be an eye or tongue. Much less can those out of the Church have a right to appoint to office in the Church. 4. It follows that the only legitimate call is from the Holy Ghost. The only legitimate vocation of the eye, hand or ear, is from him who constitutes and animates the body. So only the Spirit who constitutes and animates the Church, can call to office in the Church. 5. It follows that the whole business of him who receives the call and of the Church, is to determine the question whether or not a man is called, and if satisfied of that fact to publicly declare it. 6. It follows that every office in the Church supposes gifts. The right to teach supposes the ability to teach, as much as an eye supposes the power of vision.

7. This same analogy leads to the conclusion that the only evidence of a call to any office is the possession of the qualifications. But these qualifications are various. 1st. Regeneration, which is presupposed. 2d. Intellectual qualifications, including ability, knowledge, and orthodoxy. 3d. The spiritual qualifications, including, (*a.*) High appreciation of the importance of the office. (*b.*) A strong desire for it from proper motives. (*c.*) A willingness to go anywhere and to submit to everything in the discharge of its duties. (*d.*) A sense of responsibility or obligation, so that we can say, "Woe is me if I preach not the gospel!" 4th. Bodily qualifications; good health and the necessary gifts of utterance.

If these views of the matter be correct, what is to be thought of the multitudes who are in the ministry without this call of the Spirit? Just what is thought of those who are in the Church without regeneration They are to be recognized as Church members, and their acts as such are valid; but they are not what they pretend to be, and have no right to be where they are.

Another inference is, that it is a fearful thing to be mistaken in this matter, both for the individual and for the Church. If the blind lead the blind both will be destroyed.

CCVI. Woe is unto me if I preach not the Gospel. 1 Cor. 9: 16.

[*April* 22d, 1866.]

The gospel is God's message of mercy to mankind. It contains an exhibition of the plan, and the only plan, of salvation. It sets forth the person, the work, and the offices of Christ, and urges all men to whom it comes, to accept of Christ as their God and Saviour, and to devote themselves to his worship and service; and it assures those who do so that they shall never perish, but have eternal life.

In one sense it is every man's duty, provided he has received the knowledge of the gospel, to preach it, *i. e.*, to make it known to others. The commission and command; Go ye into all the world and preach the gospel to every creature, was given not to the apostles exclusively, nor to the ministry exclusively, but to the whole Church and to all its members. Every member has the right and is under obligation to make known this great salvation to his fellow-men. This is a right which has always been recognized and exercised by Christians. But there is an official preaching of the gospel. There is a class of men set apart according to Christ's command, to devote themselves to this work. It is to this the apostle here refers, for in the same connection he says that they who preach the gospel shall live by the gospel. This is true only of official preachers. And it was of himself as a minister that he said, "Woe is unto me if I preach not the gospel!" No man takes this honor on himself. He must be called of God. The call is by the Spirit. The office of the church is simply to authenticate that call. When a man has been thus called, licensed, or ordained to the work of the ministry, then he will be overwhelmed with woe, with the wrath of God, if he does not preach the gospel. This includes two things, the one affirmed, the other evidently implied and elsewhere directly asserted.

I. *Woe will be to the minister who neglects his work, who fails to preach, who turns off his mind and devotes his time to other avocations, unless subsidiary to his great work.*

II. *The truth implied is, that woe will be to the man who in preaching preaches anything else than the gospel; who preaches another gospel.*

I. *Men who enter the ministry should count the cost.*

They should understand what are the responsibilities which they assume, and the vows which they make. Let this then be graven on the palms of your hands. You must preach. You cannot turn back; you cannot turn aside to any other work; you cannot rightfully engage in anything which does not subserve the preaching of the gospel.

The reason for which woe is denounced on ministers who fail to preach the gospel is that men cannot be saved without it. All men are exposed to eternal death. There is but one way of deliverance from that death, and woe to him who, although officially called and dedicated to the work, fails to make that way known. If any man know of a certain preventive of or specific for the cholera, which now threatens our land, he would be a murderer if he did not make it known. So the blood of souls, the Scriptures assure us, will be required of those watchmen who fail to warn their fellow-men of their danger. It will not be a cold, heartless, perfunctory performance of this duty, which will satisfy conscience, clear our skirts, or secure the approbation of God. Our preaching must be earnest, assiduous, instructive and pointed or personal.

II. *A still heavier woe is denounced on those who when called to preach the gospel, preach something else.* If what they preach be another gospel, another method of salvation, then what Paul said must befall them. " Though we, or an angel from heaven, preach another gospel unto you than that which we have preached unto you, let him be accursed." It need not, however, be entirely another gospel. If the truth is perverted, sublimated, rendered unintelligible or unadapted to the end of convincing and converting sinners and edifying the people of God, it will bring us woe in some form and at some time. Brethren enter on your work,

1. With the firm purpose to preach the gospel; to devote yourselves to that work, and to it faithfully.

2. With the purpose of preaching nothing else; preaching only what the Bible teaches.

3. Go with the assurance that Christ will be with you, and aid and support you.

4. Be concerned only about your devotion and fidelity.

5. Your reward will not be in proportion to your talents, your popularity, or even your success, but in proportion to your devotion and fidelity.

6. Be of good courage; your labor will be short, your reward eternal.

CCVII. Proper views and motives in seeking the gospel ministry.

[*Sept. 5th*, 1852.]

The views and feelings proper for any work are determined by its design; by the means of accomplishing its end; and by its importance.

I. *The design of the ministry is the salvation of men.* 1. As salvation implies the happiness of those saved, it follows that benevolence or philanthropy is indispensable. This is often regarded as the sole or all-comprehending motive; but this might be found in a Jew or Mohammedan. There might be benevolence, though there were no God, or no Christ, or though we knew nothing of them.

2. The design of the gospel is more specific. It is the holiness of men, their reconciliation to God. Hence holiness is necessary in the minister; a sense of its value; a sincere, predominant desire to promote acquiescence to it, to bring men to forsake all sin, and to be reconciled to God.

3. But the holiness contemplated, though essentially the same with that of angels, is still peculiar. 1st. Involving penitence. 2d. Consisting specially in the love of Christ, and conformity to him. Hence the specific design of the ministry is to bring men to know, love, worship and obey the Lord Jesus. Hence it is essential that the minister should have, (*a.*) A due sense of the dignity of the Lord Jesus. (*b.*) Supreme love for him. (*c.*) Desire to see his kingdom everywhere prevail. "Lovest thou me?" is the one question which Christ asked of those who would feed his flock or gather his sheep.

II. *The proper state of mind is determined by the means by which this great end is to be accomplished.* It is not by fire and sword; not by coercion; not by intellectual power, as men would propagate a philosophy; not by subjection to a church, or the administration of magic rites as men would extend a mystery or a fraternity; but it is by *preaching Christ.* Hence there is essential, 1. A determination to use no other means.

2. A sense of our own insufficiency to render even this means effectual, and therefore a constant sense of dependence.

3. Conviction of its being indispensable, and therefore a purpose to use it diligently, and to prepare now to do so with effect.

III. *The magnitude of the work.* Nothing can be compared to it in importance. Men who are looking forward to the most important work in the world should be, 1. Grave. 2. Single-minded, having but one object in view. 3. Unembarrassed by the world. 4. Constantly exercising themselves for the work, as those preparing to run a race.

IV. *Difficulties of living under right motives.* They arise, 1. From sin and worldliness. 2. From sloth. 3. From the allurements of wealth, honor and power, or when connected with the ministry.

V. *Importance of right views.* An unconverted worldly ministry is the greatest curse to the Church and to the world; a spiritual and devoted ministry, the greatest blessing.

CCVIII. A savor of life unto life, or of death unto death.
2 Cor. 2: 14-16.
[*October 14th,* 1855.]

Exposition of the passage.

The apostle had been greatly cast down, but was comforted. He therefore thanked God who always caused him to triumph, and made him instrumental in diffusing the knowledge of Christ, which as a sweet savor was acceptable to God. The apostle himself, therefore, was acceptable to God, whether the result of his labors was the life or death of those to whom he preached. The doctrines here taught are,

I. *That the knowledge of Christ is acceptable or pleasing to God.* It is as an incense. It is pleasing to God that men should know Christ, *i. e.,* recognize him as the Son of God, and worship, trust and obey him as such. This is the end of the preaching of the gospel, and this is the end which it will ultimately accomplish. This incense shall ascend from every altar, from every dwelling, and from every heart.

II. *That ministers of the gospel are acceptable to God.* He takes delight in them, as in a sweet savor. They are peculiarly his servants. Their work is a work which he approves and delights in. This is not true in a like sense or to the same degree of any other class of men, or of any other kind of service. It is only indirectly that others, such as men of other vocations or professions, or office, diffuse the knowledge of Christ, and are therefore a sweet savor unto God.

III. *Christ himself—the knowledge of Christ, and, therefore also his ministers, are the means of life to some and of death to others.* He was set for the fall and the rise of many in Israel. He came unto judgment, that those who see not might see, and those who see might be made blind. He was the corner-stone, and also a stone of stumbling and a rock of offence. What is true of him is true of his gospel, and of ministers. Wherever the gospel goes, or wherever ministers go, they bring life to some and death to others. This truth should weigh upon our minds and produce seriousness, anxiety, solicitude lest we should be the means only of death.

IV. *The acceptableness of Christ, of the gospel and of ministers in the sight of God, does not depend on the effect produced.* It is not only when men are saved by them, that they are agreeable to God, but also when men perish for neglecting the truth. Christ when mocked, scourged and crucified, was as acceptable to God as when enthroned. The gospel is as glorious and excellent when men reject it to their own condemnation, as when they believe. And ministers, if faithful, are as well-pleasing to God when unsuccessful as when successful. This should comfort and sustain them under all their trials. The missionary who labors for years without a convert is still as incense in the estimation of God. Men do not so view the matter. Ministers through unbelief often regard themselves as rejected and disowned when no visible effects follow their labors. But God views the matter in a different light. Successful or unsuccessful, the faithful minister is equally acceptable to God.

V. *To be thus acceptable to God it is necessary,*

1. That we should not huckster the word of God. That is, 1st. We should not make gain of it, use it for our own advantage, make it a means of our own honor or profit. 2d. We should not adulterate it. It is only the pure gospel that is an ὀσμὴ εὐωδίας (odor of a sweet smell), and therefore only those who offer or diffuse the pure gospel. Adulterated truth and those who diffuse it are an offense, and as smoke in the nostrils of God.

2. We must be sincere, pure-minded, acting from pure motives.

3. We must be actuated by God, governed by his Spirit.

4. We must act as in his presence.

5. We must speak in Christ, as true Christian men and ministers, united to him and deriving all things from him.

CCIX. Ministerial Responsibility.

[*Feb. 25th,* 1855.]

I. *Ministers are officers.*

1. They are not self-called. 2. They are not commissioned by the people. 3. They are called of God. This is proved, 1st. From their titles. 2d. From the declarations of Scripture. 3d. From the actual appointment by Christ and the apostles.

II. *Their responsibility is, therefore, ultimately to God.* Not only have they a personal, but they have also an official responsibility resting upon them.

III. *They are responsible not for the results of their labors.* Though Israel be not gathered, yet they may be glorious in the eyes of the Lord. But they are responsible, 1. *For their doctrine.* They are bound to preach the truth simply and clearly. They fail in this regard, 1st. When they teach error. 2d. When they do present the truth clearly, but adulterate or dilute it with the wisdom of men, the σοφία τοῦ λόγου. 3d. When for any reason they fail to teach. They may exhort or excite, but if they fail to teach, they are unfaithful to their great vocation. As the truth is essential to holiness, the responsibility of ministers in regard to it is exceeding great.

2. *They are responsible for fidelity.* 1st. As to declaring the whole counsel of God, and not keeping back the truth through fear or favor. 2d. As to reproving sin. 3d. As to correcting the erring. 4th. As to guiding the inquiring.

3. *They are responsible for their diligence.* 1st. In study. 2d. In the discharge of all their official duties.

4. *They are responsible for their spirit and example.*

IV. *This responsibility is the greater,* 1. From the importance of the truth. It is the mysteries of God.

2. Because the honor of Christ, the interest of his kingdom, and the salvation of souls are at stake.

3. From the consequences to the minister's own soul. The ministerial office is therefore to be dreaded, and not assumed without a distinct and well-authenticated call from God. Woe to those who seek the ministry for a piece of bread, or for ease or honor.

CCX. Preaching Christ.

[*May 16th*, 1852.]

Paul frequently declares that this was his great vocation. It includes,

I. *The subject.* II. *The object of his preaching.*

I. *Christ is the proper subject of preaching.* What does this mean?

It means, 1. That the subject of preaching was not the wisdom of the world.

2. That it was the revelation concerning Christ. 1st. The nature of his person. 2d. The character of his work in all his offices. 3d. The method of salvation through him; what we must do to obtain an interest in his salvation. 4th. The duties which we owe to him.

II. *Christ as the object of preaching.*

The objects which men have are various; some of these are selfish and degrading. Some preach Christ of strife and envy. Others have objects which are legitimate, but subordinate, as the temporal well-being of men, or their eternal well-being. The true, specific and appropriate object is the exaltation and glory of Christ; that he may be known, worshiped and obeyed.

III. *Reasons why we should preach Christ.*

1. Because he is our God and Saviour. 2. Because this is requisite to men becoming Christians. 3. Because to make men Christians is the best means of glorifying God, and the only means of promoting the happiness, holiness and salvation of men.

IV. *To preach Christ is a grace.*

The reasons why it is so great a favor, are, 1. Because it is the highest service of God and Christ. 2. Because to be permitted to serve him is the highest honor and blessedness. 3. Because it is the greatest source of happiness.

Therefore, brethren, as ye go hence, go to preach Christ. Let that be your theme and that your object. If faithful, you will receive a crown of righteousness. If unfaithful, it would have been better had you never been born.

CCXI. For it is not ye that speak, but the Spirit of your Father which speaketh in you. Matt. 10: 20.

[*May 7th*, 1854.]

(Last conference of the session.)

I. *Christ's address to his messengers, as applied to ministers at present.*

1. They are to go, not as the apostles at first, solely to the Jews, but into all the world; not to this or that nation only. 2. They are to preach. 3. They are to do all the good they can. 4. They are to rely on their work for their support. 5. They are to go with the consciousness of a divine mission. 6. They are to be wise and harmless. 7. They are to speak as the organs of the Holy Ghost. 8. They must expect persecution, and be prepared to bear it. 9. They may be assured of divine protection. 10. The test of discipleship and the conditions of salvation for teacher and taught are confession and devotion. 11. God will bless those who bless them.

II. *The special topic for consideration is the 20th verse. Ministers are to speak as the organs of the Holy Ghost.*

It is a sound principle of interpretation that a comprehensive declaration or promise is to be understood in different senses, or with various degrees of latitude, according to the class of persons to whom it is applied. The same declaration may be a promise of inspiration, to the apostles, of spiritual knowledge and ability to teach, to ministers, and of spiritual illumination, to believers.

1. The sense in which the apostles were the organs of the Holy Ghost. 1st. They received their knowledge by his suggestion and revelation. 2d. They spake in words which he taught. Therefore they were to speak without premeditation.

2. The sense in which ministers are the organs of the Holy Ghost. 1st. They are to speak only what is contained in the word of God, which is the record of the teachings of the Holy Ghost; not human wisdom, not human speculations about divine things. The matter of their preaching must be what the Spirit has revealed. 2d. The manner or form, the mode of presentation, must be spiritual; that is, not metaphysical, or rhetorical, but scriptural. 3d. Hence, negatively, they are not to seek either the matter or the manner of their preaching from themselves, but by diligent study of the word of God; acting as the organs of the Spirit in communicating his messages to men. The command not to premeditate includes, (a.) prohibition of self-reliance, and, (b.) a command to rely on the Spirit. 4th. Hence, also, they are to seek and cherish the indwelling of the Spirit, for his teaching is both external by the word, and internal by his grace. 5th. Hence, further, they must not only seek the indwelling of the Spirit as a teacher, but as a sanctifier. To be the organ of the Holy Ghost as the efficient and successful agent in communicating this truth, we must be full of faith and of the Holy Ghost.

III. *There are three things then, brethren, included* in being the organs of the Spirit, which constitute the three great elements of a successful ministry. 1. Derive the matter of your preaching from the word. 2. Let the form or manner of exhibition be scriptural, *i. e.*, that which is taught by the Spirit. 3. Be yourselves full of the Holy Ghost. This last is the most important. 1st. Because it secures the others. 2d. Because the others without it must be comparatively ineffectual. 3d. Because it is the ordinance of God to make the living the channels of life. This is proved from Scripture and from experience. No false fire or fictitious zeal can supply the place of the Spirit. The holiness which flows from the presence of the Spirit gives, (a.) Assurance of zeal. (b.) Wisdom and skill. (c.) Benevolence and love. (d.) Forbearance and perseverance. (e.) Peculiar power over the heart and consciences of men.

CCXII. Ministers Soldiers of Christ.

No man that warreth entangleth himself with the affairs of this world.—2 Tim. 2: 4.

[*March 16th*, 1856.]

I. *What it is to be a soldier.*

The soldier's life is the hardest life in the world.

1. It involves more labor. 2. More privation. 3. More exposure. 4. More exertion of the faculties, *i. e.*, in watchfulness and in combat, than any other vocation.

II. *It therefore requires,*

1. Great strength of mind or body, according to the nature of the warfare, *i. e.*, strength of purpose. 2. Great patience. 3. Great activity and diligence. 4. Entire devotedness; freedom from other cares, and consecration to his work. No man can be a soldier and a farmer, or a merchant.

III. *The Christian is called a soldier, and so is the minister.*

What does Paul mean to teach concerning the ministerial office, in calling ministers soldiers?

1. *That the work* in which they are engaged is an arduous one, calling for the exertion of all their powers. They have many enemies to overcome, *within* and *without*.

Within, a. Sloth. *b.* Languor. *c.* Want of faith. *d.* Despondency. *e.* Desire of ease. *f.* Desire of fame. *g.* Love of money, love of power.

Without, a. Error. *b.* Infidelity. *c.* Disregard of the truth. *d.* Ignorance. *e.* Vice in all its forms. *f.* Malice and detraction. *g.* Satan and his emissaries.

The work is not only arduous because of opponents to be overcome, but also because of the work to be done. *a.* To teach the gospel. *b.* To instruct the young. *c.* To guide the inquiring. *d.* To comfort and edify the people of God. *e.* To visit the sick, the poor, and the prisoner. *f.* To propagate the gospel.

2. *Paul means to teach* that his work demands a man's whole time and strength. He may not (*a.*) Entangle himself with the affairs of the world. He has no right to engage in any secular occupation, except so far as it may be necessary for the prosecution of his work; he may not be a farmer, mechanic, merchant, teacher.

(*b.*) He may not allow other pursuits to distract his attention. Literature, science, politics, even general enterprises of benevolence, are all to be made subservient to his one great work—of making disciples.

3. *Paul teaches* that the minister, in the discharge of his duties, is to exhibit all soldierly qualities. *a.* Endurance. *b.* Alertness. *c.* Courage. *d.* Patience. *e.* Indomitable perseverance.

4. He teaches that the minister, like the soldier, should be animated by a spirit of loyalty. The proper motive in a soldier is loyalty to his sovereign or to his country. This is the characteristic motive. The justice of his cause, the important interests at stake, and other motives may have, and should have, their proper influence; but the great motive is his allegiance to his sovereign. So in the case of the minister, loyalty to Christ, zeal for his glory, love for his person, the desire to establish and extend his kingdom, because it is his, is the distinctive and proper motive. There are other motives, as the good of men, their improvement, happiness and salvation; but these are all insufficient and subordinate. It is the overwhelming sense of the glory of Christ, and of our obligations to him, which can alone either qualify a man for this work, or sustain him under it.

5. Paul means to teach that passive obedience is the duty of the minister. He is not the judge where he is to go, or what he is to do. He has nothing to do, but to go where he is ordered, and to do what he is required.

6. He teaches that the soldier is responsible for the faithful discharge of his duties, and for success. It is only the general who is held accountable for results. So the minister, like the private soldier, is not responsible.

7. He teaches that a crown of glory, a crown of righteousness, awaits the minister, and that crown is given only to the faithful.

CCXIII. Be thou faithful until death, and I will give you a crown of life. Rev. 2: 10.

[*April 26th*, 1863.]

Ministers are often represented as those to whom a special trust has been committed. Paul says, (πεπίστευμαι οἰκονομίαν, τὸ εὐαγγέλιον), 1 Cor. ix: 7. Gal. ii: 7. 1 Thess. ii: 4. 1 Timothy i: 11. Two things included in fidelity. First, the safe custody of what is committed, "keep that which I have committed unto thee." Second, strict adherence to our obligations and assiduous performance of our duties. A treasurer is faithful who keeps safely the treasure confided to him. A subject, or servant is faithful, who is true in his allegiance and assiduous in the performance of his duties. In the case of stewards both these ideas are included. The property of their masters is entrusted to them; and they are charged with its due administration and the guidance and government of the household. In like manner ministers are called upon to exercise fidelity in both these forms. To them a treasure has been committed for safe custody; and they are the servants of a king and master to whom they owe allegiance and devotion.

I. *The trust committed to them.* That is, ἡ παραθήκη. This is said to be "the mysteries of God;" "the gospel;" "the word of God;" "this treasure," 2 Cor. iv : 7. The thing therefore committed to the Church, and especially to ministers, is the truth—not scientific, historical, philosophical truth—but the truth of God as revealed in his holy word.

Of this treasure it is to be remarked, 1. That it is of infinite value, *i. e.*, it has a value to which it is impossible to set any limit, and of which we have no measure. It is incommensurable. Gold, silver, precious stones can no more be compared to it than light can be compared with sound. There is no standard of comparison. The truth of God stands in a category by itself. It has an intrinsic value altogether apart from its effects. There are three kinds of value. (*a.*) That which is purely fictitious and conventional. The value of rarity. As of gems, rare plants or books. (*b.*) The value of utility. (*c.*) Intrinsic worth. All these combined in the gospel. It is by itself. Its utility is beyond estimate. And its intrinsic worth is infinite. There is a sense in which the knowledge of God or of Christ is God or Christ, as blank ignorance is equivalent to the non-existence of the object of knowledge. The truths of Scripture are therefore of the highest order of truths. They relate to the highest class of subjects which can come under the cognizance of men or angels. Secondly, these truths are of infinite value measured by the standard of utility. They are essential to our own salvation; to the salvation of the world; to the best interests of society and of civilization. They are necessary to pardon; to holiness, to morality; to eternal life. No substitute can be provided for them. They and they only are the power of God, *i. e.*, the only channels through which his saving power is manifested and exercised. This infinite treasure on which so much depends is committed to you. And it is committed to you exclusively so far as your own souls are concerned, and mainly so far as your people are concerned. This therefore is a fearful responsibility.

2. It is a treasure which it is very hard to keep. Gold and silver may be put in safes or buried in the earth. But this cannot be so disposed of. It must be unconfined. The difficulty of this task is plain from the fact, that the church has so generally failed. The Greek, Latin, Protestant. (*a.*) It is committed to earthen vessels; to very feeble hands. It will not do for us to trust to our strength, or to our watchfulness. (*b.*) It is exposed to numerous enemies. Our own hearts, our own understandings, the traditions of men; the force of public

opinion; the speculations of philosophy; the assaults of false teachers; the machinations of Satan.

You must therefore feel that you have not only a great task; but a most difficult one to perform. The only thing for you to do is, first, to have a clear conception of what you have to do, not to discover truth, but simply to ascertain what is revealed as truth and to hold it fast, without adulteration; second, to determine that you will be faithful to this trust and resist all these enemies of the truth whether inward or outward; and then, look to God constantly for help, knowing that your sufficiency is of Him.

II. *The only form of fidelity is allegiance and devotion to Christ as our King and Master.*

This includes, 1. A right state of mind towards him. In pure love; consuming gratitude; entire submission; and zeal for his glory. These are motives which secure fidelity, and without which it is impossible. 2. The renunciation of any other master. You cannot serve God and mammon; Christ and Belial; the world and your Saviour. 3. Assiduity and diligence in the discharge of all your duties to yourself, to your people, to the Church and to the world.

This fidelity must be unto death: Some are very faithful for a while and then become false. How was it with Judas. With Arnold. With thousands in the world and in the Church. It is only those who persevere unto the end who are saved. Remember that your work and your danger end only in the grave, etc.

III. *The reward. I will give you a crown of life.*

" I," *i. e.*, the eternal Son of God clothed in our nature. The giver is Christ. The gift a crown of life. A crown is an ornament, a dignity and a symbol of power. This crown is one of life, not only living but consisting in life, spiritual and eternal, the highest kind of life. Imperishable, which renders beautiful; which exalts; which gives power.

CCXIV. Thy Kingdom Come.

[*Jan. 7th,* 1866.]

The kingdom of God or of Christ in the New Testament, means in general that kingdom of the Messiah which the prophets in the Old Testament predicted should be established. John the Baptist, therefore, as the forerunner of Christ, announced that the kingdom of God was at hand. Christ's kingdom was then established, and is frequently spoken of as consisting of those who recognized Christ as their king. As this recognition was either cordial or merely outward, and when cordial was also outward, the phrase came to designate the community of true believers as such, and the community of professed believers, consisting of the sincere and the insincere. As the kingdom of Christ, however, in this world is imperfect; or, in other words, as the authority of Christ is both limited in extent here on earth, and is only partially recognized even by his true disciples, the Scriptures often speak of the kingdom of Christ as still future; that is, as the time being still future, when his royal authority shall be universally recognized, and when it shall extend over the whole earth. According to one view, this is to take place before the resurrection and general judgment; according to another, it shall be after these events. Those again who adopt the former view are of two classes. First, those who look for a universal Church, a millennial prosperity of true religion, under the present dispensation of the Spirit; who think that the heathen are to be converted, the Jews restored, and religion universally to prevail, in the use of the means of grace now in force. Second, those who hold that this dispensation of the Spirit is merely preparatory; that little will be accomplished towards the conversion of the world until Christ shall come the second time. This second advent is personal and visible. He will establish his throne in Jerusalem; the Jews shall return to their own land, and acknowledge him as their Messiah; all nations shall be converted, and the Jews with Christ shall reign over all the earth in great external splendor and prosperity for a thousand years. This is the kingdom of Christ for whose coming they wait and pray. According to the common Church doctrine, what we pray for when we say Thy kingdom come, is that the authority of Jesus Christ as king shall be universally recognized, and his control over all hearts shall be absolute, and all evil be banished, and that consummation be reached which is called the kingdom of glory. That is, they pray for the state described by Paul when he says that all enemies shall be put under his feet.

The recognition of Christ as king includes, 1. So far as we are concerned, his absolute proprietorship in us and sovereignty over us as God manifest in the flesh; a proprietorship and sovereignty founded, 1st. On the right of creation. 2d. On the right of gift. 3d. On the right of redemption. This includes authority over the reason, the conscience, the affections, and the life.

2. Subjection to his will, or obedience to his laws, whether relating to moral, religious, social or political duties.

3. Devotion to his service; loyalty to him, *i. e.*, love for his person, zeal for his honor, and consecration to the promotion of his kingdom, is the characteristic principle of those who constitute his true subjects.

4. Reliance on his protection, his ability to subdue all his and our enemies and to secure the best interests of all his subjects. To doubt his power or his willingness thus to protect and bless, is disloyalty. Now when Christ's kingdom comes in the individual soul, he is

saved; when it is established in the souls of those constituting any community, they have attained all the benefits of his reign, which are to be enjoyed in this life. And when all nations shall be subdued, and Christ's reign established over all people and in every heart, the work of redemption will be accomplished, and the everlasting kingdom of our Lord shall be inaugurated in all its blessedness and glory. The great end of life, therefore, the only thing worth living for is, to secure the reign of Christ in our own souls, and to bring others to call him Lord.

CCXV. Domestic Missions.

[*Feb.* 3d, 1867.]

I. *The object of domestic missions is to supply the destitute portions of our own population with the institutions of the gospel.* There are two methods of doing this. The one is by itinerant preachers. This method was the one originally adopted in our church, and continued until a recent period of our history. The object of such itinerants was partly, to preach to the scattered population who had no opportunity to attend any place of stated worship; and partly, to organize new churches by gathering scattered members and ordaining officers over them, and thus to put them in the way of getting a minister for themselves. The other method of conducting the work of missions is to aid feeble churches in sustaining a pastor. This method, with us, has almost superseded the other. There is no reason why they should not be combined. Neither, of itself, is sufficient. Dr. C. C. Jones, when secretary of the Board of Missions, acted on the plan of aiding a church for a few years, and then abandoning it, if it did not become self-supporting. This was a disastrous policy. There are great practical difficulties in this work, because no central Board can know the necessities of every locality, and the judgment of presbyteries is often influenced by special regard to their own field and neglect of the wants of other portions of the country; they are influenced also by natural sympathy with their own members.

II. *Who are to perform this work?* Whose duty is it to see that the gospel is sustained among the people? There are two different principles on which the Church has been divided. The one is that the duty of sustaining the gospel in any one place, rests on the people of that place. This is natural, or at least plausible. The support of the municipal officers of a town or borough rests exclusively on the people of the town. It is their concern, and the concern of no one else. The same is true also of the poor. It seems unreasonable that people of one town should contribute to the support of the minister of another. This principle would be the right one provided, 1. The people felt the necessity for a minister as they do that of municipal officers, and 2. Provided the interests at stake were those of the people of that place exclusively. But neither of these things are true, and, therefore, this plan if rigorously carried out would be destructive. The other principle is that the obligation to sustain the gospel rests upon the Church as a whole. The command is to preach the gospel, *i. e.*, secure its being known, everywhere. This is the true principle, 1. Because all the considerations, except those which are personal and family, which bind us to support the gospel in one place, apply to all others. The gospel is necessary everywhere. Men will perish without the knowledge of it. The honor of Christ is promoted by the conversion of souls everywhere. The interests of morality, religion, and social order, and national prosperity are as much concerned in having the gospel in one place as in another. 2. The gospel cannot spread, and will not be sustained on the other plan. People will not send for it, nor support it. 3. The Church acts on this principle among the heathen. 4. The most aggressive and prosperous denominations act on it. 5. The state has been forced to act on it in matters of education. 6. The permanence, power and spiritual welfare of our church is deeply concerned in this.

III. *Reasons why we should devote more energy to Domestic Missions.*

1. The general reasons of the command of Christ, the value of the soul, and the necessity of religion to social and national prosperity.

2. The special reason of the greatness of the work. Compare this work in England and Scotland with the work here. The extent of the country and the sparseness of the population render it specially difficult, and therefore demanding zeal.

3. The rapid increase of our population; it is outrunning the means of supply.

4. The certainty that error and vice will prevail, if the gospel be not preached and sustained.

5. The importance of the forming period of a nation's life, and the permanency of the original type. Illustrations.

6. All other good enterprises depend on this.

CCXVI. The Knowledge of the Gospel necessary to the Salvation of the Heathen.

[*October 7th*, 1855.]

Introductory remarks.

We must be in harmony with the Bible in order to understand the Bible. A knowledge of sin and of God as sovereign is necessary to a right apprehension of God's dealings with sinners. The origin of evil, the prevalence of error and vice, the fewness of the saved, the perishing condition of the heathen, are all mysteries, which we cannot deny, and must receive on the evidence on which they rest. As to the perishing condition of the heathen, it is to be remarked,—

I. *That justice does not demand their salvation, or that they should have the means of it.* The contrary assumption has led some to assume that the light of nature is sufficient; and others, that the gospel will be preached to them hereafter. That these assumptions are unfounded is proved,

1. From the fact that justice requires only, 1st. That men should be judged according to their works, and, 2d. According to their light. This, the Scriptures teach, will be the case with the heathen.

2. Because the Scriptures teach that salvation is a matter of grace. God was not bound to provide salvation for our race. To deny this is to deny the whole gospel, and make the work of Christ a matter of debt.

3. Hence if God is not bound to provide for the salvation of any, he is not bound to provide for the salvation of all, if he chooses to save some.

4. God has ever acted on this principle, and therefore it must be right.

II. *In point of fact the heathen cannot be saved without the gospel.*

1. Because the Bible declares the light of nature to be insufficient.

2. Because it has declared faith in Christ to be necessary.

3. Because it has commanded the gospel to be preached to all nations as the means of saving them.

4. Because it has declared holiness to be necessary, and the heathen are not holy.

5. Such is and ever has been the faith of the Church. The reproach is often cast upon evangelical churches that they are uncharitable; but Greeks, Romanists and High Churchmen restrict salvation to an external body, we restrict it only to the good. All the holy will be saved.

III. *Inferences.*

1. We should be humbled under a sense of insensibility and want of faith. We exhibit the same unbelief respecting ourselves and others. It is a great sin.

2. Truths should assume in us the form of principles, and not depend on feeling. We should act under the conviction that the gospel is necessary.

3. We should consecrate ourselves to this work. We waste our lives if they are devoted to any other object.

CCXVII. Call to the Work of Foreign Missions.

[*October 12th,* 1856.]

I. *What is the work of missions?* II. *What is a call to that work?*

I. *The work of foreign missions is not a distinct part of the general work of the Church.* The commission under which the Church acts has equal reference to all parts of the field. The work of the missionary is therefore not different from the work of a minister. A man who enlists as a soldier, does not enlist for any one field. He is to go wherever he is sent.

II. *A call to the work of missions, therefore, can only be analogous to the question whether a minister is to be settled in one place rather 'than another.* How is a man to know whether he is called to settle in a city or in the country, in the east or in the west? There is no difference between these questions and the question whether he is called to go abroad or to remain at home. The question assumes that the Lord has a purpose with regard to the location of his ministers; that he makes that purpose known; and that they may ascertain what that purpose is.

1. The Lord has a purpose with regard to the location of his ministers. 1st. This is to be inferred from the general doctrine of providence, which teaches that God's purposes extend to all things, and that he overrules all things to the accomplishment of that purpose. Nothing is fortuitous. The place of our birth, of our education, our profession, and of the field of labor are all included in the plan. 2d. It is to be inferred from the doctrine of Christ's headship over the Church, and of his continual guidance of it by his Spirit, by which he gives gifts to each one according to his will and leads all his people in the way in which they should go. 3d. It follows from his peculiar relation to ministers. They are stars in his hand, and he assigns to each his sphere. They are his ambassadors, and he sends each on his own mission. They are his laborers, etc. We find therefore, that he sent Jonah to Nineveh, Paul to the heathen, Peter to the circumcision. Christ has a purpose with regard to us.

2. He makes that purpose known. 1st. This must be inferred from the nature of the case. We are rational creatures and are governed by rational means. If God has a design for us to accomplish, he must make it known or we cannot, in this matter, fulfill his will. 2d. As a matter of experience we find that God does make known his purpose. He did so, as we have seen, with regard to the prophets and the apostles, and he does so with regard to ordinary ministers. It is not to be inferred, however, that this is always done in such a way as to preclude

all investigation on our part; nor so as to prevent any danger of mistake. A man may mistake, and go counter to the will of God; and the consequences are disastrous. We ought therefore to give the question a careful consideration.

3. How does God reveal his will to his ministers, as to where they should labor? He does it first, by his inward dealings with them, and secondly, by his outward dispensations. First, as to his inward dealings. 1st. He furnishes them with the gifts requisite to some special field of labor. 2d. He addresses their understandings. He presents to them the wants of the different parts of the great field; the facilities for usefulness; the demand for laborers. 3d. He addresses their conscience. 4th. He addresses their hearts, awakens an interest in particular portions of the field, and infuses into them an earnest desire for the work.

Secondly, as to his outward dispensations. 1st. He removes obstacles out of the way, such as want of health, obligations to dependent parents, and other hindrances of a like nature. 2d. He sends messages to them by friends. 3d. He sometimes stirs up the church to call them here or there.

The duty of candidates for the ministry.

1. To feel that they are bound to go wherever God may call them; that it is not for them to choose.

2. To feel perfectly submissive, and say, Lord what wilt thou have me to do.

3. To investigate the subject; not to dismiss it, but to examine conscientiously.

4. To use all the means to come to an intelligent decision, and to keep their minds open to conviction.

The work of missions is a blessed work. 1. Because its results are so glorious. 2. Because it is so peculiarly unearthly. 3. Because the promises of God are so abundant to those who forsake houses, and lands, and friends, etc., for his sake.

CCXVIII. The harvest truly is plenteous, but the laborers are few.—Matt. 9:37.

[*April 30th*, 1854.]

I. *What is the harvest?* It is the mass of human souls. It is called a harvest, 1. Because intrinsically valuable. 2. Because designed to be saved. 3. Because it must be reaped. If let alone it will perish. 4. Because it is prepared, or ready for the sickle.

II. *This harvest is plenteous.*

The number of human beings now living on the earth, and accessible more or less to the gospel, is 800,000,000 or 900,000,000. The harvest includes not the men of this country only, nor of Europe, but of Asia, of Africa, of India, of China, and of the Islands of the sea. All these need the gospel, all are capable of salvation, all are accessible.

III. *The duty of reaping the harvest*, rests, 1. On the whole Church. 2. Specially on the ministers. 3. On each individual minister.

IV. *In what part of the field each should labor*, depends,

1. Not on the wishes of the individual, but on the will of God.

2. His will is to be determined in relation to each, first, by general considerations, and, second, by special considerations.

First, the general considerations which should determine our personal duty are such as these: 1st. The relative size of the different portions of the field. 2d. The relative proportion of laborers in those fields. 3d. Their relative importance in reference to the whole. 4th. Their accessibility and state of readiness for the gospel. 5th. The relation in which they stand to us. We have a greater duty to the people of this country than to others, just as a man is under greater obligations to provide for his own family than for others.

Second, the special considerations are, 1st. Those which relate to our qualifications. 2d. To our constitution or health. 3d. To our domestic or social obligations. 4th. To the dealings of God's providence and Spirit.

V. *Motives which should induce us to give ourselves up to this work, to go where God may send us.*

1. The command of Christ, which is explicit and obligatory, and is addressed to us as truly as though we were specially named in the commission. Disobedience as to going at all, or as to going where we ought to go, is certain to entail the greatest evils on our own soul.

2. Love to Christ and gratitude for the benefits of redemption. The special motive is love to the Redeemer, founded on his glorious excellence as God manifested in the flesh, on his love to us, and on the benefits which we receive from him. The force of this motive is seen in all the apostles and martyrs and missionaries whom God has sent and blessed.

3. The absolute necessity of the gospel to the salvation of the heathen. This is clearly the doctrine of the Bible and of the Church. If they do not hear, they cannot believe; and if they do not believe, they cannot be saved.

Let this subject, therefore, come before you in all its solemn importance, and let it weigh constantly on your minds.

CCXIX. Preparation for the Lord's Supper.
[Date not given.]

The Lord's Supper is presented under various aspects in the Scriptures.

I. *It is presented primarily as a commemoration of the death of Christ.* As the design of his death was the redemption of man, or rather of his people, to commemorate his death is to render public thanksgiving for our redemption. As redemption is deliverance from the power and condemnation of sin, preparation for this thank-offering must include, 1. A sense of sin. 2. A desire to be delivered from it, and a purpose to forsake it. 3. Belief that Christ's death is available to our deliverance, and trust in it for that purpose. 4. Gratitude and love for so infinite a blessing.

II. *It is presented as the seal of the covenant of grace, and as the acknowledgment of our acceptance of that covenant and appropriation of its benefits.* Preparation for it in this view implies, 1. A knowledge of the covenant of grace or plan of salvation. 2. An acquiescence in it, or acceptance of it for our own salvation, with all its promises and obligations; and as God therein promises for Christ's sake to be our God, we therein accept him as our God and portion; and as we promise to be his people, we therein consecrate ourselves to the service and glory of God in Christ. 3. All the sentiments of humility, faith, gratitude and love which such a transaction requires, and when intelligently and, sincerely performed, of necessity excites.

III. *It is presented as an act of communion with Christ.* The cup which we bless is the communion of his blood; the bread which we break is the communion of his body. That is, in receiving the bread and wine as the memorials of Christ, we receive his body and blood— *i. e.*, their sacrificial and saving virtue—and thus become one with him. We receive and appropriate him as our sacrifice, and as the Saviour of our souls; and he gives himself to us. It is therefore an act of intimate communion. Preparation for the Lord's Supper in this aspect requires, 1. The intelligent apprehension of the nature and design of the sacrament as the communion of the body and blood of Christ. 2. Faith in it as a means of grace, *i. e.*, as a divinely appointed channel of communicating to us Christ and his benefits. 3. The desire for this great spiritual blessing, a hungering and thirsting after this spiritual meat and drink; and, when at the table, the actual appropriation of the offered blessings to ourselves. This is feeding on him. 4. The humility, gratitude and love again, which those must feel who are thus admitted to the presence of the Lord, and receive from his own hand this spiritual food.

IV. *It is presented as an act of communion with our fellow Christians.*
All who ate of the Jewish altars professed to be Jews, and to regard
all other Jews as their brethren. All who frequented the temple of
idols were united as joint worshippers of demons. Thus, the apostle
says, all who come to the Lord's table are one body. They are one
united company of worshippers of the same Saviour, each united to him
as the living head, and therefore united to the others as members of the
same body. Preparation for the Lord's Supper in this aspect requires,
of course, 1. The recognition of the fact that all Christians are brethren,
and that their intimate union with each other in virtue of their common union with Christ, is signified and professed in coming to the
Lord's table. 2. The exclusion, on the one hand, of all feelings inconsistent with this fellowship of saints, of all malice, envying, bitterness,
&c.; and on the other hand, the exercise of the opposite sentiments of
love, mutual confidence and consideration, and sympathy. 3. The
fixed purpose always to act towards our fellow Christians as towards
those to whom we are united by the tenderest, most intimate, and most
enduring bonds.

These various aspects of the ordinance of course are consistent, and
preparation for it in one form involves preparation for it under all its
other aspects. Its essential idea, however, is thanksgiving for redemption, and therefore requires true views of the glory of the Redeemer as
the eternal Son of God clothed in our nature, proper sentiments towards
him as our divine Saviour, gratitude for his work, and devotion to his
service and glory. Any man who sincerely desires to thank the Lord
Jesus for his redemption, and who purposes to live in obedience to his
commands, is authorized and bound to come to the table of the Lord,
and aid in proclaiming and perpetuating the knowledge of his death.

CCXX. The Lord's Supper as a Means of Grace. (No. 1.)

[September 11th, 1859.]

I. *The Lord's Supper has ever been regarded as a source of power.*

1. Some attribute to it nothing more than the moral power of a
rite, significant of divine truth.

2. Others, on the opposite extreme, attribute to it an inherent, divine or supernatural power. Some attribute this supernatural power to
the elements themselves; others, to the divine word or promise which
is connected with the ordinance. These views agree, 1st. In denying
that the efficacy is due to the *ab extra* influence of the Spirit. 2d. That
it is not conditioned by the inward state of the communicant.

3. The doctrine of our church is, *First,* That the effect intended is
not regeneration, nor justification. But it is, 1st. The renewed appli-

cation of the blood of Christ. 2d. Our spiritual nourishment and growth in grace. *Secondly.* That these effects are not due to any supernatural power in the elements, or in the rite, or in him who administers it, but solely to the blessing of Christ and the operations of his Spirit. *Thirdly.* That the condition of this power, on our part, is faith. That is, if we have faith, we experience the power of the sacrament; if we have it not, we do not experience it.

II. *By faith here is not meant*, 1. The general belief of the gospel, or plan of salvation as revealed in the Scriptures; nor 2. Does it mean saving faith. It is not true that every true believer receives Christ, feeds upon him to his spiritual nourishment at the Lord's table, any more than it is true that every such believer is always spiritually edified by prayer or the reading of the Scriptures.

3. But it is faith in what the Scriptures teach concerning this ordinance. 1st. That it is a divine appointment, not a human device. 2d. That it is designed to commemorate the death of Christ. 3d. That it is a means of communion with the Lord Jesus Christ, *i. e., first,* a means of communicating to us the benefits of his death; and, *second,* a means or occasion of intercourse with our souls. Hence this includes, (*a.*) Faith in his presence in the ordinance. (*b.*) Faith that he is what he is, the Son of God in our nature, our prophet, priest and king. (*c.*) Faith that he loves us. This is indispensable. 4th. That it is a means of uniting all believers as one body. They become one by their joint participation of the same head. This is the faith requisite for profitable communion.

III. *The reason is, that without it we are not in a proper state to receive the benefits of the ordinance, and with it we are.* It constitutes the receptivity. If informed that a parent whom we had not seen for a long time was in a room awaiting us, it is plain, 1, that if we did not believe that he was there; or, 2, if we believed that the person really there was not our father; or, 3, that, although our father, he did not love us or acknowledge us as his child, then we should not be prepared to meet him. But if we believed all these three points, it would constitute our preparation, and we would not fail of being delighted by the interview. So of the Lord's Supper, if we believe that Christ is there; that he is our God and Saviour; that he loves us, then we are sure of the benefits of his presence.

CCXXI. The Lord's Supper as a Means of Grace. (No. 2.)

[*October 8th*, 1865.]

I. *By means of grace is meant the means of divine appointment for the purpose of conveying grace.*

By grace is meant, 1. Some divine gift. 2. Divine or supernatural influence of the Holy Spirit. Where there are no such means of grace, their saving gifts, so far as we know, are not conferred. To those to whom God does not send his word, he does not send salvation.

II. *The Lord's Supper is a means of grace.* What is the special gift and the special nature of the divine influence which it is intended to convey?

The Roman Catholic doctrine on this subject is,—

1. That each sacrament has its own special grace connected with it. 2. That that grace can be obtained in no other way. The benefits conveyed by baptism can be obtained only by baptism; so of orders, penance, extreme unction, &c. 3. That this gift, or the effect produced, is indelible, like the impression of a seal. Truth and error are here mixed. The error is, (1.) In asserting that the gifts conveyed by the sacraments can be obtained in no other way. (2.) In making certain rites sacraments, which are not such. (3.) In making the gift or impression indelible. The truth is, that there is a difference between baptism and the Lord's Supper. The former symbolizes the washing of the soul from guilt and pollution by the blood and Spirit of Christ; and these are the gifts specially conveyed. The latter while it (1.) sets forth the death of Christ as a sacrifice for sins, and (2.) involves an appropriation of this sacrifice to the souls of believers, is (3.) specially designed as the expression of our union with Christ and with one another. The special benefit, therefore, which it is designed to convey, is this fellowship with Christ and his people. And the special divine influence or inward grace, with which it is attended, is the consciousness of such union.

This is proved from what Paul says to the Corinthians, from the 6th chapter of John, although not directly referring to the Lord's Supper, and from the general faith of the Church manifested in calling the Lord's Supper a Communion. Hence we should specially expect and pray for this special grace when we go to the Lord's table, and we should come away cherishing the feeling that we and Christ and his people are one. Hence also it is called a feast of love, and animosities between brethren are considered a special hindrance in this ordinance.

III. *How is this grace conveyed?*

1. Not by any inherent virtue in it. 2. Not by the supernatural power of the administrator. 3. Therefore not uniformly, nor to all. Some fail entirely of the blessing; some receive far more at one time than at another. 4. But it is conveyed to believers, and to those only; that is, to those who believe, 1st. In Christ and his gospel. 2d. In the special promise of God in connection with this ordinance. 3d. To those, therefore, who appropriate its blessings by faith.

5. As faith is the subjective condition, so the Spirit is the efficient cause. It is by his working in those who by faith receive the sacraments; thus their benefits are conveyed.

In this there is an analogy with the word. 1. It does not benefit all. 2. It does not benefit the believer always in the same way or measure. 3. Its sanctifying benefit is to those who by faith receive it. 4. This faith is the fruit of the Holy Spirit, by which also all its saving fruits are produced.

INFERENCES.

1. We should greatly value the Holy Supper. Protestants are apt to go to an extreme in opposition to Catholics.

2. We should be careful in our preparation for the communion.

3. And we should see to it that we are the better, and not the worse for our attendance on the Lord's table.

CCXXII. Christian Fellowship as Expressed in the Lord's Supper.

[*January 13th,* 1861.]

The meaning of words in Scripture is often best understood by adverting to their literal signification. Thus, κοινωνία, *communion*, means having things in common, from κοινός, *common;* and οἱ κοινωνοί are those who have things, or something in common. We are said to have communion by the cup, to take part in, to partake of the blood of Christ, and by the bread to be made partakers of his body; and hence, since the bread is one, we are κοινωνοί, we have in common, we jointly partake of one and the same body, and thus become one body. There is an intimate and real union effected by this joint participation. What is it that Christians have in common in the Lord's Supper, which makes them one? The answer to this question has split churches and caused rivers of blood to flow.

1. Some say it is the real body and blood of Christ. They say either that the bread and wine are transubstantiated into the body and blood, or, that while the bread and wine retain their own nature, the body and blood of Christ are really and locally present in, with and under them, and are received by the mouth.

2. Calvin said that what believers have in common in the Lord's Supper is the power of Christ's glorified humanity, which is miraculously communicated, being received, not by the mouth, but by faith.

3. The Reformed say that what they have in common is the sacrificial virtue of Christ's body and blood. They all partake of the benefits of his death, and of his life, and in virtue of this communion they

have fellowship one with another. They are united, 1st. Not outwardly only by the profession of the same religion. 2d. Not merely as a society under one head, and one organization. 3d. Nor as a family, fold, or kingdom is united as the objects of the same care, and recipients of the same benefits. But, 4th. Inwardly and really, as partaking of the same life, clothed in the same righteousness, and animated by the same Spirit; and, therefore, 5th. They are united as members of the same body.

Concerning this fellowship of Christians, the Scriptures teach, 1. That it depends on union with Christ. It is because every believer is a partaker of Christ, is united to him, as a branch to the vine, that they are united to each other. 2. That this union is the most intimate and lasting which can exist among men. It is more intimate than the family relations, and outlasts them. I do not say that it has such a hold on the affections, but that it has its roots deeper in our nature. The family relations belong to our social and earthly life. This is a union which belongs to our spiritual and eternal life. 3. It is a catholic union. It has nothing to do with church distinctions. It underlies the differences of ecclesiastical organizations. Greeks, Latins, Lutherans and Reformed, if one with Christ, are one body; and this we are bound to recognize. It is a great sin against Christ and against his body, if we refuse to recognize as a fellow-Christian, or refuse Christian fellowship to any true Christian because he differs from us in anything whatever.

This union is Catholic, not only as uniting Christians of all denominations, but of all ages, rich and poor, learned and unlearned, barbarian, Scythians, bond and free. These distinctions are real. They are not to be ignored, but they are all superficial, outward and transient. Underneath them all is this majestic bond of union, which unites all these classes as one body in Christ Jesus.

4. This inward mystical union reveals itself in the consciousness. 1st. In a common faith. 2d. In common love, reverence and devotion to Jesus Christ. 3d. In mutual love. 4th. In common experience, hopes and aspirations.

5. It reveals itself in the conduct. 1st. By mutual recognition. 2d. By intercommunion. 3d. By mutual forbearance, and by acts of charity and benevolence.

CCXXIII. The Lord's Supper in Relation to Christ's Death.

[*March 17th*, 1861.]

I. *The Lord's Supper is a proof of the fact that Christ died.* Any commemoration of an historical fact, when such commemoration dates back to the time immediately subsequent to the event, involves of necessity the truth of the fact. As this commemoration has been uninterrupted and universal, it is the testimony of each succeeding generation to the great fact in question. We should so regard it. It is one important end to be accomplished by the ordinance, and it is a great honor to be of the number of those appointed to keep alive the knowledge of the fact.

II. *It is a continued proof that the death of Christ was the culminating point of his work.* Had it been simply designed to keep Christ in mind, it might have been his birth, or his life, or his history that it commemorated. So it has been with other great benefactors of our race. But the fact that his death was selected by Christ himself to be perpetually celebrated, shows that his death was his great work. He came into the world to die. All else was subordinate to this. He was to be remembered not as teacher or healer, but as dying.

III. *The Lord's Supper commemorates the manner and nature of Christ's death.* It was not an ordinary death, brought about by sickness or decay; but it was a death in which his body was broken and his blood shed. Neither was it a death by lawless violence, only a casualty, but a death judicially inflicted. He was condemned to die, by the man who had the power of life and death in his hands. But this mere human judgment was only the form and instrumentality under and by which a divine judgment was pronounced. It was by the determinate counsel and foreknowledge of God that he was crucified and slain. This is true not only in the sense in which all things come to pass according to the counsel of the divine will, but also in the sense that God delivered him up. He laid on him the iniquity of us all. Christ regarded his sufferings and death as imposed by the hand of God. It was to him that he looked. We are to regard the death of Christ as the offering up of his Son by the Father for the sins of the world.

IV. *It sets Christ's death forth as voluntary.* He was led, but he was led unresistingly. He laid down his life of himself. He had power to lay it down and power to take it again. Thus he is exhibited in the prophets and thus also in the evangelists.

V. *It sets forth his death in the twofold light of a sin offering and a federal offering.* The latter is the former, but the former is not always the latter.

1. As the victim bore the sins of the offerer, so Christ bore our sins.

2. As the death of the victim took the place of that of the offerer, so Christ's death was vicarious.

3. As the effect of a sacrifice was expiation and propitiation, so was Christ's death. It removed our guilt; it renders God propitious.

4. As the offerer was certainly pardoned and restored, so is the death of Christ certainly efficacious. It not merely renders salvation possible, but certain.

As a federal offering, 1. It ratifies the covenant. It is the pledge on the part of God that he will fulfill his promise. 2. Therefore it secures for the believer all the benefits of the covenant of grace.

VI. *As it sets forth Christ's death under these two aspects*, or as Christ's death was in fact both a sin offering and a federal offering, so the Lord's Supper is a commemoration of his death as a sin offering and as a federal offering. It is so to the Church, to the spectators, and to the world. It is a continued testimony to all men that Christ died for the sins of the world, the just for the unjust; that his blood is sacrificial and cleanses from all sin.

VII. *But to the believing communicant it is more than this.* It is the actual reception of the body and blood of Christ, *i. e.*, of their sacrificial benefits. He then and there, as he receives the bread and wine, receives Christ, and all his benefits for his spiritual nourishment and growth in grace. This act of appropriation is not an emotional act; it does not imply any special elevation of devout feeling, however desirable that may be; it is not an act of the understanding merely; but it is an act of faith, *i. e.*, believing, 1. That Christ died. 2. That he died a death of pain and blood. 3. That he died judicially. 4. That he died by the appointment of God. 5. That he died for the sins of men, as a sacrifice, and has been accepted as such. 6. That we are partakers of the benefits of his death. We receive them as freely offered.

CCXXIV. Retrospect of the Lord's Supper.

[*March* 13*th*, 1853.]

I. *Importance of this ordinance.*

1. It is a historical fact that the Lord's Supper is the middle point of the Christian life. Proof of this: 1. In its very perversion in so large a part of the Church. 2. In the practice of the purest churches, and in the experience of Christians. The reason for it is found in the fact that communion with Christ is the sum of Christian piety, and in the fact that such communion is more intimate and palpable in this service than anywhere else, 1. Because of its divine appointment for that end. 2. Because it is a conspicuous outward act, expressive and declarative of our union with the Lord Jesus as his worshippers, and as the members of his body. It is like the day of one's espousals. It is the public celebration of our union with Christ.

II. *Its nature appears from what has been said.*

The Lord's Supper is not a didactic service. Its primary design is not to instruct. It is like the ancient sacrifices in this respect. Instruction is involved in it, but in the act of offering the state of mind required is that of a worshipper. He comes to do, and not to learn. But it is a liturgical service; not a service for the people, but by the people. It is a mistake, therefore, when the minister puts the people in a passive relation, and addresses them as the spectators or attendants. He is but the leader of their act of worship, in which they remember Christ, lay hold of his promise, and devote themselves to him. All parts of the service should bear this character. Hence, 1. The introductory prayer should not be general, but specific. 2. The administration of the elements is a simple act, not to be connected with exhortations or instructions. How inappropriate is it to dwell at a feast on the proper mode of eating, or on the theory of digestion. 3. The concluding prayer also should be a thanksgiving for redemption. After the service, exhortations may be given.

III. *Its benefits.*

As the Lord's Supper is a κοινωνία (koinonia) or communion, and as communion implies reciprocal action between two or more parties, there is a three-fold aspect of the service, or three parties engaged and present in this ordinance. 1. Christ. 2. Believers. 3. Fellow-Christians. These are all parties, and are essential to the service.

1. Christ gives himself, his righteousness, his Spirit, and his salvation.

2. The believer receives Christ as the Son of God, as the incarnate God, as his wisdom, righteousness, sanctification and redemption. He engages, (*a.*) To renounce sin. (*b.*) To obey Christ. (*c.*) To devote himself to his service.

3. He communes with his fellow Christians. (*a.*) Recognizing them as Christians. (*b.*) Recognizing his union with them as joint members of Christ. (*c.*) Recognizing all the obligations of mutual love, forbearance and assistance arising out of this relation.

Topics to consider:—1. Importance or value of this sacrament. 2. Motives to live according to our engagements

CCXXV. Revivals of Religion.
[*February* 28th, 1858.]

Their nature; their reality; their importance; their dangers.

I. *The nature of a revival; or, what is meant by a revival of religion.* It is a familiar fact that religion in the soul is sometimes in a lower and sometimes in a higher state. The passage from the one to the other is more or less rapid. So in a church or community. There are periods of decline and periods of refreshing. So under the Old Testament dispensation. So in the times of Christ. So in the time of the

Reformation, in the time of Edwards and since. The phrase has here acquired a conventional sense. It is confined to a sudden change from general inattention to a general attention to religion, to those seasons in which the zeal of Christians is manifestly increased, and in which large numbers of persons are converted to God.

II. *The reality of any such experience in the Church is denied,* 1. By Rationalists and all who deny the supernatural operations of the Spirit of God. 2. By those who deny that the converting influences of the Spirit are ever exerted except in connection with the sacraments. 3. By those whose theory of religion does not admit of instantaneous or rapid conversions; who hold that the germ of piety implanted in baptism is by an educational process to be nurtured into conversion. 4. By those who, while admitting the facts of the Bible on the subject, seem disposed to regard them as belonging rather to the class of miracles than of the normal state of the Church. Granting the facts of supernatural divine influence, there is no objection to the theory of revivals. That is, there is nothing in them inconsistent with the nature of religion or with the modes of divine operation. It is a question of fact. These, of course, from Scripture and history are decisive.

The question of reality may be viewed in another light. That is, Whether any given religious excitement is a genuine revival or not? 1. It is of course not to be taken for granted that every such excitement is a work of God. It may be nothing but the product of acts and eloquence of men, and consist in the excitement of mere natural feelings. Much no doubt which passes for revival is more or less of that character. 2. The criteria for the decision between true and false revivals are the same as those for deciding between true and false religion. These are, First, their origin. Are they due to the preaching of the truth? Secondly, their character. Is the excitement humble, reverential, peaceful, benevolent, holy; or is the feeling manifested proud, censorious, malicious, denunciatory, schismatical, irreverent? Thirdly, their permanent fruits. This is the only certain test. The case of Beaufort, S. C. 3. Perfection not to be expected in revivals any more than in the religion of individuals. Such excitements are not to be condemned because of some evils, and those often great ones.

III. *Their importance.* This may be estimated, proximately, in two ways. 1. By the importance of the end which they are assumed to answer. The salvation of many souls and the elevation of the piety of the Church. 2. Historically, *i. e.*, by a reference to the effects which they have produced. The day of Pentecost. The Reformation. The times of Wesley in England and the times of Whitefield and the Tennants, Edwards and others in this country. Estimated by these standards, their importance is incalculable.

IV. *False views of their importance.*

1. That they are the only way in which religion can be promoted. Many say they are the hope of the Church. Many so rely upon them that they expect little or nothing except during such periods. They lie on their oars. They do little, and sink in person and zeal. 2. Another false view is that they are the best way. They are great mercies, but there are greater. When there have been years of famine a superabundant harvest is a great blessing. But it had been better had each harvest been good. There is a better state as well as a greater amount of good in the latter than in the former case. A regular normal increase is better than violent alternations. General permanent health is better than exuberant joyousness alternating with depression.

V. *Dangers.* These may be learned in two ways. 1. From their nature, or *à priori.* 2. From experience, or *à posteriori.*

1. From their nature. Excitement in proportion to its intensity in an individual or in a community calls into vigorous exercise both the good and bad elements which may be extant. It makes the self-righteous, the censorious, the vain, more so. It calls up and calls out all the evil elements in the Church. It sets them on new, unauthorized or improper means of promoting religion. The evil elements often mingle with the good, so as to be far more apparent than the good. The desolations of the thunder-storm or the flood are often more apparent than their benefits.

2. From experience we find that the following evils are apt to attend revivals. (*a.*) False teachers, false doctrines, false or improper measures, as in the Apostolic age. (*b.*) False views of religion, fanaticism, enthusiasm. (*c.*) Contempt of the ordinary means of grace, and neglect of them. (*d.*) Disparagement of religion in the eyes of serious, reflecting men. (*e.*) Denunciation and schisms. (*f.*) False views of the proper kind of preaching and neglect of the instruction of the young.

CCXXVI. Evidences of a Work of Grace.—John 3: 3.

[No date given.]

I. *As in all other cases, the test laid down by Christ applies here also.* That is, by their fruits ye shall know them. Men do not gather grapes of thorns, or figs of thistles. A good tree bringeth forth good fruit. The only evidence of the indwelling of the Spirit is the fruit of the Spirit. Narratives of experience are comparatively of little account.

1. Life in all its forms, when fully developed and in lively exercise, manifests itself beyond dispute. A tree in the spring putting forth its leaves, and in the autumn laden with fruit, every one sees is alive. It is easy to see that wheat in a field, when green and flourishing, is alive;

but no microscopic inspection will enable us to decide in many cases which of two grains of wheat will grow. Life, when only in the germ, does not reveal itself with certainty.

2. Although in many cases it is impossible to determine whether life be present or not, it is commonly easy to decide whether death is. Death reveals itself even more speedily and certainly than life. The evidence of spiritual death is in many cases so clear as to preclude all necessity of asking the question, Have we spiritual life? (*a.*) Heresy, or deliberate rejection of any fundamental doctrine of the Scriptures, is declared to be decisive evidence of spiritual death. (*b.*) So also is deliberate sinning. Not occasional transgressions, but the purpose to live in sin in any form. Be not deceived; neither fornicators nor idolaters, nor covetous, nor revilers, nor extortioners shall inherit the kingdom of God. (*c.*) Hatred of Christians. If a man say, I love God, and hateth his brother, he is a liar.

3. The Scriptures assume that a man may be deceived as to his spiritual condition. They make it his duty to examine himself, and they lay down the tests of Christian character. This question cannot be decided by any analysis of our affections. Unless they are so decided as to need no examination, they cannot be distinguished as spurious or genuine by merely looking at them. The love of God, repentance, faith, are not only ambiguous as words and phrases, but the states of mind which they express are so complex that it is next to impossible to determine certainly on their character. Hence those who are always poring over their feelings and affections, to decide whether they are regenerated or not, never get any satisfaction.

The three great evidences of grace given in the Scriptures are, *First*, the accordance of our inward apprehensions and convictions as to truth with the word of God. The natural man discerneth not the things of the Spirit. The spiritual man discerneth all things. He sees, 1. That what the Scriptures teach concerning the guilt and pollution is true. He does not inwardly dissent from it, but acquiesces in it, in its application to himself. 2. He recognizes the truth and excellence of the doctrines of the Scripture concerning God, his being, perfections, government and sovereignty; the righteousness of his law, etc. He is glad God reigns. 3. He especially acquiesces and his whole heart accords with the truth of what is said of our Lord. He is seen by the renewed to be indeed the Son of God; God manifest in the flesh, the chiefest among ten thousand. The heart goes out to him in reverence, admiration, gratitude and devotion. 4. He acquiesces gladly in what is revealed of the plan of salvation. He sees that it is suited to his case. He knows that a gratuitous method of salvation, through a righteousness and strength not his own, is what he needs.

The *second* test relates to the purposes of the heart. These are more easily determined than the feelings. 1. There is a deliberate purpose not to live in sin, to strive against it in all its forms. 2. A purpose to endeavor to grow in grace, to become more and more holy, and to this end to be diligent in the use of all divinely appointed means. 3. The purpose to devote ourselves to the service and glory of Christ. That is, the true Christian determines that neither himself nor the world shall be the ultimate end for which he lives. Such is his purpose, and therefore he determines that not his own will or interest, but the will of Christ shall be the rule of his conduct.

The *third* test is the outward fruits of holiness. If the tree be good the fruit will be good. 1. There will be kindness, justice, forbearance, benevolence in our dealing with others. 2. There will be strict morality in all that regards our duties to ourselves. 3. There will be a religious life, *i. e.*, a life of prayer, of Christian fellowship and worship, and of effort to promote religion.

CCXXVII. Method of dealing with Inquirers.

[*February 9th*, 1862.]

Every Christian, and especially every minister, will have this work to do. It is a very responsible work. It is a very difficult work.

I. *General principles suited to all cases.* The directions given will be determined by the views we entertain of the nature of religion.

1. Rationalists endeavor to suppress all concern.

2. Romanists teach men to submit to the church, and practice religious duties and penance.

3. Protestants direct inquirers to come directly to God in the way appointed in the gospel. But this general direction is modified by the peculiar views of those who give it.

1. Some place the essence of religion in submission to God, and hence the general directions to submit.

2. Some place it in the choice of God as a source of happiness, and hence the direction, "Choose God as your portion."

3. Some again place it in a volition to make the happiness of the universe the end of our being.

4. Others, in the return of the soul to God through Christ, and by faith in him. Hence the general direction to "believe."

This is the proper direction, (*a.*) Because faith is declared to be the condition of salvation. Believers are saved. Unbelievers are lost. (*b.*) Because this is the apostolic direction. (*c.*) Because neither pardon nor sanctification is otherwise to be obtained. (*d.*) Because Christ is the Alpha and Omega of the gospel.

But what is faith? What is the precise thing to be done? The exercise of this involves immediate conviction of sin.

II. *Special directions.*

1. As to ·sceptical doubts. (*a.*) Do not rely on speculative arguments mainly. Whether in dealing with heathen, philosophers, or errorists or Romanists, the true place of speculative arguments is simply to remove difficulties, to show that the truth is not inconsistent with reason or fact. They are not to be used to prove the truth, *i. e.*, to afford its positive evidence. (*b.*) But rely upon the exhibition of the truth, and upon pressing it on the conscience. (1.) Because the ground of faith is the witness of the Spirit with the truth. (2.) Because the truth is self-evidencing. (3.) Because arguments are human, while truth is divine.

2. As to Fatalists, who say nothing can be done. They plead the doctrine of election. (1.) Here again moral considerations should direct our effort. The intellectual difficulty is not first to be removed. (2.) The sinner should be urged to act as he does in other cases.

3. As to those who rely on the excuse of inability, or feel they can do nothing. (1.) It is vain to tell men they are able. (2.) This is not necessary to produce a sense of guilt.

4. The true method is to admit the fact and fall as the leper at the feet of Jesus.

5. As to those who plead hardness of heart, want of conviction of sin. Show the true place of conviction.

IX.

DEATH,

AND THE CONSUMMATION OF REDEMPTION.

CCXXVIII. Time.

[Dec. 31st, 1854.]

I. *What it is.* II. *How it should be improved.* III. *Means to that end.*
IV. *Motives to enforce the duty.*

I. *Time is duration as measured by succession.* Without succession
there could be no time. To a large extent our conception of time arises
from the imperfection of our nature. To us the distinction between the
past, present and future is palpable. But suppose that the past was as
vivid as the present. It would then be present. And, with clear fore-
sight of the future, it also would be present, and we should exist in an
unmoving state.

Time has reference to our present mode of existence. We are said
to stand on the borders of eternity. The departed are said to be in
eternity. In German idiom, the familiar expression for the dead is,
those rendered eternal.

Time then, so far as we are concerned, is that portion of our existence which we pass in this world. The flow of time is equable. It
never moves either faster or slower. To our consciousness it is, however, variable. Sometimes it is swift, when we are so occupied that we
pay no attention to its progress; sometimes slow, when we are constantly watching its motion, or when many distinct events, usually
widely separated, are crowded into a short period.

The flow of time is ceaseless. It waits for no man. It is irrevocable.
The past is gone for ever. As time is that in which events and acts
are performed, its due improvement is our primary duty.

II. *The due improvement of time requires,*

1. That it should not be allowed to run to waste, or spent in idleness.

2. That it should not be employed in doing what is evil or useless.

3. That it should be employed, (*a.*) In the service of God. (*b.*) In self-improvement. (*c.*) In doing good to our fellow-men. These are three great legitimate ends to which our time should be consecrated. All else is subordinate or included under those heads.

III. *The way to improve our time.*

1. All rules on this subject, to be of use, suppose the existence of a sense of its value, and of a purpose to turn it to the best account. Otherwise, we might as well prescribe rules for preserving life to the dead.

It must be taken for granted, then, that we possess the desire and purpose to improve our time, or rules will do us no good. The maxims of experience are,

1. A time for everything, and everything in its proper time. That is, first, there should be system, and secondly, no procrastination or delay.

2. Take care of the minutes and the hours will take care of themselves. Gather up the fragments.

3. Whatever you do, do it with your might.

4. Never be idle. Seek rest in sleep, and relaxation in change of employment.

IV. *The motives to enforce this duty.*

1. We are responsible to God for the use of our time. It is the great talent committed to our care.

2. It is short, uncertain and irrevocable.

3. Much of it has already run to waste.

4. The issues of time are in eternity. The present determines the eternal future.

CCXXIX. So teach us to number our days that we may apply our hearts unto wisdom.—Ps. 90 : 12.

[*Jan. 2d, 1853.*]

What is wisdom ? What is it to number our days ? How does the latter lead us to apply the heart unto the former ?

I. *What is wisdom ?* The fact is plain that religion is in the Scriptures often called wisdom, and wickedness, folly. The good are the wise ; the wicked are fools. But why is this? Because it implies the selection of the best means and the use of the best ends. The highest end is God's glory ; the best means, obedience to his will. It is the height of folly to select any creature good or temporary attainment as the chief end. This all but the righteous do, and therefore all but the righteous are fools.

The glory of God is the highest end,

1. Because he is infinitely superior to any other being, and to the whole universe. To know him, and to be the means of making him known is more important than all things else.

2. Because the manifestation of his glory secures all the excellence there is in the universe.

3. Because it secures all the blessedness rational creatures can enjoy. This, therefore, is wisdom. The wise are those who make God's glory the end of their being. Hence,

1. The gospel is called the wisdom of God. It is that system, (a.) Which reveals God as the highest end. (b.) Which makes known the means for the attainment of that end. (c.) And because it brings those who embrace it into the possession of wisdom, i. e., it makes them wise.

2. Hence the wisdom of men is called foolishness, (a.) Because it presents something else than God's glory as the end. (b.) Its means are futile for good. (c.) Those who embrace it are fools.

II. *What is it to number our days?*

1. To consider how few they are in the whole. 2. How few remain. 3. How many have been wasted.

III. *How does a sense of the fewness of our years lead us to apply our hearts unto wisdom?*

1. Because it leads us to see how little time we have to attain the greatest ends.

2. Because it leads us to see the folly of employing these few years to ends which can profit nothing.

3. Because it makes us feel that we are unprofitable servants, who have neglected our Master's work.

INFERENCES.

1. The duty of self-examination and reflection. We should see how we have failed in applying our hearts unto wisdom.

2. The duty of decision and renewed effort to become faithful servants.

3. The importance of availing ourselves of all the means in our power of impressing the uncertainty and value of time upon our hearts.

CCXXX. So teach us to number our days that we may apply our hearts unto wisdom.—Ps. 90 : 12.   (**No. 2.**)

[*Jan. 12th,* 1868.]

There is a remarkable difference as to this verse in the versions. The Septuagint assumes a different reading: " Cause me to know thy right hand and those cordially, or in heart, instructed in wisdom." So the Vulgate. Luther's version : " Let us remember that we must die, in order that we may be wise." De Wette: "Teach us to number our days, that we may attain a wise heart." Young: "To number our days aright, let us know; and we bring the heart to wisdom." Alexander: "The number of our days let us know, and we will bring a heart of wisdom." Our version gives the true idea; a proper estimate of life tends to wisdom.

Life is short and uncertain. To act as though it were indefinitely long, or as though the possession of it was secure, is folly. This is a folly of which most men are guilty, and to which all men are exposed. We are ourselves sensible how little we lay to heart the brevity and uncertainty of life. How much we live as though we should live always. At twenty or thirty we live and feel as to life's continuance as we did at ten or fifteen. At fifty or seventy, it is all the same. We live in the present, and the present is as real at one age as at another. It requires an effort, therefore, to bring this truth home to our minds, so that it shall really affect and control our lives.

This is difficult from the nature of the case. Duration is equable. There is nothing in time itself to mark the transition from one moment to another. The same is true of motion.

Nothing indicates the passage from one portion of space to another, but passing by some fixed object. Thus men feel in a balloon or on the ocean. Motion is noticed if the ship moves faster than the water; but not if it is only carried forward by a current. We are not sensible of the motion of the earth through space. Thus we are insensible to the flight of time. We have reason to pray that God would impress us with a sense of its rapidity, its brevity, its uncertainty. The reason in this matter must control the feelings.

There are two measures of time,—days, months and years being one, and events the other. A portion of time in which nothing specially important has occurred, may be as long as that which has determined the fate of an individual or of nations. What three years of the world's history can compare with those of our Lord's ministry? How far more important the first fifty years of the Church than the centuries that followed. How vast the consequences of the events of the Reformation period. How has the state of our country been changed by the four years of war just ended. How has the state of Europe been changed by the six weeks' campaign of the Prussian army.

So with the individual. If he is called upon to number his days he will estimate them not by hours, but by events. The years of his conversion, of his call to the ministry, of his ordination, of his entering into some special field of labor. One year may contain more to think of, more that moulds his destiny than all the other years of his life. The year a man yields to temptation may decide his fate for eternity.

The first lesson this teaches us is, the unspeakable value of time. In time we determine our eternal state. In time we do all we are ever to do for the good of others, or for our own advancement in good, or for the glory of God. This is our day for work. After this the night cometh when no man can work.

The second lesson is humility and penitential sorrow that our time has run so much to waste. What have we done? What progress in knowledge? Have we increased in piety? What have we accomplished for the Church or for the world? No man can make this review of life without being deeply sensible how greatly he has sinned; how he has wasted or allowed to lie unimproved this great talent of time which God has committed to our hearts. Regret is unavailing. Lost time and opportunity cannot be recalled.

The third lesson is that we should be brought to the solemn determination to make the most of the few days that remain. They must be few. They may be almost gone. Therefore let us apply our hearts unto wisdom. Let us be wise, wise in improving to the utmost our remaining days in living nearer to God, praying more, holding more constant intercourse with God our Saviour, in studying more, in laboring more for the good of others, for the progress of truth and holiness among men.

Fourth lesson : Gratitude to God for his forbearance and his abounding mercy to us, unprofitable servants.

CCXXXI. Death.

[*April 13th*, 1856.]

Death is the dissolution of the body, the separation of the soul from its earthly tabernacle.

I. *Death is not natural.* It is a penalty. If there had been no sin, there had been no death. Life had been immortal either here or hereafter.

II. *At death there is a separation entirely from the world.* The dead are the departed, the *verewigte.* The body is reduced to dust.

III. *The soul,* 1. does not cease to exist. 2. It does not become unconscious. Its eternal destiny is immediately decided.

IV. *The souls of the righteous are,* 1. Made perfect in holiness. How, we need not ask. 2. They do immediately pass into glory. This is proved, (*a.*) from Scripture, Christ's declaration. (*b.*) Paul's experience. (*c.*) Lazarus in Abraham's bosom. (*d.*) Christ's argument against the Sadducees. (*e.*) The universal belief of Christians.